A HISTORY OF

AMERICAN MUSIC EDUCATION

A HISTORY OF

AMERICAN MUSIC EDUCATION

Second Edition

Michael L. Mark
Charles L. Gary

The National Association for Music Education

Contents

Preface to the Second Edition

In 1988, the authors of this book were part of a committee assigned to organize a symposium at the University of Maryland, College Park, celebrating the 150th anniversary of Lowell Mason's historic experiment in teaching music as a curricular subject at the Hawes School in Boston. From that association grew the plans for writing *A History of American Music Education,* which was published in 1992. In this second edition, we continue examining the profession—its interests, accomplishments, and frustrations—and the status of music education as America and the world prepare for a new century and a new millennium.

STATUS OF MUSIC EDUCATION

Americans have been oriented to growth since the founding of the nation. If we accept continual expansion and proliferation as a measure of the health of the music education profession, then it can only be viewed as vibrant, robust, and vital. On the one hand, the downsizing, or even closing, of school music programs in the 1970s and 1980s in response to economic downturns is not as constant of a threat to the profession. And threats of the loss, or even interruption, of music offerings are not something new for music educators (see p. 165). Even when systematic music programs have been reduced, school performing ensembles seem to gain in popularity with students and communities. On the other hand, it is worrisome to note instances in which elementary music education, the historic foundation of music education in America, has been curtailed.

Another measure of the health of the music education profession might be taken by examining some aspects of MENC—The National Association for Music Education, the central professional organization of music educators.[1] Membership has increased dramatically during the past decade. The total membership in 1988 was 55,380, and by 1998 membership had grown to 67,097. Also indicative of professional health is the relocation of the MENC headquarters in 1993 to a much larger building. The move was necessitated by additional staff whose purpose was to increase service to the membership, as well as by a need for space for the materials and resources demanded by a growing publications program.

Other indicators of professional well-being might be seen in the expanding intellectual arenas of music education research and philosophy, which have developed sizable cadres of leadership; the ever-increasing number of new publications supporting special interests in the field; the state, regional, and national professional in-service conferences that continue to grow in attendance and offerings; and the state and national advocacy efforts that have matured to a level of high sophistication and that enjoy major successes in legislation favorable to music education.

NATIONAL STANDARDS FOR ARTS EDUCATION

One of the strongest measures of professional health, and probably the most significant music education event of the 1990s, was the passage of the Goals 2000: Educate America Act. This federal legislation recognized the arts as core curricular subjects, "as important to education as English, mathematics, history, civics and government, geography, science, and foreign language."[2]

History. The background of the National Standards for Arts Education is especially meaningful in regard to two historic trends that have come together in the 1990s to form a foundation for the standards. First, the criteria used to establish the standards are competency-based. For more than thirty years, MENC has advocated this approach in regard to what should be expected of students and teachers. In 1965, MENC published *Music in General Education* (see p. 316), which enumerated eleven "Outcomes" that could reasonably be expected of pupils who had spent twelve years in public schools. The competency-based approach was indicated by such phrases, as: "He will be able to sing," followed by this description: "*The generally educated person is articulate.* He uses his voice confidently in speech and song. He sings in a way that is satisfying to himself. He can carry a part in group singing. His singing is expressive."[3]

Three years later, in 1968, MENC President Wiley Housewright appointed a commission, under the chairmanship of Robert Klotman, to study the status of music teacher education. The commission adopted a competency-based approach to teacher education, and when the report was published in 1972, it contained a description of musical competencies expected of music educators with regard to 'Producing Sounds'—"All music educators must be able to: perform with musical understanding and professional proficiency; play accompaniments; sing; conduct; and supervise and evaluate the performance of others."[4] Other competencies related to the ability to organize and describe sounds, and to those personal and professional qualities that make a professional teacher.

Also during this period, the MENC National Commission on Instruction, chaired by Paul Lehman (MENC president, 1984–86), was preparing *The School Music Program: Description and Standards*. This pivotal document listed "performing, organizing, and describing" activities that should be expected of students at various grade levels. The 1974 publication was extremely influential and almost immediately began to stimulate changes by state boards of education, which have the ultimate authority in American education. The publication of the second edition of *The School Music Program* in 1986 further affirmed the leadership of MENC in raising the quality of music education.

The second historic trend that led to the development of the National Standards involves the collaborative relationship among arts education professional associations that began when four organizations representing dance, art, music, and theatre (DAMT) worked together on the IMPACT project (see pp. 341–42). When John Mahlmann moved from the position of director of the National Art Education Association to accept the executive directorship of MENC in 1983, he was influential in further coordinating the work of the four associations. Once established, the Consortium of National Arts Education Associations prompted the development of statements of ideals comparable to those of MENC for the National Art Education Association, the National Dance Association, and the American Alliance for Theatre and Education. Drawing from these statements, the Consortium sought a grant that would enable it to develop the National Standards for Arts Education. This was a period when the federal government was becoming concerned about the declining quality of public education, and a grant was forthcoming jointly from the U.S. Department of Education, the National Endowment for the Arts, and the National Endowment for the Humanities to MENC on behalf of the Consortium.

The Standards. It is interesting to compare *National Standards for Music Education* with its music predecessors, the two editions of *The School Music Program: Description and Standards.* In doing so, although the form of presentation is different, one can clearly see the lineage of the music standards. Paul Lehman, chaired the committee for the 1974 edition of *The School Music Program,* and Charles Hoffer (MENC president, 1988–90), the second. The task force for developing the National Standards was headed by Lehman, and Hoffer was a member. The two editions organized the school years K–12 into traditional but different classifications—the first divided the middle years into preadolescent and early adolescent, and the second recognized the organization of schools into elementary school, middle and junior high school, and senior high school. The National Standards organized the school years into K–4, 5–8, and 9–12 sections.

The first edition (1974) of *The School Music Program* had a tripartite division of the ways students might interact with music: performing, organizing, and describing. The 1986 edition added "notating" as a part of performing, changed "organizing" to "creating," joined the term "listening" to "describing," and added "valuing." The first sentence of the music section of the National Standards for Arts Education states: "Performing, creating, and responding to music are the fundamental music processes in which humans engage."[5] The lineage of the National Standards is apparent.

Each of the three music sections contains the same nine content standards, followed by achievement standards specific to the level. For example, one of the nine standards in music K–4 reads:

1. *Content Standard:* Singing, alone and with others, a varied repertoire of music.
Achievement Standard
Students
a. sing independently, on pitch and in rhythm, with appropriate timbre, diction, and posture, and maintain a steady tempo.
b. sing expressively, with appropriate dynamics, phrasing, and interpretation.
c. sing from memory a varied repertoire of songs representing genres and styles from diverse cultures.
d. sing ostinatos, partner songs, and rounds.
e. sing in groups, blending vocal timbres, matching dynamic levels, and responding to the cues of a conductor.[6]

The eight other content standards in each level are:

2. Performing on instruments, alone and with others, a varied repertoire of music.
3. Improvising melodies, variations, and accompaniments.
4. Composing and arranging music within specified guidelines.
5. Reading and notating music.
6. Listening to, analyzing, and describing music.
7. Evaluating music and music performances.
8. Understanding relationships between music, the other arts, and disciplines outside the arts.
9. Understanding music in relation to history and culture.

All students are expected to reach the respective achievement standards by the time they complete the fourth grade and the eighth grade. Although the phrase "before they move on" is used, there is no recommendation that students be held back because arts competency has not been demonstrated. There are two levels of achievement for high school students: proficient and advanced. All high school students are expected to demonstrate competency at the proficient level, while only those who have elected specialized courses in the various arts disciplines are expected to reach the advanced level before graduation.

Publications Resulting from the National Standards. After MENC disseminated the National Standards, it launched a specialized series of publications designed to help teachers implement them. The thirteen-book series, edited by Carolynn A. Lindeman (MENC president, 1996–98), is called "Strategies for Teaching." The books are specific in their orientation. Among the first to appear were *Strategies for Teaching K–4 General Music, Strategies for Teaching Middle-Level and High School Keyboard, Strategies for Teaching Strings and Orchestra,* and *Strategies for Teaching Elementary and Middle-Level Chorus.*

The Effects of the National Standards. It is too early to know what long-range impact the National Standards for Arts Education will have on American schools, but the initial effect must be judged as positive. The standards are voluntary, meaning that each state board of education is free to either adopt them, develop its own arts standards, or simply ignore them (at the risk of disqualifying themselves from receiving certain federal funds). To date, at least forty state boards of education have adopted some form of arts education standards, many of them based directly on the National Standards. Local school systems in those states are in various stages of developing and implementing curricula that reflect the standards of their particular states.

CURRICULUM

Music educators offer a remarkable range of musical experiences that would have amazed, and perhaps even confounded, Lowell Mason, T. P. Giddings, Frances E. Clark, Russell Morgan, Lilla Belle Pitts, and their colleagues. Music educators continually strive to keep up with multiculturalism, improvisation, technology, and interdisciplinary studies among other recent additions to school experiences. There is also a renewed commitment to lifelong learning in music, from early childhood to the senior years. The vigor that has been an essential characteristic of the profession since its inception does not seem to have been lost or overwhelmed by this fast-changing world.

Multiculturalism. The Tanglewood Declaration (see p. 312) called for numerous changes and additions to the school music curriculum, among them the musics of other cultures. We now officially recognize that the musics of the United States include those of virtually every world culture, but until 1967, school music gave scant recognition to any but traditional Western tonal music. The presentation by Barbara Reeder's Seattle students at the 1968 MENC National In-Service Conference opened the door of multicultural music education for many teachers. The subsequent attention to the rich variety of world musics has expanded rapidly since that time but never more so than during the 1990s. No music program is considered complete if it does not include musics that were considered exotic, possibly even harmful, in the past. Since then, many American music educators have had the opportunity to teach and study outside the United States and have returned with a fascination for the musics of other cultures. Others have studied in this country with musicians from other lands; and still others have had the opportunity to work with ethnomusicologists, who provide a different perspective on music. The ever-increasing number of international students in the United States has also helped stimulate interest in the musics of their native lands.

While by no means universal in American schools, it is not surprising to find students presently involved with more than Western European music. They may be listeners in general music classes, performers on non-Western instruments, or even manufacturers of the instruments themselves. These experiences bid fair to make music relate more closely to the life they face after school.

Improvisation. The inclusion of improvisation in the music curriculum is another outgrowth of the Tanglewood Symposium, which recommended that jazz become an integral component of school music study. The inclusion of improvisation in the 1994 National Standards constitutes recognition of its importance to current music education. Originally the province of instrumental instructors, improvisation is now an important tool for teachers of vocal music as well. It is no longer confined to jazz ensembles. Today we find choral teachers using improvisation to teach rhythm, form, notation, timbre, and tone quality. Vocal groups that sing traditional sacred choral music are also capable of excellent performances of vocal jazz and rap. Teachers have shared their thoughts on improvisation through articles in *General Music Today, Teaching Music,* and the *Music Educators Journal.* Some masters of improvisation, such as Wynton Marsalis, have shared their expertise with music educators as well.

Technology. Technology might well be the greatest stimulant to change in music education. Computers were used decades ago in a rather limited manner, often to teach factual information about music or to present dictation exercises. Today, more advanced technology and dramatically lower hardware prices make computer equipment available to virtually all students. The possibilities of technology in the music program are limited only by the ingenuity of music educators. Students are often ahead of their teachers in technological know-how and skill.

Classes in music technology attract and hold students who previously may have evidenced no interest in music. Teachers develop their own software programs to meet the particular needs of their students. A CD-ROM can turn a computer into a library; Internet web sites put students and teachers in touch with the world at large; music notation software allows students and teachers to be music engravers; synthesizers permit students to hear their original melodies as they would sound on various instruments while they experiment in orchestration; and teachers use sequencers to create accompaniments or prepare practice tapes for students of differing abilities. As teachers engage in more multicultural musics, the value of the Internet increases as a medium for the exchange of musical ideas, in the form of MIDI (Musical Instrument Digital Interface) files,[7] between students in different countries.[8]

Many music educators have become fascinated with this new world of electronics and adapt their teaching to take advantage of the marvelous possibilities it presents. They also have shared their ideas on the pages of *Teaching Music* or in a regular "Technology for Teaching" column that ran for four years in the *Music Educators Journal*. The column was discontinued after May 1993 because the Editorial Committee was, by that time, receiving many good manuscripts on the subject that they could publish as feature articles. An MENC web site was launched in January 1996. Workshops are offered throughout the country by colleges and universities, as well as by manufacturers of the equipment. The possibilities of technology are, as our students say, "awesome."

TEACHER EDUCATION AND CERTIFICATION

The preparation of teachers in every academic discipline has changed in the past ten years as many universities have realigned their teacher education curricula to focus more on the liberal arts. These institutions, all research universities (as differentiated from colleges and comprehensive universities), are referred to collectively as the Holmes Group. Often, the programs include a year of professional training under master teachers. The music teacher preparation program, however, is distinctly different from those in French, English literature, physics, or any other discipline. Consequently, music education has brought different problems to the table. Although the fit between new teacher education paradigms and music teacher preparation programs is not entirely comfortable, the distribution of undergraduate courses for music education majors now often attempts to include more liberal arts. There has been an increase in field experiences as well. Lisa DeLorenzo of Montclair (NJ) State College, writes, "Students [interns] see with different eyes when they have experienced a leadership role with children. . . . The most powerful lessons are those that the students discover on their own."[9]

Teacher educators recognize the necessity of adding such new music education experiences as technology, multicultural approaches, and interdisciplinary studies to the undergraduate major in music education, but the basic pattern established by Karl Gehrkens (see p. 280) remains the predominant one. Some institutions have added a fifth year, either by their own choice or by state mandate, which in some cases leads to the granting of both the baccalaureate and master's degree at the same time. Recognition of the fact that undergraduate work in music education is exceptionally demanding has led colleges and universities to raise admission standards, thereby further improving the quality of school music instruction.

In 1990, the Music Educators National Conference set up a Professional Certification Committee to grant the titles "Nationally Registered" or "Nationally Certified" to music educator members who demonstrate the competencies required of teachers of the highest quality. Seven hundred seventy-five teachers had received this recognition when the program was discontinued, in large part because MENC accepted the agenda and program of the National Board for Professional Teaching Standards (NBPTS). MENC continues to recognize those previously certified, consistent with the original plan. Now, music education leaders join leaders of other disciplines in establishing standards and assessment procedures for NBPTS to assure that teachers who meet the stringent requirements for official recognition are truly deserving of both the honor and the rewards that such an achievement brings in the form, it is hoped, of salary and promotion.

RESEARCH

Probably the dominant event in the field of music education research was the 1992 publication of the *Handbook of Research on Music Teaching and Learning*.[10] Edited by Richard Colwell, the *Handbook* contains fifty-five chapters written by more than seventy scholars. This immense volume, which examines and clarifies numerous issues to both researchers and practitioners, is of great use to the profession.

In addition to that critical publication, there have recently been new ways of looking at the subject of the identification of talent, which has long been a research interest to music educators and others. Edwin Gordon, for example, posits that any human can develop musical traits if exposed to the proper experiences early enough in life. Benjamin Bloom's study of talent bears out Gordon's thoughts on nurturing. Howard Gardner's recognition of multiple intelligences, including a musical one, has encouraged educators to ask again for a central place in the curriculum. Dr. Frank R. Wilson of Denver believes in a biological guarantee of musicianship, which prompted Franz Roehmann to ask, "What is the neurologic, physiologic, and psychological effect of a musically enriched or deprived environment during that critical period (life of the fetus); is our genetic guarantee somehow degraded, lost or postponed?"[11] The practices of the late Shinichi Suzuki are recalled. An increase in interest in early childhood education may prove to be a wave of the immediate future for researchers.

The number of Special Research Interest Groups (SRIGs) of the Society for Research in Music Education (SRME) has grown to thirteen, and each now has a newsletter and meets biannually. Interest in qualitative research has grown throughout the 1990s. The journal *Update: Applications of Research in Music Education* has been added to the list of periodicals published by MENC (after having been issued for several years by the University of South Carolina). *Update* helps bridge the gap between researchers and practitioners. The *Bulletin of the Council for Research in Music Education* continues to disseminate much of the research carried out in universities, and the number of state and regional research publications continues to grow. The premier music education research journal, MENC's *Journal of Research in Music Education,* receives so many manuscripts deserving publication that in 1998 MENC agreed to publish several enlarged issues to accommodate the increased number of articles.

MENC has taken an active interest in developing a research base related to practice, as reported in the February 1998 issue of the *Music Educators Journal.* "A Research Agenda for Music Education: Thinking Ahead," a special insert, identified broad concerns: music teaching and learning in a time of innovation and reform; music education for new, diverse, and underserved populations; and supporting and surrounding issues.

NEW PARADIGMS OF SCHOOLING

In the 1980s, public schools were the target of severe criticism in several widely disseminated major reports. Public confidence in the education establishment, once very strong, eroded throughout that decade.[12] By the 1990s, several alternatives to traditional public schooling were put into practice. For-profit companies won contracts to operate public schools on the basis of guarantees that students would perform better academically. Home schooling increased dramatically, as did the number of charter schools. In response to the new competition for both higher standards and students, public schools restructured to better serve the needs of their communities. Changes in public education include decentralization of authority within school systems—especially in the form of site-based management—as well as an ever-increasing number of magnet schools, and more community control over education policy. All of these developments hold the promise of change for music education, and all have been given attention by various constituencies within the profession.[13]

In addition, the music education profession has seen increased competition by organizations that sponsor performances for students, both in and out of school. Music educators are thus still faced with deciding whether their young musicians are being exploited for commercial purposes. On the other hand, civic groups such as symphony orchestras are helping the business of music education by sponsoring youth groups and by providing in-school appearances of professional musicians. Young Audiences and musicians supported by the National Endowment for the Arts continue to offer cultural programs in schools, some of which are coordinated with official school curricula. In and of themselves, these programs are to be applauded, but they pose questions of the apportioning of limited community resources that need to be addressed. Music educators and independent arts presenters have yet to come to terms with each other in a positive, structured manner.

MUSIC EDUCATION AND COMMUNITY

An especially positive development in the area of community relations is the "Get America Singing . . . Again" campaign led by Will Schmid (MENC president 1994–96). That project, like the one that gained widespread public recognition for the organization in its early days (see pp. 238–41), is designed to establish a common song repertoire and to promote community singing beyond the walls of the school. The heart of the project is the song literature published for community use: a song edition and an accompaniment edition of forty-three songs, with a foreword by Pete Seeger. In 1996, Cincinnati music educators staged a community sing involving thousands in Cincinnati Music Hall. Partners with MENC in the campaign have been the Society for the Preservation and Encouragement of Barber Shop Quartet Singing in America (SPEBSQSA), Sweet Adelines, the American Choral Directors Association (ACDA), and Chorus America. Other cities have seen increased community music activities as well.

Scheduling. Community actions, such as the decision to change to year-round schools or the addition to the curricula of sex education, consumer affairs, AIDS prevention, conservation and energy, and other such current affairs classes, have had a profound impact on the time given to performing music groups. Music educators continue to find creative means to deal with such innovations as block scheduling. In 1991, the U.S. Congress established the National Education Commission on Time and Learning, which published *Prisoners of Time* in 1994.[14] That report led to a recommendation by the Consortium of National Arts Education Associations that 15 percent of school time should be devoted to instruction in the arts. Although the problem of insufficient instructional time still exists, at least there is now an official policy on the subject to support arts educators as they face the problem in the future.

PARTNERSHIPS

MENC–The National Association for Music Education remains the central and preeminent organization of the music education profession, the one under which other music education organizations gather. Vanett Lawler, the second executive secretary of MENC, once commented in regard to an infant organization representing a fraction of the profession, "Better to invite them to come in under the tent than have them outside going their own way." The recent MENC leadership has heeded that advice. The structure of the organization has expanded to incorporate most of the huge variety of specialized interests that constitute the profession. The current *Member Handbook* lists nine associated organizations and nineteen auxiliary organizations, which together represent specialized interests in curriculum, musical genres, teaching methodologies, technology, business, and others.

In addition to the Consortium of National Arts Education Associations discussed above, MENC was instrumental in establishing the National Coalition for Music Education in 1990 to raise awareness of the value and importance of music in education. Joining with MENC are the National Academy of Recording Arts & Sciences, Inc., and NAMM—The International Music Products Association, both of which are prestigious, high-profile organizations that interact with the public in numerous ways that are complementary to the interest of music education. All three groups are focusing on the implementation of the National Standards for Arts Education. The Coalition planned a Music Education Summit in September 1994 involving almost fifty organizations. The ninety-some attendees found ways to promote the National Standards as a help to their own goals and the common good. Subsequent meetings were held in 1996 and 1998. The remarkable variety of specializations represented at these summits indicates how widespread and multifaceted the range of professional interests actually are.

Recently, at the suggestion of Arnold Broido of the Theodore Presser Company, MENC hosted a joint meeting with representatives of the National School Boards Association and the American Society of Composers, Authors and Publishers (ASCAP) Foundation. The participants searched for the most effective ways to inform those policy makers, who ultimately control the educational experiences and standards, of recent evidence of the benefit of music study. Attendees were informed of several reports on the benefits of music education. One, a study by Frances Rauscher and Gordon Shaw, indicated that piano study appears to give children an advantage in spatial-temporal reasoning over their peers who worked with computers or had no special training. The 1997 report of the College Board showed that students with four years of study in the arts outscored those with no arts instruction by a combined total of 101 points on the verbal and mathematical portions of the SAT.

At a second meeting, in August 1998, the group agreed to continue to "stress student achievement, equity, and excellence as we work to raise the consciousness level regarding the importance of music in school." These efforts will be directed at school board members, decision makers, and the general community.

PROBLEMS

As was the case in 1988, there is still no universally accepted philosophy underlying the practice of music education in this country. Many still relate their mission to aesthetic education, which underlies the coming together of the arts education organizations. Not that there are not alternatives available. Some thinkers have offered another approach, which encompasses any manner of participation in music.

One concern, recognized at the Tanglewood Symposium in 1967, is that a relatively small percentage of high school students have any courses in music. This situation has been only partially mitigated in those states that are now requiring an arts credit for graduation. Bennett Reimer, long a defender of music education as aesthetic education, has recently presented listening, seriously taught, as an answer and a responsibility for the profession. He says, relating his comments to the content standards of the National Standards:

> Armed with the guidance of the National Standards, we are finally in a position to expand our mission to better meet the needs of those we are pledged to serve. The most effective way we can do so

is by creating music programs that fulfill the two guidelines we have long proclaimed we need to follow—programs that are balanced and comprehensive. We are not yet there. We are not yet complete. As a result we are not yet secure in education. It is my fondest hope that as the new century begins, we will have rededicated our efforts to the highest ideal—a balanced and comprehensive music education for all students in our schools.[15]

NOTES

1. To more clearly reflect the organization's mission, in 1998, the Music Educators National Conference was renamed MENC—The National Association for Music Education.
2. Consortium of National Arts Education Associations, *National Standards for Arts Education* (Reston, VA: Music Educators National Conference), p. 11.
3. Karl L. Ernst and Charles L. Gary, *Music in General Education* (Washington, DC: Music Educators National Conference, 1965), p. 51.
4. *Teacher Education in Music: Final Report* (Washington, DC: Music Educators National Conference, 1972), pp. 5–6.
5. Consortium of National Arts Education Associations, p. 26.
6. Ibid.
7. Larry Mueth, "MIDI Technology for the Scared to Death," *Music Educators Journal* 79 (October 1993): 49–53.
8. David Beckstein, "Telecommunications and MIDI," *Teaching Music* 4 (October 1996): 49–53.
9. Lisa C. DeLorenzo, "Early Field Experiences in the Community," *Music Educators Journal* 77 (November 1990): 51–53.
10. Richard Colwell, ed., *Handbook of Research on Music Teaching and Learning* (New York: Schirmer Books), 1992.
11. Frank R. Wilson and Franz L. Roehmann, ed., *Music and Child Development* (St. Louis, MO: MMB Music, 1990).
12. Michael L. Mark, *Contemporary Music Education,* 3rd ed. (New York: Schirmer Books, 1992), pp. 19–24.
13. Ibid., pp. 114–17.
14. National Education Commission on Time and Learning, *Prisoners of Time* (Washington, DC: U.S. Government Printing Office, 1994), pp. 7–8.
15. Bennett Reimer, "Music Education in the Twenty-First Century," *Music Educators Journal* 84 (November 1997): 33–38.

BIBLIOGRAPHY

Anderson, William. *Teaching Music with a Multicultural Approach.* Reston, VA: Music Educators National Conference, 1991.

Arts Education Research Agenda for the Future. Washington: National Endowment for the Arts and the U.S. Department of Education, 1994.

Bitz, Michael. "Teaching Improvisation Outside of Jazz Settings." *Music Educators Journal* 84 (January 1998).

Bloom, Benjamin. *Developing Talent in Young People.* New York: Ballantine Books, 1985.

Boswell, Jacquelyn. "Human Potential and Lifelong Learning." *Music Educators Journal* 79 (December 1992).

Britton, Allen P. "MENC: Remembrances and Perspectives." *The Quarterly Journal of Music of Teaching and Learning* (Summer 1994).

Colwell, Richard, ed. *Basic Concepts in Music Education II.* Nivot, CO: University of Colorado Press, 1996.

———. *Handbook of Research on Music Teaching and Learning.* New York: Schirmer Books, 1992.

Consortium of National Arts Education Associations. *National Standards for Arts Education: What Every Young American Should Know and Be Able to Do in the Arts.* Reston, VA: Music Educators National Conference, 1994.

———. "Summary Statement: Education Reform and the Arts." Reston, VA: Music Educators National Conference, 1994.

Csikszentmihalyi, Mihalyi. *Talented Teenagers: The Roots of Success.* Cambridge: Cambridge University Press, 1996.

DeVito, Albert. *Computer, MIDI, Desktop Publishing, Dictionary.* Milwaukee: Kenyon Publications, 1991.

Elliott, David. "Music, Education, and Musical Values." In *Musical Connections: Tradition and Change,* ed. Heath Lees. Auckland, NZ: International Society for Music Education, 1994.

———. *Music Matters.* New York: Oxford University Press, 1995.

Fowler, Charles, and David Elliott. *Winds of Change.* Marie McCarthy, ed. College Park, MD: University of Maryland, 1994.

Frederickson, Scott. "Teaching Beginning Vocal Improvisation." *Music Educators Journal* 90 (January 1994).

Gardner, Howard. *Frames of Mind: The Theory of Multiple Intelligences.* New York: Basic Books, Inc., 1983.

Gary, Charles L. "A Tradition of Progress: 75 Years of the *MEJ.*" *Music Educators Journal* 76 (April 1990).

———. *Transforming Ideas for Teaching and Learning the Arts.* Washington: U.S. Department of Education, 1997.

Griswold, Harold E. "Multiculturalism, Music, and Information Highways." *Music Educators Journal* 81 (November 1994).

Hall, Marianne. "Dance in the Music Classroom." *Teaching Music* 6 (August 1998).

Jorgensen, Estelle R. "Towards an Enhanced Community of Scholars in Music Education." *The Quarterly Journal of Music Teaching and Learning* (Spring 1990).

Labuta, Joseph A., and Deborah Smith. *Music Education: Historical Contexts and Perspectives.* Upper Saddle River: Prentice Hall, 1997.

Lehman, Paul. "The National Standards: From Vision to Reality." *Music Educators Journal* 81 (September 1994).

Mahlmann, John J. "Maximizing the Power of Coalitions." *Association Management* 47 (September 1995).

Mark, Michael. *Contemporary Music Education,* 3rd edition. New York: Simon and Schuster Macmillan, 1996.

Moody, William, ed. *Artistic Intelligence and Implications for Education.* New York: Teachers College Press, 1990.

National Commission on Music Education. *Growing Up Complete: The Imperative for Music Education.* Reston, VA: Music Educators National Conference, 1991.

National Education Commission on Time and Learning. *Prisoners of Time.* Washington: U.S. Government Printing Office, 1994.

Opportunity-to-Learn Standards for Music Instruction: Grades PreK–12. Reston, VA: Music Educators National Conference, 1994.

Perspectives on Implementation: Arts Education for America's Students. Reston, VA: Music Educators National Conference, 1994.

Reese, Sam, and Adam Davis. "The Systematic Approach to Music Technology." *Music Educators Journal* 85 (July 1998).

Reimer, Bennett. "Music Education as Aesthetic Education: Past and Present." *Music Educators Journal* 75 (February 1989).

———. "Music Education as Aesthetic Education: Toward the Future." *Music Educators Journal* 75 (March 1989).

———. *A Philosophy of Music Education,* 2nd edition. Englewood Cliffs, NJ: Prentice-Hall, 1989.

Reimer, Bennett, and Ralph Smith, eds. *The Arts, Education, and Aesthetic Knowing.* Chicago: National Society for the Study of Education, 1992.

Reimer, Bennett and Jeffery E. Wright, eds. *On the Nature of the Musical Experience.* Niwot, CO: University of Colorado Press, 1992.

Roads, Curtis. *Computer Music Tutorial.* Cambridge: MIT Press, 1996.

Small, Christopher. *Music, Society and Education.* Middletown, CT: Wesleyan University Press, 1996.

Stake, Robert. *Evaluating the Arts in Education: A Responsive Approach.* Columbus: Charles E. Merrill Publishing Co., 1975.

Swannick, Keith. *Music, Mind and Education.* London: Routledge, 1988.

The Vision for Arts Education in the 21st Century. Reston, VA: Music Educators National Conference, 1994.

Volk, Terese M. *Music, Education, and Multiculturalism.* New York: Oxford University Press, 1998.

Wilson, Frank R. *Tone Deaf and All Thumbs.* New York: Random House, 1988.

Preface to the First Edition

Music has been a part of every known society. Its functions vary in different societies, but it is commonly used for ritual, work, entertainment, pageantry, therapy, communication, and of course aesthetic satisfaction. The transmission of the knowledge of music, what we call music education, has also been part of the culture of all societies. From the simplest teaching by imitation to the complex systems of music education we know today, the history of music education informs us that music has been considered worthy of study and practice by all people.

Now, at the end of the twentieth century, we live in an era of greater international cooperation, in which cultural differences tend to be recognized and respected. Many of us have learned to cherish the uniqueness of every culture and to recognize how each enriches our contemporary technological society. This was not always the case. When Europeans were still new to America, they kept most of the old ways alive here. The European heritage influenced American cultural life profoundly. As a result, the study of any aspect of American history, including music education, must reflect its precedents in other countries.

Although the contributions of African and Asian heritages to music education are significant, their influence on practices in the broad, formal music education setting became universal only after public-school music education was well established in the United States. For this reason, in Part I, we begin our examination of American music education with its Western precedents. Part II deals with the nature of the New World and those who made the earliest contributions to American music instruction. Part III reviews the political, cultural, and musical conditions and events from the beginning of the United States of America through its first seventy-five years. Part IV treats the evolution of the music education profession, and Part V reviews American music education after the middle of the twentieth century.

The distinguished American composer Howard Hanson once told a radio audience:

The development of music in the public schools, in my opinion, constitutes the most significant progress that has been made in the music development of the United States. It is not too much to say that this movement has not only national but world significance. In public school music, America has indeed surpassed itself and given to the countries of the old world a lesson and an example.

What is the nature of the phenomenon to which Hanson referred? How did such a blossoming occur on the outskirts of Western civilization? From whence came the seeds? Who brought them to the New World? How was a new society able to support such a flowering while at the same time conquering a continent and populating it with people from around the world? What circumstances nurtured this growth? Who took charge of these events and stimulated the growth of American music education? This book will examine these questions as it recounts the history of an American experiment—universal education in music.

The authors hope that students preparing to devote their professional lives to music education will profit from a better understanding of its triumphs and shortcomings and will be inspired by a knowledge of some of the dauntless, and even heroic, figures who have gone before. It is possible, too, that practicing music educators may also find inspiration and enhanced regard for their historic and noble profession.

Primary sources were consulted whenever possible. A considerable body of information on the history of music education, however, has also been recorded in respected research journals and in the theses and dissertations produced in American universities. Much use was made of these secondary sources. The authors are grateful to all of the scholars whose works were consulted, but we confess that we did not hesitate to verify some of the material against available primary sources when discrepancies were discovered.

The authors wish to thank the Music Educators National Conference and its members for the use of many quotations from the *Journal of Research and Music Education*, the *Music Educators Journal*, and many other publications that represent a great portion of American music education over the past 84 years.

The authors are also indebted to Dr. Cyrilla Barr and Father Alexander DiLella of The Catholic University of America; Dr. Allen Britton, Dean Emeritus of the School of Music of the University of Michigan; and Dr. George Heller of the University of Kansas; as well as to Carolyn Westbrook of Towson State University for her assistance with the illustrations for this book. Finally, we wish to express our appreciation to Maribeth Anderson Payne, Jane Andrassi, and Robert Axelrod of Schirmer Books for their support, help, and patience as this work progressed.

MICHAEL L. MARK   CHARLES L. GARY
Towson State University   The Catholic University of America

A HISTORY OF

AMERICAN
MUSIC
EDUCATION

PART I

THE WESTERN HERITAGE

1

THE HEBREWS OF THE
OLD TESTAMENT

This history of music education in Western civilization begins with the Hebrews because in their culture, unlike others, music was part of the lives of all the people and not just the domain of professional musicians. The Hebrews were unusual among ancient peoples in believing that music was not an invention of the gods with the power to influence morality and affect behavior.[1] To the Hebrews, music was a human invention; they used it in worship and work, and probably for enjoyment as well.

THE HEBREWS IN EGYPT

The Hebrews probably participated in the musical life of Egypt during their enslavement there, but it was not until their deliverance that we learn of their universal participation:

> Then Moses and the people sang this song to the Lord, saying, I will sing to the Lord, for he has triumphed gloriously; the horse and his rider he has thrown into the sea. . . . Then Miriam . . . took a timbrel in her hand and all the women went out after her with timbrels and dancing. And she led them in the refrain then; Sing unto the Lord, for he has triumphed gloriously; the horse and his rider he has thrown into the sea.[2]

Music had been a part of their life long before the Hebrews became captives in Egypt, but it is likely that their musical skills and knowledge were enriched during many generations in the Egyptian musical environment. Throughout their enslavement the Hebrews had the opportunity to observe an organized system of music that included singing, dancing, and all of the instruments mentioned in the Old Testament except the shofar.

MOSES

The highly ethical and humanitarian religion of the Hebrews was based on the concept that all men and women were equal before God. Music was considered a way of serving God, and everyone was expected to be involved. Moses, the leader of the Hebrews during their deliverance, was well trained in music, and he probably understood the relationship between Egyptian music and religious observances thoroughly. He might even have attended the special school for liturgical music in Memphis.

Moses has been identified as the first true music educator as we understand the term today.[3] Not only did he mold the Hebrews into a nation bound together with a unique ethical religion during their forty years of wandering in the wilderness, but he must also have insisted that they study music to maintain their skills. He demonstrated the use of music, and he composed and taught.[4]

THE HEBREWS IN CANAAN

When the Hebrews arrived in Canaan, they established a distinctive culture that employed poetry and music. Scholars have speculated that pictorial art and sculpture were not part of their lives because they were forbidden to make graven images.

Universal Participation in Music. Folk songs of a highly rhythmical nature accompanied working in the fields, picking grapes, and treading the grapes in the winepress. The Bible gives the texts of several war songs as well as accounts of events involving masses of people singing in processions. Much of this music was undoubtedly learned through the family or while participating in those activities.

The central aspect of Hebrew life was religion, and the Bible provides clues to the role music played in it. By the time of the prophet Samuel (c. 1020 B.C.), poetry and singing had advanced to a high level. Samuel and David (Israel's second king) are thought to have organized the complex use of voices and instruments that became an integral part of the religious service. Sendry cites the Babylonian Talmud as indicating that the sacrificial act was invalidated by the lack of singing.[5] Werner indicates that the Talmud "hints that lack of correct singing annulled the value of the sacrifice."[6]

Music in the Religious Service. The musicians of the temple at Jerusalem, the Levites, were the descendants of Aaron. They were professionals who were permitted to serve only when they reached the age of thirty. Their training was supposed to begin at the age of twenty-five, but because they were required to master so much music by rote, they probably began earlier. Another group of professional musicians, the bards, were paid well enough for their services at weddings, banquets, and other religious and civic celebrations to be stable members of the community.

Music Instruction for Religion. Although professional temple musicians originally sang for religious services, the people eventually joined in. At first they might have only interjected amens and hallelujahs, but the parallelism of their poetry, going back to the Sumerians hundreds of years before, lent itself to responsorial singing. Some of their psalms were written to encourage participation. Psalm 147, verses 1 and 7, demonstrates the principle and the Hebrews' faith in music.

1. (CALL) Praise ye the Lord: for it is good to sing praises unto our God. (RESPONSE) For it is pleasant: and praise is comely.
7. (CALL) Sing unto the Lord with thanksgiving; (RESPONSE) Sing praise upon the harp unto our God.

Responsorial chanting or reading of the psalms is still the practice of Jews and Christians alike.

There was also a formal structure for learning music. Representatives of the people, *Anshe Maamad*, traveled to Jerusalem each year from every part of the kingdom.[7] These "bystanders" were taught in a synagogue within the temple by outstanding Levites. Two of these early music educators—Rabbi Joshua ben Hananya and his disciple, Rabbi Johanen ben Zakkai—are known by name.[8] The laypersons then returned to their own synagogues (there were 394 of them at one time) to share the new songs with their neighbors.

SUMMARY

In the context of the history of music education, the most important aspect of the music of the ancient Hebrews is not the contribution of the professional musicians but rather the concept of each individual's worth and his or her right and duty to "sing unto the Lord." The Hebrew culture provided a model for universal participation in music and music education. The model did not continue throughout Western history, but it has resurfaced in the democratic educational system of the United States.

NOTES

1. Edward Dickenson, *Music in the History of the Western Church* (New York: Scribner's, 1902), p. 14.
2. Exod. 15:1, 20, 21.
3. Alfred Sendry, *Music in Ancient Israel* (New York: Philosophical Library, 1969), p. 482.
4. Deut. 31:13, 19, 22.
5. Sendry, *Music in Ancient Israel*, p. 169.
6. Eric Werner, "Music," *Interpreter's Dictionary of the Bible*, vol. 3 (New York: Abingdon Press, 1962), p. 460.
7. A. Z. Idelsohn, *Jewish Music in Its Historical Development* (New York: Tudor, 1948), p. 21.
8. Werner, "Music," p. 463.

BIBLIOGRAPHY

Dickenson, Edward. *Music in the History of the Western Church*. New York: Scribner's, 1902.

Gradenwitz, Peter. *The Music of Israel: Its Rise and Growth Through 5000 Years*. New York: Norton, 1949.

Heaton, E. W. *Everyday Life in Old Testament Times*. New York: Scribner's, 1956 .

Idelsohn, A. Z. *Jewish Music in Its Historical Development*. New York: Tudor, 1948.

The Interpreters Bible, The Holy Scriptures in the King James and Revised Standard Versions. Vol. 1–12. Nashville: Abingdon, 1952.

Rothmuller, Aron M. *The Music of the Jews*. New York: Barnes, 1954.

Saminsky, Lazare. *Music of the Ghetto and the Bible*. New York: Block, 1934.

Sendry, Alfred. *Music in Ancient Israel*. New York: Philosophical Library, 1969.

—— and Norton, Mildred. *David's Harp*. New York: New American Library, 1963.

Werner, Eric. "Music." *Interpreter's Dictionary of the Bible*, vol. 3. New York: Abingdon, 1962.

——. *The Sacred Bridge*. Jersey City, NJ: Da Capo Press, 1979.

White, John Manchip. *Everyday Life in Ancient Egypt*. London: Balsford, 1963.

2

THE AGE OF ANTIQUITY

GREECE

The Greeks came to the Mediterranean basin around 1000 B.C.; Greek culture dates to about a century later, 900 B.C. In the Mediterranean area they found a highly developed musical system that included poetry and dancing among the conquered peoples. The Greeks respected the people under their domination and incorporated the best parts of their cultures into their own. They often adopted the music of other cultures and modified it to suit their own needs and tastes.

Greek Democracy. One of the fundamental beliefs of Greek civilization was that man lives in an orderly universe in which it is possible to seek truth and virtue. Man's rational powers enable him to achieve happiness and fulfillment. A democratic system of government was established to reflect this belief. The affluent and comfortable life of Greek citizens, however, was based on a caste system, the lowest level of which consisted of slaves.

The Greek citizen sought wealth because it permitted a life of satisfaction, meaning the proper balance between the intellectual and the physical. When Athens blossomed during its Golden Age (beginning around 500 B.C.), it contained beautiful buildings, attention was paid to the arts, and it had a highly developed educational system. All of these facets of Greek society reflect the belief that the human condition was the primary goal in life. The city provided a wealth of cultural, intellectual, and athletic opportunities that supported high materialistic and spiritual standards of life.

Sophistry. The freedom of Greek society provided an atmosphere in which intellectual curiosity was prized. Many scholars tried to understand the world by examining the universe and man's relationship to it. Numerous schools of philosophy developed, but one, Sophistry, had the greatest influence on Athenian life. The Sophists—teachers who held the highest humanistic ideals—believed in the concept of the balanced individual, whose ability to discipline and control himself was the basis of his own satisfaction and happiness. The Sophists gained political control of the city-state and were thus able to enforce their teachings, but as has been demonstrated throughout history, political and intellectual authority do not mix well. Over time, Sophist beliefs evolved from idealistic convictions to a dogmatism that corrupted their political authority. They no longer believed in divine force, having concluded that "man is the measure of all things"; since there is no higher force, man makes his own rules. This doctrine inevitably leads to the authority of one person—the one with political power. New ideas about the nature of virtue and citizenship were rejected because they threatened those in power. Eventually, Athenian society began to decay because its government no longer supported traditional humanistic ideals. Instead, a perversion of those values permeated the government, leading to decadence and corruption.[1]

Education was an important aspect of Greek life, and many contemporary Western educational ideas and beliefs started there. The three-tiered organization of education—primary, secondary, and tertiary (where boys were prepared for the military)—was created by the Greeks. The state supported the tertiary level in Athens and all three levels in Sparta.

Greek educational systems were often built on music (including poetry) and gymnastics to purify the soul and develop the body. The goal of Greek education was pragmatic—to influence both the body and the soul to develop citizens capable of participating in Greek society and worthy of receiving its benefits. The educational systems of both Sparta and Athens included music as an integral part of the curriculum. Music education was necessary because music festivals, contests, and singing societies were integral to the culture of Greece, and adults were expected to participate.

It is possible that the Greeks invented collective schooling when schoolboys attended schools accompanied by their slaves.[2] (Girls did not attend school.) The first level was the music school. There students learned poetry and how to accompany themselves on the lyre. They studied at the music school from the ages of seven to fourteen, when they began their secondary education. The work in music was done largely on an individual basis, and so it is likely that some boys attended in the morning and others in the afternoon.[3] School began shortly after daybreak and ended before sunset. The boys went home for their meals. Solon passed a law preventing schools from remaining open after sunset. Classes were held straight through the weekend, with no break. The fourth-century philosopher Teles referred to gymnastics trainers, literary masters, music masters, and painters as the four chief burdens of boys.

Pythagoras (582–507 B.C.). The Greek mathematician Pythagoras, who influenced the study of music throughout much of Western history, taught that music and arithmetic were integral to each other. His observation of the relationship of the sides of a triangle led him to conclude that mathematical relationships are universal and do not vary in individual cases. So it was with his acoustical observations. He found that when a vibrating string is halved, its vibration rate is doubled, and the pitch is an octave higher. Such mathematical relationships were the foundation for the study of the scientific aspects of music.

According to the Pythagorean view, music was a "microcosm, a system of sound and rhythm ruled by the same mathematical laws that operate in the whole of the visible and invisible creation."[4] The Pythagorean school valued music because it is governed by the same mathematical laws that govern the universe, which can be understood through knowledge of its mathematical proportions. One who understood musical proportions could understand the harmony of the universe. Music as a mathematical science became an important subject of study and remained so for many centuries.

Sparta, the warrior city-state, educated its young people to be soldiers who were completely faithful to the state. For that reason, physical training was of utmost importance and included riding and sports, for both men and women. Sparta had a musical culture that was reflected in its educational system. Plutarch tells us that Sparta was the real musical capital of Greece in the seventh and early sixth centuries. When sacrifices were made to the city's deities, there were solemn processions in which children paraded to the accompaniment of singing. Festivals, held throughout the year, were an important part of Spartan life; they included athletic and musical competitions and are thought to have reached a high artistic level.

Plutarch mentioned two music schools. The first, which existed for the first two-thirds of the seventh century, was noted for its vocal and instrumental solos; the second, which lasted from the end of the seventh century to the beginning of the sixth, specialized in choral lyrics and produced musicians and poets of renown.

The purpose of education was to prepare men to be soldiers, with everything directed toward that end. Students learned to read and write and received musical training, but not for its aesthetic value: They learned music because it helped develop loyalty to the state and was a natural accompaniment to the activities of war.

Athens, like Sparta, was a city-state, but its cultural and artistic values were sharply different. Originally, all parts of Greece had similar levels of culture and education. In the sixth century the Athenians became the first to end the practice of keeping its men armed at all times, even within the city. They eventually adopted a less violent, more civilized life-style. By the fifth century, Athenian life, culture, and education had become predominantly civilian.

The art of Athens, originally only music, was characterized by playing the lyre, dancing, and singing. The word "music" later came to mean the fine arts, and most of what we know of Greek art is found in forms other than music, including architecture and sculpture, poetry, and dancing. The arts were taught in schools, where children learned drawing, dancing, and music. Drawing and painting teachers were added to the staffs of Athenian schools in the fourth century.

Greek students learned both instrumental and vocal music. Two instruments, the lyre and the aulos (a type of oboe), were essential to Greek music and therefore to Greek music education. By the second century B.C. the aulos had lost its popularity, and only the lyre was taught to children. Students learned to sing as well as play. Some school examinations in the third century included a test in accompanied singing and a lyre solo.[5] Boys were excused from the study of poetry and music after the age of fifteen.

More important was choral singing, which was performed in unison and accompanied by an instrument, usually the aulos. Choirs were required for religious ceremonies held by the city. The ceremonies played an important part in the education of Greek youth, but choral singing was not necessarily a major part of the curriculum. The music was simple, and a master could prepare the chorus in a few rehearsals. The ceremonies were held at the time of certain feasts and were accompanied by intertribal competitions. Each tribe was represented by its choir, which was sponsored by one of its rich citizens. The Hellenistic tradition emphasized not only excellent performance and high artistic quality but also competition. As competition intensified, some choirs began to use professional musicians rather than amateurs. The increasing use of professionals was one of the factors that caused the decline of musical amateurism and thus of music in Greek education.

A school charter of the second century describes how schools were to be organized. They were to have three literature teachers, two gymnastics teachers, and one music teacher. Since the music teacher was a specialist, he earned more than the others. He taught only the boys in the last two years of school and at the *ephebia*, where young men served their military obligation. At school the music instructor taught the lyre (with and without plectrum) and "music," which meant either singing or mathematical theory. Some school charters in other parts of Greece required no music at all.

The Decline of Music in Education. Until about the fifth century, music had been simple in nature and easy to play. It eventually declined in educational importance because it was no longer within the technical ability of amateurs to perform—it had become complex and required technical proficiency. Starting late in the fifth century, musical performance became the province of specialists. Conservative educators insisted on keeping music in the curriculum as it had been when it was performed by amateurs, but Aristotle and others questioned its value if students could not hope to perform it satisfactorily.

MUSIC IN GREEK EDUCATION

Plato (c. 427–347 B.C.). Plato's writings have influenced education throughout Western history because he was concerned with the education of the ideal citizen. Plato's teacher, Socrates, had accepted his death sentence willingly rather than disobey Athenian law, despite the fact that it reflected Sophist corruption. His idealism was passed on to his student, much of whose philosophy was dedicated to defining the ideal political state. That state, described in the *Republic,* was quite different from the actual one in which he lived, and the idealized educational system he advocated was that of an earlier time in Greek history.

Plato's ideal state included an educational system with two basic elements—music and gymnastics. Gymnastics and field sports, the curriculum of his sports school, were important pastimes of children and adults because they developed the "civic virtues of disciplined courage, self-control, friendly cooperation, and loyalty to the group and its ideals" (*Republic, Laws*).

Organized games were valued not only because they developed the body and character but also because they were useful "with a view to war and the management of home and city." Sports competitions were held monthly, with the entire community participating. Education in gymnastics was actually training for community festivals, greater festivals in honor of deceased leaders, and the twelve annual military field days. Gymnastics training prepared citizens for warfare, helped them maintain physical fitness, and developed positive civic virtues.

A Balanced Education. Plato's dialogue between Socrates and Glaucon in the *Republic* established a rationale for balance in education:

> There are two arts which I would say some god gave to mankind, music and gymnastics for the service of the high-spirited principle and the love of knowledge in them—not for the soul and the body except incidentally,

but for the harmonious adjustment of these two principles by the proper degree of tension and relaxation of each.

Then he who best blends gymnastics with music and applies them most suitably to the soul is the man whom we should most rightly pronounce to be the most perfect and harmonious musician, far rather than the one who brings the strings into unison with one another.

Upon receiving Glaucon's agreement with this statement, Socrates asked: "And shall we not also need in our city, Glaucon, a permanent overseer of this kind if its constitution is to be preserved?"[6] It appears that Socrates was advocating the appointment of a supervisor of music and gymnastics.

Plato believed that the affect of music (meaning music, literature, and dancing) on children influenced their values and behavior, and he advocated censorship over the music used in education. The purposes of music in education were to help children develop a perception of idealized community life and to prepare them to participate actively in it as responsible citizens. The use of improper music, poetry, and stories would defeat these purposes.

Education in music is most sovereign, because more than anything else rhythm and harmony find their way to the innermost soul and take strongest hold upon it, bringing with them and imparting grace, if one is rightly trained, and otherwise the contrary. And further, because omissions and the failure of beauty in things badly made or grown would be most quickly perceived by one who was properly educated in music, and so, feeling distaste rightly, he would praise beautiful things and take delight in them and receive them into his soul to foster its growth and become himself beautiful and good. The ugly he would rightly disapprove of and hate while still young and yet unable to apprehend the reason, but when reason came the man thus nurtured would be the first to give her welcome, for by this affinity he would know her.[7]

Plato's ideal education actually reflected the "good old days," when it consisted of gymnastics for the body and music for the soul.

The Education of Leaders. Plato believed that basic education was appropriate for ordinary citizens but was insufficient for training future leaders. Those selected to lead would not necessarily be the best musicians and athletes, who are trained by repetition which does not develop scientific insights. Without such insights, one could not know the truth. He called music "guesswork" because it appeals to the emotions rather than to the intellect. According to Plato, art is revelation and can contain deep meaning, but such is not always the case; it can also be a faint imitation of reality. Thus, art is sometimes truth and sometimes not. The artist never knows whether his works are true. Also, the arts must be interpreted, and each listener interprets differently. Therefore, the arts do not offer a rational approach to truth and are not suitable for intense study and practice by those who would be leaders.

Future leaders needed to study science, but not that of Pythagoras, who observed and categorized physical phenomena. Plato believed that people are misled by sensory impressions, so truth can be discovered only by the intellect. The revelation of the physical nature of the universe is external to the phenomenon under study. The scientist is actually a spectator. Plato preferred the abstract study of science, in which the philosopher-scientist separates science from the empirical method and studies pure theory. This is done through the dialectic method, which is an inductive means of discovering truth by asking the right questions. The subjects to be studied by the dialectic method were arithmetic, geometry, astronomy, and harmonics. These four mathematical subjects, later known as the quadrivium, constituted the core of classical higher studies. Students were expected not only to have basic functional knowledge of each subject but also to perceive the pure essence of each subject as well. In other words, they were expected to discover truth with the mind only, independent of sensory experience.[8]

Harmonics, or music, was the study of acoustics. Musical tones and their relationships were merely the rudimentary basis of the purely intellectual study of harmonics, which led students into the purely intellectual realm of reason. The dialectic examination of what Plato called the natural harmony of numbers was his means of investigating why some numbers are harmonious and others are not. This is why harmonics was considered a science and included in the higher education curriculum.[9] Having completed the study of the quadrivium, future leaders went on to study philosophy, by which they could learn the truth that enabled them to be leaders.

Aristotle (384–322 B.C.) desired that the school curriculum reflect the needs of both the community and the individual. His scientific writings covered the theoretical sciences (physics, mathematics, metaphysics), practical sciences, and productive sciences, which included the creation of artificial things such as the arts. He agreed with his teacher, Plato, on the importance of music in education but viewed it somewhat differently. He wrote:

> The customary branches of education are in number four; they are—(1) reading and writing, (2) gymnastic exercises, (3) music, to which is sometimes added (4) drawing. Of these, reading and writing and drawing are regarded as useful for the purposes of life in a variety of ways, and gymnastic exercises are thought to infuse courage. Concerning music a doubt may be raised—in our own day most men cultivate it for the sake of pleasure, but originally it was included in education, because nature herself, as has been often said, requires that we should be able, not only to work well, but to use leisure well . . . our fathers admitted music into education,

not on the ground either of its necessity or utility, for it is not necessary, nor indeed useful in the same manner as reading and writing, which are useful in moneymaking, in the management of a household, in the acquisition of knowledge and in political life, nor like drawing, useful for a more correct judgement of the works of artists, nor again like gymnastic, which gives health and strength; for neither of these is to be gained from music. There remains, then, the use of music for intellectual enjoyment in leisure; which is in fact evidently the reason of its introduction, this being one of the ways in which it is thought that a freeman should pass his leisure. . . . It is evident, then, that there is a sort of education in which parents should train their sons, not as being useful or necessary, but because it is liberal or noble.

Aristotle proposed that students should not be trained to compete with professionals but should study music to develop musical taste. His words describe what he wanted to see happen in the schools. This did not happen, however, and educators continued to offer the music instruction of archaic times. They were not successful because the societal conditions that affected music instruction had changed radically. Music and gymnastic instruction were static and inappropriate for the times, and by the first century B.C. they had all but disappeared from the liberal curriculum of Greek schools. Education became predominantly literary.[10]

ROME

The Romans, conquerors of Greece and much of the rest of Europe and the Mediterranean area, emulated the Greeks by absorbing the best of the cultures they conquered. In fact, the Greek educational system was adopted almost in its entirety. Unlike the Greeks, the Romans were not innovative and made relatively insignificant contributions to the history of music. Roman art and music, like practically all other Roman creations, were produced by professional artists and musicians, often slaves influenced by Hellenism. The one important original Roman educational contribution was the study of the law to prepare students for legal careers. Probably the greatest contribution of Rome to Western culture is the creation of its legal system to govern a vast empire.

When the Romans first realized the vitality of Greek culture, they were enthralled with the singing and dancing characteristic of Greek life. Romans were more somber, though, and they eventually reacted against this aspect of Greek culture. Music was not considered an appropriate activity for boys, and it was barely tolerated for girls. Although it was sometimes included in Roman education, it had no standing of real strength in the curriculum and little respect among educators.

In this regard, music in Roman education was similar to music in Greek education during the last two centuries of independence.

There was music in ancient Rome, and it had a part in Roman life. The musicians were artisans, however, and did not come from the aristocracy. The making of music was the work of professionals, usually slaves, whose education consisted of instruction in those subjects they needed to do the work required of them. Thus, some slaves studied music in order to become professional musicians.

Music as a mathematical science was sometimes studied by the scientifically gifted as part of their secondary education. Secondary education was available to relatively few students, virtually all of them belonging to the aristocracy. There is evidence of teachers of mathematics from the first to the fourth centuries whose teachings included music as a scientific subject.

The sons of aristocrats often aspired to careers in politics and law, both highly respected professions. The successful politician or lawyer needed to be persuasive, and so the study of rhetoric was integral to his education. Quintilian, the famous professor of rhetoric, recommended the study of music because it helped the orator to learn effective declamation and movement. He articulated no other reason to include music in the educational program.

Athenaeus, a Greek who lived in Rome about A.D. 200, wrote books about Roman life. In his *Deipnosophistai* (*Sophists at Dinner*) he quotes Theophilus from *The Harp Singer*: ''A mighty treasure, good sirs, and a constant one, is music for all who have learned it and are educated.''[11] In the same work, Athenaeus describes those who lived in Arcadia, where the law required that from infancy boys be trained in singing hymns to heroes and to the gods. He thus provides additional evidence of the functional importance of education in music in classical societies.

SUMMARY

Music was an important part of life in the classical world, and the thinkers of Greece and Rome investigated and reflected on the relationship between man and music. Their insights have influenced all Western societies to follow. The writings of the ancients may not appear to apply to this account of the development of universal music education because they were concerned only with an elite group that was supported by a much larger number of slaves and others lower than themselves in the societal stratum. Without their contributions, however, Western intellectual and cultural history would have developed quite differently, and contemporary American music education would probably be different as well.

NOTES

1. Michael L. Mark, *Source Readings in Music Education History* (New York: Schirmer, 1982), pp. 3–4.
2. Edward Power, *Main Currents in the History of Education* (New York: McGraw-Hill, 1962), p. 47.
3. Percival R. Cole, *A History of Educational Thought* (London: Oxford Univesity Press, 1931), p. 26.
4. Donald J. Grout, *A History of Western Music* (New York: Norton, 1973), p. 7.
5. H. I. Marrou, *A History of Education in Antiquity* (New York: Sheed and Ward, 1956), p. 135.
6. From Plato, *Republic*: III, *The Collected Dialogues of Plato*, ed. Edith Hamilton and Huntington Cairns (Bollingen Series 71, 1961, reprinted by the Princeton University Press, 1984), pp. 654–56.
7. From Plato, *Protagoras* in *The Collected Dialogues of Plato*, ed. Edith Hamilton and Huntington Cairns (Bollingen Series 71, 1961, reprinted by the Princeton University Press, 1984), p. 322.
8. Ibid.
9. Mark, *Source Readings in Music Education History*, p. 6.
10. Ibid., pp. 138–42.
11. From Athenaeus, *The Deipnosophists*, trans. Charles Burton Gulick (Cambridge, MA: Harvard University Press, 1937), p. 362.

BIBLIOGRAPHY

Athenaeus. *The Deipnosophists.* Translated by Charles Burton Gulick. Cambridge, MA: Harvard University Press, 1937.

Grout, Donald J. *A History of Western Music.* New York: Norton, 1988.

Hamilton, Edith, and Cairns, Huntington, eds. *The Collected Dialogues of Plato.* Bollingen Series 71, 1961, reprinted by the Princeton University Press, 1984.

Mark, Michael L. *Source Readings in Music Education History.* New York: Schirmer, 1982.

Marrou, H. I. *A History of Education in Antiquity.* New York: Sheed and Ward, 1956.

Power, Edward. *Main Currents in the History of Education.* New York: McGraw-Hill, 1962.

3

MUSIC EDUCATION FROM THE EARLY CHRISTIAN ERA TO THE REFORMATION

MUSIC IN THE EARLY CHRISTIAN ERA AND THE MIDDLE AGES

Two major figures in the history of music and music education, St. Augustine and Boethius, emerged as the Roman Empire declined and Western civilization began its descent into the Dark Ages. St. Augustine spent much of his life considering the appeal of music to the emotions. Boethius, who has been referred to as both the last of the Romans and the first of the Scholastics (medieval scholars), was instrumental in maintaining the status of music as a mathematical subject.

St. Augustine (354–430). The many conquered peoples of the vast Roman Empire did not have the benefits of Roman citizenship and had little or no opportunity to lead meaningful and fulfilled lives. When the Edict of Milan (A.D 313) legalized Christianity, with its promise of a better afterlife, the new religion spread throughout the empire in a relatively short time. Christian education also developed and flourished.

The major church figure in relating classical (Greek) thought on music to the Church was St. Augustine. Aurelius Augustinus was born in what is now Algeria. He received a Roman education and became a teacher of rhetoric in Carthage, Rome, and Milan. After a dissolute and pagan youth he reformed under the influence of St. Ambrose and converted to Christianity in 387. In 396 he founded a monastery in Hippo (Algeria); later he became the bishop of Hippo.

Augustine influenced Christianity profoundly. Through his writings, he created the intellectual framework that allowed Christianity to become the predominant European religion. He wrote little on education but nevertheless influenced European education throughout the Middle Ages, when it was a function of the church rather than of the secular state. His major work about music, *De Musica*, reviewed Greek musical practices and theory and merged them with Christian doctrine. *De Musica* prepared the way for the development of music as an integral part of Christian life.[1]

Augustine embodied the division between the theoretical aspect of music as a mathematical science and its ability to stir the emotions. Reflecting the Greek attitude, he acknowledged the dominance of reason over emotion but conceded the aesthetic influence of music on himself. Augustine feared that the beauty of music would overcome the piety of worshipers and was torn between the two positions. He described his uncertainty about the proper use of music in *Confessions*:

> The pleasures of the ear did indeed draw me and hold me more tenaciously, but You have set me free. Yet still when I hear those airs, in which Your words breathe life, sung with sweet and measured voice, I do, I admit, find a certain satisfaction in them, yet not such as to grip me too close, for I can depart when I will. . . . At times indeed it seems to me that I am paying them greater honour than is their due—when, for example, I feel that by those holy words my mind is kindled more religiously and fervently to a flame of piety because I hear them sung than if they were not sung. . . . Yet there are times when through too great a fear of this temptation, I err in the direction of over-severity—even to the point sometimes of wishing that the melody of all the lovely airs with which David's Psalter is commonly sung should be banished not only from my own ears, but from the Church's as well. . . . Thus I fluctuate between the peril of indulgence and the profit I have found: and on the whole I am inclined . . . to approve the custom of singing in church, that by the pleasure of the ear the weaker minds may be roused to a feeling of devotion.[2]

Augustine's ambivalence was characteristic of the Middle Ages, when music was both the "property of theory, the subject of speculation and remote abstraction, and an art which can exist by virtue of its own merits."[3] Boethius, on the other hand, stated that the true musician approached music not through the senses but through the faculty of reason. To him, *ars musica* (musical art) was not art as Augustine recognized it but music theory. He did not consider the musician a performer but rather one who could speculate about music.[4]

The Seven Liberal Arts. "Liberal" means free; thus the "free" arts were the means by which one achieved spiritual and intellectual maturity. In the hierarchical society of the Roman Empire the liberal arts were fit for freemen but not for others. Higher learning was divided into two groups of subjects during the decline of the Roman Empire and throughout the Middle Ages. The basis for the division of studies reaches back to the Greeks, whose various spiritual and intellectual endeavors were known as "disciplines" (*disciplinae*) by the Romans. The disciplines were categorized into many divisions, which were reduced to seven in the fifth century A.D. The trivium was the lower level of disciplines, the quadrivium the higher.

The trivium, which consisted of grammar, logic, and rhetoric, helped the student develop eloquence in preparation for teaching, discourse, and preaching. The quadrivium consisted of arithmetic, geometry, astronomy, and music. Kresteff wrote:

> The quadrivium, regarded as leading to a higher sphere of spiritual activity, had objectives which were to be reached by following . . . the fourfold road to intellectual excellence. . . . It constituted the only way by which one could penetrate into the mysteries of physical and spiritual realities and gain knowledge of the ultimate reason and truth dwelling beyond them.[5]

The trivium used the arts in a utilitarian manner. They were included for the usefulness of their practical applications. The quadrivium, conversely, was the vehicle by which the mind could learn the secrets of the universe.

Music, a theoretical subject, was a quadrivial discipline. As the Middle Ages progressed, however, two applications of music were recognized. *Musica disciplina,* as part of the quadrivium, was related to mathematics and held the possibility of revealing to the scholar the secrets of physical reality. The other application was music as an art, or *musica sonora. Musica sonora* was communicated by the voice and musical instruments. It was the antithesis of *musica disciplina,* not only because it was known through the senses rather than by reason but also because it appealed to the emotions and influenced behavior. The two divisions of music reflected the practical study of music as a means of worship and the purely theoretical study of music as a mathematical science. *Musica sonora* and *musica disciplina* developed in parallel fashion until about the end of the ninth century.

Boethius (475–525). The way for the study of music as a quadrivial discipline was prepared by Boethius, a Roman statesman and scholar whose work *De Institutione Musica* preserved Greek music theory and was studied by musicians for over a millennium. Greek musical theory, divorced from actual Greek music, was a discrete body of knowledge throughout the Middle Ages. *De Institutione Musica* was one of the major reasons for that particular view of music.

De Institutione Musica, one of four works about the quadrivium, was so influential that it was studied throughout the Middle Ages and at Oxford University until the nineteenth century. One part of it was a translation of *Introduction to Music,* a Pythagorean treatise by Nicomachus, and another part was one division of Ptolemy's three-part *Harmonics.* By the twelfth century *De Institutione Musica* was obsolete, but it did not die. Instead, Boethius's work was revised and condensed by Johann de Muris and continued in use. Boethius described the study of music as follows:

> That which is most knowable is most harmonious; only quantities, magnitudes, forms, essences, are knowable, and the discipline of music concerns itself with essences consisting of related quantities; those related quantities which are easiest to know are the proportions, the essences, the most harmonious sounds.

The writings of Boethius appealed to scholars because of his emphasis on reason. He believed that music communicates on a lower level, through the emotions. On the highest level music communicates truth because, through reason, man can abstract mathematical proportions from musical sounds and thereby come to know incorporeal essences. Moreover, reason finds as much pleasure in contemplating these harmoniously related essences as the ear finds in the fleeting experience of corporeal sound.[6]

Boethius's description of music as a mathematical science took the form of mathematical axioms and proofs. The music theorist, by studying the mathematical proportions of music, would apply reason to understand the mysteries of the universe through its proportions and harmony. The Pythagorean theorists and Boethius agreed that the motions of the planets created pitches. They believed that the planets move at velocities so great that their sounds are beyond the capacity of human hearing. "Music is a sensuous form of the all-embracing cosmic harmony, conceivable only through the intellect, and not perceivable through human senses."[7] This is what was meant by the phrase "music of the spheres."

MUSIC EDUCATION IN THE MIDDLE AGES

Although theorists studied music as a mathematical subject, it was also practiced as a living art. The education of musicians was important because music was an integral part of the church service. In the fourth century the church founded the *scholae cantorum* (singing schools) to train singers and composers for the church. These schools were expanded by Pope Gregory near the end of the sixth century. The curriculum included instruction in singing, playing an instrument, harmony, and composition. The singing schools were one of the few means by which young boys could become educated and enter a profession. Some education in music was also offered for secular purposes. For example, knights needed music instruction to compose and render love songs and ballads of a heroic nature, which was expected of them.

THE CAROLINGIAN EMPIRE

With the fall of Rome and the ensuing invasions by Germanic invaders, education in Europe declined and the classical Greek heritage lost much of its influence. Charlemagne, who ruled from 768 to 814, encouraged and supported the revival of education, and the Carolingian Empire rekindled the spirit of ancient Greece. It also partly revived its methods.

The Cathedral School of Metz (742–766), founded by Bishop Chrodegang, was a center of learning for the clergy as well as for promising children. Charlemagne was impressed by the work of Bishop Chrodegang and by the liturgical music of the Benedictine monks. He ordered that the musical practices of St. Benedict and Bishop Chrodegang be implemented in the singing school at Metz and at his own palace school. Charlemagne employed singers from the singing schools in Rome and sent talented young men to Rome for thorough training. These men later imparted music education throughout the empire by establishing schools at sees and monasteries.

Charlemagne's Letter on the Necessity of Studies in 787 resulted in the establishment of schools in monasteries and cathedrals, where boys learned reading, singing, computing holidays on the calendar, and Latin. Since neumes, the musical notation of the time, were not specific enough to permit the accurate reading of music, the ability to sing psalms, sacred songs, and hymns from memory was a major goal of the general education of boys. Students were also expected to learn the philosophy of music and aesthetics, which was known as theory.[8]

There were three types of schools—monastery, cathedral, and parish. The parish, or church, schools provided elementary instruction. The rudiments of reading, writing, and psalm singing were taught in the parish schools. Eventually, the convent schools built near the monasteries made education available to girls. The cathedral and parish schools offered intermediate-level instruction. They began as schools of music to prepare musicians for the church, but by the end of the eighth century they taught the seven liberal arts. The highest level of instruction was offered at the universities and at some of the better cathedral and monastery schools, as well as at the court schools.[9] The great medieval musicians were trained at the cathedral and monastery schools and became teachers in them. Most of the educated men who were not of the nobility owed their good fortune to musical ability, which gained them admission to the cathedral and monastery schools.[10]

Medieval society changed through the centuries, and by the twelfth century new teaching methods and institutions were necessary. Yet even then, the Greek influence remained alive in the form of liberal education based on the trivium and the quadrivium.

NEW KINDS OF SCHOOLS

The cathedral schools eventually disappeared because of competition from the new universities and city schools, especially in Germany. As trade increased and the nobility consolidated authority, the cities grew in wealth and power. The city merchants respected education and encouraged the founding of new schools, even in cities where cathedral schools already existed. They appreciated the necessity of educating people to be conscientious citizens as well as to enter the service of the church. Although the cities sponsored and controlled the schools, the clergy did the teaching. The curriculum, which was of a religious nature, included music because there was a need for priests who could sing the Mass at cathedrals, parish churches, and chapels.

Eventually, a new type of institution—the private school—was founded to offer practical education in the vernacular to both boys and girls. It was the precursor of the elementary school. By the end of the Middle Ages, many city dwellers had learned to read in city and private schools.

THE DEVELOPMENT OF EXACT NOTATION
AND THE TEACHING OF MUSIC READING

Until musical notation was developed sufficiently to permit a reasonably exact realization of the composer's musical intentions, music education consisted of training in singing. As notation developed, however, the emphasis in education began to shift to music reading. Two important figures in the development of exact notation were Odo of Cluny and Guido d'Arezzo.

Odo of Cluny (?–942). St. Odo of Cluny was a choir singer who became head of the abbey of Cluny. One of his works about the theory of music was *Enchiridion musices* (also known as *Dialogus de musica*). In the *Enchiridion*, Odo presented a systematic use of letters to represent musical pitches. It was the first time letters had been used this way, and the system became standard during the Middle Ages. The letters ran the gamut from A to G. Odo wrote of how he trained singers to sight sing with his system:

You have insistently requested, beloved brothers, that I should communicate to you a few rules concerning music, these to be only a sort which boys and simple persons may understand and by means of which, with God's help, they may quickly attain to perfect skill in singing. You asked this, having yourselves seen and heard and by sure evidence verified that it could be done. For indeed, being stationed among you, with God's help alone I taught certain actual boys and youths by means of this so that some after three days, others after four days, and one after a single week of training in it, were able to learn several antiphons and in a short time to sing them without hesitation, not hearing them sung by anyone, but contenting themselves simply with a copy written according to the rules. With the passage of not many days they were singing at first sight and extempore and without a fault anything written in music, something which until now ordinary singers had never been able to do, many continuing to practice and study singing for fifty years without profit.[11]

Guido d'Arezzo (c. 990–1050) was arguably the most important early music teacher. A choirmaster, he was responsible for the development of another systematic method for teaching young boys to sing a melody from notation. He had them memorize the familiar hymn "Ut queant laxis" ("Hymn to St. John"). The beginning tone of each of the first six phrases is one note higher than the preceding one in the major scale. Thus, they were taught to recall the initial syllables of each verse (*ut, re, mi, fa, sol, la*), which are used today to teach the rudiments of music. (Now we use *do* rather than *ut*, and we add *ti* above *la*.) The most critical element was the accurate location of the half step between *mi* and *fa*, which has characterized all of the many variants of the system from the eleventh century to the present.

Guido also invented a method for teaching improvisation, or creative composition. The method, described in Chapter 17 of his work *Micrologus*, was intended to teach not only music theory but creativity and sensitivity as well.[12]

The Development of the Musical Staff. Theorists of the Middle Ages searched for a method to notate music accurately. Around the middle of the ninth century, neumes (signs) were placed above the text to indicate that a melody was to ascend (/), descend (\), or both (∧). The practice of scribes was to copy neumes at various heights to indicate the melody more precisely. In the tenth century an unknown scribe drew a horizontal red line to represent the pitch f and arranged the neumes around the line. Later, a second line, usually yellow, was added to indicate the note c'. In the eleventh century Guido described a four line staff in use.[13] Letters were placed on the staff to indicate the lines for f, c', and occasionally g'. These letters evolved into what we now recognize as G, F, and C clef signs. With the invention of the staff, which eventually was produced without the original colors, pitches could be written exactly as they were to be performed. Precise written notation was an achievement that revolutionized the study of music and helped unify the liturgy because the same music could now be sung in churches throughout Christendom. Thus, music education was a pivotal factor in standardizing the religious service and strengthening the church. Van Waesberghe points out that an error in ascribing an earlier age to a sixteenth-century manuscript denied Guido his just due for many years.[14]

The Guidonian Hand. What we recognize as the Guidonian hand was not actually Guido's invention. Developed in the late thirteenth century, it was called *manus musicalis* until the end of the fifteenth century, when the name *manus Guidonis* appeared in B. Ramos de Pareja's *Musica practica* (1482). Virtually every music textbook during the Late Medieval and Renaissance periods contained a drawing of the Guidonian hand. Each joint of the open left hand represented one of twenty notes. Pupils sang intervals as the teacher pointed to his open left hand. This crude method proved historically important as an early system of teaching music by means other than rote. Previously, except for pedagogical experiments like Odo's, music had been taught by rote with as much imitation as was necessary for memorization.

Notation and Music Education. Systematic notation brought with it the necessity for instruction in its use, and for centuries afterward the goal of practical music education was sight singing rather than rote learning. For the first time, composers wrote music for singers who could perform it as it was conceived. Notation became the major subject of study in the cathedral and court schools, and the better students went on to study polyphony and composition. The significance of Guido's work was that it made the intricate and detailed notation of Renaissance polyphony possible. It permitted music to become a more creative art and to contribute to the intellectual developments that led to the Renaissance. At the same time, the other subjects of the curriculum continued to be presented by rote.[15]

Despite his contribution to practical music education, Guido believed that utilitarian knowledge of music was of less value than theoretical knowledge. He echoed both Plato and Boethius when he wrote "There is a great difference between musicians and singers. The latter perform, while the former know that which music consists of. For he who executes what he does not know is termed a beast."[16]

THE MEDIEVAL UNIVERSITIES

The monastery schools of the seventh and eighth centuries were the genesis of the medieval universities. The monks operated two kinds of monastery schools—internal schools (*scholae interna*), for students who planned to take religious vows, and external schools (*scholae externa*), for

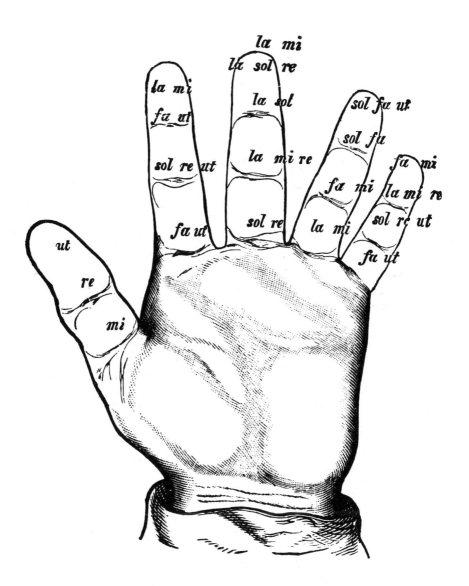

FIGURE 3–1 The Guidonian Hand. From *The History of Music*, vol. 1, by Emil Naumann. London: Cassell & Co., LTD, 1888.

students who did not plan to enter a religious order. The interest of the monks in the external schools declined as the millennium approached because they feared that worldliness would not serve them well. The cathedral schools then filled the void left by the demise of the external schools. These schools did not continue for long, but their contribution to music education was significant because they were closely connected with singing schools, where music was practiced as an art rather than studied as a science. It was in these singing schools that the great Franco-Flemish musicians were educated.

During the latter part of the twelfth century, the cathedral school of Notre Dame gradually merged with several church schools in Paris and developed into a new kind of institution—the university. Because of its location in a major urban center, the university was able to draw the most outstanding scholars from all parts of Europe. The Sorbonne at Paris was not the earliest European university, but it was the first to develop from cathedral and church schools. Others with similar roots soon followed. Oxford and Cambridge were both established near the end of the twelfth century, Cologne in 1388, Prague in 1348, and Vienna in 1365. Other universities were founded in Erfurt (1379) and Heidelberg (1385) by order of the territorial princes.

The medieval universities continued the tradition of the seven liberal arts. Upon completion of the trivium, students were awarded the baccalaureate in arts. Many continued their education to complete advanced degrees that qualified them for entrance into the professions (law, medicine, and theology). Students who completed their study of the seven liberal arts were doctors, licensed to teach throughout Christendom. In the German universities the new teacher was expected to begin his career with lectures on music, and so failure in music disqualified the student for a teaching license.

The study of music in medieval universities reflected Greek thought on music as a science as it had previously influenced education in Rome and in the monastery and cathedral schools. Music theory (*Musica speculativa*) continued as the study of music as a mathematical science, but practical, or applied, music (*musica practica*) provided universities with rich musical lives. Many faculty members were also music theorists and composers, some among the most highly respected of their time. They brought the study of music as an art to the university. Practical music did not have the same academic respect as music theory, but it provided an atmosphere in which musical creation and performance flourished. This was especially true in Paris, where some of the most distinguished composers lectured and participated in the musical life of the university. The already rich musical atmosphere was enhanced by the Notre Dame choir and the king's personal chapel choir. The directors of these organizations were also university officials. The Notre Dame singing school was actually a preparatory school for the university, and many of its students went to the Sorbonne as choristers supported by scholarships. The University of Salamanca was the first to establish a chair of music as one of its endowed professorships. This chair, founded in the thirteenth century, encouraged musical *ars* as well as *scientia* by requiring that composition be taught.

Practical music enriched university life in many ways. Religious observances accompanied by music were held constantly. The academic year opened with a Mass sung in the cathedral or church, and Masses were celebrated every day throughout the year. The student body was composed of various groups, called nations. Each used music to celebrate the feast days of their patron saints and for other ceremonies. There was also much pageantry that called for music. The informal musical activities of students revealed their love of music as a practical art. These activities sometimes took so much of their time that the universities invoked rules against them to protect the academic time of the students.

THE RENAISSANCE

The focus of intellectual development during the Renaissance was on both the past and the future. The backward focus reestablished and strengthened the bond with the ancient classical cultures of Greece and Rome based on the introduction of many works just being rediscovered in the West; at the same time, the creative geniuses of the Renaissance advanced and enriched the intellectual status of mankind. The musical Renaissance was a time of new and innovative musical practices, as the Church encouraged and supported composers in developing their art to new heights. The European universities continued the musical practices of the Middle Ages into the Renaissance. The academic aspect of the subject declined in importance by the middle of the fourteenth century, however, because of the static quality of music theory, which continued to focus on ideas formulated in ancient Greece. By the middle of the sixteenth century music was no longer a part of the curriculum in most universities. Only the University of Salamanca continued its tradition of an endowed chair of music.[17] In fact, the medieval scholastic system continued in Spain until the seventeenth century, with music taught as an integral part of the science of mathematics.[18]

Music continued to be taught, but musicians had the title of music director, rather than professor. It was a position of less distinction and salary. Music directors were contracted to lecture occasionally in mathematics courses, to give private instruction, and to participate in the music of festivals and pageants.

THE PROTESTANT REFORMATION AND EDUCATION

St. Benno, bishop of Meissen, is credited with restoring public singing of the Divine Office in the eleventh century, but the practice did not spread beyond his see. One of the results of the Reformation four hundred years later was the establishment of a participatory musical role for the congregation. Several educators contributed to the development of what is known as humanistic education. The work of Erasmus set the stage for further educational development by Martin Luther, John Calvin, and John Marbecke, each of whom made a distinctive contribution to his own branch of Protestantism.

Desiderius Erasmus (1469–1536) promoted both classical and biblical studies. He argued that the two were complementary. Erasmus was inspired by the ancient scholars, especially Quintilian. He wrote two books that strongly influenced classical education—*The Right Method of Instruction* and *The Liberal Education of Boys*. The latter set forth the goals of education. Erasmus believed the educated man to be knowledgeable, honest, and capable of independent judgment. "Erasmus is really saying that the essential purpose of education is to lead the individual toward autonomy, both intellectual and moral. Or, to put it in another way, sound education is the essential condition of real wisdom."[19] Erasmus also wrote textbooks and guides to help teachers and students in their study of classical literature. His most significant contribution was the development of a theory of humanistic education in which a bond was established between classical knowledge and sound moral character. This concept persisted for centuries and profoundly influenced American music education (Chapter 8).

Martin Luther (1483–1546). The Protestant Reformation began with Luther's attack on the papacy because of the sale of indulgences for the reconciliation of sinners. The posting of his Ninety-five Theses on the door of the castle church at Wittenberg in 1517 signaled Luther's break with Rome and the beginning of the Reformation, a religious and social movement that was to transform virtually every European nation and eventually affect nations of every continent.

The Reformation influenced education in many ways. First, attendance at schools and universities declined because the revolution disrupted society. Monasteries closed, and with them their schools. Educational foundations, scholarships, and endowments were embezzled by princes and other nobles. Many positions held by learned men were abolished for lack of students. These problems resulted partly from the religious warfare precipitated by the Reformation and partly from the spread of Protestantism, which diminished the need for Catholic schools.[20] Because one of the primary reasons for education until the sixteenth century had been to prepare for work in the church as priests, nuns, and monks, there was less reason to educate children.

One of the major educational outcomes of the Reformation was the transfer of education from the church to the state. Enrollment in schools and universities declined drastically because civil governments were unprepared to sponsor educational systems. The remaining Catholic elementary schools and the new Protestant elementary schools seldom offered instruction in more than reading, writing, arithmetic, morals, religion, and sometimes manual work. They continued as schools for the elite in most countries until much later, when they became common schools for the benefit of all children.

Martin Luther was a vigorous and influential spokesman for universal education. He believed that education should be provided for the children of the common people as well as those of the wealthy. In fact, Luther and Melancthon, the educational preceptor of Germany, devised a plan to create the first public-school system since the Roman Empire. The school system developed slowly, however, and it was centuries before compulsory education laws were enacted by most nations. As new educational systems were built throughout the sixteenth century and thereafter, revised educational programs were necessary to reflect the cultural, social, and religious changes taking place in Europe. Luther recommended that music, poetry, history, and the "whole course of mathematics" be added to the normal curriculum of reading, writing, and arithmetic.

Luther, who was himself musical, advocated the teaching of singing and instrumental music. He believed that "singing good music makes a man more reasonable and well-mannered . . . [as] general education produces an orderly society."[21] In fact, he so esteemed music that he valued only theology higher. His words echoed those of the Greek philosophers in their discussions of the effects of music on character:

> Let this noble, wholesome, and cheerful creation of God be commended to you. By it you may escape shameful desires and bad company. At the same time you may by this creation accustom yourself to recognize and praise the Creator. Take special care to shun perverted minds who prostitute this lovely gift of nature and of art with their erotic rantings; and be quite assured that none but the devil goads them on to defy their very nature which would and should praise God its Maker with this gift. . . .[22]

Luther wanted children to study music and to enjoy it. He believed that teachers should be musicians, and the schools established under the influence of his religious teachings included music in the curriculum. There were three divisions of schools. The first, *Evangelical schools,* provided elementary education. The two others were both *Latin schools,* which provided secondary education. Luther recommended the study of music in all three divisions. He was helped in promoting music education by Georg Rhau, a composer and printer, and Johann Walther, a composer and teacher. Rhau printed music for the church and schools, and helped unify them by laying a foundation for Protestant music. Walther edited and compiled much of the Protestant German school music.[23]

John Calvin (1509–1564), called the "Protestant Pope," was a French Protestant reformer, theologian, and educator whose convictions and powerful leadership led to divisions in Protestantism. His chief work, *The Institutes of the Christian Religion,* gave the basis of his reformist ideas. It contained the seeds of Calvinism as it would come to be in Europe and as the religion carried to the New World by the early settlers in New England. The doctrines of the *Institutes* led Calvinists to abandon all the sacraments except baptism and the Lord's Supper (which they considered merely a symbolic memorial). All rites and ceremonies for which they could find no biblical authority were eliminated from the church service. They discarded vestments, holy-water fonts, stained-glass windows, sacred images, incense, and organ music, as well as the crucifix. Their form of worship stressed the reading of scripture, the preaching of sermons, and the singing of psalms without instrumental accompaniment. The most important teaching was that of salvation.

Calvinists believed in predestination, meaning that from birth people were predestined by God for salvation or damnation. The "elect," or "saints," would go to heaven and the others to hell, regardless of their deeds during life, although a good life was considered evidence that one was a member of the elect. The Calvinist way of life came to be know as "puritanical," as described by the later English Calvinists, and it was the English Puritans who brought Calvinism to the New World.

Calvin believed that music was to be enjoyed when combined with reverence for God and not as a secular pleasure. His strict convictions were reflected in his educational ideas. One of his tenets was that church music should consist only of the congregational singing of psalms as translated into the vernacular language and set to "moderate" melodies. These sedate tunes were newly composed by Louis Bourgeois, or, as with Luther, adapted from popular songs. *The Geneva Psalter* of 1565 was a three-part setting by Claude Goudimel intended for use at home. It is likely that these psalms were sung in America by French Huguenots during their ill-fated attempts to establish settlements in Florida and South Carolina. English Protestants who took refuge on the Continent from the persecutions of Queen Mary (1553–1558) adopted Calvin's beliefs. These Pilgrims and the Puritans carried his teachings with respect to music and education to New England.

John Marbecke (c. 1510–c. 1585), a theologian and Henry VIII's organist at St. George's Chapel in Windsor Castle, wrote *The Book of Common Prayer noted* (1550), a musical setting of Bishop Thomas Cranmer's Anglican service (1544). The accentual nature of the English language requires a different treatment of melody than plainsong. Marbecke's setting made congregational participation in the Anglican service possible. He adapted parts of Gregorian chant, using a simple monotonic style for the prayers and the Apostles' Creed, modulation in the recitation of the psalms, and a songlike manner in the canticles and works taken from the Mass.[24]

EDUCATION IN THE SEVENTEENTH CENTURY—
THE AGE OF REALISM

During the seventeenth century the newly emerging middle class, composed in large part of people in mercantile and manufacturing occupations, needed education to prepare them for work. Earlier, when there was no middle class, little occupational education was needed by peasants, artisans, and tradesmen. Now, however, nations began to depend on the middle class for their wealth and influence. Schools, especially the academies, began to offer education of a more practical nature. Some influential educational figures were John Comenius, John Locke, and Richard Mulcaster. Comenius and Locke emphasized the need for new curricula, and Comenius and Mulcaster stressed universal education.

John Amos Comenius (1592–1670) was born in Bohemia (now Czechoslovakia) and later settled in Poland, where he wrote and ministered to his coreligionists, the Brethren. He was an educational reformer whose writings influenced education in Europe, Asia, and America. His *Gate of Languages Unlocked* went through 106 editions, 80 in his lifetime. *The World Through Sense Pictures* had 116 editions, the last 9 in the twentieth century. According to his philosophy, pansophy, all true things must be in harmony with true religion, including true philosophy and true art. He applied pansophy to the art of teaching in *The Great Didactic*, in which he discussed the teaching of music and art specifically in terms of curriculum and method.[25] His recommendations included singing well-known melodies and the elements of advanced music for those with musical aptitude. Also, students were to learn psalms and hymns by heart. He wrote about how children learn music and what they should accomplish:

> Music is especially natural to us; for as soon as we see the light we immediately sing the song of paradise, thus recalling to our memory our fall, A, a! E, e! I maintain that complaint and wailing are our first music, from which it is impossible to restrain infants; and if it were possible, it would be inexpedient, since it contributes to their health; for as long as other exercises and amusements are wanting, by this very means their chests and other internal organs relieve themselves of their superfluities. External music begins to delight children at two years of age; such as singing, rattling, and striking of musical instruments. They should therefore be indulged in this, so that their ears and minds may be soothed by concord and harmony.

In the third year the sacred music of daily use may be introduced; namely, that received as a custom to sing before and after dinner, and when prayers are begun or ended. On such occasions they ought to be present, and to be accustomed to attend and conduct themselves composedly. It will also be singing the praises of God. In the fourth year it is possible for some children to sing of themselves; the slower ones, however, ought not to be forced, but permitted to have a whistle, a drum, or pipes, so that by whistling, drumming, and piping they may accustom their ears to the perceptions of various sounds, or even to imitate them. In the fifth year it will be time to open their mouths in hymns and praises to God, and to use their voices for the glory of their Creator.

These things parents, in singing or playing with children, may easily instill into their minds; the memory is now more enlarged and apt than previously, and will, with greater ease and pleasure, imbibe a larger number of things in consequence of the rhythm and melody. The more verses they commit to memory, the better will they be pleased with themselves, and the glory of God be largely promoted. Blessed is the home where voices resound with music.[26]

John Locke (1632–1704) was born in England. He attended Oxford University, where he was awarded the bachelor's degree in 1655 and the master's degree in 1658. His primary interest was society and its problems. To him, the most important goal was the security of society and of the individual. He recognized that most people could not learn to perform difficult and complex music well and recommended that music have last place among the accomplishments of students because it wasted so much of a young man's time to gain only moderate skill. He had "amongst Men of Parts and Business seldom heard any one commended or esteemed for having an Excellency in Musick." However, he recommended music as a form of recreation to "divert and delight pupils wearied with Study or Dancing." Locke considered dancing instruction important because it "gives graceful Motions all the Life, and above all things Manliness, and a becoming Confidence to young Children."

Richard Mulcaster (1530–1611) was the headmaster of the Merchant Taylor's School of London, the alma mater of the poet Edmund Spenser. Mulcaster's educational beliefs influenced other educators in Europe and America. He believed that a child's interests and abilities should be considered when developing educational programs. He was also a leader in universal education and the use of English as the language of instruction (as opposed to Latin). The Boston Latin Grammar School, founded in 1635, reflected his educational aims and ideals. His curriculum for children included reading, writing, drawing, singing and playing. He wrote about music as a subject of study:

When *Music* shall teach nothing, but honest for delite, and pleasant for note, comlie for the place, and semelie for the person, sutable to the thing, and serviceable to circumstance, can that humor corrupt, which bredeth such delite, being so everiewhere armed against just chalenge, of either blame or misliking?[27]

MUSIC INSTRUCTION IN GERMAN SCHOOLS

Music in German Schools. Music was a curricular subject in some German schools, normally at the secondary level; the Latin school usually required choral singing. The same was true of the Protestant gymnasium. In the sixteenth century the headmaster of the Protestant gymnasium in Strasbourg instructed the music teacher with the words "It is your duty to teach that the psalms which are sung in the church and school are to be sung not haphazardly but artistically and correctly."[28] In Germany, elementary level students learned music principles by rote and sang by ear. At the intermediate level, boys progressed to music theory and part singing and composed in class. Students in the upper level studied more advanced theory and were expected to master sight singing and part singing. Some German schools had excellent music programs and even offered instrumental instruction. Boys not only sang in school but also earned money by singing at weddings, funerals, and other social and civic occasions.[29]

School music in Germany flourished because of its close relationship to the church. With the coming of the Enlightenment, rationalist thinking changed the role of music in education, which was no longer closely tied to religion. Formerly, music was taught by parish schoolmasters, who were also organists; they were replaced by part-time, virtually untrained music teachers. The quality of school music declined drastically, and it was not until the end of the nineteenth century that serious attention was given to the problem. In 1910 a law was passed requiring music teachers to pass a state examination after three or four terms of study. Music education in Germany still consisted primarily of singing lessons at that time,[30] as it does even today.

Private Music Instruction. Music was also taught outside the schools. Private music instruction was always available in European countries. Adults and children studied singing and instruments for their own enjoyment. In the eighteenth century claviers were purchased by many middle-class people to play for pleasure. Keyboard instruction books were available for self-instruction or for use by private teachers. Unlike current instruction books, they consisted mostly of written explanations, and musical notation was used only for examples. It was not until the nineteenth century that methods books contained more music.[31] Even then, however, many still consisted mostly of text, with musical examples interspersed. An example is the American book *Materia*

Musica, or Materials for the Pianist; A Class Book, Containing the Principles of Music, Applied To Piano-Forte Playing. Adapted for private tuition, but more especially arranged and adapted for the use of Schools for Young Ladies, Normal Schools, and other Seminaries of Learning (J. C. Engelbrecht, Boston: Oliver Ditson & Company, 1868). The few examples of notation in the book demonstrate pitch, rhythm, intervals, trills, and other aspects of music, but there is no piano music.

The Beginnings of Music Conservatories. Music education throughout most of Western history was a privilege of the elite, or at least of those who could afford to pay for their schooling. Ironically, the roots of the conservatory, the training school for professional musicians, were Italian charitable institutions for orphans and other underprivileged children. In Italy conservatories of music developed from the asylums, or *ospedali*, for orphaned and illegitimate girls; they were called *ospedali* because they were originally attached to hospitals. The oldest institutions of this kind were in Venice (Ospidale dei Mendicanti, 1262; della Pietà, 1346), but the name "conservatory" came from Naples, where similar institutions were called *conservatorio* (Conservatorio Santa Maria de Loreto, 1537; Sant' Onofrio a Capua, 1576). The educational programs of the four *ospedali* in Venice and the Neapolitan *conservatorio* were strong in musical training. The girls learned vocal and instrumental music and sang in choirs, and public concerts were presented frequently. The musical atmosphere was conducive to excellence in performance, and the concerts were well attended.

During the eighteenth century twelve hundred different operas were performed in the theaters of Venice. The public supported the *ospedali* music programs not only because of its love of good music but also because of its insatiable desire for new music, which created a virtually endless need for well-trained musicians. Both Rousseau and Goethe wrote about the beauty of the concerts they heard at the *ospedali*.[32] Grout quotes a letter in which a concert is described:

> They are reared at public expense and trained solely to excel in music. And so they sing like angels, and play the violin, the flute, the organ, the violoncello, the bassoon. . . . Each concert is given by about forty girls. I assure you there is nothing so charming as to see a young and pretty nun [the girls were not nuns] in her white robe, with a bouquet of pomegranate flowers in her hair, leading the orchestra and beating time with all the precision imaginable.[33]

Most of the Italy's greatest composers in the seventeenth and eighteenth centuries—including Monteverdi, Cavalli, Lotti, Galuppi, and Porpora—taught in the *ospedali* and wrote music for the students there. Many had been *ospedali* students themselves. Antonio Vivaldi (1678–1741) was employed from 1704 to 1740 at the Ospedale de Pietà in Venice as conductor, composer, teacher, and general superintendent of music. It was here that most of his nonoperatic music was performed for the first time. Eventually, the *ospedali* broadened their functions to include musical training for people other than orphaned and illegitimate girls.

Conservatories in other countries, which began later, did not originate in charitable asylums. Most of the world's great conservatories outside of Italy were established in the nineteenth century, with the exception of the Stockholm Kungliga Musikhögskolan (1771) and the Paris Conservatoire National de Musique (1784). Yet choir schools continued to provide an education and practical musical experience as late as the nineteenth century; both Hayden and Schubert were students at choir schools.

SUMMARY

We have seen two concrete examples of the decline of music education in societies that had prized it at one time. In both cases—latter-day Greece and the Renaissance universities—music instruction no longer paralleled the use of music in the society that sponsored it. Those who controlled music instruction refused to make it relevant to the needs of society, and so it waned.

The long heritage of music education throughout the vast expanse of Western history reflects an educational system for the wealthy and titled and for those who enter the service of the Church. We will see in the next chapter that when music became a part of the American school curriculum, it was in the democratic context of universal education. Music, like other subjects, was to be taught to all children. It is this fact that differentiated American public music education from its historical precedents and permitted it to influence American society as no previous music education system had since that of the ancient Hebrews.

NOTES

1. A. D. Kresteff, "Musica disciplina and musica sonora," *Journal of Research in Music Education* 10 (Spring 1962): 13–29.
2. From F. J. Sheed, trans., *The Confessions of St. Augustine* (New York: Sheed & Ward, 1943), pp. 242–44.
3. Kresteff, "Musica disciplina," p. 16.
4. Ibid., p. 27.
5. Ibid., pp. 14–15.
6. C. Bower, "Boethius' *The Principles of Music*, an Introduction, Translation, and Commentary" (Ph.D. dissertation, George Peabody College for Teachers, 1966), p. 393.

7. M. F. Bukofzer, "Speculative Thinking in Medieval Music," *Speculum* 17 (1942): 165.
8. Ernest F. Livingstone, "The Place of Music in German Education from the Beginnings Through the 16th Century," *Journal of Research in Music Education* 15 (Winter 1967): 243–44.
9. Livingstone, "The Place of Music," p. 262.
10. Allen P. Britton, "Music in Early American Public Education: A Historical Critique," *Basic Concepts in Music Education*, pt. 1, ed. Nelson Henry (Chicago: National Society for the Study of Education, University of Chicago Press, 1958), p. 197.
11. Odo of Cluny. "Enchiridion musices," ca. 935, in Oliver Strunk, *Source Readings in Music History: From Classical Antiquity through the Romantic Era* (New York: Norton, 1950), pp. 103–116.
12. Samuel D. Miller, "Guido d'Arezzo: Medieval Musician and Educator, *Journal of Research in Music Education* 21 (Fall 1973): 240–42.
13. Donald J. Grout and Claude V. Palisca, *A History of Western Music,* 4th ed. (New York: Norton, 1988), p. 81.
14. Jos. Smits van Waesberghe, *Musica Disciplina* 5 (1951): 15–53.
15. Livingstone, "The Place of Music," p. 247.
16. Nan Cooke Carpenter, *Music in the Medieval and Renaissance Universities* (Norman, OK: University of Oklahoma Press, 1958), p. 25.
17. Ibid., p. 268.
18. Donald W. Forrester, "An Introduction to Seventeenth-Century Spanish Music Theory Books," *Journal of Research in Music Education* 21 (Spring 1973): 65.
19. Edward J. Power, *Main Currents in the History of Education* (New York: McGraw-Hill, 1970), p. 271.
20. Harry G. Good and James D. Teller, *A History of Western Education,* 3rd ed. (New York: Macmillan, 1969), p. 152.
21. Joe E. Tarry, "Music in the Educational Philosophy of Martin Luther," *Journal of Research in Music Education* 21 (Winter 1973): 361.
22. Ulrich S. Leupold, ed., *Luther's Works,* vol. 53: *Liturgy and Hymns* (Philadelphia: Fortress Press, 1965), pp. 321–24.
23. Tarry, "Music in the Educational Philosophy," p. 363.
24. Edward Dickenson, *Music in the History of the Western Church* (New York: Scribner's, 1902), p. 337.
25. John Amos Comenius, *The Great Didactic,* trans. and ed. M. W. Keatings (London: A. & C. Black, 1923).
26. Will S. Monroe, *Comenius' School of Infancy* (Boston: D. C. Heath, 1908), pp. 48, 49.
27. From Richard Mulcaster, *Mulcaster's Elementaire (1582)* (London: Oxford University Press, 1925), pp. 5, 6.
28. Clyde William Young, "School Music in Sixteenth-Century Strasbourg," *Journal of Research in Music Education* 10 (Fall 1962): 129. Quoted from Martin Vogeleis, *Quellen und Bausteine zu einer Geschichte der Musik und des Theaters im Elsass, 500–1800* (Strassburg: Le Roux & Cie., 1911), p. 250.
29. Ernest F. Livingstone, "The Place of Music in German Education Around 1600," *Journal of Research in Music Education* 19 (Summer 1971): 144–67.
30. Bernhard Binkowski, "Personalities in World Music Education No. 9—Leo Kestenberg," *International Journal of Music Education* 14 (1989): 48.

31. Marvin J. Bostrom, "Eighteenth Century Keyboard Instruction Practices as Revealed in a Set of Master Lessons," *Journal of Research in Music Education* 13 (Spring 1965): 33–39.
32. Will and Ariel Durant, *Rousseau and Revolution: A History of Civilization in France, England, and Germany from 1756, and in the Remainder of Europe from 1715 to 1789.* (New York: Simon and Schuster, 1967), pp. 233–34.
33. Charles de Brosses, "Lettres familières sur l'Italie, Paris, 1885, I, 193–94," quoted in Donald Jay Grout, *A History of Western Music,* 3d ed. (New York: Norton, 1980), p. 404.

BIBLIOGRAPHY

Augustine of Hippo: Selected Writings. Translated by M. T. Clark. New York: Paulist Press, 1984.

Binkowski, Bernhard. "Personalities in World Music Education No. 9—Leo Kestenberg." *International Journal of Music Education* 14 (1989).

Bostrom, Marvin J. "Eighteenth Century Keyboard Instruction Practices as Revealed in a Set of Master Lessons." *Journal of Research in Music Education* 13 (Spring 1965).

Bower, C. "Boethius' *The Principles of Music,* an Introduction, Translation, and Commentary." Ph.D. dissertation, George Peabody College for Teachers, 1966.

Britton, Allen P. "Music in Early American Public Education: A Historical Critique." *Basic Concepts in Music Education.* Edited by Nelson Henry. Chicago: National Society for the Study of Education, the University of Chicago Press, 1958.

Bukofzer, M. F. "Speculative Thinking in Medieval Music." *Speculum* 17 (1942).

Carpenter, Nan Cooke. "The Study of Music at the University of Oxford in the Middle Ages (to 1450)." *Journal of Research in Music Education* 1 (Spring 1953).

———. "The Study of Music at the University of Paris in the Middle Ages." *Journal of Research in Music Education* 2 (Fall 1954).

———. *Music in Medieval and Renaissance Universities.* Norman, OK: University of Oklahoma Press, 1958.

———. "Music in the Medieval Universities." *Journal of Research in Music Education* 3 (Fall 1955).

Dickenson, Edward. *Music in the History of the Western Church.* New York: Scribner's, 1902.

Durant, Will and Ariel. *Rousseau and Revolution: A History of Civilization in France, England, and Germany from 1756, and in the Remainder of Europe from 1715 to 1789.* New York: Simon and Schuster, 1967.

Forrester, Donald W. "An Introduction to Seventeenth-Century Spanish Music Theory Books." *Journal of Research in Music Education* 21 (Spring 1973).

Good, Harry G., and Teller, James D. *A History of Western Education,* 3rd ed. New York: Macmillan, 1969.

Grout, Donald J., and Palisca, Claude, *A History of Western Music,* 4th ed. New York: Norton, 1988.

Hamilton, Edith, and Cairns, Huntington, eds. *The Collected Dialogues of Plato.* Bollingen Series 71 1961, reprinted by the Princeton University Press, 1984.

Harman, Alec. *Man and His Music: Medieval and Renaissance Music.* New York: Schoken, 1969.

Harman, Alec, and Milner, Anthony, *Man and His Music: Late Renaissance and Baroque Music.* New York: Schocken, 1969.

Kresteff, A. D. "Musica Disciplina and Music Sonora." *Journal of Research in Music Education* 10 (Spring 1962).

Livingstone, Ernest F. "The Place of Music in German Education from the Beginnings Through the 16th Century." *Journal of Research in Music Education* 15 (Winter 1967).

———. "The Place of Music in German Education Around 1600." *Journal of Research in Music Education* 19 (Summer 1971).

Longyear, R. M. "Music at the Hohe Karlsschule, 1770–1794." *Journal of Research in Music Education* 12 (Summer 1964).

Lord, C., trans. *Aristotle: The Politics.* Chicago: University of Chicago Press, 1984.

Mark, Michael L. *Source Readings in Music Education History.* New York: Schirmer, 1982.

Marrou, H. I. *A History of Education in Antiquity.* New York: Sheed and Ward, 1956.

Miller, Samuel D. "Guido d'Arezzo: Medieval Musician and Educator." *Journal of Research in Music Education* 21 (Fall 1973).

Power, Edward J. *Main Currents in the History of Education.* New York: McGraw-Hill, 1970.

Schrade, L. "Music in the Philosophy of Boethius." *Musical Quarterly* 33 (1947): 188–200.

Sheed, F. J., trans. *The Confessions of St. Augustine.* New York: Sheed & Ward, 1943.

Smith, Samuel. *Ideas of the Great Educators.* New York: Barnes & Noble, 1979.

Strunk, Oliver. *Source Readings in Music History: From Classical Antiquity Through the Romantic Era.* New York: Norton, 1950.

Tarry, Joe E. "Music in the Educational Philosophy of Martin Luther." *Journal of Research in Music Education* 21 (Winter 1973).

van Waesberghe, Jos. Smits. *Musica Disciplina* 5 (1951).

Walker, Robert. *Music Education: Tradition and Innovation.* Springfield, IL: Charles C. Thomas, 1984. Chapter 3: "Music Education in Modern History: Religion, Social Training, and Good Taste."

Young, Clyde William. "School Music in Sixteenth-Century Strasbourg." *Journal of Research in Music Education* 10 (Fall 1962).

PART II

THE NEW WORLD: AMERICA

4

EARLY MUSIC
EDUCATION
IN THE NEW WORLD

THE SPANISH AND NATIVE AMERICANS

Musical cultures flourished in America long before European explorers arrived. Successful music education programs have been documented to almost 150 years before Columbus discovered America.

The Incas. The earliest known structured music education system in America was that of the Incas, in what is now Peru, around 1350. Music instruction was given in schools for the children of the royal family and the nobles of the empire. The curriculum was described by a Spanish observer who wrote:

> They did not teach from writings, because they had none. But by rote and by actual participation they inculcated the rites, precepts, and ceremonies of their false religion. They taught the grounds and reasons for their system of laws, and how to apply them in governing subject peoples; . . . also how to speak elegantly and correctly, how to bring up their children,

and how to regulate their households. In addition, the amautas (masters) taught poetry and music.[1]

The four-year course of study culminated in oral examinations that tested the students' knowledge of wars, conquests, and sacrifices as celebrated in song. Young women also received music instruction. Musically talented girls from nine to fifteen years of age were placed in a nunnery where they were trained in singing and flute playing so they could entertain at banquets of the royalty and nobility.

The Spanish found that the native Indians throughout the Andean region were receptive to European music and capable of becoming highly proficient performers. The Franciscans, Dominicans, and Augustinians used music as the principal tool to evangelize the Indians. In all of their schools—from Quito, the northernmost city of the Inca empire, to Copacabana on Lake Titicaca—music was the main subject. The pupils even learned advanced European polyphony at Quito.[2]

The Jesuit fathers came to Peru in 1568. Their schools traditionally emphasized the classics, but in Lima they saw that the Indians responded so enthusiastically to European music that it prepared the way for their conversion. Like the religious orders that preceded them, the Jesuits also made music the principal subject in their schools. In 1600 the church at Santiago del Cercado had two organs, four sets of shawms, two trumpets, viols, and other instruments. As more Indians were converted to the Catholic faith, both the quantity and quality of European music, even the most complex polyphony of the Renaissance, became part of the religious lives of the Indians. The music of the churches and cathedrals rivaled that of Europe.[3]

The Aztecs. Hernando Cortes conquered Mexico in 1521, after a two-year military campaign, and Spain became ruler of Mexico. At that time Spain was the only European country to have conquered a part of the New World and colonized it, and the prestige and wealth that Mexico brought it was the envy of other European countries.

Pedro de Gante. The response of the Aztecs to European music was similar to that of the Incas. The rich culture of the defeated Indians was destroyed as the Spanish colonized Mexico and converted the Indians to Christianity. This was done by missionaries sent to instruct and acculturate the Aztec people. Pedro de Gante, a Franciscan lay brother from Flanders, arrived in 1523 and within a year had opened a school for the sons of native chiefs in Tezcoco. The school was housed in a building provided by the Aztec emperor Ixlilxochitl. Here de Gante taught reading, writing, singing, playing instruments, copying musical manuscripts, and constructing instruments. At night he preached and taught Christian doctrine.[4] By 1527 the school had been relocated to Mexico City, after the extensive damage of Cortes's military campaign was repaired. Many of the students in De Gante's school later became teachers in small villages.[5] In addition to music and academic subjects, de Gante also taught arts and crafts, stonemasonry, carpentry, sewing and embroidery. By 1529 he had five hundred students; eventually he taught about one thousand students each year.[6] Heller wrote:

> Fully 100 years before any sizeable colonization efforts were noticeable in North America, his students in Mexico City were singing European music, copying Franco-Flemish polyphony, playing and building violins and organs, and composing and teaching music in the European style.[7]

De Gante also spread the Spanish-Catholic heritage beyond Mexico City. He erected churches and schools in the countryside and staffed them with his graduates. He may have built as many as one hundred churches in the Valley of Mexico.[8]

By 1536 a university had been established in Mexico. A printing press was set up in 1539, and an Ordinary of the Mass was printed on it in 1556. This, the first book printed in America, was followed shortly after by 11 other liturgical books. Only 14 liturgical books with music were printed in Spain during the same period.

The Spanish also established music instruction in what is now U.S. territory. In 1540 Francisco Coronado conquered the area that became New Mexico, leaving priests there after he departed. One of these priests, Juan de Padilla, had been a music teacher, and he taught music to the Indians. By 1630 there were Spanish friars in 25 missions serving 60,000 Indians. Each mission had a school similar to the one established by Pedro de Gante. The New Mexico missions were destroyed in the 1680s, but the Spanish continued to establish schools in Texas, New Orleans, and California. Music was the principal subject in these schools.[9]

THE FRENCH AND NATIVE AMERICANS

The French explorer Jacques Cartier landed on the coast of Labrador in 1534 and gave thanks with a sung Mass. Some Indians told him greatly exaggerated stories of fabulous wealth to be found in the New World, tall tales of a Kingdom of Saguenay, inhabited by white men who had mines of gold, silver, and rubies and who grew spices. Among them were men with only one leg who flew like bats and never ate.[10] Cartier believed the stories. The French wanted to profit from Canada as the Spanish had from Mexico, and, accompanied by Donnaconna, chief of the Huron Indians, Cartier convinced the king of France that Canada offered a golden opportunity. As they continued to explore Canada, the myth of Saguenay was dispelled. However, the French did establish trading posts, where fur was bartered with the Indians for axes and other iron tools. Unlike the Spanish in Mexico, the French did not enslave the natives as they colonized Canada; they established a lucrative fur trade and founded settlements in what is now the province of Quebec.

The king of France wanted to assert his country's dominion in the New World. To do so, it was necessary to convert the Indians to Christianity. The French settlers, like the Spanish, also brought Christianity to the Indians with the use of music. A French teacher wrote from near Quebec in 1675: "The nuns of France do not sing more agreeably than some savage women here; and, as a class, all the savages have much more aptitude and inclination for singing the hymns of the Church." The missionary work, including music instruction, was so successful that in 1668 the Iroquois received papal permission to celebrate their services, including the Mass, in their native language rather than in Latin.[11]

The French established colonial settlements as far south as Louisiana. Because one of their purposes was to convert the Indians, they built mission schools in many parts of Canada, in the Great Lakes areas, and along the Mississippi River Valley all the way to the Gulf of Mexico. A mission school was begun in Maine in 1640, and five years after New Orleans was founded in 1718 a boys' school was opened in Louisiana by the Capuchin Fathers. In 1727 the French Ursuline nuns established a school for girls in New Orleans. Other French mission schools were founded in Detroit (1755) and Saint Louis (1764). Every mission, regardless of its size, had a school, and one of the subjects taught at the French mission schools was singing.[12]

The practice of conquering native populations and converting them to Christianity is morally controversial. Many feel that the Indians benefited, but others view it as corrupt and disrespectful of established systems of belief. Regardless of the issue of morality, there is little doubt that the Europeans provided excellent and effective music education and that they were successful in using music for conversion. Their achievement offers further evidence of the historical value of music education to the Catholic Church and to Western civilization, but it had little influence on the development of American music education patterns.

EARLY IMMIGRANT GROUPS TO THE NEW WORLD

What we know as uniquely American music education began with the founders of the English colonies in New England—the Pilgrims and the Puritans. Before examining the musical and educational practices of the English settlers, we will first look at those of several other European immigrant groups that came to America later but still early in the colonial period. Like the English immigrants, they too sought religious freedom.

William Penn was a Quaker who exchanged a debt of about £16,000 owed to his father for a large amount of land west of the Delaware River. It was originally called Sylvania and later Pennsylvania. Penn offered land and religious freedom to anyone who wished to settle in Pennsylvania. He was especially sensitive to the need for religious freedom because the Quakers had come to the New World in 1653 to escape religious and political repression only to be persecuted by the Puritans in Massachusetts. By 1776 more than 100,000 members of various religious groups resided in Pennsylvania. They included Anglicans, Catholics, Lutherans, Mennonites, Moravians, Pietists, and Quakers. Other groups from several European countries settled in Maryland and other colonies to the south. Many were musically sophisticated and often included music in their school curricula.[13] Britton wrote: "What is important to remember is that these Americans saw to it that music was taught in the first schools they organized."[14]

Other Religious Sects. Some of the most musical of the early immigrants to America were members of religious sects whose philosophical roots go back to the early dissident actions of the Bohemian martyr John Huss (1369?-1415). Unlike their Lutheran neighbors, who maintained a revised liturgical service, these brethren developed a form of worship that placed emphasis on individual conduct over doctrine. Congregational singing was important in Luther's service, but it became integral to the lives of the sects led by Jacob Ammen (Amish) and Menno Simon (Mennonites) and to the Moravians. Music was taught in the schools they established in America, and it was a part of their daily community life.

The Moravians were a branch of the Unity of Brethren, the church of Comenius. The stature of Comenius as an educator was such that although he did not travel to America, he was invited to be president of Harvard College. After fleeing Bohemia and Poland and finding refuge on the estate of Count Zinzendorf in Saxony, the Moravians developed a missionary purpose. As a result, the first of the group to emigrate to the New World came as missionaries to the Indians and blacks in the new colony of Georgia in 1735.

The missionary work in Georgia was not successful, and various Moravian groups went on to establish homes in Bethlehem (1741), Nazareth (1744), and Lititz (1748), Pennsylvania. They soon established other congregational communities, called *Gemeinen*, and a community in Salem, North Carolina, in 1766. Moravian settlements became the most vital centers for European-style music in the colonies because of their musical training in Germany and the importance of music in daily community life. Not all of the music-making was confined to churches. Homes and Brethren Houses (where the Collegium Musicum played every evening) also hosted much music-making. The trombone choirs for which Bethlehem is still famous played from a tower into the open air. The Moravians also brought a strong choral tradition from Germany.

The most famous Moravian composer was John Antes (1740–1811), the first composer of chamber music in America. The Moravians not only composed much of their own music but also brought to America works of European composers, including Johann Cristoph Bach and Johann Ernst Bach. The Moravians founded the first American *collegium musicum* (1744), organized the first American trombone choir, built organs, and presented the first American performances of major European oratorios and symphonies. During the time when the hardships of American frontier life hampered the development of a serious musical culture, the Moravians composed and performed a prodigious amount of vocal and instrumental music.

Music played an integral part in Moravian life partly because it was a means of preserving their traditions. Of more fundamental importance, it was guided by religious impulse as a means of spiritual uplift and praise. Christian Ignatius Latrobe (1758–1836) wrote:

> All that learn this science in their schools, are taught to consider the practice of it, whether vocal or instrumental as leading to the same grand point, namely, in the service of the Lord, and the promotion of His glory on earth.[15]

The rich Moravian musical heritage incorporated a strong emphasis on music education. It was essential to educate children in music to maintain their religious practices, but they also believed in the necessity of developing aesthetic sensibilities.[16] The purpose of music education was clarified in a Moravian publication: "That the youth should become musicians is by no means a necessary result, not even a desirable one; we would only insist that music should have its sway in the whole formation and refinement of mind and heart."[17] There was a song session (*Singstunde*) of about forty-five minutes almost every school day during which the children sang hymns and chorales. In this way, the children became familiar with the church service and learned to participate in it.[18] Later in their school careers, students performed the "best sacred literature in the preclassical and classical idiom: solo songs, anthems, cantatas, and oratorios."[19]

The Moravians also valued instrumental music highly. Piano and organ instruction was included in school music experiences, as was the study of orchestral instruments. Music was an important part of the biannual commencement exercises. In the nineteenth century the exercises included not only vocal and instrumental solos but music by full orchestra and chorus as well.[20] Individual instrumental study was the norm except for those boys who were preparing to perform with the church trombone choir. On June 5, 1759, when the school at Nazareth was to be dedicated, the boys who were moving from Bethlehem to the new school sang some hymns before lining up for the ten-mile march; they were played off by a trombone choir. This scene could not have been duplicated anywhere else in the colonies. The trombonists were trained in the Moravian schools as part of their regular instruction and at no cost to them.[21]

The Moravian music education tradition had weakened by the middle of the nineteenth century, when public education began to incorporate music instruction into its curriculum. By that time, church authority had also diminished, which further reduced the place of music in education. Eventually, Moravian music education resembled American public school music education.[22] Moravian music never gained much favor outside the Moravian community, but the sect influenced American musical life with its *collegia musica* and their first performances of European oratorios and symphonies.[23]

The Moravians were more musically influential than their own activities indicate. They met Charles Wesley and George Whitefield, the Methodist preachers, during their sea journey to Georgia in 1735. The preachers were so impressed by the singing of the Moravians that they decided to give hymn singing more importance in their work. The long-term musical effect on the American South through Methodism and itinerant preachers such as William Walker ("Singin' Billy") was enormous.

The German Seventh-Day Baptists. Johann Conrad Beissel founded the Ephrata Cloister of Seventh-Day Baptists (Lancaster County, Pennsylvania) in 1732 as a semimonastic community. His preaching inspired his followers to separate from the Dunkard Church and establish a new community at Ephrata. Beissel composed over one thousand hymns and musical settings based on the Old Testament. His music was complex, with up to eight often antiphonal parts, and in a unique style that bore little resemblance to European music. He also founded and trained a chorus to sing his music. Because he was a mystic, Beissel's hymns exalted the mystical life. He was among the first to compose sacred music in the New World, and his treatise on harmony (the preface to his 1747 hymnbook) might have been the first published in America.[24] The Ephrata Cloister contributed to American colonial life through its printing press, which produced a steady output of books for almost a century.

Many beautifully illuminated manuscripts have survived since Beissel's time, and contemporary musicians have lead groups singing the unique material. Beissel's comments on teaching music suggest that he was acquainted with the problems of teaching children. He once noted that much diligence is required to produce quality sounds and added, "If one (a student) seems to be totally incapable, let him desist for a time, in order that he may not become entirely discouraged."[25]

The Mennonite sect was founded in Zurich, Switzerland, in 1525 and spread to Germany, Austria, Holland, Russia, and America (including Canada). The Mennonites settled in Philadelphia and Germantown, Pennsylvania, and later in the Midwest. They brought with them a hymnbook published in Germany in 1583; a newer edition, published in 1742, is still used in Pennsylvania and Ohio. The 1940 edition of the *Mennonite Hymnary* contains music drawn from Lutheran, Catholic, and Jewish sources dating to the sixteenth century.

Mennonite Christopher Dock, a German pacifist who arrived in America in 1714, opened a school in Skippak, Pennsylvania, in 1718. After several years he turned to farming because the school did not have sufficient support. His true calling was teaching, however, and after a few years of leading summer schools in Germantown, he reopened the school in Skippack and alternated his days with another school in Salford. Dock continued his grueling schedule until his death. He was found dead on his knees at a prayer desk in one of the schools in 1771. One of his pupils, Christopher Saur, a printer in Germantown, persuaded Dock to write a treatise (*Schul Ordnung*) on how to conduct a school. The second edition, which appeared in 1770, contained a description of a note board to be used in teaching music to children. The board, which was black, had three five-line staffs etched on each side. Dock said, ''The freedom has been given to me, in singing, to sing both hymns and psalms. So I have sung with them both hymns and songs.''[26]

Other Pietists, under the leadership of Johannes Kelpius, left Germany to establish a community near Philadelphia. Their strong belief in education supported a highly structured curriculum. In the latter seventeenth century pietist leader August Hermann Francke (1663–1727) founded the Halle Foundation, a group of schools at Halle—including a Latin school and a scientific school—for children whose parents could not afford to educate them, and a school for teachers. About two thousand students attended these schools by the middle of the eighteenth century. The curriculum was called ''realist'' because actual objects, such as minerals, wood, and glass, were used to study science. A *Realschule*, or Realist School, was founded in Berlin in 1747 with a Latin-scientific curriculum. The Realist movement spread to America in the eighteenth century, when Benjamin Franklin founded a Realist school in Philadelphia. Other similar schools were established later. The Pietists, who were musical, used elaborate music for their services, often accompanied by viols, oboes, trumpets, and kettledrums.

The Shakers originated in the English Quaker Church in 1706. Mother Anne Lee led a nine-member sect, the United Society of Believers in Christ's Second Coming (also called the Millennial Church), to America in 1774. They settled in New York State, and before Mother Anne's death Shaker colonies had been established in Massachusetts, Maine, Rhode Island, and New Hampshire. New colonies were later founded in the Midwest. There were more than six thousand members at one time, but the numbers began to decline after the Civil War, mostly because of their belief in celibacy. They also believed in separation and equality of the sexes, divine revelation, the millennium, confession, and the second coming of Christ.

The first Shaker hymnal, *Millennial Praises,* contained some original compositions. During the Great Revival (1837–1847), "vision songs" (so called because they were received as gifts through the air) were added. Many of them were set to nonsensical syllables, or an unknown "tongue." An important part of the service was dancing, usually improvised. Because of their bodily movements, they became known as the "Shaking Quakers." They later introduced organized dances. Being celibate, they had little need for the musical education of children, although they provided education for the children of converts.

Several kinds of notation were used in Shaker tune books, including shape notes, American Indian notation, numerical notation, and traditional round notes (after 1870). Most Shakers used a notational system that consisted of the first seven lower-case letters of the alphabet, either written in a straight line or in the approximate direction of the melody. The staff was not always used.[27] Shaker music, like Shaker furniture, buildings, and all other aspects of their lives, was characterized by its functional simplicity. From their inventive genius came the circular saw, the flat broom, and other devices familiar to us today. Their appealing simplicity can be readily perceived in the tune "The Gift to Be Simple," which Aaron Copland used in *Appalachian Spring.*

The key to the importance of music education in the various German communities is the richness of community musical life. Music was thoroughly integrated into everyday life, and so music education was also a normal and important part of general education. In this way the cultures of the early American German communities and the ancient Hebrews were similar.

THE NEW ENGLAND COLONIES

The mainstream of American music education emerged from the British settlements in New England. The English colonists arrived in two groups, the first in 1620 and the second in 1630. Both left England during the Reformation to seek religious freedom.

The Reformation. Although many early churchmen (St. Paul, St. John Chrysostom, St. Jerome, St. Augustine) advocated the singing of psalms by all Christians or struggled to have congregational singing during services (St. Benno of Meissen), education in music performance during the Middle Ages was restricted to the clergy, for the most part. One of the distinctive features of the two largest denominations resulting from the Reformation was the involvement of the congregation in singing spiritual songs.

Martin Luther. In 1524, seven years after nailing his ninety-five theses to the door of the church in Wittenberg, Luther, with the assistance of Johann Walther and Conrad Rupff, published a songbook. In the forward Luther wrote that he had the hymns set in four parts specifically to attract young people, who needed to be trained in music. As has been discussed, education was an essential part of Luther's church and of its many evangelical offshoots. His emphasis on teaching music to all believers began a new phase of the use of music in one branch of Western society.

Luther's desire to give every member of the congregation a participatory role in the new German service resulted in setting many hymns in the vernacular. These were sung in unison by the congregation and in four parts by the choirs in cathedrals and larger churches. A practice of alternating stanzas of a hymn between the choir and the people was reported. Luther realized that the older members of the church would be apt to resist joining in such a radical change in the service. He therefore concentrated on seeing that the children learned the hymns and sang them in church. He even seeded the congregation with choirboys who could carry the people along. Eventually the tunes became well loved and were set polyphonically by such musicians as Ludwig Senfl, Johann Eccard, and J. S. Bach. The psalmody that the other large Protestant movements developed was much simpler.

The Puritans. When Henry VIII (1491–1547) broke with Rome and established his own church, the style of worship did not change dramatically, as it had on the continent. Services were merely Anglicized without eliminating such ritualistic matters as kneeling to receive the sacraments or elaborate vestments for the clergy. Under Henry's successor, Edward VI (1537–1553), the *Book of Common Prayer* was introduced and the forty-two Articles of Religion were published (later replaced by thirty-nine articles). During the reign (1553–1558) of Mary Tudor, papal authority was reestablished by Parliament and the laws against heresy were restored. During Mary Tudor's reign the reformers were subjected to cruel punishments and life in general was made difficult for them. Being constantly at risk of harsh persecution, they fled to the continent. They found sanctuary in Strasbourg, Frankfurt-on-the-Main, Emden, Wesel, Zürich, and Geneva. Between eight hundred and one thousand remained on the continent until Elizabeth was crowned in 1558. The English exiles, all Protestants, were divided into two groups—Anglican and Calvinist. The Calvinists became familiar with psalmody while in Switzerland.[28]

When the dissenters returned to England after Elizabeth's accession, they became strong advocates of psalmody, a new style of religious music. In 1562 the Sternhold and Hopkins *Whole Book of Psalms* was published, and Day's four-part edition appeared a year later. By this time dissenting Englishmen referred to themselves as Puritans, a term designed to indicate that they wished only to purify the church, not abandon it.

The Pilgrims. Others took a stronger position. In 1582 Robert Browne published treatises advocating separation from the established church. It was Browne who first defined a church in terms of a congregation of like-minded people. A group who believed strongly in his teachings fled to Holland to escape persecution from Queen Elizabeth, who was committed to the unity of church and state. After a little over ten years in Holland, this group, the Pilgrims, feared that their children might grow up speaking Dutch. They chose to found their own community in the New World, where they could have their own land and worship as they pleased. The Separatists were musical people, and their founder, Robert Browne, was a good lutenist. Edward Winslow, himself a Pilgrim, described the departure of the Pilgrims from their coreligionists in Holland:

> They that stayed at Leyden feasted us that were to go, at our pastor's house, being large; where we refreshed ourselves, after tears, with singing of psalms, making joyful melody in our hearts, as well as with the voice, there being many of our congregation very expert in music.[29]

In 1620 a group left Holland for Southampton, England. There they joined friends from London who had acquired financial backing and the ship *Mayflower*. The group arrived in America in 1620. On Cape Cod, where they landed first, most of the adult men signed the Mayflower Compact, which had been drawn up by Miles Standish and other leaders of the group. Under this compact they formed a "civil body politic" and committed themselves to "all due submission and obedience" to the just and equal laws to be passed by the government. They reboarded the *Mayflower* and arrived at Plymouth, which had already been named by Captain John Smith on his earlier explorations. The Plymouth Colony was established, and William Bradford was elected governor after the death of the first governor. Thus, early in the American experience English colonists established a means of self rule under law. The newly established government, however, was a theocracy.

One of the most important possessions of the Pilgrims was the *Book of Psalms*, by the Reverend Henry Ainsworth. It had been written for them in Holland and published in 1612. It had 342 pages and 39 psalm tunes, some of which were English, Dutch, and French. The tunes were written in a variety of meters so that all 150 psalms could be used. Ainsworth's *Book of Psalms* was the official psalter of the Plymouth Colony as late as 1692, when the settlement merged with the Massachusetts Bay Colony.

The Puritans came to America in 1630 in 17 ships carrying 1,000 men, women, and children. They established the Massachusetts Bay Colony as a community where their religious ideals could be practiced. Within twenty years they numbered over 20,000.

The Puritans, being Calvinists, believed in predestination and simplicity of worship. This meant there were to be no professional musicians or musical instruments in their churches. The music of their church consisted of biblical psalms set to folk songs; like the people themselves, it was spare and severe. Their psalm book was written by English exiles in Geneva, who derived it from the French psalter. It was known as *The Whole Book of Psalms*, or more informally, the Sternhold and Hopkins. The 1562 edition contained sixty-five tunes. Music was also a minor part of community life. Drums and trumpets substituted for bells in calling people to church and warning them of Indian attack. Part of the trade with the Indians was in the form of Jew's harps, which were imported to be bartered as well as to be played by the Puritans themselves.

Having come from a musical country, the Puritans were a musical people. They believed, however, that psalmody was the only music appropriate for worship and faithfully avoided indecent songs, which were plentiful in seventeenth-century England. These they considered the "nourishment of vice and the corruption of faith."[30] Gilbert Chase wrote that the Puritans were neither antagonistic nor intolerant toward music. "They judged music according to the way it was used."[31] Psalmody was their preferred music.

Despite the harshness of their lives, six years after arriving in America the Puritans founded Harvard College, where their leaders were to be trained. By 1663 the curriculum included six subjects—political philosophy, ethics, astronomy, geometry, physics, and languages (Latin and Greek). Although the early curricular offerings did not include music, the students learned to sing from notation, and music was a part of their daily lives. The Reverend Thomas Symmes of Bradford, Massachusetts, described "Regular Singing" at Harvard in his 1720 essay, "The Reasonableness of Regular Singing, or Singing by Note":

> It was studied, known and approved of in our College, for many years after its first founding. This is evident from the Musical Theses which were formerly printed, and from some writings containing some tunes, with directions for singing by note, as they are now sung; and these are yet in being, though of more than sixty years standing; besides no man that studied music, as it is treated of by Alstead, Playford and others, could be ignorant of it.

The musical theses and other writings containing tunes were later lost when Harvard Library was destroyed by fire.

The Bay Psalm Book. The first book printed in the English colonies was *The Whole Booke of Psalmes Faithfully Translated into English Metre.*

Whereunto is prefixed a discourse declaring not only the lawfullness, but also the necessity of the heavenly Ordinance of Singing Scripture Psalmes in the Churches of God, otherwise known as *The Bay Psalm Book.* The Committee of Thirty, a group of ministers, compiled the book to correct some of the textual inaccuracies in the Sternhold and Hopkins. The work was actually done by the Reverend John Eliot, Thomas Weld, and Richard Mather (grandfather of Cotton Mather). The ministers were educated men, familiar with Hebrew. They desired translations truer to the original meanings.

Another reason for the new psalter was the many meters used in the old books, which tended to confuse the congregation. The Ainsworth had fifteen, and the Sternhold and Hopkins seventeen. *The Bay Psalm Book,* printed in 1639, had only six meters. Perhaps the reason the translations were not as accurate as the ministers wished was that setting the psalms in metrical English was a popular pastime in the seventeenth century for educated gentlemen, and there were countless settings done by amateurs. The new book was printed in Cambridge on Stephen Day's press, which had been sent from England in 1638.

The Bay Psalm Book was popular on both sides of the Atlantic. It went through 70 editions over a 30-year period—18 of them in England and 22 in Scotland. The definitive edition was the third; it was known as *The New England Psalm Book.*

The Bay Psalm Book initially had no music, possibly because no one in the colony could engrave the plates. People were expected to use other books for the tunes to which the psalms were to be sung. The enormously popular Sternhold and Hopkins originally had unharmonized tunes, but the 1563 edition was in four parts. The Puritans sang unison in church, although they were encouraged to use the part books at home. The Reverend Henry Dunster, the founding president of Harvard College, did the first major revision of *The Bay Psalm Book* in 1651. The seventh and eighth editions are unknown and could have had notation, but the first edition known to contain music was the ninth (1698); it was also the first known book to include music printed in the colonies. It contained thirteen tunes for treble and bass. The notes were diamond-shaped, and there were no bars. Instead of the text being printed below the notes, the solmization letters were placed there to help the singers find the correct pitch. This was probably the first example of solmization letters used in this way in America; it later became an important and widespread teaching device.

The quotation above from Reverend Symmes, which mentions the English publisher and composer Playford, concerns Playford's book *An Introduction to the Skill of Music,* published in 1654. Several new editions were issued, and the book was popular in New England as a means of self-instruction in the rudiments of music. The tunes that appeared in the ninth editon of *The Bay Psalm Book* were taken from the eleventh edition of Playford's book.

MUSICAL LIFE AND MUSIC EDUCATION
IN THE SOUTHERN COLONIES

The cultural life of New England was rather bleak compared to that of the areas to its south. While psalmody occupied the minds of the musical leaders of Boston and the rest of New England, music performance was becoming a part of the lives of other regions. European music was performed by both touring European musicians and Americans, and public performances were normal community activities. Secular music was popular in the South in addition to religious music, which contributed to the development of a concert life.

Unlike the North, the South had a class society in which music was a privilege of the upper class. The southern colonies fostered a manorial culture imitative of that in Europe. European musicians and dancing masters emigrated to the South, where they readily found employment as instructors and performers. As the need for music outgrew the supply of artists and teachers, musicians and dancing masters became itinerant, traveling from plantation to plantation to perform, teach, and play the organ in churches. Music instruction in this system was available only to the children of the wealthy. Robert Carter owned a plantation in Northern Neck, Virginia. He owned a pianoforte, harpsichord, guitar, violin, German flutes, and an armonica (an invention of Benjamin Franklin). There was a school on the plantation for his two sons, five daughters, and one nephew. The schedule was as follows:

7–8 A.M.	School
9:30	Breakfast
9:30–12:00	School
12:00	Play
2:00	Dinner
3:30–5:00	School
8:00	Supper

Carter stressed music in his children's education. He hired a music master to teach the girls piano and harpsichord, and he himself taught guitar. The children were excused from some schooltime on Tuesdays and Thursdays to practice. Dancing was also important. One boy was flogged for skipping dancing school. In other places, parents would sometimes band together to build schoolhouses and hire schoolmasters. It was not unusual for girls to be sent to boarding schools, where music and dancing were generally offered.[32] Most of the rest of the southern people were denied the privilege, which is one of the reasons that the northern singing schools spread to the South so successfully.

Comparison with New England. The southern colonies viewed education in a fundamentally different way than the northern colonies. The Puritans who ruled the New England theocracies believed in public education for everyone. As early as 1635 a schoolmaster was hired in Boston, and in 1636 a school committee was appointed and a teacher hired in Charleston, Massachusetts. In 1642 the Massachusetts Bay Colony passed the first public education law in the colonies, the Massachusetts School Law of 1642, which required town officials to compel parents to provide an elementary education for their children. The law did not require the establishment of schools. It specified minimum educational essentials and permitted towns to comply as best they could. The second law, the Massachusetts School Law of 1647, required that every township of at least fifty families appoint a teacher for the children and that reading and writing be taught. Towns of one hundred or more families had to "set up a grammer schoole, the master thereof being able to instruct youth so farr as they may be fited for the university [sic]." Of special importance, this law legalized taxation for the support of education. The third education law, the Massachusetts School Law of 1648, specified what was to be taught and provided a rationale:

> For as much as the good education of children is of singular behoof and benefit to any Common-wealth; and whereas many parents and masters are too indulgent and negligent of their duty in that kinde. It is therefore ordered that the Select men of everie town, in the severall precincts and quarters where they dwell, shall have a vigilant eye over their brethren and neighbours to see, first that none of them shall suffer so much barbarism in any of their families as not to indeaver to teach by themselves or others, their children and apprentices so much learning as may inable them perfectly to read the english tongue, and knowledge of the Capital lawes; upon penalties of twentie shillings for each neglect therein. Also that all masters of families doe once a week (at the least) catechize their children and servants in the grounds and principles of Religion. . . . And further that all parents and masters do breed and bring up their children and apprentices in some honest lawfull calling, labour or imployment, either in husbandry, or some other trade profitable for themselves, and the Common-wealth, if they will not or can not train them up in learning to fit them for higher imployments.[33]

Similar legislation was passed by the legislatures of Connecticut, Plymouth, and New Hampshire within a few decades. These laws required practical education that embraced vocational and religious training. Music, not being appropriate for the curriculum in such a school, was taught privately in the singing schools.

Education, a private matter in the South, was usually a privilege of the wealthy. Another reason for the regional dissimilarity was the strikingly different demographic characteristics of the two regions. While New England had many cities, towns, and villages that provided the population density necessary to establish public schools, the South had fewer population centers. The county or parish was the nucleus of local government and social activity, and the plantation was the primary cultural unit. Virginia, for example, had only one village, Jamestown, and no towns until the eighteenth century. Without population centers, there were not enough children of the wealthy to populate public schools. John Peyton Little's comments on education in Virginia are typical of southern thought on education:

> It is better to place education under church influence, than under that of the State. . . . The government cannot, itself, educate the communities; it can only act by a cloud of irresponsible and ignorant school masters; nor would it be right for it to exercise the power, if it possessed the ability of imparting a good education. . . . Schools originated and sustained by private, or denominational enterprise, are best; of such kinds are the schools of Richmond.[34]

Charleston, South Carolina, was a major cultural and musical center of colonial America. Its population included musicians and dancing masters from Europe, the West Indies, and the colonies to the north. The mixed population was reflected in the variety of musical cultures that developed. The first known opera performance in America (*Hob in the Well*) took place in 1735 in Charleston. The first American musical society, the Saint Cecilia Society, was founded there in 1762 to sponsor public concerts. The cultural life of Charleston was fashioned after that of European capitals. Touring companies from England would land in Charleston and work their way north, presenting works by Thomas Arne and Charles Dibdin. Musicians with the troupes would frequently advertise their availability as teachers while in town.

Other Musical Cities in the South included Williamsburg, Virginia, where the first known playhouse in America was founded in 1722, and Upper Marlboro, Maryland, where *The Beggar's Opera* was performed in 1752. It was the first opera production in America to include an orchestra.

Plantation Life in the South involved music in many ways. The landowners and their families were often gentlemen musicians who performed for themselves and for their friends. Young ladies were expected to be able to accompany their own singing on a keyboard instrument, and it was common practice for a gentleman to bring a gift of sheet music to a lady upon whom he called. The southern landowners also sang in their churches. Like their counterparts in the cities, they valued amateurism in the arts and looked down upon those who earned their living as musicians. However, they needed music teachers and employed them for private instruction in voice and the playing of instruments.

The music of the plantations that most affected the cultural life of the nation was that of the slaves, whose rich African musical heritage was modified to meet the unhappy conditions of their existence. Their strong musical traditions helped sustain them in their bondage, and their musicality was well recognized and respected by their white masters. Music was one of the few positive things in the lives of the slaves.

When ministers and other whites became concerned about the spiritual needs of the slaves, they introduced them to Christianity. The emotionalism and exuberance of revivalist Christianity, especially in the form of the evangelical denominations (such as the Methodists and the Baptists) and the numerous smaller sects appealed to the blacks. They responded enthusiastically and quickly to the music of these denominations, adapting it for their own needs and developing a gospel music tradition that evolved into a vital and popular contemporary genre. The later development of black music into jazz is a well-known story and one that has had worldwide musical and cultural impact.

The Philadelphia Region benefited from the many German immigrant groups that settled in proximity to it. The musical lives of the religious sects and of the German and Swedish settlers who did not belong to religious communities enriched the region and gave it a reputation for musical culture.

The cultural life of the city itself began later. The Quaker prohibition against music and theater was codified into law, but even that could not prevent public theater performances. Despite the laws prohibiting their activities, musicians and dancing masters were active early in the eighteenth century. In 1710 a dancing master found employment in Philadelphia, and public concerts were probably given before the first recorded concert in 1757. Musical life in the city finally began to flourish during the second half of the eighteenth century. The first professional theatrical performance was given in 1749. The antitheater law was repealed later in the century, and in 1791 a theater was built in Philadelphia. In 1781 *The Temple of Minerva*, an oratorio composed by Francis Hopkinson, was performed to an audience that included General and Mrs. George Washington. Hopkinson is better known as a signer of the Declaration of Independence, but he was also a judge, poet, painter, and organist of Christ Church in Philadelphia. In 1784 the German Reformed Church sold over 2,000 tickets to a concert of American music performed by 50 instrumentalists and 250 singers. The concert concluded with Handel's Hallelujah Chorus.

New York was slower than the southern cities in developing a strong musical life, but concerts were performed there in 1736 if not before. Ballad operas were presented in the early 1750s. Imitations of London's "pleasure gardens" offered New Yorkers another opportunity to hear professional singers.

Baltimore did not become a town until 1730, but by the time of the Revolution it had over 6,500 inhabitants and public concerts. It attracted a number of European musicians immediately after the war, including Alexander Reinagle and Rayner Taylor.

SUMMARY

Music education in colonial America outside of New England consisted for the most part of private instruction in voice, keyboard, and orchestral instruments, usually taught by European immigrants. Formal systems of mass music education did not develop in places where the population attended concerts and other musical events and where music performance was the realm of the professional musician. As in ancient Rome, music was performed by professional musicians for the pleasure of those in the highest level of society. The music profession was not highly regarded, and it was unusual for middle and upper-class people to aspire to it. Active participation in music was an amateur undertaking, and it would have been unseemly for ladies and gentlemen to be too proficient in musical performance. Music was an integral aspect of the lives of southern slaves and not simply a reward for their labor at the end of the day. In communities such as those settled by Germans, where music was completely integrated into life activities, music education was also integrated. Formal music lessons might be available, but generally there was an informal approach to learning music. Children lived musically and assimilated it as they did other life experiences. The remarkable musicality of the southern blacks, as well as that of the German religious sects, illustrated the fact that the most successful education is that which is closely related to life activities and which fosters skills the student will need to assume a place in the adult community. A similar phenomenon was evident in the culture of the ancient Hebrews, among Greek citizens, and in the European *scholae cantorum*, where music was a major part of the lives of children.

NOTES

1. Garcilaso de la Vega, *Primera Parte de los Commentarios Reales* (Lisbon: Pedro Crasbeeck, 1609), fol. 95, c. 2. In Robert M. Stevenson, "Music Instruction in Inca Land," *Journal of Research in Music Education* 8 (Fall 1960): 110.
2. Ibid., pp. 112–13.
3. Ibid.

4. George Heller, "Fray Pedro de Gante, Pioneer American Music Educator," *Journal of Research in Music Education* 27 (Spring 1979): 23–24.
5. Lota M. Sell, "The First Teachers of European Music in America," *Catholic Historical Review,* New Series 2 (October 1922): 372–78.
6. Heller, "Fray Pedro de Gante," pp. 21–28.
7. Ibid., p. 24.
8. Ibid.
9. Allen P. Britton, "Music in Early American Public Education: A Historical Critique," *Basic Concepts in Music Education,* pt. 1 (Chicago: National Society for the Study of Education, University of Chicago Press, 1958), p. 199.
10. Samuel Eliot Morison, *The Oxford History of the American People* (New York: Oxford University Press, 1965), p. 40.
11. *The Jesuit Relations and Allied Documents,* ed. Reuben G. Thwaites, vol. 60 (Cleveland: Burrows Brothers, 1896–1901), p. 145.
12. James A. Burns, *The Catholic School System in the United States: Its Principles, Origin, and Establishment* (New York: Benzinger Brothers, 1937), p. 86.
13. Britton, from J. F. Saschse, *The German Sectarians of Pennsylvania 1742–1800,* 2 vols. (Philadelphia: The Author, 1899–1900), p. 198.
14. Ibid.
15. *Church Music and Musical Life in Pennsylvania in the 18th Century,* vol. 2 (Philadelphia: Pennsylvania Society of the Colonial Dames of America, 1927), p. 21.
16. C. I. Latrobe, ed., *Hymn-tunes Sung in the Church of the United Brethren* (London: The Editor, ca. 1806).
17. Harry H. Hall, "Moravian Music Education in America, ca. 1750 to ca. 1830," *Journal of Research in Music Education* 29 (Fall 1981): 226.
18. Hall, from "Our Boarding Schools," *The Moravian Church Miscellany* 5: (1854): 257–62.
19. Hall, "Moravian Music Education," p. 227.
20. Ibid., p. 228.
21. Hall, from M. Haller, *Early Moravian Education in Pennsylvania.* Published as vol. 15, *Transactions of the Moravian Historical Society* (Nazareth, PA: The Moravian Historical Society, 1953).
22. Hall, "Moravian Music Education," p. 233.
23. Ibid.
24. Donald M. McCorkle, "The Moravian Contribution to American Music," *Music Library Association Notes* 13 (December 1956): 597.
25. Lloyd G. Blakely, "Johann Conrad Beissel and Music of the Ephrata Cloister," *Journal of Research in Music Education* 15 (Summer 1967): 123.
26. *Church Music and Musical Life in Pennsylvania,* p. 51.
27. Nancy Kirkland Klein, "Music and Music Education in the Shaker Societies of America," *Bulletin of Historical Research in Music Education* 11 (Winter 1990): 38–40.
28. Hamilton C. Macdougall, *Early New England Psalmody: An Historical Appreciation 1620–1820* (Brattleboro, VT: Stephen Daye Press [reissued by Da Capo Press], 1940), p. 7.
29. Gilbert Chase, *America's Music,* 2nd ed. (New York: McGraw-Hill, 1966), from Winslow, *Hypocrasie Unmasked* (1646), quoted in Pratt, *The Music of the Pilgrims* (Boston: Oliver Ditson Company, 1921), p. 8.
30. H. W. Foote, "Musical Life in Boston in the Eighteenth Century," *Proceedings of the Antiquarian Society,* New Series 49 (1940): 293–313.

31. Chase, p. 6.
32. Julia Spruill, *Women's Life and Work in the Southern Colonies* (New York: Norton, 1972), pp. 102, 196. Much of Spruill's information was taken from Philip V. Fathien, *Journals and Letters, 1767–1774,* edited for the Princeton Historical Association by John Rogers Williams, Princeton, NJ, 1900.
33. Sol Cohen, ed., *Education in the United States: A Documentary History,* vol. 1 (New York: Random House, 1974), pp. 394–95.
34. John Peyton Little, "History of Richmond," *Southern Literary Messenger* 17 (October 1851): 234–36, quoted in Ivan W. Olson, "The Roots and Development of Public School Music in Richmond, Virginia 1782–1907" (Ph.D. dissertation, University of Michigan, 1964), p. 64, and James A. Keene, *A History of Music Education in the United States* (Hanover, NH: University Press of New England, 1982), p. 60.

BIBLIOGRAPHY

Barth, Pius Joseph, O.F.M. "Franciscan Education and the Social Order in Spanish North America (1502–1821)." Ph.D. dissertation, University of Chicago, 1945.

Blakely, Lloyd G. "Johann Conrad Beissel and Music of the Ephrata Cloister." *Journal of Research in Music Education* 15 (Summer 1967).

Blume, Friedrich. *Protestant Church Music.* London: Norton, 1974.

Britton, Allen P. "Music in Early American Public Education: A Historical Critique." *Basic Concepts in Music Education,* pt. 1. Chicago: National Society for the Study of Education, University of Chicago Press, 1958.

Brooks, Henry M. *Olden-time Music: A Compilation from Newspapers and Books.* Boston: Ticknor and Company, 1888.

Brumbaugh, Martin G. *The Life and Works of Christopher Dock.* Philadelphia: Lippincott, 1908.

Bullock, Henry Allen. *A History of Negro Education in the South: From 1619 to the Present.* New York: Praeger, 1967.

Burns, James A., C.S.C. *The Catholic School System in the United States: Its Principles, Origin, and Establishment.* New York: Benzinger Brothers, 1937.

Chase, Gilbert. *America's Music,* 4th ed. New York: McGraw-Hill, 1988.

Church Music and Musical Life in Pennsylvania in the 18th Century, vol. 2. Philadelphia: Pennsylvania Society of the Colonial Dames of America, 1927.

Cohen, Sol, ed. *Education in the United States: A Documentary History,* vol. 1. New York: Random House, 1974.

Hall, Harry H. "Moravian Music in America, ca. 1750 to ca. 1830." *Journal of Research in Music Education* 29 (Fall 1981).

Heller, George. "Fray Pedro de Gante Pioneer American Music Educator." *Journal of Research in Music Education* 27 (Spring 1979).

Klein, Nancy Kirkland. "Music and Music Education in the Shaker Societies of America." *Bulletin of Historical Research in Music Education* 11 (Winter 1990).

Little, John Peyton. "History of Richmond." *Southern Literary Messenger* 17 (October 1851).

Macdougall, Hamilton C. *Early New England Psalmody: An Historical Appreciation 1620– 1820*. New York: Da Capo Press, 1969.

McCorkle, Donald M. "The Moravian Contribution to American Music." Music Library Association *Notes* 13 (December 1956).

Morison, Samuel Eliot. *The Oxford History of the American People*. New York: Oxford University Press, 1965.

Nettl, Paul. *Luther and Music*. New York: Russell & Russell, 1967.

Olson, Ivan W. "The Roots and Development of Public School Music in Richmond, Virginia 1782–1907." Ph.D. dissertation, University of Michigan, 1964.

Sell, Lotta M. "The First Teachers of European Music in America." *Catholic Historical Review*, New Series 2 (October 1922).

Spruill, Julia Cherry. *Women's Life and Work in the Southern Colonies*. New York: Norton, 1972.

Stevenson, Robert M. "Music Instruction in Inca Land." *Journal of Research in Music Education* 8 (Fall 1960).

5

THE NEW ENGLAND ROOTS OF AMERICAN MUSIC EDUCATION

New Englanders participated in musical activities in their secular lives, but most of their musical activity was related to worship. Since they lived in a political theocracy where religious music, especially psalmody, was favored and encouraged, special importance was attached to it. There was not much concert life; most music was made by the people themselves in the form of psalmody and eventually some secular music. In fact, there was a ban on theater productions in Boston, but people got around it by scheduling "Moral Lectures," which were readings of dramatic works. Even *Beggar's Opera* was performed in this way, without music or acting.

The authorities wanted religious life to remain strong, and they recognized that the people had to be sufficiently educated in music to support the church service. For that reason, it was in New England that a formal system of music education for the masses developed; here the American music education philosophy of music for the masses was conceived. Ironically, mass music education emerged from a fundamental difference in the way congregations sang psalm tunes.

OPPOSING PRACTICES IN PSALM-TUNE SINGING

The Regular Way and the Old Way. There were two methods of singing psalm tunes, both imported from the Old World. The "regular way" consisted of singing by note, or reading music. The "old way," which originated in England for the benefit of illiterate parishoners, developed into a tradition there and in the New World where there were soon many who could not read music. Each line of a psalm was read by a deacon. A precentor, who led the congregational singing, gave out the pitch for the tune. The line was then repeated by the congregation to a prescribed tune that was part of their memorized repertoire. This practice was known as "lining out." The process was repeated for each line of the psalm. The fundamental purpose of lining out was to satisfy the Calvinist requirement that worshipers "heard, understood, and sang the biblical words."[1] It must be remembered that the words were the more important element to the early New Englanders, although no doubt the opportunity to raise one's voice after listening to a three-hour sermon was welcome in any form. Lining out was the common practice in seventeenth-century English churches and still exists in many Baptist churches in the mountain areas of Kentucky, Virginia, and North Carolina.[2]

The old way became known as that of the unsophisticated country people who had not learned to read musical notation. When city people used the phrase "old way," it was normally a derogatory reference. Their attitude showed little understanding of conservative rural Americans. The country people probably enjoyed singing psalm tunes in this manner and preserved the tradition because it suited their musical taste. If the precentor was musical, the congregational response was likely to be musical. Often, though, the tune was in a too high or too low a key, the tempo dragged, and the precentor would alter the tune and add embellishments. These practices resulted in the decline of the quality of church music during the first few generations in the New England colonies. George Hood characterized the state of music in seventeenth-century New England churches in his book *History of Music in New England* as being so completely neglected that by the beginning of the eighteenth century few congregations could sing more than three or four tunes. Their sparse repertoire became corrupted because they could not read music. The same tunes were sung differently from one congregation to another and from one person to another. The Reverend Cotton Mather wrote in 1721, "It has been found . . . in some of our congregations, that in length of time, their singing has degenerated into an odd noise, that has more of what we want a name for, than any Regular Singing in it."[3] This poem was written on a panel of a pew in a New England church:

COULD poor king David but for once   But could St. Paul but just pop in,
To S—m Church repair,   From higher scenes abstracted,
And hear his Psalms thus warbled out,   And hear his gospel now explain'd,
Good Lord, how would he swear!   By ——, he'd run distracted![4]

The decline of the quality of psalmody has been attributed to the exigencies of life in the New World, where people had to clear forests, find food, clothe themselves, and take care of the countless details of building a society in the wilderness. There was little time to maintain their rich European musical traditions. Gilbert Chase points out that during the same period a similar decline occurred in England and Scotland, where people presumably had the time and the means to maintain their musical skills. The quality of church singing in the Old World appears to have been quite similar to that in America. Doctor Burney, Samuel Johnson's friend, wrote in his *History of Music* (1789) of church singing in England, or what he called "bawling out":

The greatest blessing to lovers of music in a parish church is to have an organ in it sufficiently powerful to render the voices of the clerk & those who join in his outcry wholle inaudible. Indeed all reverence for the psalms seems to be lost by the wretched manner in which they are sung.

Dr. Millar Patrick wrote of lining out in Scotland:

Singing of the psalms, inexpressibly dreary, was made worse by the importation from England of the practice of "lining"—the precentor reading or intoning each line before it was sung. Such a practice, necessary where the people had few or no psalters or where they were in general illiterate, was absurd in Scotland, where the people could read; yet it established itself so firmly in favor that in some cases congregations suffered serious secessions when it began to be abandoned.[5]

An amusing account of "deaconing" in Scotland is given by Lightwood:

The 1645 Westminster Assembly, as it is called, ordained that "where many of the congregation cannot read, it is convenient that the minister, or some other fit person appointed by him and the other officers, do read the psalm, line by line before the singing thereof." . . . Our Puritan forbears were not overblessed with a sense of the ludicrous, or they would have been much exercised to sing, say verse 3 of the 50th Psalm with decorum. For this is what would take place. The Clerk would give out the first line, "The Lord will come and He will not"—and then the congregation would repeat the extraordinary statement. Then the clerk would read, "Keep silence, but speak out"—and this paradoxical remark would then be solemnly sung by the congregation. . . . This custom continued in use for many years. The Scotch did not take to it kindly at first, for they could not see why they should be made to suffer merely because their English brethren could not read; but by degrees it became almost a second nature with them, and in the end they were loath to give up the custom . . . it gradually gave way to two lines being read at once, which remained the practice for some years after 1860, especially among Nonconformists, who, at any rate in country districts, retained the custom of giving out two lines at a time until quite recently.[6]

Unlike Lutherans, the lack of musicality in congregational singing was of little concern to Calvinists, to whom the only important element of music was the text. People were expected to sing with understanding and sincerity.[7] Bullinger said in a sermon published in 1569:

Let no man think, that prayers sung with man's voice are more acceptable to God, than if they were plainly spoken or uttered; for God is neither allured with the sweetness of man's voice, neither is he offended, though prayer be uttered in a hoarse or base sound. Prayer is commended for faith and godliness of mind, and not for any outward show.[8]

Considering that parallel events took place in Europe and that Calvinism had a strong influence on the New England churches, it is likely that the New England settlers deliberately chose to ignore musical notation in favor of deaconing because that was their traditional manner of singing and they thought it most pleasing to God. Chase theorizes that the popularity of deaconing in New England resulted in a florid style by the more musical singers that left the less-musical congregants to their own devices. They might have sung more slowly and at a lower pitch, while the more musical singers added embellishments and sang faster and higher.

THE REFORM MOVEMENT LAYS THE GROUNDWORK FOR FORMAL MUSIC EDUCATION

The time had come for people to become musically literate. This was to be no easy task after several generations of declining musical skills in the New World. By the early part of the eighteenth century the ministers had begun to campaign vigorously to change to the regular way. The ministers, contemporaries of J. S. Bach, were vocal and sometimes strident in their sermons and writings, which were their vehicles for instituting change. The most influential minister was Reverend John Tufts, of Newbury, Massachusetts, who not only preached sermons that disparaged musical illiteracy but also wrote the first American textbook meant to solve the problem. The pioneering work of Tufts led to the *singing school*, which influenced American music and music education for over a hundred years. Tufts was the most significant figure in American music education until the 1820s, when Lowell Mason led it in a new direction.

An Introduction to the Singing of Psalm-Tunes (1721). The earliest practical attempts to improve the situation were in the form of music texts, the first or second of which was *An Introduction to the Singing of Psalm Tunes* by Tufts. Although several dates have been given for the publication of the first edition, the most likely is 1721. No copies of the first (1721) or second editions have been found. Lowens points out that the first known reference to the work is in a newspaper advertisement placed by the publisher:

> A small Book containing 20 Psalm Tunes, with Directions how to Sing them, contrived in the most easy Method ever yet Invented, for the ease of Learners, whereby even Children, or People of the meanest Capacities, may come to Sing them by Rule, may serve as an Introduction to a more compleat Treatise of Singing, which will speedily be published. To be Sold by Samuel Gerrish Bookseller; near the Brick Church in Cornhill. Price 6d.[9]

The "more compleat Treatise of Singing" probably refers to Thomas Walter's more elaborate *Grounds and Rules of Musick Explained* (Boston, 1721), which was also announced by Gerrish in the *Boston News-Letter* of May 15 and 21, 1721.[10] The title page of the third edition (1723) of Tufts's *Introduction to the Singing of Psalm Tunes* read:

> An introduction to the art of singing psalm-tunes; in the most plain and easy method ever yet made known. Or, a collection of the best psalm-tunes in two parts, fitted to the meanest capacity. First contrived by the Reverend Mr. Tufts. The third edition. With an addition of the basses of the tunes printed from a copper plate correctly engraven. Boston: Printed by T. Fleet, for Samuel Gerrish, near the Brick Meeting-House in Cornhill. 1723.

"The Publisher's Preface" was optimistic about the success of the book:

> THERE has been of late a wonderful, and laudable Inclination in multitudes of People, both Old and Young, to learn to Sing according to the Rules of Music; and the Reformation that has been already made, begins to be visible in many Congregations, both in this Town, and many Towns in the Country. . . . It is plain that the following easy Method of singing the Psalm-Tunes, has been greatly Instrumental of promoting this good Work; it has answer'd its End far beyond what was first expected.[11]

The book has special significance for American music education because it was intended to help children, as well as adults, learn to sing.[12]

Tufts was the first American to devise an innovation in musical notation to simplify music reading. He abandoned traditional round notes and substituted the first letters of the four solmization syllables— F(a), S(ol), L(a), and M(i)—on the staff. The four syllables represented the seven notes of the scale. The practice of singing with four syllables was known as *fasola* singing. The letters represented pitches by their placement on the appropriate lines and spaces of the musical staff. *Fa, sol, la* were sung for the first three tones of the scale and *fa* was then sung one half-step higher than the *la* for the fourth tone. *Sol* and *la* followed for steps five and six, and *mi* was used for the seventh tone—the leading tone one-half step below the tonic *fa*, which began the new octave. The practice of identifying the keynote by the placement of *mi* became an important part of the knowledge imparted through the singing schools. Four-note solmization systems, sometimes called Lancashire Sol Fa, were adopted by both British and American singing school composers. Carried into the South in the early nineteenth century, it was still in isolated use in the twentieth. Andrew Adgate, in his *Rudiments of Music*, gave instructions for modifying the syllables when accidentals appeared in the notation:

If a sharp comes before any particular note, that is not found in the cliff, we change its vowel into E, and give it the sound of E in me, as long as the sound is affected by the accidental sharp: The same alteration takes place when a note that is flat at the cliff has a natural set before it. Sometimes after the beginning of a tune, and when me has an accidental flat or natural set before it, we may change E into A, sounded as in hall.[13]

Tufts indicated duration with punctuation. A period after a letter note signified a half note, a colon a whole note, and no punctuation meant a quarter note.

The solmization system was not actually Tufts's invention. It had been used in the 1698 edition of the *Bay Psalm Book*. Letter notation was not new even then, having been used in Europe for one hundred and fifty years. It first appeared in a French psalter in 1560. Letter notation was also used that same year in England in John Day's edition of the Sternhold and Hopkins psalter. This simple system was adequate for the traditional psalm tunes but not for more complex music.[14] It is possible, but arguable, that Tufts reinvented the system, not knowing it had been used earlier. Tufts's notation did not become popular but was nevertheless important because it was a model for others who devised more effective notations.

An Introduction to the Singing of Psalm Tunes had an appendix, in which the rudiments of music, instructions for tuning the voice, musical notation, intervals, scales, clefs, and meter signatures were presented. The book became the prototype for numerous other books published throughout the eighteenth century. The third edition, published in 1726, is the earliest still in existence. It contained thirty-seven English

[7]

DIRECTIONS

For Singing

The TUNES which follow.

THE Letters F, S, L, M, mark'd on the feveral Lines and Spaces in the following Tunes, ftand for thefe Syllables, viz. *Fa, Sol, La, Mi,* and are to fhew you,

I. The Diftance of the Notes one from another in each Tune, or to give you the true Pitch of every Note. Therefore obferve, From *Mi* to *Fa,* and from *La* to *Fa* afcending ; or, from *Fa* to *La,* and from *Fa* to *Mi* defcending, are but half Notes, or Semitones. From *Fa* to *Sol,* from *Sol* to *La,* and from *La* to *Mi* afcending; or, from *Mi* to *La,* from *La* to *Sol,* and from *Sol* to *Fa* defcending, are whole Notes, or Tones. *Mi* is the Principal Note, and the Notes rifing gradually above *Mi,* are *Fa, Sol, La, Fa, Sol, La,* and then *Mi* again : And the Notes fall-

FIGURE 5–1 Directions for reading Tuft's distinctive notation from *An Introduction to the Singing of Psalm Tunes.* Reproduction from the collections of the Library of Congress.

psalm tunes with two harmony voices. Of special interest is the "100 Psalm Tune New" (no. 23), which was probably written by Tufts. If so, it could be the first complete composition by a native American composer.[15]

The third edition also contains an interesting paragraph with an air of prophecy:

> What a great addition it would be to the pleasure of Singing, if we had more *Female* Voices assisting in that Holy Exercize, and the sweet and sprightly Voices of our Children. *Women* have certainly greater advantages to attain the Skill of Singing than *Men.* They have generally good Voices, and more Leisure then Men have; and their obligations to Praise GOD are as full, and binding. And as to our Children, how affecting the Sight, how vast and charming the Pleasure to have them sweetly joining with us in our *Family Worship,* as well as in *Public* Assemblies, in singing for the Praises of their Great CREATOR; and this even by some almost as soon as they can speak plain, and begin to read. O that this time for the *Singing of Birds* were come![16]

The Reverend Thomas Symmes was another articulate reformer. He wrote a pamphlet entitled *The Reasonableness of Regular Singing, or Singing by Note* (1720), subtitled *An Essay to revive the true and ancient mode of Singing psalm-tunes according to the pattern of our New-England psalm-books.* Symmes described singing by note as follows:

> Now singing by note is giving every note its proper pitch, and turning the voice in its proper place, and giving to every note its true length and sound. Whereas, the usual way varies much from this. In it, some notes are sung too high, others too low, and most too long, and many turnings or flourishings with the voice are made where they should not be, and some are wanting where they should have been.[17]

The Reverend Thomas Walter of Roxbury, Massachusetts, also published a manual on singing the regular way. Like Tufts, Walter was a graduate of Harvard College. He was a nephew of Cotton Mather. His book *The Grounds and Rules of Music Explained or An Introduction to the Art of Singing by Note* was published in Boston in 1721. It was printed by James Franklin, whose brother Benjamin was an apprentice in his shop at that time. The subtitle read *An Introduction to the Art of Singing by Note. Fitted to the meanest Capacities.* In the book, Walter wrote:

> Once the tunes were sung according to the rules of music but are now miserably tortured, and twisted, and quavered, in some churches, into an horrid Medley of confused and disorderly Noises. . . . Our tunes are, for Want of a Standard to appeal to in all our Singing, left to the Mercy of every unskilful Throat to chop and alter, twist and change, according to their infinitely divers and no less odd Humours and Fancies. . . . I have

observed in many places, one man is upon this note while another is upon the note before him, which produces something so hideous and disorderly as is beyond expression bad.

Justifying the change to the Regular Way, he wrote:

Somebody or other did compose our tunes, and did they, think ye compose them by rule or by rote? If the latter how come they are prick'd [written] down in our Psalm books?

The Grounds and Rules of Music Explained used conventional notation, probably because Walter thought it would be received more readily than a new and unfamiliar system like that of Tufts. The book had twenty-four tunes in three parts and the introduction included "Some brief and very plain Instructions for Singing by Note."

In 1728 the Reverend Nathaniel Chauncey listened to an objection to regular singing: "It looks very unlikely to be the right way because the young people fall in with it; they are not want to be so forward for anything which is good." Chauncey's answer was

As old men are not always wise, so young men are not always fools. They are generally more free of prejudices than the Elderly People. Their present age disposes them to Mirth, and it should be a joyful and acceptable thing unto Elderly People to see them foremost to improve their Mirth according to Scripture's direction.[18]

FIRST MUSIC EDUCATION CONFLICT

The groundwork for formal music education was laid by ministers who wanted to improve the quality of music in their churches by returning to traditional music-reading practices. The "Regular Way" was resisted fervently by some congregations and gradually accepted by others. The change began in the cities, where the citizens had more exposure to European musical traditions and standards. The "Old Way" persisted in rural areas before a reform movement began to influence the conservative country people.

The reform work of the New England ministers influenced American education far beyond their dreams. Their work had significant results in the establishment of a formal system of music education to provide music instruction to the masses and eventually led to school music education as we know it today.

THE SINGING SCHOOL MOVEMENT

The Reverend Thomas Symmes asked in 1723:

Would it not greatly tend to promote singing of psalms if singing schools were promoted? . . . where would be the difficulty, or what the disadvantages, if people who want skill in singing, would procure a skillful person to instruct them, and meet two or three evenings in the week, from five or six o'clock to eight, and spend their time in learning to sing?[19]

The agitation of Symmes and other ministers succeeded as singing schools, remarkably like the one suggested by Symmes, began to be established. The movement toward the regular way gained momentum quickly. As early as 1722 there was a Society for Promoting Regular Singing in Boston. Reverend Walter gave a lecture at a meeting of the society. It was entitled "The sweet Psalmist of Israel: A Sermon Preach'd at the Lecture held in Boston, by the Society for promoting Regular and Good Singing, and for reforming the Depravations and Debasement, our Psalmody labours under, In Order to introduce the proper and true Old Way of Singing."[20]

The term "singing school" refers to a movement in which music teachers, or singing masters, held classes in communities where people desired to learn to sing by note. Britton points out that singing schools were similar to *scholae cantorum* and other choir schools centuries earlier in Europe[21]. Like the earlier European schools, the singing school served both musical and social purposes. It prepared people to be effective members of the church congregation while providing a social opportunity for people with similar interests and abilities. The singing school, like its earlier European counterparts, also provided a livelihood for numerous music teachers, called singing masters, many of whom were composers as well. They emulated the European kapellmeisters.[22]

The Great Awakening. The rapid expansion of interest in the singing school can only be understood in relation to the explosive revival of the period. With its roots in pietism, the "awakening" is generally credited to Theodorus Frelinghusen in the Middle Colonies in 1725. Nine years later Jonathan Edwards at Northampton, Massachusetts, set New England ablaze with revivalism. An Englishman, George Whitefield, helped spread the movement during his seven visits to America. One of his seats of operations was the Independent Presbyterian Church in Savannah, Georgia. The awakening not only stimulated interest in church music but is also generally acknowledged to have had a positive effect on moral standards and the place of the church in the community and, possibly through its influence on the individual, the furtherance of a democratic spirit.

One aspect of the movement grew from the beliefs of the Wesley brothers, John and Charles, in England. Charles Wesley, the "poet of the revival," considered music of primary importance in religion, and when he began his evangelistic work in 1735 he immediately concentrated on singing. The people who followed his teachings, later called Methodists, were communicants of the Church of England. The great music of the Church of England was concentrated in the cathedrals and other places where professional choirs performed. Although new music was written for the church, metrical psalms were seldom set to involved music. Charles Wesley, aware that the common people desired to participate in the music of worship, wrote about 6,500 hymns. His hymns and those of Dr. Isaac Watts gained quick acceptance on both sides of the Atlantic. By 1740 hymns had become an integral part of the service. J. Spencer Curwen noted:

> We must call to mind that hymns, heartily sung by a whole congregation, were an unknown element in public worship at the time when Wesley and Whitefield's work began. . . . John Wesley, although like his brother Charles, a member of the Church of England, in describing the ordinary service of the parish Church refers to "the drawl of the parish clerk", the "screaming of the charity children", and "scandalous doggerel of Hopkins and Sternhold." It is easy to understand how welcome the new hymn-tunes were, with their pulsating, secular rhythms, their emotional repetitions, the fugal tunes, the iterations of words in cumulative sequences after the "sleep of formalism. . . . The Methodists with their hymns and their singing burst like heralds of new life. Crowds were drawn to their services simply by the irresistible charm of the music. To sing hymns was to be a Methodist. The Independents were not long in joining the movement, the Church of England pursuing its conservative way."[23]

A second great revival, occurring at the turn of the century, swept through the rural South and the newly settled West. Both the new hymns and the compositions of many of the singing masters made music an important part of this highly emotional movement.

A Notational System had been invented centuries earlier in Europe to overcome the difficulties of preserving music as composers intended it to be performed and to assist students in learning to read and write music. The American singing school likewise motivated musicians to invent new notational systems so their students could learn to read music more easily. The most important new notation was shape notes. Shape notes not only helped educate students but also provided a medium for the preservation of a body of music composed with that particular kind of notation. Shape notes will be discussed more fully later.

The singing school was a popular movement that did not select talented students to the exclusion of others. Unlike the earlier European choir schools, the singing school was an entirely private enterprise. The church had supported the choir schools in Europe, but the singing schools had no similar support from government, churches, or a wealthy aristocracy. Students paid the singing master directly for his services. Sometimes a barter system operated, with the master being paid in corn or other staple or with a room during his stay in town if he was itinerant.

How Singing Schools Operated. A singing master would set up a singing school in a classroom, church, courthouse, home, tavern, or other convenient place; the most common location was an extra room in the meeting house.[24] Classes usually met in the evening, from one to five times each week, and lasted from a few weeks to six months. The singing master would advertise his singing school with a newspaper announcement or by posting broadsides (posters). Information about tuition, schedule of class meetings, and other pertinent information would be included.

The singing master might run another singing school in a nearby community simultaneously or devote himself exclusively to one singing school at a time. The culmination of the singing school was the singing lecture, which consisted of a concert by the students and a sermon by a minister. If there was no sermon, it was called a singing assembly. At the conclusion of the school the itinerant singing master would go on to another community to set up a new singing school. He might carry with him a variety of merchandise to sell along the way or in the new community to supplement his tuition income. He might also provide services in addition to teaching singing, especially if he had another occupation like wheelwright, carpenter, mason, or tanner. The singing master might spend part of the year working at home at another occupation and travel part of the year, or he might travel all the time.

The students would be expected to buy tune books from the singing master. The tune books contained both instructions for reading music and a collection of music, including psalms, hymns, and other music to be sung in class. Most of the music was composed by singing masters, sometimes by the one selling the book.

Fisher described what was probably a typical singing school, one established just after the Revolutionary War in Baltimore and the first in that city. He wrote:

> Ishmael Spicer opened a school in the Court House during the early part of November 1789. The school met four evenings a week; its sole purpose was the improvement of "church musick." Tuition was set at two dollars and a half per quarter for each student. Spicer announced that he would teach not only the most improved tunes of the different churches in Baltimore, but also the rules of music from the "newest and most approved plan in America.[25]

The system of teaching was that of Andrew Adgate, who had founded an institute for vocal music in Philadelphia around 1785. The plan used a progressive arrangement of musical elements to assist in note reading with the four sol-fa syllables. This was similar to the system used by many singing masters at that time.[26]

Students attended singing schools to learn music reading and to improve their voices, and because it gave them an opportunity to exercise a love of singing. The singing school was also an institution that gave people a place to socialize. Most students were young adults who welcomed the opportunity to come together in an activity approved by their elders. Birge quotes former singing-school students in their reminiscences about singing schools. Henry Perkins wrote: "Those were halcyon days. We not only sang every exercise, tune, and anthem to do, re, mi . . . but at the close . . . we escorted the prettiest girl, to our way of thinking, home." A jaded Yale undergraduate wrote:

> At present I have no inclination for anything, for I am almost sick of the World & were it not for the Hopes of going to the singing-meeting tonight & indulging myself a little in some of the carnal Delights of the Flesh, such as kissing, squeezing, &c. &c. I should willingly leave it now.

Obviously, the social aspect of the singing school was as important as the musical. The singing schools were established to satisfy a religious need, but they served a secular need as well. The music was mostly of a religious nature at first; secular music was added gradually.

In time, the singing schools became a rural phenomenon. They began in New England during the 1720s. As they multiplied and thrived there, they also spread rapidly to southern and middlewestern rural areas. Early singing classes were taught by John Salter in Charleston in 1730, Will Tuckey in New York in 1754, Josiah Davenport in Philadelphia in 1757, and James Lyon, also in Philadelphia, in 1750.

As the cities absorbed more European immigrants throughout the eighteenth and nineteenth centuries, urbanites developed appreciation for European music. Interest in psalmody and church hymns not only began to decline, but urban Americans came to disdain it and to regard singing school music as that of the unsophisticated and unrefined country people. As the influence of the singing schools grew in the rural regions, it declined in the cities where they began. Singing schools existed in all rural areas of the country, but they continued longer in the South because public schools in the North eventually usurped their functions. The development of choral societies (Chapter 7) had a similar effect on the singing schools. The singing schools contributed to American cultural life for two centuries, from the early 1700s to the early 1900s.

Britton states that the singing school can be categorized as an "evening" or "night" school, a group of schools or classes organized to provide instruction in subjects not offered in the public school curriculum.[27] Students attended evening schools voluntarily and at their own expense to study such diverse subjects as languages, surveying, dancing, sewing, handicrafts, and others. When the subjects were proven to be of lasting interest to citizens and when the public schools were ready to offer instruction in them, some, like music, were absorbed into the curriculum.[28] The decline of the singing schools in the latter half of the nineteenth century was caused in great part by this phenomenon. More and more public schools began to offer free music instruction in competition with the singing schools, for which people had to pay. Had it not been for the singing schools, however, it is unlikely that music would have been adopted by large numbers of public schools. The first teaching methods came from the singing schools, as did the first cadre of public school music teachers.

THE TUNE BOOKS

The texts used in singing schools were called "tune books." Typically oblong-shaped, they were known as end-openers. About 1,400 tune books were published, many with distinctive, often long-winded titles similar to those published in England. For example, one book was entitled *The Delights of Harmony; or, Norfolk Compiler, Being a new collection of psalm tunes, hymns and anthems; with a variety of set pieces. From the most approved American and European authors. Likewise, the necessary rules of psalmody made easy. The whole particularly designed for the use of singing schools and musical societies in the United States. By Stephen Jenks . . . Dedham, Mass. . . . 1805.*

Tune books were both music texts and collections of choral music. They included an appendix in which the rudiments of music were presented. This practice went back at least to printer John Day's four-part psalters, including the Sternhold and Hopkins (1562), which had sections on theoretical instruction. The inclusion of the rudiments of music began in the New World with John Tufts's *Introduction* and Thomas Walter's *The Grounds and Rules of Musick Explained* and continued through the nineteenth century. Fundamental information on music reading was presented in some of the tune books. Others presented more elaborate and complex material, going far beyond the rudiments to more advanced music theory. By the latter part of the nineteenth century, tune books often included complete lesson plans.

The Pedagogical Sections of Tune Books were more or less standardized until the early part of the nineteenth century. They began with the four-note gamut, followed by the proportional values of notes and rests, "other characters," "rules to find the mi," including an explanation of the four-syllable fa-sol-la system, and meter signatures. Then there is information on the tonic, "Lessons for Tuning the Voice," and interval exercises, called "The Intervals Proved," which employed the intervals commonly used in singing the music in the tune book. This was a standard order of presentation, and it contained no exercises or review questions.[29] It was an atomistic approach to learning, in which students learned each aspect of music reading separately before putting them together.[30] Students were expected to learn the rudiments before they did much singing.

In the early part of the nineteenth century, when the concepts of the Swiss educator Johann Pestalozzi (see Chapter 7) began to influence American education, the pedagogical presentations of tune books changed. The principles of Pestalozzian instruction were adapted for music instruction. These principles, which were quite different from those that supported the pedagogical presentations in earlier tune books, changed both the nature and course of music instruction in the United States.

When Lowell Mason undertook to apply Pestalozzian principles to a teaching method, he developed a new format that influenced the teaching of music throughout the country. In the ninth edition of the *Boston Handel and Haydn Society's Collection of Church Music*, he presented the instructional material in lessons, rather than as expository material, and supplied questions for the teacher to ask the students, as well as the expected responses. In 1830 Elam Ives divided instruction into three "departments"—rhythm, pitch, and dynamics—and Mason began to use those headings in 1839. The new pedagogy made students "active" rather than "passive" by mixing the instructional material with musical exercises, which permitted them to apply new concepts as they were learned. The introductory section began with a discussion of rhythm, rather than the gamut, which dealt with pitch. The principle of "one thing at a time" was observed in presenting such complex topics as transposition, modulation, and chromatic scales at the end of the introduction.[31]

The addition of exercises to the pedagogical section was the most fundamental change made by Mason in his *Modern Psalmist* (1839). After the publication of that book, virtually all other tune books included similar exercises interspersed with the introductory texts. The question-and-answer format was modified to a presentation of review questions, and instruction was divided into rhythm, melody, and dynamics in that order. These changes in instructional format transformed the introductory sections of tune books into an entirely different format.[32]

Notation was one of the most interesting aspects of the tune books because many authors devised new notational systems to simplify music reading. The first was Tufts's *Introduction*, and many others followed. The most revolutionary method of notation was the shape note system, in which a different shape was assigned to each of the four syllables. Singers could ascertain the pitch by the shape of the note rather than by its placement on the staff. This notation was also referred to as "patent notes" and derisively as "buckwheat notes."

The first to use shape notes were William Little and William Smith in *The Easy Instructor*, followed by Andrew Law in *The Art of Singing*. *The Easy Instructor*, published in 1798, was orthodox in everything but the shapes of the notes. Little and Smith used a triangular note head for *fa*, a round note for *sol*, a square for *la*, and a diamond for *mi*.[33] The shapes conformed to the then-current Anglo-American solmization system, in which major scales began and ended on *fa*. Minor scales began on *la*.

The Easy Instructor, which was received enthusiastically, was a commercial success. Numerous editions came out from 1805 to 1831, and tens of thousands of books were sold. The various editions followed the trends in tune books from the earlier New England fuging tunes to the later reform movement in tune-book pedagogy. With the Pestalozzian changes brought by Lowell Mason and his colleagues, supporters of shape notes began to favor a seven note system. Jesse Aikin's system was widely accepted, and many others were developed. Most used the same shapes but assigned them to different notes.

The Mason brothers, Lowell and Timothy, published their highly successful *Ohio Sacred Harp* in both traditional notation and shape notes. Although the Masons, especially Lowell, favored and actively promoted traditional notation, they realized that their book would appeal to the rural people of the Ohio Valley only if it was printed in shape notes. Eight editions, the first probably in 1832, were published.[34]

Andrew Law devised a slightly different shape note system. He used the same shapes as Little and Smith, but they signified different notes. The diamond was *mi*, the square *faw* (*fa*), the circle *sol*, and the triangle *law* (*la*). Law did not use the musical staff because the shape notes made it redundant. He had published the *Musical Primer* in 1780 in round notes, but the fourth edition (1803) was in shape notes. His

FIGURE 5–2 Page 95 of *Choral Harmonie*, by Isaac Gerhart and Johann J. Eyer. Harrisburg, PA: John Eyer, 1818.

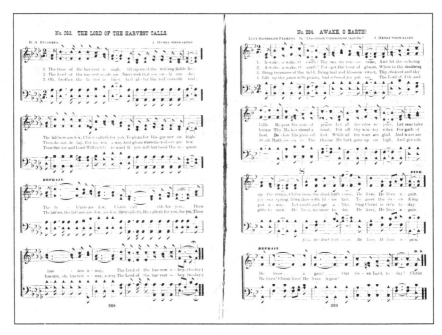

FIGURE 5–3 Pages 268 and 269 from *Psalms, Hymns and Spiritual Songs No. 3 for Church, Sunday-school and all Societies of Religious and Musical Endeavor*, by J. Henry Showalter, Geo. B. Holsinger, S. J. Perry, and J. G. Perry. West Milton, OH: Showalter, Holsinger & Perry Bros., 1837.

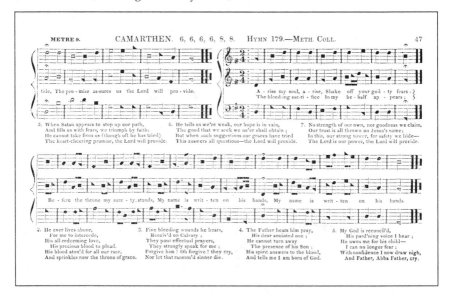

FIGURE 5–4 Page 47 of *A Compilation of Genuine Church Music, Comprising a Variety of Metres, All Harmonized for Three Voices. Together with a Copious Elucidation of the Science of Vocal Music*, by Joseph Funk. Harrisonburg, VA: Joseph Funk & Sons, 1847.

FIGURE 5–5 Page 27 of *52 Hymns of the Heart Selected by C. C. McCabe, with an Appendix of Favorite Solos and Choruses.* Philadelphia: John J. Hood, 1882.

system, without the musical staff, did not succeed. He had overlooked the fact that shape notes were intended to lead to an understanding of regular staff notation.

Many versions of shape notes appeared throughout the nineteenth century, and some continued to be published in the South into the twentieth century. For a large part of the rural South, shape notes entirely replaced conventional notation in the nineteenth century. Shape notes came to be associated with rural people. Eventually, there was so much derision of shape notes by people who favored traditional notation, especially in the North, that the novel system was abandoned. Ironically, shape notes were of great help to people who wanted to learn to read music, and the loss of the system meant the end of an educational tool of proven value.

The Music of the Tune Books included several types of pieces. The most prevalent were psalm tunes and hymn tunes, which were similar in form. Psalms and hymns were homophonic and usually from eight to twenty-two measures in length. The liveliest form was the fuging tune, which had two parts. The first section was homophonic and ended on the tonic or dominant; the second section contained imitation of up to two measures and was repeated, making an *ABB* form. The strongly rhythmic fuging tune became very popular, but it was not actually a fugue. Its counterpoint was simplistic imitation by relatively untrained composers.

According to Temperley, the fuging tune developed in the early part of the eighteenth century in England from the British version of the singing school.[35] It evolved as the itinerant English singing master, like his American counterpart, traveled from one parish to another to teach music. Country choirs developed from these schools. These choirs had the technical proficiency to go beyond the simple anthems of the service and attempted more challenging music, which included new psalm tunes in place of the more familiar ones. Psalmody flourished in the country because of the choirs, and as time went on the music reflected the characteristics of the individual choirs. The old psalm tunes had one note to a syllable, but melismas began to change the melodies. Later an "alleluia" was added to the end of each line of the text. Lines began to be repeated, especially the last, which changed the form of the traditional tune. Then, some lines were sung only by individual parts or pairs of parts. Finally, some sections were sung in counterpoint, with parts of the text overlapping. The fuging tune that we have come to recognize, with a section in four-part imitative counterpoint, developed in the 1740s.[36]

Although the fuging tune was not an invention of the New World, it was well loved in New England. In *Poganuc People* (1879) Harriet Beecher Stowe described a scene in which Billings's tune "Majesty" was sung around 1820:

If there were pathos and power and solemn splendour in the rhythmic movements of the churchly chants, there was a grand, wild freedom, an energy of motion in the old "fuguing" tunes of that day that well expressed the heart of a people courageous in combat and unshaken in endurance. The Church Chant is like the measure motion of the mighty sea in calm weather but those old "fuguing" tunes were like that same ocean aroused by stormy winds, when deep calleth unto deep in tempestuous confusion, out of which at last is evolved union and harmony. It was a music suggestive of the strife, commotion, the battle-cries of a transition period of society, struggling onward towards dimly seen ideals of peace and order. Whatever the trained musician might say of such a tune as old *Majesty,* no person of imagination and sensibility could hear it well rendered by a large choir without deep emotion, and when back and forth from every side of the church came the different parts shouting—

On cherubim and seraphim
Full royally he rode,
And on the wings of mighty winds
Came flying all abroad.

there went a stir and thrill through many a stern and hard nature, until the tempest cleared off in the words—

He sat serene upon the floods
Their fury to restrain,
And he as Sovereign Lord and King
Foreveremore shall reign.

And when the Doctor rose to his sermon the music had done its work upon his audience in exalting their mood to listen with sympathetic ears to whatever he might have to say.

The "set piece" was sometimes a longer sectional composition with changing moods and meters, chordal and imitative treatment, and occasional solo passages; it could also be a shorter piece in *AAB* form in homophonic style. The "anthem" was an extended through-composed piece with several sections of different moods and meters. Each section was thematically unrelated. The anthem was written for mixed voices in two, three, and four parts, with occasional solo parts. The "sentence" was a short scriptural text set to music, usually only one or two periods, and homophonic. By the middle of the eighteenth century, hymns by such composers as Isaac Watts and Charles Wesley were also being included in tune books.

THE SINGING MASTERS

There were probably thousands of singing masters during the two centuries in which singing schools existed. Little or no information is available on the vast majority of them, but some left writings describing their musical training, teaching, and lives in general. Most earned a major part of their income from other occupations, but some were able to live adequately on their income from teaching music. Those who were the most enterprising and able did well.

Many singing masters became itinerant because the increasing popularity of singing schools resulted in a shortage of singing masters. Traveling teachers could serve several communities. The singing masters were similar to other traveling peddlers, craftsmen, and artisans— they traveled from community to community to sell their wares or services, and, having exhausted their business temporarily, moved on to the next community. *Dwight's Journal of Music* published a letter in 1859 from W. S. B. Matthews, a singing master who later became well known as a piano teacher and music editor. In one week he gave 28 private lessons on the piano or melodeon, 3 singing schools in 3 different towns, 3 choir rehearsals (Catholic and Baptist), 2 public-school music classes, and 4 Sunday services. He was pleased with the pay. He wrote in a letter to John Sullivan Dwight, who published it in his *Journal of Music* of December 24, 1859:

> Private lessons, 50¢ each; public school, one dollar each; singing classes, for twelve lessons, one dollar per scholar. Conventions anywhere from $25 to $100 for three days. The first sum is about the customary price to a local conductor. Choirs $100 per annum each.

The three singing schools numbered 75, 50, and 70 students. Matthews stated that the activities described in his letter were typical for music teachers in the West.

Although Matthews's income was good, it was also uncertain. Singing masters were affected by economic conditions and by their ability to provide what the students wanted. If the students were not pleased with the teaching or with the music they sang, they could simply cease patronizing that particular singing master. The singing schools catered to the taste of their students for obvious reasons.

EARLY AMERICAN COMPOSERS

The first native-born American composers were James Hopkinson and James Lyon, both well-educated and respected citizens. They adopted the contemporary European style of composition favored by the American upper class of the time. Hopkinson's songs were similar to those of such English composers as Thomas Arne and William Shield. The Reverend James Lyon published a collection in Philadelphia in 1761 known as *Urania* (the complete title was *Urania, or a Choice Collection of Psalm-Tunes, Anthems, and Hymns, From the most approved Authors, with some Entirely New, in Two, Three and Four Parts. The whole Peculiarly adapted to the Use of CHURCHES and PRIVATE FAMILIES. To which are Prefixed The Plainest & most Necessary Rules of Psalmody). Urania* covered 198 pages, much longer than any previous American tune book. All but six of the pieces were by English composers. Most of the elaborate modern British music had not been published before in America.[37] The others were composed by Lyon himself. The importance of *Urania* is that it was an early collection of church music presented in an expensive, ornate edition usually associated with the more extravagant European publishing standards. These composers contributed little to the development of American music because they adhered to European practices and standards rather than adapt their talents to American needs.

Some other important tune books published in America were two books by Josiah Flagg, the *Collection of the Best Psalm Tunes* (1764) and *Sixteen Anthems* (1766), William Tans'ur's *Royal Melody Complete* (Newburyport, 1767; originally published in London, 1755), and Aaron Williams's *Universal Psalmodist* (Newburyport, 1769; originally published in London, 1763). By the end of the 1760s the tune-book repertory had grown quite large but consisted mostly of European tunes. At least eighty new collections were published between 1770 and 1800.[38] During that time the proportion of American music increased dramatically as native-born American composers began to compile collections that relied heavily on their own music.

THE YANKEE COMPOSERS

The singing school movement not only constituted the first formal system of mass music education in the colonies but also nurtured the first American school of musical composition. A group of New England composers, people of more modest circumstances than Hopkinson and Lyon, developed a new American style that had significant influence on both American music and music education. Many of the singing masters were composers as well as teachers, compiling their own tune books to sell to students, who constituted a ready-made audience for their works. A few of these composers and teachers were college graduates, but most were tradesmen, craftsmen, or artisans whose love of music led them to become singing masters. They had to be indifferent to the disrespect that American society held for musicians at that time. In fact, music was not even considered a profession—it was something done in addition to one's ''real'' work.

The Music of the Yankee composers was of a folkish character. It was simple, flowing, and rhythmically strong. Modal progressions, unusual dissonances, open fifths, and parallel fifths and octaves distinguished it from European music, except that found in Tans'ur's collection. Most of the texts were religious, and more came from the poetry of Isaac Watts than from any other author. This first American school of musical composition was simple in comparison with European music, but it had its own rugged strength.

William Billings (1746–1800) was the best known of the Yankee composers. Billings apprenticed himself to a tanner, probably at the age of fourteen, and worked at that craft throughout his lifetime. His enthusiasm for life sprang from his great love of music. He was lame in one leg, had one eye, a deformed arm, and a harsh voice, and was addicted to snuff. He was married and had at least six children. In the term of his day, he was "without any address," meaning that he lacked social grace. He had unbounded enthusiasm for music and frequently exclaimed his love for it. In one outburst he shouted, "Great art thou O Music! and with thee there is no competitor." Billings had no formal schooling after the age of fourteen, when his father died. He was a gifted musician and probably had music lessons from a local choirmaster. Billings also studied Tans'ur's *Musical Grammar*. One of his personal characteristics was supreme self-confidence, which left him unconcerned about his lack of musical training. He wrote:

> Perhaps it may be expected by some, that I should say something concerning Rules for Composition; to these I answer that Nature is the best Dictator, for all the hard, dry, studied rules that ever was prescribed, will not enable any person to form an air. . . . It must be Nature, Nature must lay the Foundation, Nature must inspire the Thought.
> . . . For my own Part, as I don't think myself confin'd to any Rules for composition, laid down by any that went before me, neither should I think (were I to pretend to lay down Rules) that any one who came after me were any ways obligated to adhere to them, any further than they should think proper; so in fact, I think it best for every Composer to be his own Carver.[39]

As a composer who followed his own rules, Billings wrote psalm settings, hymn settings, anthems, canons for chorus, and patriotic songs. One of his most successful compositions was the tune "Chester," which was included in *The New England Psalm Singer* (1770). His second book, *The Singing Master's Assistant* (1778), contained additional new patriotic verses written by Billings. "Chester," with its patriotic text, became the marching and battle song of the Continental Army during the Revolutionary War. As always, his enthusiasm was boundless as he described the fuging tune:

> There is more variety in one piece of fuging music than in twenty pieces of plain song. . . . Each part seems determined by dint of harmony and strength of accent, to drown his competitor in an ocean of harmony, and while each part is thus mutually striving for mastery, and sweetly con-

tending for victory, the audience are most luxuriously entertained, and exceedingly delighted; in the mean time, their minds are surprisingly agitated, and extremely fluctuated. . . . Now the solemn bass demands their attention, now the manly tenor, now the lofty counter, now the volatile treble, now here, now there, now here again O inchanting! O ecstatic! Push on, push on ye sons of harmony (from *The Continental Harmony,* 1794).

In his second book, *The Singing Master's Assistant*, Billings included "Rules for Regulating a Singing-School." Having conducted singing schools, he was aware of the legal and disciplinary problems faced by singing masters. He wrote:

As the well being of every society depends in a great measure upon GOOD ORDER. I here present you with some general rules, to be observed in a Singing-School.

1st. Let the society be first formed, and articles signed by every individual; and all those who are under age, should apply to their parents, masters or guardians to sign for them: the house should be provided, and every necessary for the school should be procured, before the arrival of the Master, to prevent his being unnecessarily detained.

2d. The Members should be very punctual in attending at a certain, hour, or minute, as the master shall direct, under the penalty of a small fine, and if the master should be delinquent, his fine to be double the sum laid upon the scholars.—Said fine to be appropriated to the use of the school, in procuring wood, candles, &tc.

3d. All the scholars should submit to the judgment of the master, respecting the part they are to sing; and if he should think fit to remove them from one part to another, they are not to contradict, or cross him in his judgment; but they would do well to suppose it is to answer some special purpose; because it is orally impossible for him to proportion the parts properly, until he has made himself acquainted with the strength and fitness of the pupil's voices.

Billings's fourth point cautions against unnecessary conversation, whispering, or laughing because it is impolite.[40] McKay and Crawford infer from these rules that the scholars were young and probably more interested in singing for recreation than for instruction or devotion.

The first singing school Billings is known to have taught was in 1769, when he and an associate placed an advertisement in the *Boston Gazette*: "John Barrey & William Billings Begs Leave to inform the Publick, that they propose to open a Singing School THIS NIGHT, near the Old South Meeting-House, where any Person inclined to learn to Sing may be attended upon at said School with Fidelity and Dispatch."

Billings's first tune book, *The New England Psalm Singer, or American Chorister,* was published in 1770, when he was twenty-four. It was engraved by Paul Revere. His other books were *The Singing Master's Assistant* (1778), which was called "Billings Best," *Music in Miniature* (1779),

The Psalm Singer's Amusement (1781), *The Suffolk Harmony* (1786), and *The Continental Harmony* (1794). Billings was the only tune-book compiler of his time to include only his own music in his publications, with the exception of *Music in Miniature*. Here he included eleven borrowed songs, ten from Europe and one, "Royalston," attributed to Abraham Wood of Massachusetts.[41]

The New England Psalm Singer was an important publication because it was the first published compilation of entirely American music and the first tune book of a single American composer.[42] *The Singing Master's Assistant* was Billings's most popular collection. It went through four editions, although only the publication information and prefatory material varied from one edition to the other. The music was the same in each. *The Singing Master's Assistant* was the first tune book published in America after the Revolutionary War began. It ended a four-year pause in the publication of music collections.

Billings's popularity declined toward the end of his life, and he was unable to support his family on his musical income. He earned money at several jobs, including trade inspector, scavenger (street cleaner), hogreeve (a town officer responsible for impounding stray hogs), and leather sealer.[43] Even so, he was still unable to earn enough to support his children. In 1790, when he was forty-four years old, his friends held a benefit concert for him. Notwithstanding the gain he might have received from the concert, a month later he had to mortgage his house. He continued to compose throughout the decade but earned little from his music.

Billings died in poverty in the year 1800. At the time of his death he owned only the heavily mortgaged house and four pieces of furniture. His funeral was announced in the *Columbian Centinel* : "Died— Mr. William Billings, the celebrated music composer. His funeral will be tomorrow at 4 o'clock, P.M. from the house of Mrs. Amos Penniman, in Chamber-street, West-Boston." Mrs. Penniman was his daughter, and he had probably lived in her house for some time. He was reportedly buried in an unmarked pauper's grave in Boston Common, but that is unlikely because a town ordinance of 1795 ended burials there since it was so crowded with graves.[44]

Supply Belcher (1751–1836) was a tavern keeper in Stoughton, Massachusetts, before moving to Stoughton, Maine, where he became known as the "Handel of Maine." There he was a schoolteacher, choir director, justice of the peace, and representative in the Massachusetts legislature (Maine was a part of Massachusetts until 1820). He published *The Harmony of Maine* in Boston in 1794. Belcher composed both simple and elaborate pieces, but his music was best known for its appealing simplicity, which caused him to be compared with Stephen Foster.

Daniel Read (1757–1836) was one of the most popular Yankee composers. He was born in Rehoboth, Massachusetts, and lived in New

Haven, Connecticut. After his service in the Continental Army, he became a bookseller and publisher in New Haven. He overcame his poverty and became a manufacturer of ivory combs, a director of the library, and a composer, compiler, and publisher of sacred music. Read published *The American Singing Book* in 1785, *An Introduction to Psalmody* in 1790, and *The Columbian Harmonist* in 1793. He also founded a monthly periodical, *The American Musical Magazine*, intended to contain "a great variety of approved music carefully selected from the works of the best American and European composers." His music continues to this day to be sung in rural areas of the United States.

Oliver Holden (1765–1844) of Dorchester, Massachusetts, is known primarily for his song "Coronation," which became the tune most used for the hymn "All Hail the Power of Jesus' Name." He operated a music store, was a choir director and singing school master, dealt in real estate, and was a Mason, a preacher, and a member of the Massachusetts House of Representatives. He compiled *The American Harmony, The Union Harmony,* and *The Massachusetts Compiler.* As an unenthusiastic supporter of the new American music, he wrote:

> It is to be lamented that among so many American authors so little can be found well written or well adapted to sacred purposes, but it is disingenuous and impolitic to throw that little away while our country is in a state of progressive improvement.

Justin Morgan (1747–1798) of Springfield, Massachusetts, taught school, kept a tavern, and bred horses (he was the breeder of the Morgan horse). In 1788 he moved to Randolph, Vermont, where he was town clerk. He spent much time teaching singing schools, to which he rode on the original Morgan horse. He did not publish collections of music but is known for some of his individual songs. One, "Montgomery," is a fuging piece still popular with American rural hymn singers. His lengthy "Judgment Anthem" is filled with pictorialism, shifting tonalities, and contrasting textures.

Jeremiah Ingalls (1764–1828) also moved from Massachusetts to Vermont, where he was a tavernkeeper and a deacon of the Congregational church. He led the choir, taught singing schools, and composed and compiled music. He was also at various times a farmer and a cooper. His collection was *The Christian Harmony, or Songster's Companion.* It contains secular tunes used as settings for sacred texts. His best-know piece is "Northfield," which, like Morgan's "Montgomery," is still sung in rural areas.

Andrew Law (1748–1821) came from loftier beginnings than his musical colleagues, and he disdained their music. He was a grandson of

Governor Law of Connecticut, earned a master's degree from Brown University, studied divinity privately, and was ordained in 1787. Law wrote only one tune that was widely used, "Archdale." He published *Plain Tunes* in Boston in 1767 and *The Select Harmony* in 1779. *The Musical Primer* was published in 1780, but it is the fourth edition of that book (1803) that is especially significant because it contained a "new plan of printing music." The innovation was shape notes, used in place of traditional round notes. The four shapes were diamond, square, round, and triangular. Explaining the lack of a musical staff, Law wrote: "The characters are situated between the single bars that divide the time in the same manner as if they were on lines, and in every instance where two characters of the same figure occur their situations mark perfectly the height and distance of their sounds." The four shapes corresponded to the *mi fa sol la* syllables of John Tufts.

Law's shape note system gained support from some prominent people, but others objected to it because it was novel and not in general use. He was an unlikely innovator, being much more conservative than many of his fellow New England musicians. Although his early music had been similar to that of the other New England composers, his taste changed, and he turned against that school of composition. In the preface to *The Musical Primer* he disparaged the shallow music used in churches. He criticized the works of his contemporaries:

> Hence the dignity and the ever varying productions of Handel, or Madan, and of others, alike meritorious, are, in a great measure, supplanted by the pitiful productions of numerous composuists, whom it would be doing too much honor to name. Let any one acquainted with the sublime and beautiful compositions of the great Masters of Music, but look round within the circle of his own acquaintances, and he will find abundant reason for these remarks.[45]

BLACKS AND THE SINGING SCHOOLS

White parishioners were not the only patrons and teachers of singing schools; evidence exists of blacks having participated as well. Cotton Mather organized a Society of Negroes, who were instructed in singing as early as 1674. As late as 1854, the Reverend Hanks conducted a singing school for blacks in a Wilmington, North Carolina, church with a mixed congregation and at the same time a singing school for whites in a church with a white congregation. [46]

Newport Gardner (1746–1826?) was a slave of the Gardner family. He is thought to have studied music with Andrew Law in Providence, Rhode Island, in 1783. He then conducted his own singing school in Newport, Rhode Island. He was described in an 1830 book by John Ferguson as follows:

> Newport Gardner . . . early discovered to his owner very superior powers of mind. He taught himself to read, after receiving a few lessons on the elements of written language. He taught himself to sing, after receiving a very trivial initiation into the rudiments of music. He became so well acquainted with the science and art of music, that he composed a large number of tunes, some of which have been highly approved by musical amateurs, and was for a long time the teacher of a very numerously-attended singing school in Newport.[47]

Gardner obtained his freedom in 1791 and was made a deacon of the Congregational Church.

"Frank the Negro," according to Andrew Law, directed a singing school in New York City in 1746 with as many as forty scholars.[48] There were undoubtedly other black singing masters as well.

THE DECLINE OF THE SINGING SCHOOL

The music of the singing school was rooted in American tradition and represented an early popular heritage. When the new country was established after the Revolutionary War, Americans went about restoring relations with European countries. Immigrants began to arrive, and most of them settled in the large eastern cities. As the economy grew and wealth began to accumulate, some people acquired the means to enjoy the best of European culture. A new reform movement, this one against the New England style, began to develop. Andrew Law, who had composed for so long in the New England style, wrote that as his knowledge of the "sublime and beautiful compositions of the great Masters of Music had grown, he sought to substitute serious, animated, and devout music for that lifeless and insipid, or that frivolous and frolicsome succession and combination of sounds" that had been created by the New England composers. Elias Mann wrote in his tune book (1807) that he had included "none of those wild fugues, and rapid and confused movements, which have so long been the disgrace of congregational psalmody."

The new reform movement was similar to that of a century earlier, when the New England ministers promoted singing schools to improve the music in their churches. They had used the word "science" to describe that which was new and desirable (music reading) and which should replace the old and useless. Again, at the beginning of the nineteenth century, the word "science" was used for the same purpose, but this time to try to replace the New England style with the European. New England music was "unscientific" because it did not conform to the new norm, European music. Throughout the nineteenth century, the Yankee music was reviled and disdained by music critics and music historians. In 1848, Augusta Brown wrote an article for *The Musician and Intelligencer* of Cincinnati that demonstrated the widespread feeling of inferiority in regard to Yankee music. She wrote:

> The most mortifying feature and grand cause of the low estate of scientific music among us, is the presence of common Yankee singing schools, so called. We of course can have no allusion to the educated professors of vocal music, from New England, but to the genuine Yankee singing masters, who profess to make an accomplished amateur in one month, and a regular professor of music, not in seven years, but in one quarter, and at the expense, to the initiated person, usually one dollar. Hundreds of country idlers, too lazy or too stupid for farmers or mechanics, ''go to singing school for a spell,'' get diplomas from others scarcely better qualified than themselves, and then with their brethren, the far famed ''Yankee Peddlars,'' itinerate to all parts of the land, to corrupt the taste and pervert the judgment of the unfortunate people who, for want of better, have to put up with them.

Brown's statement summarizes the attitude of the nineteenth century genteel class of music lovers toward the music of the Yankee composers and the singing schools.

In addition to the change in musical taste by city dwellers and others of refined cultural tastes, the decline of the singing schools was also caused by the growing belief that the public schools should include music in the curriculum. Lowell Mason, a highly respected champion of music in public education, was instrumental in the replacement of vernacular practices with the cultivated European tradition. As more and more public school systems throughout the country adopted music as a tax-supported curricular subject, the need for singing schools declined. Many of the singing masters eventually abandoned their singing school careers and became music teachers in public schools.

THE FIRST NOSTALGIA REVIVAL

Although early New England music was a thing of the past in most parts of the North by the latter part of the nineteenth century, many Americans remembered it as the music of their youth. At least one American singing master capitalized on the old music by presenting concerts of the old music. Calling himself Father Kemp and dressing archaically in colonial-style clothes, this musician performed New England music all over the country in the 1880s in at least a thousand concerts. He also sold songbooks featuring the music of early New England composers. Father Kemp stated in the preface:

> Permit me to say, that my business has led me into an extensive acquaintance with the masses, my knowledge of music, my familiarty with the

wants and wishes of the people, qualify me in some good degree for this service. I have exercised my best discrimination in selecting such pieces only as are most popular with the majority, in different sections of the land. . . . I have snatched several old songs, that were going over the chasm of forgetfulness. They are not to be found in any of the published works. They were mostly written in that happy vein, in which the Old Folks cheerfully adapted themselves to circumstances. I send this forth confident that our patrons, and all lovers of genuine music, will give it welcome. I hope it will find its way into the hands of the masses . . . that their original power may yet be felt in stirring up souls to an active interest in holy things;—and as they have been a medium of rapture in the past, so may they be in the future, until we shall take, from their soul-subduing sounds, that spirit of humility which so adorned the life of our *Great Exemplar,* preparing us for that endless song upon which the fathers have entered.

Choral Societies, or Musical Associations (sometimes called singing clubs), were another phenomenon related to the singing school, but they eventually assumed greater importance in American society (Chapter 8). One of the best known was the Stoughton (Massachusetts) Singing Society, which developed in 1774 from a singing school led by William Billings, although he did not establish the society. Many European immigrants had arrived in the United States by the beginning of the nineteenth century, and a large number of them were from Germany, where choral singing was highly respected. The choral societies were primarily amateur associations that performed choral works of length and technical difficulty. At first, the choral societies and singing schools performed the same repertoire, but eventually the societies took on longer and more demanding works. The purpose of the singing schools continued to be singing instruction. The choral societies also performed oratorios, and some performed Handel's *Messiah,* Mozart's *Requiem,* and Masses by Haydn and Beethoven early in the nineteenth century.[49] At least one hundred choral societies existed in Massachusetts between 1785 and 1840, all dedicated to "improvement in sacred music."[50] According to Nitz, by 1825 practically every New England singer had made a successful transition from the native fuging tune to European psalmody in the churches, and many musicians had mastered the European style well enough to perform the oratorio literature.[51]

The choral societies were helpful in some communities by having vocal music adopted into the school curriculum because the schools could then provide trained singers to the societies. Choral societies continued their activities throughout the nineteenth century and in some places into the twentieth. During the second half of the nineteenth century, joint concerts involving more than one society became popular. The choral societies helped elevate the musical taste of the public and influenced the choice of music used in public school music programs in some communities.[52]

FIGURE 5–6a The cover of *Father Kemp's Old Folks' Concert Tunes*. Boston: Oliver Ditson Co., 1889.

SUMMARY

The singing school movement exemplifies American education at its most characteristic. The singing masters answered a demonstrated need of the people by providing instruction that their students were willing to pay for. If the instruction had not been effective, the wrong music used, the schedule inconvenient, or anything else about the school seriously wrong, the people would not have attended. It was a popular movement that gave the public what it wanted. The singing schools demonstrate that effective instruction is not the exclusive domain of

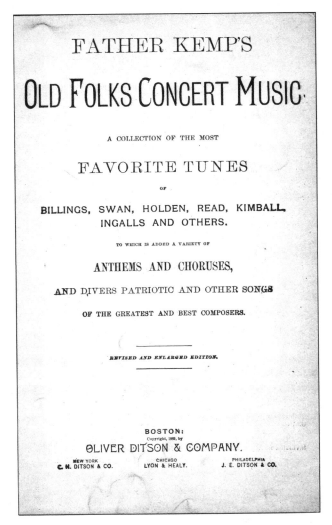

FIGURE 5–6b The title page of *Father Kemp's Old Folks' Concert Tunes*. Revised and enlarged edition. Boston: Oliver Ditson & Co., 1889. Note discrepancy in titles of cover and title page.

comprehensive schools and that good musicians and teachers can earn a living in a democratic capitalist society by being sensitive to what the public wants and needs.

Also of great importance, the singing schools provided a model for the further development of a formal system of music education in America. They proved that the masses could learn to read music and enjoyed doing so, and that the public wanted to participate in music. The singing schools also provided a large cadre of experienced teachers who became the early public school music teachers. If not for them, it is likely that the growth of school music would have been slower for lack of music teachers.

Finally, the singing masters were teachers, composers, and performers. The composers of the music most popular with the people were also the teachers of those people. At that time in America's history, musical composition, performing, and teaching were combined and there was little reason for the public to perceive a distinction between the three activities. Apart from the singing schools, it has been rare for composers to be involved in mass music education in American history. The singing schools provided a natural setting for musicians to develop their talents in all aspects of music. The people saw the singing masters as musicians, not composers or performers or teachers.

NOTES

1. Nicholas Temperley. "The Old Way of Singing: Its Origins and Development," *Journal of the American Musicological Society* 34 (Fall 1981): 533.
2. Temperley, "The Old Way of Singing," p. 539.
3. Cotton Mather, *The Accomplished Singer.* "Intended for the assistance of all that sing psalms with grace in their hearts: but more particularly to accompany the laudable endeavours of those who are learning to sing by Rule, and seeking to preserve a REGULAR SINGING in the Assemblies of the Faithful." 1721.
4. The *American Apollo*, Boston, April 20, 1792. In Edward S. Morse, *Olden-Time Music: A Compilation from Newspapers and Books* (Boston: Ticknor and Company, 1988), p. 21.
5. Millar Patrick, *Manual of Church Praise* (Edinburgh: Church of Scotland, 1932), p. 43.
6. Ibid., p. 80.
7. Temperley, "The Old Way of Singing," p. 514.
8. Heinrich Bullinger, "Of the Form and Manner How to Pray to God," 1569, IV, 196. *The Decades of Henry Bullinger,* ed. T. Harding (Cambridge: Parker Society Publications, 1849–1852).
9. *Boston News-Letter,* January 2/9, 1721. In Irving Lowens, "John Tufts' *Introduction to the Singing of Psalm-Tunes (1721–1744):* The First American Music Textbook," *Journal of Research in Music Education* 2 (Fall 1954): 89–90.
10. Lowens, "John Tufts' *Introduction,*" p. 90.
11. Theodore M. Finney, "The Third Edition of Tufts' *Introduction to the Art of Singing Psalm-Tunes,*" *Journal of Research in Music Education* 14 (Fall 1966): 166.
12. Ibid.
13. Andrew Adgate, *Rudiments of Music,* 3rd ed. Philadelphia: John M'Culloch, quoted in Allen P. Britton, "Theoretical Introductions in American Tune Books to 1800" (Ph.D. dissertation, University of Michigan, 1949), p. 196. Also quoted in Keene, *A History of Music Education in the United States.*
14. Irving Lowens and Allen P. Britton, "*The Easy Instructor* (1798–1831): A His-

tory and Bibliography of the First Shape Note Tune Book," *Journal of Research in Music Education* 1 (Spring 1953): 31.

15. Irving Lowens, "John Tufts' *Introduction to the Singing of Psalm-Tunes* (1721–1744): The First American Music Textbook," *Journal of Research in Music Education* 2 (Fall 1954): 89–102.

16. John Tufts, *An Introduction to the Singing of Psalm Tunes*, 3rd ed. (Boston, 1723), pp. 4-5.

17. Thomas Symmes, "The Reasonableness of, Regular Singing, or, Singing by Note" (Boston: B. Green, for Samuel Gerrish, 1720), p. 18, quoted in David P. McKay and Richard Crawford, *William Billings of Boston* (Princeton: Princeton University Press, 1975).

18. Nathaniel Chauncey, *Regular Singing Defended, and Proved to Be the Only True Way of Singing the Songs of the Lord. . . .* (New London: printed and sold by T. Green, 1728).

19. Symmes, "Reasonableness of, Regular Singing," p. 12.

20. *New England Courant*, March 5, 1712, quoted in Gilbert Chase, *America's Music*, 2nd ed. (New York: McGraw-Hill), p. 27.

21. Allen P. Britton, "The Singing School Movement in the United States, *Report of the Eighth Congress, New York, 1961, of the International Musicological Society*, vol. 1, *Papers*, Jan Larue, ed. (Kessel: Baerenreiter, 1962), pp. 77–79, vol. 2.

22. Ibid., offprint, pp. 89–90.

23. J. Spencer Curwen, *Studies in Worship-Music*, p. 24, quoted in Hamilton C. Macdougall, *Early New England Psalmody: an Historical Introduction 1620–1820*. (Brattleboro, VT: Stephen Daye Press, 1940), pp. 134–137.

24. James A. Keene, *A History of Music Education in the United States* (Hanover, NH: University Press of New England, 1982), p. 19.

25. *Maryland Journal and Baltimore Advertiser*, October 30, 1789, in James L. Fisher, "The Roots of Music Education in Baltimore," *Journal of Research in Music Education* 21 (Fall 1973): 215.

26. Fisher, "The Roots of Music Education," pp. 216–17.

27. Britton, "The Singing School Movement in the United States," pp. 89–90.

28. Ibid., p. 90.

29. Phil D. Perrin, "Pedagogical Philosophy, Methods, and Materials of American Tune Book Introductions: 1801–1860," *Journal of Research in Music Education* 18 (Spring 1970): 65.

30. Allen P. Britton, "Theoretical Introductions in American Tune Books to 1800" (Ph.D. dissertation, University of Michigan, 1949), reported in Perrin, p. 66.

31. Perrin, p. 67.

32. Ibid., p. 68.

33. Irving Lowens and Allen P. Britton, "The Easy Instructor (1798–1831): A History and Bibliography of the First Shape Note Tune Book," *Journal of Research in Music Education* 1 (1953): 148.

34. James Scholten, "Lowell Mason and His Shape-Note Tunebook in the Ohio Valley: *The Sacred Harp, 1834–1850*," *Contributions to Music Education* 15 (Fall 1988): 48.

35. Nicholas Temperley, "The Old Way of Singing: Its Origins and Development," *Journal of the American Musicological Society* 34 (Fall 1981): 512.

36. Nicholas Temperley and Charles G. Manns, *Fuging Tunes in the Eighteenth*

Century (Detroit: Detroit Studies in Music Bibliography Number Forty-nine, Information Coordinators, 1983), pp. 4–7.

37. McKay and Crawford, *William Billings of Boston*, p. 22.
38. Ibid., p. 24.
39. Billings, *New England Psalm Singer,* (Boston: Printed by Edes and Gill, 1770), p. 19.
40. William Billings, *The Singing Master's Assistant* (Boston: Draper and Folsom, 1778), pp. 16–17, quoted in McKay and Crawford, *William Billings of Boston.*
41. Richard Crawford and David P. McKay, "The Performance of William Billings' Music," *Journal of Research in Music Education* 21 (Winter 1973): 318.
42. McKay and Crawford, *William Billings of Boston*, p. 41.
43. Rose Dwiggins Daniels, "William Billings: Teacher, Innovator, Patriot," *Music Educators Journal* 74 (May 1988): 25.
44. Hans Nathan, *William Billings: Data and Documents* (Detroit: The College Music Society, 1976), p. 46.
45. John Grashel, "The Gamut and Solmization in Early British and American Texts," *Journal of Research in Music Education* 29 (Spring 1981): 66.
46. Nancy Ring, "Black Musical Activities in Ante-bellum Wilmington, North Carolina," *The Black Perspective in Music* 8 (Fall 1980): 146.
47. Eileen Southern, *The Music of Black Americans* (New York: Norton, 1971), pp. 80–81.
48. Ibid., p. 81.
49. Fisher, "The Roots of Music Education," p. 223.
50. Donald Nitz, "The Norfolk Musical Society 1814–1820: An Episode in the History of Choral Music in New England," *Journal of Research in Music Education* 16 (Winter 1968): 320.
51. Nitz, "The Norfolk Musical Society," p. 328.
52. Fisher, "The Roots of Music Education," pp. 222–23.

BIBLIOGRAPHY

Britton, Allen P. "The How and Why of Teaching Singing Schools in Eighteenth Century America." *Bulletin of the Council for Research in Music Education* 99 (Winter 1989).

Britton, Allen P. "Music in Early American Public Education: A Historical Critique." *Basic Concepts in Music Education* (National Society for the Study of Education, pt. 1.) Chicago: University of Chicago Press, 1958.

———. "The Singing School Movement in the United States." *Report of the Eighth Congress, New York, 1961, of the International Musicological Society,* vol.1, *Papers.* Ed. Jan Larue. Kassel: Bärenreiter, 1961.

Britton, Allen P., and Lowens, Irving. "Daniel Bayley's 'The American Harmony': A Bibliographical Study." *Papers of the Bibliographical Society of America* 49 (1955).

———. "Unlocated Titles in Early Sacred American Music." Music Library Association *Notes* 2 (December 1953).

Brooks, Henry M. *Olden-Time Music: A Compilation from Newspapers and Books.* Boston: Ticknor and Company, 1888.

Buechner, Alan C. "Yankee Singing Schools and the Golden Age of Choral Music in New England." Ed.D. dissertation, Harvard University, 1960.

Covey, Cyclone. "Did Puritanism or the Frontier Cause the Decline of Colonial Music?: Debated in a Dialogue between Mr. Quaver and Mr. Crotchet." *Journal of Research in Music Education* 6 (Spring 1958).

Daniels, Rose Dwiggins. "William Billings: Teacher, Innovator, Patriot." *Music Educators Journal* 74 (May 1988).

Elward, Thomas J. "Thomas Harrison's Patented Numeral Notation System." *Journal of Research in Music Education* 28 (Winter 1980).

Finney, Theodore M. "The Third Edition of Tufts' *Introduction to the Art of Singing Psalm Tunes*." *Journal of Research in Music Education* 14 (Fall 1966).

Fisher, James L. "The Roots of Music Education in Baltimore." *Journal of Research in Music Education* 21 (Fall 1973).

Foote, Henry Wilder. "Musical Life in Boston in the 18th Century." *Proceedings of the American Antiquarian Society* 46 (1939).

Grashel, John W. "The Gamut and Solmization in Early British and American Texts." *Journal of Research in Music Education* 29 (Spring 1981).

Keene, James A. *Music and Education in Vermont, 1700–1900*. Macomb, IL: Glenbridge Publishing, 1987.

Lowens, Irving. "John Tufts' *Introduction to the Singing of Psalm-Tunes* (1721–1744): The First American Music Textbook." *Journal of Research in Music Education* 2 (Fall 1954).

Lowens, Irving, and Britton, Allen P., "*The Easy Instructor* (1798–1831): A History and Bibliography of the First Shape Note Tune Book." In Irving Lowens, *Music and Musicians in Early America*. New York: Norton, 1964.

Macdougall, Hamilton C. *Early New England Psalmody: An Historical Introduction 1620–1820*. Brattleboro, VT: Stephen Daye Press, 1940.

Manual of Church Praise. Edinburgh: Church of Scotland, 1932.

Nitz, Donald. "The Norfolk Musical Society 1814–1820: An Episode in the History of Choral Music in New England." *Journal of Research in Music Education* 16 (Winter 1968).

Perrin, Phil D. "Pedagogical Philosophy, Methods, and Materials of American Tune Book Introductions: 1801–1860." *Journal of Research in Music Education* 18 (Spring 1970).

Ring, Nancy. "Black Musical Activities in Ante-bellum Wilmington, North Carolina." *Black Perspectives in Music* 8 (Fall 1980).

Scholes, Percy A. *The Puritans and Music in England and New England*. London: Oxford University Press, 1934.

Scholten, James W. "Amzi Chapin: Frontier Singing Master and Folk Hymn Composer." *Journal of Research in Music Education* 23 (Summer 1975).

———. "Lowell Mason and his Shape-Note Tunebook in the Ohio Valley: *The Sacred Harp, 1834–1850*." *Contributions to Music Education* (Fall 1988).

———. "Lucius Chapin: A New England Singing Master on the Frontier." *Contributions to Music Education* (Winter 1976).

Southern, Eileen. *The Music of Black Americans*. New York: Norton, 1971.

Temperley, Nicholas, and Manns, Charles G., *Fuging Tunes in the Eighteenth Century*. Detroit: Detroit Studies in Music Bibliography Number Forty-nine, Information Coordinators, 1983.

Temperley, Nicholas. "The Old Way of Singing: Its Origin and Development." *Journal of the American Musicological Society* 34 (Fall 1981).

Wolf, Edward C. "Johann Gottfried Schmauk: German-American Music Educator." *Journal of Research in Music Education* 25 (Summer 1977).

PART III

EARLY AMERICAN EDUCATION

6

EDUCATION FOR A NEW DEMOCRACY

BUILDING A NATION

Differences among Americans. The victory of the loose confederation of American colonies over the world's mightiest power, England, might be considered miraculous. The astonishing defeat of the British at Yorktown, however, by no means assured the success of a new country on the North American continent. When the new nation was created after the Revolutionary War, the states had little in common with each other, except for their brief colonial experience in working together, to achieve the common goal of political freedom and their shared pride in victory. Not only were there political, social, cultural, and linguistic differences among Americans, but there were regional and ideological conflicts and commercial rivalries as well.

When the Constitution was ratified in 1788, the country consisted mostly of farms and small communities from Canada to Florida. Only two cities, New York and Philadelphia, had more than 25,000 inhabitants. A prosperous middle class had begun to develop in the port cities, and their interests were different from those of both the poor farmers and the rich plantation owners. Tension between economic classes of people was inevitable. There was some manufacturing in New England, but the South depended on slavery to support its agricultural economy. This strained relations between the new northern and southern states and exacerbated regional differences.

Religious differences were intensified because many Anglicans in such states as Virginia and South Carolina, where the Church of England was dominant, were Loyalists and had not supported the fight for freedom. Both the Anglicans and the Puritans of New England abhorred the Quakers. Even Puritan New England was of two minds by this time. The extraordinary religious revival that swept Europe in the 1730s and 1740s was communicated to America by Jonathan Edwards, the "Artist of Damnation." Edwards, and other evangelists who followed him, rekindled the hellfire-and-brimstone Calvinistic belief in many Americans. Others, mostly intellectuals, emulated the movement toward rationalism in Europe and became liberals.

The people felt more loyalty to their states than to the nation, and many considered themselves more allies of the citizens of other states than fellow countrymen. Americans themselves were very different from each other. There were wealthy merchants in New England and the middle states and planters in Virginia and the Carolinas. All states had many small farmers and skilled workers of modest means and in the South there were slaves. Refugees from persecution on the continent spoke many languages other than English. Some states had a history going back over one hundred fifty years while Georgia had been settled for only a little over fifty years and a Crown colony for even less.

Another barrier to unity among Americans was the problem of transportation. It was as far from Savannah to Richmond as it was from London to Aberdeen, and that far again to Boston. The few roads that existed were primitive.

The members of the confederation shared the responsibility for an enormous debt incurred during the War of Independence, but they had no form of government capable of raising money. Perhaps the only issue on which there was universal agreement was their opposition to a strong central government, which they feared would resemble the repressive British rule.

Fortunately, the American people had an optimistic self-confidence, possessed rich natural resources, and were led by dedicated intellectuals who were able to envision a new democracy growing from the loose confederation. It was not until four years after the Revolutionary War that a compromise could be agreed upon by the fifty-five representatives to the Constitutional Convention. When Benjamin Franklin emerged from the final session, he was asked, "What have you given us?" His reply, "A republic, if you can keep it," forecast the struggle of the nation's early years.

THE EUROPEAN INTELLECTUAL BASIS
OF AMERICAN DEMOCRACY

The Enlightenment, or Age of Reason. The European intellectual revolution of the late seventeenth and early eighteenth centuries is known as the Enlightenment. It was a reaction against the Reformation that preceded it. European philosophers gradually redirected thought away from religion as the ultimate authority and toward science and reason. Rational thought, as opposed to religious faith, came to be seen as the means of understanding the universe and man's place in it. There was a new confidence in knowledge as the basis of power. The great thinkers of the Enlightenment completely rejected revelation and the religious authority that accompanied it. The Enlightenment swept across Europe and found its way to the New World, leaving secularization in its path and loosening the hold of Puritanism in New England. Nine American colonies recognized an official state church before the Revolution. After the war, none did.

The movement was also referred to as *humanism*, because it taught that man controlled the means to his own improvement and could not rely on divine power to change his life. Knowledge was the central focus of humanism, and schools were needed to help people attain the knowledge they needed. A system of education that would reflect democratic principles and prepare citizens to maintain them had to be created. Some of the important ideas for the new educational system came from such European intellectual leaders as Descartes, Rousseau, and Pestalozzi.

René Descartes (1596–1650) was a French philosopher and scientist. His philosophical and educational theories opposed the authoritarian system of education that had survived in Europe for many centuries. His own philosophical exploration began with universal doubt. He proposed that the only thing that could not be doubted was doubt itself. From this came his phrase *Cogito, ergo sum* (I think, therefore I am), which confirmed the existence of the self. From the certainty of the self he continued to find proof of other things and finally of God. Since God exists, the physical world must be real because God would not deceive people with illusions. If the perceptions of humans are real, then they are capable of studying and understanding the world.

Descartes's philosophical doctrine led him to important scientific work. As a scientist and philosopher, he proposed that children could learn about the world through scientific and mathematical studies. His educational system was free of the influence of medieval scholasticism and recognized the ability of people to learn by means of their own perceptions. He was highly influential in the modernization of education to include science and mathematics.

Jean Jacques Rousseau (1712–1778) was a Swiss-French philosopher author, political theorist, and composer. His political thought was expressed in *The Social Contract*, one of his most influential works. His educational philosophy is contained in *Émile*, in which he described the idealized education of Émile. Knowledge was drawn from Émile, rather than imparted to him, thus nurturing his native abilities. Rousseau proposed an educational system that would allow people to freely develop their potential. He also proposed a free social order in which rational people would choose to honor the general will. It is not surprising that Rousseau's democratic ideals for both society and education would find ready acceptance in the New World.

The Constitution of the United States of America guaranteed the rights of individual citizens and allowed for the pursuit of happiness, whatever that might mean for each person. These guarantees created the conditions for the flowering of American civilization and culture. The new American ideals were consonant with those of the Enlightenment, which held that man determines his own future through his rational powers. Thomas Jefferson's Declaration of Independence, which provided the rationale for the Constitution, drew heavily on the thinking of English philosopher John Locke, especially his *Second Treatise of Government*; Locke had also written a charter for the Carolinas. Jefferson expressed in elegant, powerful prose ideas drawn from Locke and such other Enlightenment thinkers as Rousseau, Voltaire, and Thomas Paine.

> We hold these truths to be self-evident, that all men are created equal, that they are endowed by their Creator with certain inalienable Rights, that among these are Life, Liberty, and the Pursuit of Happiness.

Though Jefferson was in France in 1787, his influence was felt strongly at the Constitutional Convention. Many contributed to the document, but James Madison is credited with being the "Father of the Constitution." With its ratification, the United States of America officially supported the belief in the perfectibility of man, the inevitability of progress, and the power of reason.

Ratification of the Constitution. The process of approval by the several states established the basis for the two-party system that has characterized American politics ever since. The Constitution gave the term *"federal"* specific meaning by confirming a "sovereign union of sovereign states." The federal government was made sovereign within limitations specified in the Constitution.

Until 1865, a major characteristic of national politics was the rivalry between the Jeffersonian Republicans and the Federalists. The Republican Party represented the interests of the agricultural-slaveholding interests of the South and the Federalist Party the mercantile-shipping-financial interests of the large seaport cities from Massachusetts to South Carolina. Under the leadership of Alexander Hamilton, the Federalists had worked for the adoption of a constitution that mandated a strong central government to make decisions for the masses. The Jeffersonian Republicans were the party of the agrarian South. They advised caution in regard to oligarchy and to strong central government. It was only after the promise of amendments to the original document, which would specifically spell out limitations on the central government in a bill of rights such as was found in most state constitutions of the time, that there was a possibility for the document to be ratified. Article VI, section 2, made clear that the laws of the federal government were to be the supreme laws of the land, but the Tenth Amendment specified: "Powers not delegated to the United States by the Constitution, nor prohibited by it to the States, are reserved to the States respectively, or to the people." It is from this clause that the authority of the states to establish and maintain public education is derived. Education became the responsibility of the states because it was not specifically identified as a function of the federal government.

Delaware was the first state to ratify the Constitution, in December 1787. New Hampshire, the ninth state to ratify, cast the deciding vote the following June. Not until Virginia and New York followed suit later that summer, however, could there be any certainty of launching a viable nation. North Carolina and Rhode Island did not approve the Constitution until the first Congress met in 1789 and began to approve a bill of rights.

THE CULTURAL LIFE OF THE YOUNG NATION

Arts, Letters, and Sciences. After the Revolutionary War, the attention of Americans was occupied by commerce and politics, but many young people turned to intellectual and artistic pursuits. Noah Webster, a twenty-five-year-old Hartford schoolmaster and occasional singing master,[1] said in 1778, "America must be as independent in literature as she is in politics, as famous for arts as for arms." He published his famous speller and later Webster's *American Dictionary.* Creative activity began to flourish about that time, and many Americans wrote school texts, various kinds of literature, poetry, and music. American art also began to blossom. John Trumbull painted *Battle of Bunker Hill, Death of Montgomery,* and *Declaration of Independence.* Charles Willson Peale of Annapolis undertook to paint all of the distinguished American generals and naval officers of his day. Washington sat for him at least seven times. The natural sciences flourished during the same period, and in 1780 the American Academy of Arts and Sciences was founded in Boston. Ten years later the first American historical society was established, also in Boston, where a number of histories of the war and of various places in the colonies were written.

EDUCATION IN THE YOUNG UNITED STATES

The founders of the new nation made certain assumptions about the place of education in a democracy. This was particularly true of the Jeffersonian Republicans, who placed their faith in the ability of the common man to govern himself. The Republicans viewed education as the means of preparing people for self-government. Unfortunately, educational opportunities were scarce in the southernmost of the thirteen original states. Massachusetts had passed a law in 1642 requiring towns with fifty or more householders to provide an elementary school. Five years later communities with more than a hundred families had to offer grammar-school education to prepare boys for college. Schools were provided in the South only when one or more plantation owners chose to do so. Before the Revolution, many of the children of this select group had been sent to England for their schooling; other rural children were fortunate if they learned to read and write.

A NEW PERIOD IN AMERICAN EDUCATION

The Academy. The end of the American Revolution also marked the beginning of a fruitful period in education. Latin grammar schools (secondary schools) taught Latin in preparation for college. Pupils studied the writings of Aesop, Virgil, Cicero, Ovid, St. Paul, Corderius, and the Bible. The rudiments of Greek were taught in some Latin grammar schools, also to prepare students for college entrance requirements. College domination of secondary schools began in the colonial era and lasted until the twentieth century. Latin schools prepared students only for the ministry, the magistracy, or teaching in a Latin school; they were unpopular because they did not meet the practical needs of American society.

A new institution, the academy, came into being under the leadership of Benjamin Franklin. Franklin recognized the need for a more practical type of school than was available at that time. He proposed the establishment of an academy in Pennsylvania in which youths might "learn things that are likely to be most useful and most ornamental, regard being given to the several professions for which they are intended." A mathematical, English, and classical school were to be included. The academy opened in 1751, was chartered in 1753, and received a new charter as a college in 1755. This new kind of school, which dominated American education for almost a century, was characterized by an emphasis on English language, literature, and oratory; the introduction of science courses; and nonsectarian control of the institution, which was governed by a self-perpetuating board of trustees.

Franklin's academy began a movement that expanded rapidly. It gradually replaced the old Latin school as the dominant secondary school and profoundly affected secondary and higher education because it offered a new kind of liberal education and a vocational foundation not available in the Latin schools. Most of the academies were private schools, however, and their substantial tuition costs prevented them from serving a great proportion of the population.

Early Public Schools. The last years of the eighteenth century were dominated by the many complex requirements of building a new nation. Another conflict with England, the War of 1812, consumed more energy and resources but helped further unify the diverse nation. There was little time to develop a viable educational system. Even when attention was given to education, Americans showed little interest in common schools. This was because many people associated the term "public school" with "pauper school." A South Carolina law of 1710 established "indigent" schools. Even the most humble Americans did not want to admit to themselves or others that they could not afford to educate their children. When school laws were passed around 1800, insufficient funds were allocated to implement them properly or private entrepreneurs took advantage of the provisions. Some private academies in Vermont were rechartered as county grammar schools, which were then granted public lands.[2]

Jefferson's Contribution to Education. Jefferson considered a system of public education necessary to preserve the democracy he had helped establish. He wanted it to be secular and independent not only of religious influence but of religious coercion such as that of the New England educational systems under Puritan theocratic government. Jefferson's educational ideal required a social environment that permitted people complete religious freedom. He was a member of a committee that proposed sectioning Virginia into *hundreds* and establishing an elementary school in each hundred to teach reading, writing, and arithmetic at public expense. He also proposed a plan to create a secondary-school system throughout the state. Those advanced students who could afford to pay tuition would do so, and the others would receive scholarships. The plan for elementary education was rejected by the state legislature in 1779 and again in 1817. Nevertheless, he had sensitized leaders of many states to his political theories and the importance of education. He lived to see a groundswell movement develop to bring about a universal system of education.

Jefferson suggested reconstructing the curriculum at the College of William and Mary, his alma mater. He proposed adding a professor of ethics and fine arts who would be responsible for such subjects as sculpture, painting, gardening, music, architecture, oratory, poetry, and criticism. The Anglican board of control rejected Jefferson's proposal.

The Common School Movement. The country mounted several crusades in the third decade of the nineteenth century. Among them were drives for the prohibition of alcoholic beverages, the establishment of more humane institutions for the mentally insane, a ten-hour workday, and the creation of common schools. A call for free public schools by the Workingmen's Association in 1820 developed into a unified nationwide effort that became known as the movement for common schools. Among the leaders were Horace Mann and Henry Barnard (see Chapter 8), two men who led remarkably parallel lives. They were graduates of Brown and Yale respectively. Both became lawyers, then legislators, and both became involved with the reform movements of the period. Both served as state superintendents of common schools, founded educational journals to help the cause, and eventually served as university presidents. Mann's advocacy of universal education was a manifestation of Jefferson's belief in human equality and perfectibility; the nonsectarian educational system he guided as secretary to the Massachusetts board of education became a model for other states.

Horace Mann (1796–1859), a descendent of Puritans, was one of the most influential educational reformers in American history. He rejected the Calvinist doctrine of human wickedness in favor of the belief that education could be an instrument in developing human perfection.[3] This was a revolutionary position because it advocated education for all people. As secretary to the Massachusetts state board of education (1837), Mann exerted positive leadership in Massachusetts and created an excellent model of nonsectarian education to be emulated by other states. It was in Massachusetts that music education was first established as a public-school curricular subject. Although Mann had nothing to do with that, he supported music education and in doing so helped it gain a foothold in the curriculum. His best-known writings are the twelve *Annual Reports.* The seventh report (1844)[4] contains a lengthy rationale for public school music and a tribute to it.

Professional Meetings.   One of the vehicles for communicating to educators and common citizens about common schools was professional meetings. Among the more influential organizations that sponsored such meetings were the American Lyceum in the East and the Western Literary Institute and College of Professional Teachers in Ohio.

Frontier Education.   The people of the frontier democracy believed that if education was not to be private, then it should be administered by the local community. The result was many small school districts with insufficient means of support. One of the tasks of the common school movement was to persuade the populace that public education should be free of tuition. Decisions on what should be in the curriculum were also necessary. At first, schools were planned to cost as little as possible; it took years of work before Nathan Guilford could get the citizens of Ohio to provide sufficient tax support for public schools.[5] Although they voted their support in 1824, the 1829 City Directory indicates that most of the Cincinnati schools were still private in that year.

As the citizenry gained experience with public education, people eventually became more willing to pay more for better schools. A low tax, optional to school districts, became a mandatory tax, which meant higher taxes but more adequate school funding. Some states offered financial aid to local areas on the condition that the districts maintain schools for a specified length of time with their own funds. This allowed the schools to stay open longer each year and to raise the salaries of teachers. By these means the principle of tax-supported schools was established.

By 1840 the free school was becoming a part of the American educational system. The common school was the cornerstone. During much of the nineteenth century universal education, as represented by the common school, meant eight years of schooling; however, the groundwork for secondary education had been laid as part of the public school system. In 1824 Massachusetts passed a law requiring a public secondary school for every community with five hundred or more families. Boston had established such a school three years earlier. It was the English classical school, which became the English high school under the new law. The curriculum, which was practical in nature, was intended to prepare boys for the kinds of work they would do as adults. The early high schools were oriented somewhat toward vocational training, but they provided a good education in English as well. Latin and Greek classics were read in English.

The curriculum established by the 1824 law included history, bookkeeping, algebra, geometry, and surveying. Towns with a population of over four thousand were required to add Greek, Latin, rhetoric, and logic. The law began a movement that spread quickly through New England and the Midwest. The tradition of private secondary schools continued in New England and the Middle States, but in the new states of the Northwest Territory the high school usually served as the secondary school for all children.

By the middle of the nineteenth century the United States was well on its way to becoming a manufacturing nation. The quality of its manufactured goods quickly became competitive with those of the world's leading manufacturing country—England. Some manufactured items were even better than those made in England. At that time the American literacy rate was higher than that of England because of the common schools. Although there is no solid evidence of a higher literacy rate improving American manufactured goods, a better educated work force is likely to turn out better products. If this was indeed the case, then the common school movement proved its worth to the new nation by helping make it competitive with established world powers.

The Federal Government and Public Education. Two months before the United States Constitution was completed, the Continental Congress passed a piece of legislation of critical importance to education. This was the Northwest Ordinance of July 13, 1787, written mostly by General Nathan Dane, Rufus King, and Manasseh Cutler. Benjamin Rush, Washington's surgeon general and a signer of the Declaration of Independence, was also influential in promoting education through the ordinance. Rush was not only the outstanding physician of his day but also a strong advocate of free schools, higher education for women, and the abolition of slavery. Having helped make certain that Pennsylvania would ratify the Constitution, he wrote, "The form of government we have has created a new class of duties to every American."

Several of the terms of the Northwest Ordinance reflected the ideals of the Declaration of Independence. It recognized the equality of all men by prohibiting slavery in the territory or any of the states it anticipated developing from the vast acreage within it. It guaranteed trial by jury and freedom of worship, and it encouraged education by setting aside for school support one section (640 acres) of every township of six square miles. Two whole townships were set aside for a future university.

SUMMARY

The problems associated with founding a new nation delayed the establishment of a system of public education, even though many of the leaders had made clear that such a structure was essential to their vision of what the new nation should be. Within forty years, however, the need became critical and leaders rose to the challenge of achieving the vision. This nationwide system of public education was a prerequisite for the flowering of school music during the rest of the nineteenth century.

NOTES

1. Harry N. Warfel, *Noah Webster: Schoolmaster to America* (New York: Macmillan, 1936), pp. 124–25.
2. James A. Keene, *Music and Education in Vermont 1700–1900* (Macomb, IL: Glenridge Publishing, 1987), p. 66.
3. Louis B. Wright, et al. *The Democratic Experiment* (Glenview, IL: Scott Foresman, 1968), p. 230.
4. *Life and Works of Horace Mann: Annual Reports of the Secretary of the Board of Education of Massachusetts for the Years 1839–1844* (Boston: Lee and Shepherd, 1891), pp. 445–63.
5. Eugene H. Roseboom and Francis P. Weisenburger, *A History of Ohio* (Columbus: Ohio Historical Society, 1969), p. 144.

BIBLIOGRAPHY

Butts, Freeman, and Cremin, Lawrence, *A History of Education in American Culture*. New York: Holt, Rinehart and Winston, 1953.

Darling, James. *The Music Teachers of Williamsburg*. Williamsburg: Colonial Williamsburg Foundation, WS-104, n.d.

Jefferson, Thomas. *Notes on the State of Virginia*. New York: Harper and Row, 1964 (originally H. W. Derby, Torch Books, 1861).

Keene, James A. *Music and Education in Vermont 1700–1900*. Macomb, IL: Glenridge Publishing, 1987.

Life and Works of Horace Mann: Annual Reports of the Secretary of the Board of Education of Massachusetts for the Years 1839–1844. Boston: Lee and Shepherd, 1891.

Molnar, John. *Songs from the Williamsburg Theatre*. Williamsburg: Colonial Williamsburg Foundation, WS-108, 1977.

Morison, Samuel Eliot. *The Oxford History of the American People*. New York: Oxford University Press, 1965.

Roseboom, Eugene H., and Weisenburger, Francis P. *A History of Ohio*. Columbus: Ohio Historical Society, 1969.

Wand, J. W. C. *Anglicanism in History and Today*. New York: Thomas Nelson and Sons, 1962.

Warfel, Harry N. *Noah Webster: Schoolmaster to America*. New York: Macmillan, 1936.

Wright, Louis B. *The Democratic Experience*. Glenview, IL: Scott Foresman, 1968.

7

THE PESTALOZZIAN EDUCATIONAL REFORM MOVEMENT

American public education was young and inexperienced in the early nineteenth century. Educators sought models of successful education methods in other countries. The most influential teacher of youth at that time was Johann Pestalozzi, whose work affected education throughout Europe as well as in the United States.

JOHANN HEINRICH PESTALOZZI

Pestalozzi (1746–1827) formulated educational theories that have influenced thinking about elementary education and the relationship between children and adults to the present. He also demonstrated his methods and techniques successfully. Like other Enlightenment thinkers, he was inspired by Rousseau's *Émile*. Pestalozzi's *Inquiry into the Course of Nature in the Development of the Human Race* reflects knowledge of Hobbes and Locke.

Pestalozzi studied theology at the University of Zürich but was unable to enter the ministry because of his political activity in a Swiss reformist organization. After a failed attempt at farming, he opened a school for abandoned peasant children at Neuhof (new farm), his farm near Zürich. There he had as many as fifty children in his charge at one time. They ran the farm, received instruction, and were well cared for, but in 1780 the school closed for lack of funds. Pestalozzi then decided to write about education, and between 1780 and 1797 he produced *The Evening Hours of a Hermit, Leonard and Gertrude,* and *Illustrations for My ABC Book,* among others. In 1798 he accepted a teaching position in a convent in Stans, where he taught seventy children who had been orphaned by the Napoleonic wars. Although the Swiss government honored him for his work there, the French government, which controlled the area, closed the school to convert it into a military hospital.

Pestalozzi accepted a position at Burgdorf and later another position as master of a local school for children older than those with whom he had worked previously. The classroom problems he encountered there motivated him to learn more about teaching, and he petitioned successfully for the use of a castle in Burgdorf for research, teacher training, and the development of educational materials. Here textbooks and other materials about the Pestalozzian method were prepared. In 1801 he published his most influential book—*How Gertrude Teaches Her Children.* Again the French government forced him to end his work, and he left Burgdorf. In 1804 he opened a school in Yverdon, which he operated until his retirement in 1825.

Pestalozzi, who was committed to social reform throughout his life, believed that education was the only means to elevate the social and economic status of impoverished Swiss peasants, who lived in a feudal society and had little opportunity for improvement. He was distressed by their misery and sought to give them dignity through education. He replaced strict discipline and the established memorization teaching method with one based on love and understanding of the individual child.

A singing method based on Pestalozzian principles was adopted in Switzerland and other German-speaking countries between 1810 and 1830. The first national system of music education, based on Pestalozzian principles, was established in the German state of Prussia.

THE FUNDAMENTALS
OF PESTALOZZIAN EDUCATION

Pestalozzi was more concerned with specific principles of teaching than with universal theories of education. He advocated educational reform that would permit pupils to relate life activities to education, thus making education more pragmatic. The purpose of education was to prepare people to live the best lives possible at the level of their particular station in life.

The two broad goals of his educational reform were morality and citizenship. To achieve these goals, the education of children must influence the three major capacities—the moral (most important), physical, and mental faculties.

Morality. To Pestalozzi, morality took precedence over even religion. First, people had to have the right feelings toward others because it is not possible to love a corporeal God if there is no empathy for humans. Pestalozzi exemplified this principle in his early work with children by demonstrating love of others despite the punishing physical requirements of his position. He had about eighty students whom he fed, clothed, and cared for around the clock practically by himself. Music was part of his plan to develop morality in children. The singing of national songs was meant to create patriotic feelings but more importantly to inspire devotional feelings.

The Physical Faculty must be developed if the individual is to be balanced. Thus, physical education was an important part of Pestalozzian education. Pestalozzi saw physical development as a way to maintain good health and to correct certain physical problems. He also maintained that physical exercise sharpened the senses, thus increasing perceptual ability.

The Mental Faculty had to be trained if the child was to be able to impose limits on the independence achieved by means of moral development. Moral and intellectual education were to proceed together to help the pupil achieve self-realization. The purpose of self-realization was to strengthen the ability to make correct judgments about moral questions.

Pestalozzi believed that people learn from their life experiences. To him, the first teacher, and the source of truth, was nature. People learn through their senses, which are the means by which the intellect develops.[1] Sights and sounds precede symbols. When the child is young the sense impressions are unclear, but they gradually become more organized and meaningful. Learning comes from sounds (spoken and sung), the study of form (measurement and drawing), and the study of number. There is a natural progression of study from the simple to the complex in each modality. Pestalozzian teaching principles include bringing together all things related to each other, subordinating all unessential things, arranging all objects according to their likenesses, strengthening sense impressions of important objects by allowing them to be experienced through different senses, arranging knowledge in graduated steps so that differences in new ideas will be small and almost imperceptible, making the simple perfect before going on to the complex, and distrusting precociousness.[2]

Pestalozzian Music Instruction. Although Pestalozzi valued music in education, he did not teach it, nor was it part of his educational system. Rainbow theorizes that Pestalozzi viewed the purpose of music as moral, rather than cognitive, even though he regarded the study of music as an intellectual activity.[3] Pestalozzian pedagogical principles were incorporated into a music method by Michael Traugott Pfeiffer and Hans Georg Nägeli, entitled *Gesangbildungslehre nach Pestalozzischen Grundsätzen, Pädagogisch Begründet von Michael Traugott Pfeiffer, Methodisch Bearbeitet von Hans Georg Nägeli* in 1812.[4] Nägeli was a colleague and disciple of Pestalozzi. He had organized singing classes in Swiss schools because he believed that group singing would promote social unity and religious values, as well as stimulate a desire for good music. Nägeli was also concerned that uneducated adults spend their leisure time in worthwhile pursuits that would enrich their lives and promote social values. Much of the adult Swiss population was uneducated, and there was little organized musical life in Switzerland outside of the large towns. In 1805 Nägeli formed the Zürich Singinstitut, a musical organization consisting of a mixed choir and a children's choir. The public performances demonstrated how well such an organization could serve the community.[5]

In the music instructional method of Nägeli and Pfeiffer, music was studied in the context of three main elements—rhythm, melody, and dynamics. Rhythm was studied first because it appeals most directly to the young child and because it is closely related to number; melody was studied next and then dynamics. The elements were not integrated until notation was introduced. Theoretically, they were introduced in the same order in which children perceive them, thus correlating the method with Pestalozzi's principles. Elfand describes the practice, which was not as ideal as the theory:

> The method left a great deal to be desired, for in Pfeiffer's manual with over 250 pages of highly detailed exercises, there was no singing of songs! Singing verse was postponed until all the theoretical exercises were completed but this happy event rarely if ever occurred.[6]

Eventually, the method was adapted to practical needs, and practical singing was added. Harmony had been omitted intentionally by Pfeiffer but was added by Kübler in his manual *Anleitung zum Gesangunterrichte in Schulen.*[7] There is no reason to believe the Kübler book was actually Pestalozzian in concept. This issue will be discussed later in reference to the work of Lowell Mason.

PESTALOZZIAN INFLUENCE ON AMERICAN MUSIC EDUCATION

William Channing Woodbridge. There was no unified system of music education in public or private schools during the early days of

American public education. One of the first to suggest the value of music as a regular part of the curriculum was William Channing Woodbridge. On August 24, 1830, Woodbridge delivered a speech in Representatives Hall in Boston before the American Institute of Instruction entitled "On Vocal Music as a Branch of Common Education." By arrangement with Lowell Mason, a group of boys were present to demonstrate the rewards of music instruction by singing three songs—"The Morning Call," "The Garden," and "The Rising Sun."

Woodbridge was an influential speaker, and his enthusiasm for music was persuasive to many others. He was a geographer and a minister, but like many other Americans he had a deep and sincere interest in developing the common schools. Woodbridge traveled to Europe for his health, and while there he studied instructional methods. He was well received in Europe because his reputation as a geographer preceded him. He had published *Rudiments of Geography,* an important text, but the 1824 edition of his *Universal Geography* established him as a foremost scholar in his field. During his second trip (1824–1829) he observed Nägeli employing the principles of Pestalozzi in his instruction. Those principles, modified for music instruction, were:

1. To teach sounds before signs—to make the child sing before he learns written notes or their names.
2. To lead the child to observe, by hearing and imitating sounds, their resemblances and differences, their agreeable and disagreeable effects, rather than explaining these things to him. By this principle, the child was to be an active, rather than passive, learner.
3. To teach but one thing at a time—rhythm, melody, expression are taught and practiced separately before the child is called to the difficult task of attending to all at once.
4. To make children practice each step of each of these divisions, until they master it, before passing to the next.
5. To give the principles and theory after practice, and as an induction from it.
6. To analyze and practice the elements of articulate sound in order to apply them to music.
7. To have the names of the notes correspond to those used in instrumental music.[8]

Woodbridge was impressed both with what he observed and with the corroborating opinions of Swiss and German educators. He was convinced that music should have a place in the American school curriculum and that the Pestalozzian approach was superior to that of American singing schools. On his return to Connecticut, he gained the confidence of an American music teacher, Elam Ives, Jr., who carried out an experiment in teaching music by means of Pestalozzian principles with some Hartford children.

Elam Ives, Jr. (1802–1864), was born in Hamden, Connecticut. He was a church choir director and singing school master. Little is known of his early musical training, but by the age of twenty-eight he was well established in Hartford, Connecticut. In 1830 he and his family left Hartford for Philadelphia, where he established the Philadelphia Music Seminary, of which he was principal. His pupils gave a concert in Constitution Hall in New York on May 27, 1836. During the concert, Ives announced that he planned to move to New York, where he would establish a new musical seminary. On September 1, 1836, he presented a concert by his New York pupils. He remained in New York almost until the end of his life. Ives later returned to Hamden, where he died in 1864. He wrote many books and art songs from 1830 to 1860 but is virtually forgotten in American music history. His impact on music education was much greater, and it is his work as a teacher that is historically significant.

Ives was the first to apply Pestalozzian principles to music teaching in the United States. In spring and summer 1830, he and Woodbridge translated some European materials. From the summer through September, Ives used the materials to teach a volunteer class of about seventy children ages six to twelve. This was the "Hartford Experiment." There is no record of whether it was successful, but, according to Rich, the experiment was inconclusive.[9] Woodbridge, however, reported that the children were "trained in a few months to sing in a manner which surprised and delighted all who heard them." Ives thought well enough of what he had done to prepare two books that demonstrated Pestalozzian principles. A few months later, Ives had completed the manuscript of his *American Elementary Singing Book* and delivered it to his publisher. It may have been the first American music book to advocate Pestalozzian principles.[10] The second book was *The Juvenile Lyre*, published in 1831.

LOWELL MASON

Lowell Mason (1792–1872), the "father of singing among the children" in the United States, was one of the central figures in the long and laborious process of bringing about the adoption of music as a public school subject. Mason was born in Medfield, Massachusetts, to a prosperous family. His father was town treasurer and a member of the state legislature who sang in the church choir and played several instruments. He owned a dry goods business. Lowell's grandfather had been a singing school teacher and a schoolmaster. The boy's family had a strong New England traditional music heritage. He attended the singing school of Amos Albee and later studied music with Oliver Shaw, a Ded-

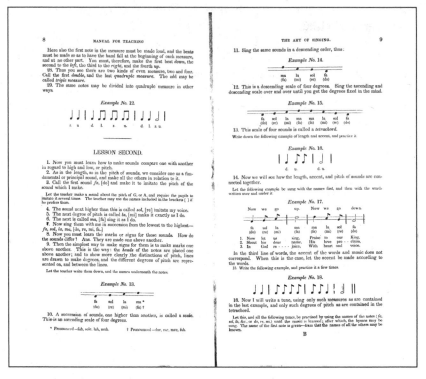

FIGURE 7-1 Pages 8 and 9 of *A Manual of Instruction in the Art of Singing,* by E. Ives. Philadelphia: American Sunday School Union, 1831.

ham musician. He played the organ, piano, flute, clarinet, and other instruments.

Mason traveled to Savannah, Georgia, in 1812. No one knows why he went to Savannah, but Keating theorizes that the city attracted him because it "must have seemed tropical and remote."[11] Florida was still owned by Spain, and Savannah was the southernmost city in the United States. He quickly found work in a store owned by Edward Stebbins that sold a variety of merchandise. Mason and Stebbins had met at the Independent Presbyterian Church in Savannah. Four years later he was made a partner, and the firm became Stebbins & Mason.[12] This was to be only one of many occupations for the ambitious and hardworking Mason. He began offering singing schools to church choir members like those he had directed earlier in Massachusetts. In 1815 he became organist and choirmaster of the Independent Presbyterian Church, where he began to compose anthems and hymns. In that same year he helped organize an interdenominational sabbath school and became its first superintendent. His organizational ability earned him the position of secretary of several organizations, including the Savannah Fencibles (his militia unit), the Savannah Missionary Society, the Sabbath School

Teachers Association, the Georgia Bible Society, the Savannah Religious Tract Society, and the Union Society. He also worked in the dry goods store and was town librarian, which required his service three evenings a week. In 1820 he became a clerk in the Planter's Bank, where he worked until returning to Boston in 1827.[13]

Mason's musical life in Savannah prepared him for the music leadership position he would assume later in Boston. He studied harmony and counterpoint in Savannah with Frederick Abel, a recent immigrant from Germany. His instruction included translating master choruses into English and realizing the figured bass. He also organized concerts, advertised as "Grand Oratorios." They included choruses by Handel, Haydn, Mozart, and others, and solos, duets, hymns, and anthems. Mason was producer, director, performer, program note writer, advertiser, and ticket seller.[14]

The Boston Handel and Haydn Society Collection of Church Music. Mason compiled his first collection of sacred music while in Savannah. It contained some of his own compositions and melodies from instrumental works of Handel, Mozart, Beethoven, and other European composers. They were adapted for singing by adding the words of familiar hymns and arranged for three and four voices with figured bass for organ or piano. When the work was completed in 1820, Mason traveled to Philadelphia and other cities to seek a publisher but was not successful. His fortune changed, though, when he met Dr. George K. Jackson, organist of the Handel and Haydn Society of Boston. Jackson was impressed with the collection and recommended that the society publish it. He called it "much the best book of the kind I have seen published in this country." *The Boston Handel and Haydn Society Collection of Church Music* was printed in 1821 and copyrighted in 1822. Mason's name appeared in the preface, but he was not identified as the editor. Years later he explained, "I was then a bank officer in Savannah and did not wish to be known as a musical man, and I had not the least thought of making music my profession."[15] The collection went through twenty-two editions, and both Mason and the Handel and Haydn Society earned handsome profits from it. The income brought financial stability and security to the society and made Mason reconsider becoming a professional musician.

Mason went back to Savannah but returned to Boston in 1826 to lecture on church music. In 1827 he accepted the position of choirmaster of Dr. Lyman Beecher's church. Still not convinced that he could support his family as a musician, he took a second position as a bank teller. He found that the bank position was not necessary, though, and eventually gave it up. In 1827 he became president of the Handel and Haydn Society, but in 1832 he resigned to allow more time for teaching music and singing to children. Mason continued his work as a church musician, and on July 4, 1832, he directed the junior choir of the historic Park

Street Church in Boston in the premiere performance of "America." His friendship with Samuel Francis Smith was a factor in the creation of Smith's poem.[16] In 1829 he began to publish children's music books. The *Juvenile Psalmist, or The Child's Introduction to Sacred Music*, came out in 1829, and *The Juvenile Lyre* in 1831. Mason claimed that *The Juvenile Lyre* was the "first school song book published in this country." He became deeply involved in school music, but that part of his career is of such singular importance that it will be reviewed later.

With George J. Webb and other Boston musicians, Mason founded the Boston Academy of Music in 1832. Here he planned to apply Pestalozzian principles to the teaching of music to children. The academy was a great success. It had as many as fifteen hundred students in the first year, and instruction was free. Separate classes were offered for adults and children. The academy sponsored the translation of Fetis's *Music Explained to the World; or, How to Understand Music and Enjoy its Performance*, which was an early attempt at music appreciation, perhaps the first in the United States. The Boston Academy of Music operated until 1847.

Mason was prolific as a compiler of music collections. He published over twenty collections, helping to satisfy the demand that he himself created for the new, more sophisticated music that bore no resemblance to that of earlier New England composers. Lowell Mason the composer wrote mostly hymns, anthems, and school songs. For the most part, his compositions were commonplace, although a number of his hymns have remained popular to the present day.

Mason traveled to Switzerland and Germany in 1837 to study Pestalozzian methods. He returned to Europe in 1851 and stayed for fifteen months, much of the time in England. When he came back to the United States in 1853 he established his headquarters in New York City and lived in Orange, New Jersey. He died at his home in 1872 at the age of eighty. Three of his four sons were influential in music. The youngest, William, was a pianist and teacher; Lowell, Jr., and Henry founded the Mason & Hamlin Company, which manufactured pianos and organs. Mason's grandson, Daniel Gregory Mason, became a prominent composer.

Lowell Mason's influence on American musical life was profound and long-lasting. His many activities involved him in various business arrangements, from which he realized a healthy financial gain. There has been a tendency to view him as a promoter like P. T. Barnum because of his ability to persuade people to like what he offered. For example, the change in public attitude toward the new science of music, as opposed to the old fashioned hymnody, was due in part to his persuasiveness and promotional ability. Some historians have suspected that his motives were not inspired purely by music or the public good but by profit as well. An example is *The Sacred Harp* (1837), compiled by Mason and his brother Timothy. It was published in regular notation as well as in shape notes, although one of Lowell Mason's goals was to have shape notes replaced by round ones. The shape note version sold well in the South and West to those who could read only shape notes, and the Masons earned handsome royalties from the sales. Lowell Mason denied responsibility for the patent note edition, however:

> The Proprietors of "Masons' Sacred Harp" have (contrary to the express wishes and views of the authors) prepared and stereotyped an edition of the Harp of 232 pages, in PATENT NOTES, under the belief that it would be more acceptable to singers in the west and south, where Patent Notes are generally used.[17]

One must wonder whether Mason approved the shape note edition to increase his profit. It is not difficult to imagine, however, the publisher of Mason's collections going against his wishes and violating his ideals in publishing the shape note edition. Regardless of who was responsible for the patent note edition, Mason was a solid businessman who realized great profit from his musical career. He provided an early example of how a musician in a democratic capitalistic society can prosper for both his own benefit and that of the public.

MASON AND THE NINETEENTH-CENTURY AGE OF PROGRESS

The Enlightenment, or Age of Reason, of the eighteenth century gave way to the Age of Progress in nineteenth-century America. The word "science" characterized the new age. It was synonymous with "progress," meaning the new, as opposed to the old and the old-fashioned. The United States was becoming ever more industrialized, and society was changing rapidly because of mechanization. The workplace was affected first, and later other aspects of life also began to change. Americans looked forward to the future and rejected the old. In music, this attitude manifested itself in the form of disapproval of the old-fashioned psalmody in favor of newer, more scientific music, such as that being composed by European composers at that time. Lowell Mason was a strong promoter of this attitude, and *The Boston Handel and Haydn Collection of Church Music* was a case in point. After nine editions, which earned huge profits for Mason, he wrote in the tenth edition (1831):

> Is it to be supposed that in psalmody, science and taste have accomplished all that they can accomplish? and is it desirable that all attempts at improvement should be checked? This is impracticable if it were desirable. . . . Unless, therefore, it be maintained that the present psalm and hymn tunes cannot be improved, and that no better can be substituted in their stead, or else, that bad tunes are as valuable as good ones, there may be as valid reasons, founded in public utility, for introducing alterations into

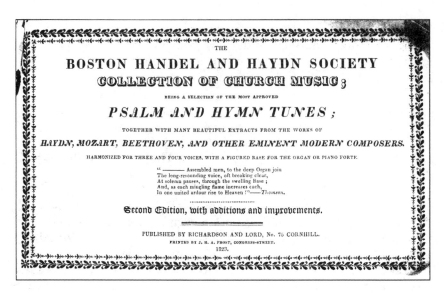

FIGURE 7–2a The title page of *The Boston Handel and Haydn Society Collection of Church Music.* Boston: Richardson and Lord, 1823.

FIGURE 7–2b Page 199 of *The Boston Handel and Haydn Society Collection of Church Music.*

text books of psalmody, as for introducing alterations into text books on arithmetic or grammar.

Mason profited from his promotion of the new music. A thorough revision of the *Handel and Haydn Collection* began the profits flowing anew as the people tried to keep up with the new taste in music. By then the old psalmody had fallen into disfavor. Few people in this progressive age could resist the new music or wanted to be labeled old-fashioned, especially if that term was associated with poor taste. Thus, the tenth edition contained fewer imitative and fuging pieces and less light music in deference to the "good sense and improved taste of the public." By this time Mason had achieved great stature in the community, and he was musically influential. He played a major role in changing the musical taste of great numbers of Americans. His influence extended into the field of education, and he was equally responsible for changing the attitude of the public toward music in the schools.

THE IMPLEMENTATION OF PESTALOZZIANISM IN AMERICAN MUSIC EDUCATION

Woodbridge was an effective promoter of Pestalozzianism in music instruction and of music as a branch of common education. Not only did he influence Mason and Ives, but he became a highly vocal advocate of public-school music. His collaboration with Mason in August 1830, in which he presented "On Vocal Music as a Branch of Common Education" to the American Institute of Instruction, was only the beginning of a long and energetic campaign to promote public-school music.[18] That particular lecture was his best known, and he presented it several times. He was also editor of the *American Annals of Education and Instruction*, through which he spread his ideas. He also promoted public-school music by means of children's choir performances.

Mason and Woodbridge. The association between Mason and Woodbridge, which began with the latter's speech at the 1830 meeting, continued for some time with important consequences. It is possible that Woodbridge and Ives changed Mason's thought about the ability of children to sing. Mason prepared *The Juvenile Psalmist* in 1829 at the request of the Boston Sabbath School Union. This small square book begins, like other singing school books, with a presentation of the rudiments of music. After thirteen pages of questions on the staff, clefs, notes, rests bars, slurs, sharps, flats, solmization, key signatures, and time, there is a paragraph in six-point type:

> Many persons, and even some teachers of music, seem to suppose that a knowledge of the rules is the principal thing to be acquired in learning to

sing. This is a great mistake . . . the great difficulty to be overcome in singing is the proper management of the voice. To acquire this is no easy task, and years of daily practice are indespensably necessary to any considerable degree of proficiency. The constant practice of the ascending and descending scales in both modes is recommended.

A page of scales follows, and the book concludes with twenty-eight hymn tunes. If Mason wrote the above paragraph, as one must assume since he is listed as the sole author of the volume, why is it placed so inconspicuously after all the matter that he claims any twelve-year-old could learn in a few lessons? Did the Sabbath School Union require the rudiments because of the long tradition of the tune books? Or was Mason not practicing in his teaching what he was preaching in his prefaces? The "years of daily practice" phrase bears out the conviction expressed in his 1826 address on church music that children must be taught music as they are taught to read.[19] His idea of how this might be done seems to have begun to change after his contact with Woodbridge.

The Juvenile Lyre, compiled by Ives and Lowell Mason and published in 1831 by Carter, Hendee & Company (Boston), was described years later by Mason as the "first school song book published in this country." Written at Woodbridge's urging, it marks the beginning of Mason's maturation as a teacher of children. The subtitle, *Hymns and Songs, Religious, Moral and Cheerful for Use of Primary and Common Schools,* gives substance to Mason's later claim that it was the first book intended for America's public school children. The message of the preface differed from that in the *Psalmist* because it was devoted to the new idea of democratic music-making. The preface also included the rationale for music instruction that would support the introduction of music education throughout the country for almost a century—the development of the moral, physical, and intellectual capacities of students. The health aspect of the rationale probably came from the British tune-book compiler William Gardiner, whose work Mason admired. Gardiner, who promoted the healthful aspects of singing, elaborated on it in his book, *The Music of Nature* (1832). He pointed out that the Germans, who sang frequently and robustly, were seldom afflicted with consumption. He also discussed the curative powers of music.[20] Pemberton refers to the *Lyre's* preface as a "landmark document of the early 1830s" because it provided the rationale needed by laypersons to accept music in the schools, and it also served as a manifesto to music educators of the time.[21]

"Proof of the very general, if not universal, power to understand the distinctions of musical sound, and to control, in accordance with them, the modulations of the voice, are multiplying," wrote Ives, or was it Mason under the influence of Woodbridge? Both signed the preface, which is the only indication of authorship. John suggests that the book is largely that of Ives, who would have been flattered to be associated with a man ten years his senior and the widely acclaimed editor of the *Handel and Haydn Society Collection*. It should be noted that the very first song is "The Morning Call," which Mason's students had sung a year earlier at the time of Woodbridge's speech. The two other songs sung at that time are also included.

The preface to the *Lyre* refers to the "change . . . in the public mind" in regard to the favored few blessed with musical talent. Had such a change taken place as well in Mason's thinking under the careful tutelage of William Woodbridge? As editor of the *American Annals of Education and Instruction* and through his public lectures, Woodbridge continued to champion the cause of music as a branch of common education. He also promoted the idea that all children could be taught to sing through public performances by children's choirs. Pemberton cites George Root's *Autobiography* as the source for an account of how Woodbridge wrote out Pestalozzian lesson plans for Mason to use in teaching a group of children that met at the Park Street Church. Samuel A. Eliot, later mayor of Boston, wrote about concerts given in June 1832:

> Never shall we forget the mingled emotions of wonder, delight, vanquished incredulity and pleased hope, with which the juvenile concerts were attended. The coldest heart was touched, and glistening eyes and quivering lips attested the depth and strength of the feelings excited in the bosoms of parents and teachers; while the happy little pupils themselves seemed to have acquired a new sense, as they certainly had gained a new source of enjoyment.Their excitement was so great as to make frequent repetitions dangerous, and the concerts were discontinued, notwithstanding the urgent solicitation of many to whom they were equally new and delightful.[22]

The success of the children led to a tuition-free class for adults that attracted five hundred people.

The Boston Academy of Music was incorporated in March 1833, due in large part to Woodbridge's efforts. He served as recording secretary and helped publicize it, especially in the *American Annals of Education and Instruction*. One of the objectives of the academy was the introduction of "vocal music into schools, by the aid of such teachers as the Academy may be able to employ, each of whom shall instruct classes alternately in a number of schools."[23] Lowell Mason and George J. Webb were hired as professors. The original intention of the founders was to have the academy provide professional musicians to offer music instruction in the schools. The directors of the academy were about fifty businessmen and professionals, some influential in the community, who gave the academy sufficient prestige to be regarded seriously in negotiations with the School Committee of the City of Boston for the adoption of music in the schools.

Four individuals assumed leadership roles in the Boston Academy of Music. Before the academy was established, George H. Snelling, a member of the Boston Primary School Board, responded to Woodbridge's influence and authored a report in which it was resolved that systematic vocal instruction should be introduced on an experimental basis in one school in each district.[24] The report was accepted by the Boston School Committee but subsequently ignored. Snelling became a member of the academy. T. Kemper Davis was an attorney and also a member of the academy. He signed an 1836 petition of twenty-four citizens to include music in the schools and was chairman of a committee on music reporting to the school committee. Samuel A. Eliot was president of the academy from 1835 to 1847 and was mayor of Boston during the time that negotiations were being carried out with the Boston School Committee (1837–1838). The fourth leader was Lowell Mason. Influential among Boston's music teachers, he was known and respected in the community.

The Boston Academy of Music immediately attracted a large number of students, necessitating the hiring of George J. Webb as assistant professor. Webb was an Englishman trained as a pianist. He had come to Boston in 1830 and was organist at Old South Church.

The academy operated vocal music programs in private schools, sponsored public lectures on music, offered its own music classes to children and adults, and worked for the general improvement of church music and the development of support for the idea of music in the common schools. Professors from the academy taught music at the Asylum for the Blind (later Perkins Institute), thus providing an early occurrence of music in special education.[25] Joseph A. Keller taught violin to a group of boys during the year 1835–1836.[26] Eventually the academy had a large choir, its own orchestra to assist with oratorios, and by the 1840s it sponsored the performance of symphonic music. In addition to teaching the public and providing public performances, the Boston Academy of Music was also highly successful in its role as a demonstration school.

The Manual of the Boston Academy of Music. In 1834 Lowell Mason published his *Manual of Instruction of the Boston Academy of Music, for Instruction in the Elements of Vocal Music on the System of Pestalozzi.* The book was a great success and became the handbook of singing school teachers throughout the country. One of Mason's biographers, Arthur Lowndes Rich, wrote: "The demand for copies of the *Manual* was very great; its circulation extensive, and the principles there developed were adopted and practised by a considerable number of teachers."[27] The final edition, the eighth, was published in 1861. In that edition, as in its predecessors, Mason comments on his "Sources of Information" in order to authenticate his tie to Pestalozzianism, the magic word among American educators of the day. Among those sources he mentions the *Gesangbildungslehre* of Pfeiffer and Nägeli. Howard Ellis made a detailed comparison of the *Manual*, the Pfeiffer and Nägeli work, and Kübler's *Anleitung zum Gesangunterrichte in Schulen* in 1957 and observed that the Pfeiffer and Nägeli book is much closer to the methods advocated by Pestalozzi than the Kübler work. In fact, the *Manual of the Boston Academy* is little more than a translation of Kübler, a fact that Mason himself divulged in a footnote in his *Carmina Sacra: or Boston Collection of Church Music*. Nevertheless, he never altered the "Sources of Information" statement in any subsequent editions of the popular *Manual*.

Mason's Reputation. Mason's unfortunate subterfuge in regard to the authorship of the *Manual* has caused him to be considered a plagiarist and raised real doubts about his true understanding of Pestalozzianism. No one has ever questioned his powers as a teacher, however, and his accomplishments with children, adults, and especially neophyte teachers were essential to the success of vocal music in the schools of the country. Mason has been defended to a degree by Efland, who established connections between Kübler's work and Pestalozzianism, thus

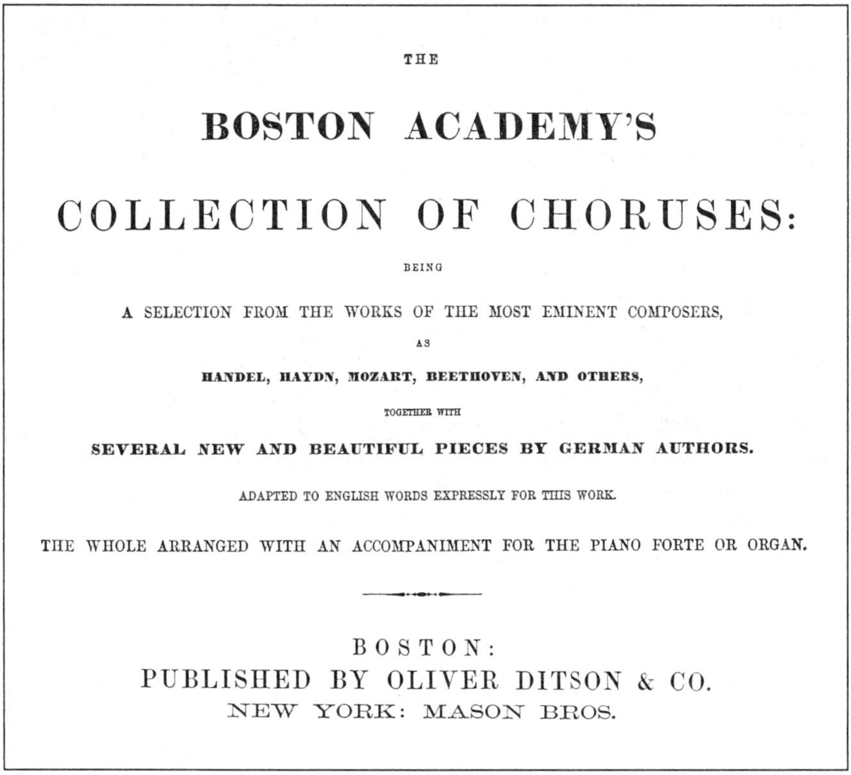

THE

BOSTON ACADEMY'S

COLLECTION OF CHORUSES:

BEING

A SELECTION FROM THE WORKS OF THE MOST EMINENT COMPOSERS,

AS

HANDEL, HAYDN, MOZART, BEETHOVEN, AND OTHERS,

TOGETHER WITH

SEVERAL NEW AND BEAUTIFUL PIECES BY GERMAN AUTHORS.

ADAPTED TO ENGLISH WORDS EXPRESSLY FOR THIS WORK.

THE WHOLE ARRANGED WITH AN ACCOMPANIMENT FOR THE PIANO FORTE OR ORGAN.

BOSTON:
PUBLISHED BY OLIVER DITSON & CO.
NEW YORK: MASON BROS.

FIGURE 7–3a The title page of *The Boston Academy's Collection of Choruses*. Boston: Oliver Ditson & Co., 1836.

FIGURE 7–3b Page 15 of *The Boston Academy's Collection of Choruses.*

providing some credibility to Mason's leadership as a Pestalozzian music teacher.[28]

Apart from the matter of Mason's sources is the use of the name Pestalozzi in connection with American music education. It became so closely associated with perceived excellence in music instruction that the name became a generic term that implied quality but not necessarily authentic Pestalozzianism. An example is a book compiled by George W. Pratt and J.C. Johnson, *The Pestalozzian School Song Book; Containing, in the First Part, A Complete Course of Instructions in the Elementary Principles of Music, with Copious Exercises and Songs, Systematically Arranged for Practice* (Boston: A.N. Johnson, 1853). The preface states:

> The name, "Pestalozzian School Song Book," has been selected, as not inappropriate to a work of this kind, in view of the important services rendered by Pestalozzi to the cause of Elementary education, in all its branches.

This was the reason for including Pestalozzi's name in the title. The method presented in the book is very much like that of the traditional tune books of earlier times and is hardly Pestalozzian. It is apparent that the compilers hoped to profit by claiming to follow the Pestalozzian method.

More on Mason's Pedagogical Methods. Further insight into Mason's methods of teaching is provided in the preface to *The Boston Academy's Collection of Church Music,* a publication he prepared for the academy in 1835 and which was already in its sixth edition one year later. This book offers "Introductory Rules" that Mason says were prepared with great care:

> According to the Pestalozzian system of instruction and as a result of much experience. The advantages of this system are so great that it only requires to be known to be universally adopted. It requires, however, to be studied by the teacher until he becomes familiar with the leading principles on which it always proceeds. The elementary principles of music presented in this way afford a pleasing, useful, and intelligent study as well to that as to the scholar; they must be *understood* and not merely *committed* to memory. It has been supposed by some that the principal difference between the Pestalozzian and the old method of instruction consists of the use of the Blackboard. This is by no means true. It is believed, that on either method, the Blackboard may be of essential service, but it is not supposed to be any more necessary to the Pestalozzian than to the old system of teaching. The true ground of the distinction between the two, lies not in the use of the Blackboard, but in the admirable analysis of the elementary principles of music furnished in the Pestalozzian method, and in the practical mode of presenting these principles to the mind of the pupil.

Twenty-four pages of "Elements" follow. They are organized into sections of six to ten ideas and a similar number of questions to be asked for each section. The note that follows points out that it is not necessary to commit these elements to memory, although it is all right to do so. It suggests the use of a light rod for pointing to the blackboard and beating time, and it encourages rote singing because "it (a) affords variety and gratifies the pupils; (b) has a tendency to improve the voice; and (c) gives the teacher a chance to correct faulty tone production." It could, therefore, "occupy profitably one quarter of the time" of the first six or even twelve lessons, "after which the pupils will have made so much progress as to be able to sing from a knowledge of the elementary principles of music." Singing by rote and using the words is to be "given up entirely . . . the use of the syllables of solmisation should be substituted for it." These introductory remarks conclude with the observation that vocal music cannot be taught in a short time as it is more difficult than learning Latin or Greek because it demands a cultivation of taste which can only be brought about by "industrious, patient, and persevering practice."

These words explain how music teaching in America's nineteenth-century schools came to be so concerned with teaching children to read music through drill with syllables. Mason, who was in no way humble, called himself the "father of singing among children in this country."[29]

The Music Convention Movement: The Beginnings of Teacher Education. Singing societies already existed in many small towns, and it was natural for them to want to join forces for contests, to perform larger works than could be handled alone, and for musical development. In 1829 Henry E. Moore set up a singing school convention using the New Hampshire Central Musical Society of Goffstown as a nucleus. Held for two days in Concord, New Hampshire, in September 1829, the convention attracted church choir directors, singing school masters, and interested singers from the various societies in the region. Similar meetings were held in Pembroke in 1830 and Goffstown in 1831, but records of further meetings are unavailable.

One of the stated purposes of the Boston Academy of Music was "to form a class of instruction in the methods of teaching music, which may be composed of teachers, parents and all other persons desirous to qualify themselves for teaching vocal music." Another was "To establish a course of scientific lectures . . . for teachers, choristers and others desirous of understanding the science of music." Mason took it upon himself to establish the academy as the center of the new convention movement and himself as leader. *The Manual of the Boston Academy of Music* became the text for most singing school masters. In August 1834, Mason and George Webb held a class for eleven men and one woman. All were from Massachusetts, Connecticut, or New Hampshire. The sessions consisted of lectures on teaching methods, discussion of problems, and classes in psalmody, harmony, and voice culture. In the evenings there was choral practice, and a concert concluded the convention. The next summer the "class-convention," which had increased in size, contained students from Maine, New York, and Pennsylvania. By 1836 the meeting had been extended to ten days of lectures on teaching methods, discussion of questions of music education and of church music, and planned debate. It attracted twenty-eight students in addition to members of previous classes who returned to attend lectures, as all alumnae were invited to do. At the conclusion of the 1836 class-convention, the students unanimously passed ten resolutions that reflect the attitude of music directors of the time:

1. RESOLVED, That the introduction and application of the Pestalozzian System of teaching music, form a new era in the science of music education in this country; and, that in pursuing our labors as teachers, we will conform ourselves as far as circumstances will admit, to that system, as published in the *Manual of the Boston Academy of Music.*

2. RESOLVED, That, in order to diffuse a knowledge of music through the community, it is necessary to teach it to our youth; and that it is desirable, and practicable, to introduce it into all our schools, as a branch of elementary education.

3. RESOLVED, That it is the special duty of the Christian Church to cultivate, and encourage the cultivation of Sacred Music generally, as a powerful auxiliary to devotion.

4. RESOLVED, That it is a source of deep regret to this Convention, that, in so many instances, Religious Societies and Parishes, instead of exerting a fostering care and influence over the cause of Sacred Music, neglect it, suffer it to fall into unskillful hands, and thus, not only wound the cause itself, but make it a detriment, rather than a help, to the best interests of the church.

5. RESOLVED, That Singer Choirs too infrequently, in conducting their part of divine worship, attempt the performance of music too difficult, and with which they are not sufficiently familiar, thereby detracting from the solemnity and devotion of the exercise.

6. RESOLVED, That in pursuing our labors as Teachers and Choristers, we will strive to avoid as far as in us lies, any thing like invidious rivalry; and that we will assist each other in our profession as we have opportunity.

7. RESOLVED, That, notwithstanding we have to contend with the prejudice of some, the opposition of others, and the indifference of many, yet we find in the progress of musical education for a few years past, abundant encouragement to perservere in our labors, and not become weary in well-doing.

8. RESOLVED, That the sentiment which prevails in some places, that to occupy a place in the Choir, is not respectable, and, therefore, to assist in one of the most delightful services of the house of God, is not an honorable and dignified employment, is a sentiment founded in ignorance and prejudice; and that those who cherish such a sentiment themselves, or give countenance to it in any way, are endeavoring to subvert an ordinance which God himself has established.

9. RESOLVED, That, in the opinion of this Convention, a good moral character is an Indispensable qualification for a Teacher of Sacred Music, or for a Chorister.

The tenth resolution expressed thanks to Professors Mason and Webb for their ''Earnest endeavors and unremitted exertions to qualify us as teachers of vocal music.''

The 1838 convention, called the ''American Musical Convention,'' attracted two groups of students. One consisted of teachers interested in the methods classes; the other expected more emphasis on the convention itself, with its meetings and election of officers. This division did not affect the 1838 meeting, but within a few years it led to a split in the attendees characterized by hard feelings and political intrigue. George Webb severed his connection with the Boston Academy of Music and started his own classes in competition with those of Mason. The conflict is described in interesting detail by Robert John.[30] The difference was eventually resolved, and the American Musical Convention continued to train musicians for school and church positions. The academy convention was organized in 1840 under the name ''The National Music Convention.'' From that time, conventions grew and spread as singing schools had earlier. They attracted skilled musical leaders, most of whom were trained or at least influenced by Lowell Mason. Mason took his conventions on the road during the 1840s. They were held as far west as Cleveland, but his favorite location was Rochester, New York. Birge wrote of the conventions:

> The Music Convention became our first national school of music pedagogy, harmony, conducting and voice culture, and thousands of young people in all parts of the country received training in these fundamentals under the leadership of such men as Thomas Hastings, George J. Webb, William B. Bradbury, George F. Root, Isaac B. Woodbury, Benjamin F. Baker and Luther O. Emerson, all of whom possessed outstanding qualities of leadership. They were all authors of many tune books and collections, for which there was a continuous demand.[31]

In a letter to his friend H. S. Perkins, C. M. Cady of Chicago wrote:

> For 30 years I have watched the effects of these gatherings upon cities, counties and states in which they have been held under such men as Hastings, Mason, Woodbury, Root and a host of younger conductors. Without exception, so far as my observation has extended, they have resulted in good in many ways, prominent among which are the following:
>
> 1. They have inspired participants with enthusiasm for musical improvement, whether as individuals, choirs, or congregations, and buried petty jealousies under lofty aims.
> 2. They have not only led to better voice culture, better choirs and heartier congregational singing, but have been powerful agents in the introduction of sight singing into the public schools.
> 3. They have familiarized the public with grand choral effects and the works of the great masters, and to that extent shown the superiority of the sublime over the merely pretty and beautiful.[32]

The Normal Institute. The music conventions lasted for about thirty years and led to another development: they served musical leaders interested in teaching and choral singing. Eventually, those with a greater interest in teaching wanted more of the convention devoted to pedagogy and those interested in choral singing wanted more time for choral practice. Another kind of convention, the normal institute, was developed under the leadership of Mason and George Root. Mason had had considerable experience with teachers institutes, having given music lectures at institutes organized for Massachusetts teachers by Horace Mann and for Rhode Island teachers by Henry Barnard.

When Mason was about to move from Boston to New York, Root approached him with the idea of a three-month normal music institute to be held in New York. Mason was almost sixty at that time and wealthy from his book income. When he hesitated, Root offered to do all the organizing, and the institutes of the 1850s were held with great success. The normal institute drew students from all over the country. Courses were offered in methods, theory, voice, and piano. This, and similar normal institutes, had the services of outstanding teachers such as William Mason, William H. Sherwood, Frederick W. Root, W. S. B. Mathews, Julia Ettie Crane, Luther Emerson, William W. Killip, Theodore F. Seward, Charles C. Perkins, and George B. Loomis. Mason continued with the institutes until 1862, when he was seventy, giving his last one in Wooster, Ohio.

The institutes were normally held in the summer, and some eventually developed into conservatories of music.[33] The other aspect of music conventions, choral singing, also developed separately into choral organizations.[34]

Lyceums. Another avenue of general education that occasionally offered special musical training was the lyceum movement. This was a form of adult education that featured such well-known figures as Ralph Waldo Emerson, with his message of American individualism. Sometimes referred to as the "Isaiah of the American democratic faith," he told a Phi Beta Kappa audience at Harvard in 1837 "We have listened too long to the muses of Europe. We will walk on our own feet; we will work with our own hands; we will speak our own minds."[35]

Teacher education was a major concern of the movement. Both Woodbridge and Mason used the lyceums presented in various communities to promote the value of vocal music as a subject for the common school curriculum. It is probably coincidental that the last year of the American Lyceum was the same year (1839) in which Massachusetts established its first normal school. Local lyceums continued, however, and after the Civil War lyceum bureaus reinvigorated the movement and served small towns throughout the nation. When the Chautauqua Institution was established in western New York, music instruction became an important part of its program, as it did in some of the imitators that also used the name "Chautauqua." The original Chautauqua, which operated as a degree granting institution from 1883 to 1898, contributed to the development of summer programs in higher education, to instruction by correspondence, and to university extension work. Instruction in music began there in 1875.[36]

SUMMARY

Education became a subject of great interest to Americans after they had weathered the many problems of establishing a new nation. As institutions were developed to provide the desired instruction, there arose individuals who were anxious for music to become part of the curriculum. Chief among them were William Woodbridge, who introduced Pestalozzian pedagogy to the United States, and Lowell Mason, who cooperated with Woodbridge in proving to the public that all children could be taught to sing. Together they paved the way for music in American schools.

NOTES

1. A. Theodore Tellstrom, *Music in American Education: Past and Present* (New York: Holt, Rinehart and Winston, 1971), pp. 24–27.
2. Arthur D. Efland, "Pestalozzi and 19th Century Music Education," *International Journal of Music Education* 3 (May 1984): 21–22.
3. Bernarr Rainbow, *The Land without Music*, London: Novello & Co. Ltd., 1967, reported in Efland, "Pestalozzi and 19th Century Music Education," p. 22.
4. Arthur Efland, "Art and Music in the Pestalozzian Tradition," *Journal of Research in Music Education* 31 (Fall 1983): 171–72.
5. Henry Raynor, *Music & Society Since 1815* (New York: Taplinger, 1978), p. 89.
6. Efland, "Pestalozzi and 19th Century Music Education," p. 23.
7. G. F. Kübler, *Anleitung zum Gesangunterrichte in Schulen* (Stuttgart: J. B. Metzler'shen Buchhandlung, 1826).
8. Lowell Mason, *Manual of the Boston Academy of Music for Instruction in the Elements of Vocal Music on the System of Pestalozzi* (Boston: Carter, Hendee, 1834), pp. 25–28.
9. Arthur L. Rich, *Lowell Mason: "The Father of Singing Among the Children"* (Chapel Hill: University of North Carolina Press, 1946), p. 15.
10. Robert W. John, "Elam Ives and the Pestalozzian Philosophy of Music Education," *Journal of Research in Music Education* 8 (Spring 1960): 47.
11. Mary F. Keating, "Lowell Mason in Savannah," *Bulletin of Historical Research in Music Education* 10 (July 1989): 74.
12. Carol A. Pemberton, *Lowell Mason: His Life and Work* (Ann Arbor, MI: UMI Research Press, 1985), p. 15.
13. Ibid.
14. Ibid., p. 80.
15. Rich, *Lowell Mason*, p. 9.

16. Ernest K. Emurian, *Stories of Our National Songs* (Boston: W.A. Wilde, 1957), pp. 25–33.

17. Lowell and Timothy Mason, *The Sacred Harp or Eclectic Harmony: New Collection of Church Music* (Cincinnati: Truman and Smith, 1837), prefatory page.

18. Estelle R. Jorgensen, "Engineering Change in Music Education: A Model of the Political Process Underlying the Boston School Music Movement (1829–1838)," *Journal of Research in Music Education* 31 (Spring 1983): 69.

19. Pemberton, *Lowell Mason*, p. 41.

20. William Gardiner, *The Music of Nature* (Boston: Wilkins & Carter, 1837), p. 450.

21. Carol A. Pemberton, "A Look at the *Juvenile Lyre* (1831): Posing a Rationale for Music in the Schools," *Bulletin of Historical Research in Music Education* 11 (January 1990): 17–32.

22. Samuel A. Eliot, "Address Before the Boston Academy of Music on the Opening of the Odeon," in Jorgensen, "Engineering Change in Music Education," p. 70.

23. Bruce D. Wilson, "A Documentary History of Music in the Public Schools of the City of Boston, 1830–1850," vol. 2 (Ph.D. dissertation, University of Michigan, 1973), p. 29.

24. Wilson, "A Documentary History," pp. 80–87.

25. Pemberton, "A Look at the *Juvenile Lyre*," pp. 69–70.

26. Rich, *Lowell Mason*, p. 45.

27. Ibid.

28. Arthur Efland, "Art and Music in the Pestalozzian Tradition," *Journal of Research in Music Education* 31 (Fall 1983): 165–79.

29. *An Address on Church Music* (New York: Mason and Law, 1851), pp. 13–14.

30. Robert W. John, "Origins of the First Music Educators Convention, *Journal of Research in Music Education* 13 (Winter 1965): 207–19.

31. Edward Bailey Birge, *History of Public School Music in the United States* (Washington, DC: Music Educators National Conference, 1928), pp. 28–29.

32. H. S. Perkins's address at the convention of the Music Teachers National Association, 1887, reported in Birge, pp. 29–30.

33. Birge, *History of Public School Music*, pp. 31–32.

34. Ibid.

35. Ralph H. Gabriel, *The Course of American Democratic Thought* (New York: Ronald Press, 1946), p. 14.

36. L. Jeanette Wells, *A History of the Music Festival at Chautauqua Institution* (Washington, DC: Catholic University of America Press, 1958), pp. 4–12.

BIBLIOGRAPHY

Birge, Edward Bailey. *History of Public School Music in the United States.* Washington, DC: Music Educators National Conference, 1928.

Efland, Arthur. "Art and Music in the Pestalozzian Tradition." *Journal of Research in Music Education* 31 (Fall 1983).

———. "Pestalozzi and 19th Century Music Education." *International Journal of Music Education* 3 (May 1984).

Emurian, Ernest K. *Stories of Our National Songs*. Boston: W. A. Wilde, 1957.

Gabriel, Ralph H. *The Course of American Democratic Thought*. New York: Ronald Press, 1946.

Gardiner, William. *The Music of Nature*. Boston: Wilkins & Carter, 1837.

John, Robert. "Elam Ives and the Pestalozzian Philosophy of Music Education." *Journal of Research in Music Education* 8 (Spring 1960).

———. "Origins of the First Music Educators Convention." *Journal of Research in Music Education* 13 (Winter 1965).

Jorgensen, Estelle R. "Engineering Change in Music Education: A Model of the Political Process Underlying the Boston School Music Movement (1829–1838)." *Journal of Research in Music Education* 31 (Spring 1983).

Keating, Mary F. "Lowell Mason in Savannah," *Bulletin of Historical Research in Music Education* 10 (July 1989).

Kübler, G. F. *Anleitung zum Gesangunterricht in Schulen*. Stuttgart: J. B. Metzler'-shen Bucchandlung, 1826.

Mason, Lowell. *Carmina Sacra: or Boston Collection of Church Music*. Boston: Wilkins and Carter, 1841.

———. *Manual of the Boston Academy of Music for Instruction in the Elements of Vocal Music on the System of Pestalozzi*. Boston: Carter, Hendee, 1834.

Pemberton, Carol A. "A Look at *The Juvenile Lyre* (1831): Posing a Rationale for Music in the Schools." *Bulletin of Historical Research in Music Education* 11 (January 1990).

Pfeiffer, M., and Nägeli, H. G. *Gesangbildungslehre nach pestalozzichen Grundsatzen Padagogisch begrundet von H. G. Nägeli*. Zurich: Nägeli, 1810.

Raynor, Henry. *Music and Society Since 1815*. New York: Taplinger, 1978.

Rich, Arthur L. *Lowell Mason: "The Father of Singing Among the Children."* Chapel Hill: University of North Carolina Press, 1946.

Tellstrom, A. Theodore. *Music in American Education: Past and Present*. New York: Holt, Rinehart and Winston, 1971.

Wells, L. Jeanette. *A History of the Music Festival at Chautauqua Institution*. Washington, DC: Catholic University of America Press, 1958.

Wilson, Bruce. "A Documentary History of Music in the Public Schools of the City of Boston, 1830–1850." Ph.D. dissertation, University of Michigan, 1973.

Woodbridge, William C. "Lectures on the Pestalozzian System of Music." *American Annals of Education and Instruction* 4 (1834).

———. "On Vocal Music as a Branch of Common Education." *American Annals of Education and Instruction* 3 (1833).

———. "On Vocal Music as a Branch of Common Education." *American Institute for Instruction*. Boston: Hilliard, Gray, Little & Wilkins, 1830.

8

THE BEGINNINGS OF
MUSIC IN AMERICAN
SCHOOLS

The establishment of music in American schools could only have been possible in a musical society. Thanks to the singing schools and other musical experiences available in the United States, by the early part of the nineteenth century appreciable numbers of Americans were participating in musical activities. Gradually, the public realized the value of music to society. With this realization, the way was prepared for music to enter the public school curriculum. Even so, more needed to be done before Americans were willing to spend their tax money on music in public education.

Singing Societies. Singing schools usually lasted twelve or sixteen weeks, but they were often the genesis of permanent singing societies. One of the earliest societies was in Thetford, Vermont, and Lyme, New Hampshire, which were neighboring villages on either side of the Connecticut River. It had a written document of organization as early as 1781.[1] The society with the longest continuous existence is that of Stoughton, Massachusetts, where William Billings had conducted singing schools. Establishing the founding date as 1786, Stoessel notes that it antedates the Berlin Singakademie by five years.[2] He also comments on the rapid growth of singing societies in America; by 1812 they outnumbered those in Germany. The Handel Society at Dartmouth College dates from 1807, and its name indicates interest in European music rather than that of the singing school.[3] Other Massachusetts towns with early choral societies were Dunstable and Dorchester. Birge reported that the latter challenged the Stoughton group to a contest in 1790.[4] Stoughton won by singing the Hallelujah Chorus from *Messiah* from memory.

The most famous singing society was the Boston Handel and Haydn Society, organized in 1815. The first concert of the society featured a chorus of one hundred (ten of whom were women), an orchestra of about twelve pieces, and an organ. Nine hundred forty-five tickets were sold, and the net proceeds were $533. After the successful inaugural concerts, the society was called the "wonder of the nation."[5] An article about the society in the *Columbian Centinel* describes the public attitude toward singing and sacred music:

HANDEL & HAYDN SOCIETY.

We are happy to see it announced in the papers that this respectable Society have appointed a time to favour the public with an opportunity of listening to their performances. If we are correctly informed of the principles upon which the Society is instituted, it is certainly entitled to public support and patronage. Among its members are almost all the principal vocal performers of Sacred Music in this and several of the neighbouring towns, and we feel confident that their powers, united with those of many of the principal professional and amateur performers of instrumental music, will furnish an intellectual repast that must prove highly gratifying to the lover of Sacred Music. We have been favoured with a copy of the Constitution of this Society, and are pleased to find that their views are liberal and commendable; they exclude no sect, but cheerfully unite with all in singing the high praises of God. Their members are not entitled to any compensation for their services, and the monies that may be collected at their public performances are appropriated to the discharge of all incidental expences and the surplus for purchasing scarce and valuable music. One of their most important objects is to create and cherish in the community a love of Sacred Music and to improve the style of its performance; and as their members emanate from every Society of public worshippers, each may reasonably expect to derive some benefit from the united exertions of the whole. We ardently wish them to perservere in their labours, and most sincerely say, "Peace be within thy walls, and prosperity within thy palaces."[6]

Singing societies were not restricted to New England. The Saint Cecilia Society of Charleston, South Carolina, probably dates from 1762. The Ukrainian Academy Chorus of Philadelphia performed full oratorios in that city and in New York shortly after the Revolutionary War. Both the New York Choral Society and the New York Sacred Music Society were founded in 1823.

MUSIC EDUCATION OUTSIDE OF BOSTON

Joseph Neef. Twenty years before Woodbridge returned from Switzerland full of enthusiasm for Pestalozzian education, Joseph Neef, one of Pestalozzi's assistants, was brought to the United States by philanthropist William Maclure. Neef was born in 1770 in Alsace, and he knew French and German. He mastered Greek, Latin, and Italian in a monastery school before joining Napoleon's Army of the Rhine at the age of twenty-one. As a member of the Second Brigade he took a round above his nose at the battle of Arcole and carried it with him for the rest of his life. During his hospital recuperation he read the writings of Pestalozzi, and on his release he became an instructor of languages and gymnastics at Burgdorf.[7] His view of education was holistic. He sang with his pupils on the march, swam, played with them to strengthen their bodies, and worked with them to make them intelligent realists. When the American geologist Maclure met Neef in Paris, he persuaded the educator to return to America with him to introduce Pestalozzian education there. This was twenty years before William Channing Woodbridge's return and twenty years too early. Americans were not yet ready for Pestalozzianism.

Communitarian Societies. After directing schools near Philadelphia (where the future Admiral David Farragut was one of his pupils) from 1809 to 1812, Neef moved to Kentucky. There he alternately kept school and farmed until Maclure recommended him to Robert Owen, who was then moving his utopian community to New Harmony, Indiana. Owen had established a comprehensive educational program in his model mill town in New Lanark, Scotland, and had sent his sons to Philipp Fellenberg's school at Hofwyl. Maclure proposed an educational system that Owen liked, and Owen turned the New Harmony school over to Maclure.

Music was an important part of the life of New Harmony, and both Owen and Maclure wanted it to be a part of the curriculum. Maclure hired Marie Louise Fretageot to conduct the preschool (ages two to five), Neef and his wife and daughters to direct the higher school (ages five to twelve), and Casimir P. d'Arusmont to run a trade school. All of the teachers had had Pestalozzian training.[8] Neef remained in New Harmony until 1828, when he went to Cincinnati to run singing schools. He later went to Steubenville, Ohio, as a singing master and eventually returned to farming in Indiana.

Owen bought the town of Harmony from George Rapp, whose dissident Lutheran group had established a town of the same name in western Pennsylvania in 1804. In 1814, two years before the territory was admitted to the United States, the Rappists moved to Indiana.

When Rapp sold the Indiana property to Owen in 1825, the Harmonie Gesellschaft returned to Pennsylvania to set up Economie (now Ambridge). Music was an important part of life and education in all the communitarian settlements, as it was in the German communities of eastern Pennsylvania. The Harmonie Society physician, Johann Christoph Mueller, is reported to have spent his mornings teaching music in the school.[9]

These examples of school music in closed communities such as New Harmony and Economie do not provide a representative picture of American school activities in the first decades of the nineteenth century. They are, however, a part of the history of music education in the United States, and there is no way to know what effect they may have had on neighboring towns in the developing West.

Preliminaries to Establishing Music as a Curricular Subject. The decade 1830–1840 was critical and significant in the establishment of vocal music programs in American schools. Those who were instrumental in bringing vocal music to the public school curriculum used many approaches, including gratis teaching, the interest of church officials, and the natural attractiveness of children's voices. They had allies among city officials and the agencies of the common school movement. Vocal music first became a part of the curriculum in Boston, but communities throughout the East and the new West worked for the same goal.

There was singing in private schools before the common schools came into existence. In the earliest years of public education some teachers trained children to sing and occasionally presented them in public concerts. Widespread interest in school music was evident. The Boston Academy of Music reported in 1835 that letters requesting information about how to introduce music as a branch of common education had been received from Georgia, South Carolina, Virginia, Illinois, Missouri, Tennessee, Ohio, Maryland, New York, Connecticut, Vermont, New Hampshire, Maine, and Massachusetts.[10]

When the Marquis de Lafayette made his reunion tour of the United States in 1824, six hundred schoolchildren in Cincinnati sang to him. A group of young boys in Massachusetts introduced the Reverend Samuel Smith's patriotic song "America" at a service in the Park Street Church on July 4, 1831. Many schools had opening exercises at which hymns were sung. Singing was a routine activity in schools for devotional and recreational purposes, but it was not yet an educational activity in itself.

Early Public School Music. It was not unusual for individual teachers in America's earliest public schools to use singing in their schoolhouses. This was undoubtedly the case with such men as Justin Morgan and Thomas Fessenden in Vermont, both of whom not only "instructed village schools'' but were also accomplished enough to be successful singing school masters in the evenings.

Morgan was primarily interested in farming, horse breeding, and composing. His library, which included Scott's *Lessons in Elocution*, Dilworth's *Arithmetic*, and Noah Webster's *A Grammatical Institute*, Part II, indicates that references to him as ''teacher of children'' meant more than teaching singing schools.[11] Lawyer Fessenden was a cellist and singing school master who earned his way through Dartmouth (class of 1796) by teaching in village schools and holding singing schools at night.[12] It is likely that Morgan and Fessenden sang with their young students in village schools during the short school terms.

Horace Barnes, in Wheaton, Illinois, was not only able to keep his pupils interested in their studies but also aroused in them a love for singing. ''It was always the best part of the day to me,'' Judge Elbert Gary later told Ida Tarbell, his biographer. George L. White, born in Cadiz, New York, in 1838, had no formal education after age fourteen but became a schoolteacher before entering the Union Army. He was musical, like his blacksmith father, and his schools were famous for their singing. After the war, he found himself in Nashville working for the Freedmen's Bureau. He became the first treasurer of Fisk University and the originator and first director of the famed Jubilee Singers, a name he coined in Columbus, Ohio, during their initial tour.

The concern of citizens for education and for music instruction is seen in some early actions taken in Keene, New Hampshire. On March 7, 1780, the townspeople voted that ''singing in public worship be performed without reading line by line as they sing.'' In 1797 the town appropriated five hundred dollars for a school. Five years later sixty dollars was appropriated ''to teach people to sing.'' There is no indication of a connection between these events, but they were expressions of the willingness of the public to tax itself for education, including music education.[13]

Until the country came to accept the concept of the founding fathers that democracy depended on universal education and that this meant publicly supported schools for all children, school music was dependent on the talents and whims of individual schoolmasters. Fortunately, the movement for common schools, which enhanced the possibilities for music education, coincided with an outgrowth of the singing schools—the establishment of singing societies by people interested in music.

THE BEGINNINGS OF SCHOOL MUSIC IN BOSTON: MUSIC BECOMES A CURRICULAR SUBJECT

In 1836 two petitions by Boston citizens and a memorial from the Boston Academy of Music were submitted to the Boston School Committee. All three documents called for the introduction of vocal music instruction in the public schools. The school committee appointed a special committee on music, chaired by T. Kemper Davis, to study the petitions and make recommendations. The special committee examined the work of the Boston Academy of Music to understand the value of music instruction. It also sent a questionnaire to the principals of five private schools that already offered music as a curricular subject. On August 24, 1837, after due consideration, the Davis committee recommended that vocal music be introduced on an experimental basis in four public schools under the supervision of the Boston Academy of Music. The recommendations of the Davis committee were contained in a lengthy report that reflected the extent and depth of the committee's investigation into the desirability of public school music. Music instruction was recommended on the basis of three utilitarian reasons—intellectual, moral, and physical development. This rationale had been published in 1831 in the preface of *The Juvenile Lyre*. The 1837 report states:

There is a threefold standard, a sort of chemical test, by which education itself and every branch of education may be tried. Is it intellectual—is it moral—is it physical? Let vocal Music be examined by this standard.

Try it *intellectually*. Music is an intellectual art. Among the seven liberal arts, which scholastic ages regarded as pertaining to humanity, Music had its place. Arithmetic, Geometry, Astronomy and Music, these formed the *quadrivium*. Separate degrees in Music, it is believed, are still conferred by the University of Oxford. Memory, comparison, attention, intellectual faculties all of them, are quickened by the study of its principles. It is not ornamental only. It has high intellectual affinities. It may be made, to some extent, an intellectual discipline.

Try music *morally*. There is,—who has not felt it,—a mysterious connection, ordained undoubtedly for wise purposes, between certain sounds and the moral sentiments of man. This is not to be gainsaid, neither is it to be explained. It is an ultimate law of man's nature. "In Music," says Hooker, "the very image of virtue and vice is perceived." Now it is a curious fact, that the natural scale of musical sound can only produce good, virtuous, and kindly feelings. You must reverse this scale, if you would call forth the sentiments of a corrupt, degraded, and degenerate character. Has not the finger of the Almighty written here an indication too plain to be mistaken? And if such be the case, if there be this necessary concordance between certain sounds and certain trains of moral feeling, is it unphilosophical to say that exercises in vocal Music may be so directed and arranged as to produce those habits of feeling of which these sounds are types. Besides, happiness, contentment, cheerfulness, tranquility,—these are the natural effects of Music. These qualities are connected intimately with the moral government of the individual. Why should they not, under proper management, be rendered equally efficient in the moral government of the school?

And now try music *physically*. "A fact," says an American physician, "has been suggested to me by my profession, which is, that the exercise of the organs of the breast by singing contributes very much to defend them from those diseases to which the climate and other causes expose them." A musical writer in England after quoting this remark, says, the "Music Master of our Academy has furnished me with an observation still more in favor of this opinion. He informs me that he had known several persons strongly disposed to consumption restored to health, by the exercise of the lungs in singing." But why cite medical or other authorities to a point so plain? It appears self-evident that exercise in vocal Music, when not carried to an unreasonable excess, must expand the chest, and thereby strengthen the lungs and vital organs.

Judged, then by this triple standard, intellectually, morally, and physically, vocal Music seems to have a natural place in every system of instruction which aspires, as should every system, to develope man's whole nature. . . .

What is the great object of our system of popular instruction? Are our schools mere houses of Correction, in which animal nature is to be kept in subjection by the law of brute force and the stated drudgery of distasteful tasks? Not so. They have a nobler office. They are valuable mainly as a preparation and a training of the young spirit for usefulness and happiness in coming life. Now the defect of our present system, admirable as that system is, is this, that it aims to develop the intellectual part of man's nature solely, when for all the true purposes of life, it is of more importance, a hundred fold, to feel rightly, than to think profoundly.[14]

The report concluded with several resolutions, the most significant of which were the following:

RESOLVED, That in the opinion of the School Committee, it is expedient to try the experiment of introducing vocal Music, by Public authority, as part of the system of Public Instruction, into the Public schools of this City.

RESOLVED, That the experiment be tried in the four following schools, the Hancock school for Girls, in Hanover street; the Eliot school, for Boys, in North Bennett street; the Johnson school, for Girls, in Washington street; and the Hawes school, for Boys and Girls, at South Boston.[15]

RESOLVED, That this experiment be given in charge to the Boston Academy of Music, under the direction of the Board, and that a Committee of five be appointed from the Board to confer with the Academy, arrange all necessary details of the plan, oversee its operation, and make quarterly report thereof to the Board.

The school committee approved the report on September 19, 1837. There was disagreement, however, on the need to appropriate funds from the common council of the city of Boston for the experiment. The council refused to do so, and the experiment was jeopardized. When Lowell Mason returned from Europe in October 1837 he agreed to teach at the Hawes School in South Boston with no salary. The school committee agreed to this on November 14, 1837.

The final agreement represented several compromises necessary to implement the plan for school music instruction. Only one school, rather than four, would receive music instruction. There would be no public funds for music instruction. Of great importance, the experiment was controlled by the Boston School Committee rather than by the Boston Academy of Music.[16]

Lowell Mason taught music at the Hawes School during the 1837–1838 school year. When the mayor of Boston, Samuel Eliot, requested a report on music instruction from the school that year, the reply praised the effect of music on the students and the quality of Mason's instruction:

> Many who at the outset of the experiment believed they had neither ear or voice, now sing with confidence and considerable accuracy; and others who could hardly tell one sound from another, now sing the scale with ease; sufficiently proving that the musical susceptibility is in a good degree improvable. The alacrity with which the lesson is entered upon, and the universal attention with which it is received, are among its great recommendations; they show that the children are agreeably employed; and we are certain that they are innocently employed. We have never known, when, unless extraordinary engagements prevented, they were so glad to remain a half-hour or more, to pursue the exercise after the regular hours of session. They prefer the play of a hard musical lesson to any out-of-door sports; of course understanding that there are some exceptions. Of the great moral effect of vocal music, there can be no question. A song introduced in the middle of the session, has been invariably followed with excellent effect. It is a relief to the wearisomeness of constant study. It excites the listless, and calms the turbulent and uneasy. It seems to re-nerve the mind, and prepare all for more vigorous intellectual action.[17]

During the school year Mason exhibited his students in performance. One of the performances was visited by a reporter from the *Boston Musical Gazette,* who was impressed by the progress of Mason's almost four hundred students. He wrote:

> The performance of the scholars under his management was truly remarkable for a readiness in answering every question put to them. The rudiments, as far as they had progressed, seemed to be perfectly familiar, and they appeared to thoroughly understand every illustration upon the blackboard. . . . The time and expense required can be but small, and the exercise must be a pleasurable relaxation from severer studies. All instruction is given by means of the black board, and no book is used except the little note book of songs; of course everything is done by familiar illustration; slow indeed, as it should be, but sure.[18]

On August 6, 1838, the subcommittee visited the program and expressed satisfaction with it. On August 14, the annual school exhibition was held in the South Baptist Church. It began with the song "Flowers, Wild Wood Flowers."[19]

The Magna Charta of Music Education. The exhibition concert, a great success, convinced many people that music should be included in the school curriculum. On August 28, 1838, the Boston School Committee approved a motion to instruct the committee on music to appoint a teacher of vocal music in the public schools of Boston. By this action, music was approved for what may have been the first time in the United States as a subject of the public school curriculum, like English and mathematics, to be supported with school funds. Music had been taught in schools before but never as an integral subject of the curriculum. This landmark action was referred to in the annual report of the Boston Academy of Music (July 1, 1839) as the "Magna Charta of Music Education."[20]

Lowell Mason was appointed superintendent of music, the first supervisor of music in the United States. He had the authority to hire his assistants to teach music. Their terms of employment did not require the approval of the superintendent of schools but rather were a private matter between Mason and themselves. Mason hired Jonathan Woodman, organist of the Boston Academy, as his only assistant in the first year. Some of Mason's former students, A. N. Johnson, G. F. Root, A. J. Drake, and J. A. Johnson, were appointed soon after to teach music in the Boston grammar schools and in two suburbs. All enjoyed later careers of distinction, and Root gained fame as a composer. By 1844 Mason was teaching in six schools and supervising ten teachers in ten other schools; he ran the program for seven years.

Despite Mason's success in developing and supervising the music program, he was open to public criticism. As is true of almost any successful public figure, he had enemies. There were numerous music teachers in Boston, and some were jealous of Mason's success. One was H. W. Day, a Boston tune book compiler, singing school master, and editor of the *American Journal of Music and Musical Visitor.* Day charged Mason, a Congregationalist, with operating the music program on a sectarian basis because all of the music teachers were Congregationalists like himself. Theocratic Massachusetts had once taxed all its citizens to support the Congregationalist Church. In 1845 the only teacher who was not a Congregationalist, Benjamin F. Baker, had been fired. The eager and activist Unitarians rallied behind Baker.

The most damaging attack was Day's criticism of Mason's financial arrangement with the schools. Mason received one hundred thirty dollars per year for each school with a music program. The teacher was paid eighty dollars, twenty dollars was spent for piano rental, and Mason kept the remaining thirty dollars. Day charged that Mason earned too much money for his position. Finally, Day attacked Mason's teaching, saying that he did not really understand Pestalozzianism and that his students learned little.[21]

A campaign of letters and newspaper articles by Day over an extended period persuaded the Boston School Committee that Mason had to be replaced. Wilson analyzed the situation as follows:

> Day had escalated a previous state of professional animosity among musicians into a continual and public state of seige upon Mason. The School Committee was without doubt embarrassed by Day's editorializing, which, in effect, made members out to be goats for allowing Mason to work the schools for personal financial gain and aggrandizement at the expense of the city.[22]

The committee did not accuse Mason of impropriety or incompetence, and despite the flimsy evidence it gave him no opportunity to defend himself before voting to relieve him of his position. He lost his job in 1845 without official warning or recourse.[23] Mason's friend on the committee, Charles Gordon, wrote about why Mason was fired: "The only reason given . . . was, that as you had held the office for several years . . . it was proper to give Mr. Baker . . . the encouragement of the office."[24]

Mason retained strong political support among former school committee members and from Horace Mann, Josiah Quincy, Jr., the next mayor of Boston, and others. He was rehired within six months of losing his job and stayed with the Boston public schools until 1851.[25]

THE SPREAD OF SCHOOL MUSIC

Boston was an important center for intellectual and cultural leadership, but other cities and regions of the new nation also demonstrated deep interest in education and music. As Lowell Mason learned when he moved to Savannah, the port cities of the Middle States and the South were more closely tied to the musical life of Europe than New England, where native singing masters had dominated the musical scene for so long. New York, Connecticut, Maryland, the District of Columbia, New Jersey, Kentucky, and Ohio all had localities where music appears to have been introduced into the schools at an early date.

New York. The opening of the Erie Canal in 1825 did more than pave the way for New York City to become the financial center of the world; it also created a future for cities along its course. Schools in such cities as Utica, Palmyra, and Buffalo showed an early interest in school music. Palmyra reportedly considered a proposal for adding music to the school curriculum as early as 1831.[26] Music was reported to have been taught in the schools of Buffalo in 1837.[27] Although the exact date is questionable, the process of introducing music into the curriculum included interested citizens, singing societies, and school boards.[28]

Ebenezer Leach taught music at the gymnasium in Utica about the time of the Palmyra proposal (1831), according to Sunderman, but it was 1845 before music was officially adopted.[29] New York City and the Public School Society hired Darius E. Jones to teach music at School Number 10 in 1836. There was concern about the expense involved and the possibility that it might interfere with the teaching of other subjects. Several cities in the state had early starting dates for school music programs— Rochester (1842), Oswego County (1842), Alleghany County (1844), and Syracuse (1852). The spread of school music over most of the regions of the state may be explained by the ease of transportation on the Erie Canal and the rivers, as well as by the number of New Yorkers who attended Mason's conventions in Boston and New York City.

Maryland. Levi Wilder, a singing school master as well as secretary of the Boston Academy 1836 Class-Convention, introduced music to the schools of Baltimore in 1843. He was helped by citizens from Germany. A concert was given by his students in July of that year. William Tarbutton was hired to join Wilder in 1845. In 1844 Wilder published the second edition of a tiny (5 inch by 3 ¾ inch) book entitled *Musical Elementary Embracing Inductive Steps on the Rudiments of Music, Part 1.* The introductory material sheds light on Wilder's methods of teaching. He recommends not using the book until after the children have sung songs by rote "for a long time." He suggests that the children have the printed words of the songs during this period. The lessons in the book are to be "passed over with the book in hand, interspersed with such illustrations from the teacher as may be thought necessary." Then the students were assigned to commit the facts to memory before the next meeting. Much use of the blackboard or, "far better," large cards was recommended.[30]

District of Columbia. The city of Washington hired John Hill Hewitt, the first music teacher in the city schools, in 1843. Hewitt, the eldest son of composer James Hewitt, was employed to teach for an hour during each of two days of the week. This schedule is reminiscent of Lowell Mason's year of voluntary teaching. Hewitt's students performed so well in an examination at the end of the year that the school board extended the teaching to more schools and awarded Hewitt a salary of $175.

The schools of the port city of Georgetown (later part of Washington) had the benefit of a year of free teaching by a Mr. Daniel in 1857. It led to the hiring of a "music master" in 1864, but before that time Mr. Daniel had been hired by the city council of Washington to teach in the schools of the capital. From 1860, when Daniel began in Washington, music has continued as a regular part of the curriculum.

Connecticut. Despite the presence of such early promoters of school music as William Channing Woodbridge and Elam Ives, Connecticut was slow in introducing music into the school curriculum. This was due, in part, to strong resistance to the idea of common schools. Henry Barnard, like Woodbridge, was a graduate of Yale and an admirer of Pestalozzi and Fellenberg. He was instrumental in persuading the state legislature to create the State Board of Commissioners of Common Schools. As the first secretary of the board, Barnard founded the *Connecticut Common School Journal*. In 1837 the Connecticut General Assembly voted to collect educational data. Questionnaires were sent to all Connecticut schools in 1838. Eight questions were about music instruction:

> Can you sing by note? Can you play any instrument? Do you teach or cause singing in school, either by rote or by note? Do you use singing as a relieving exercise for ill humor or weariness in schools? Do you use any instrument, or have any used, as an accompaniment to singing? Do you teach to use the proper musical voice in singing? Do you do so from ear, or from knowledge of the physiology of the vocal organs? How many of your pupils prove on trial unable to understand music, or acquire even a moderate degree of proficiency in the practice?[31]

This was probably the first attempt in the United States to collect data on music instruction on a widespread basis and perhaps the earliest example of research in music education. Unfortunately, Barnard's position was eliminated shortly thereafter, and Connecticut did not continue its leadership in music education. However, shortly before leaving the state to become commissioner of schools in Rhode Island, Barnard reported that "Vocal music has been introduced to some extent with the happiest results."[32]

Rhode Island. Barnard was more successful with music in Rhode Island. Providence was one of the many cities that introduced music in the schools in 1844, one year after he became the commissioner of schools.

Pennsylvania. In the late 1830s Pennsylvania state legislator Chauncey Holcomb attempted to amend the school law of 1832 to support compulsory music instruction. The amendment failed in committee because the idea was novel and threatened the success of the complete bill in the legislature. Holcomb was a champion of compulsory music education and spoke about it before learned societies. He discussed the historical descriptions of how music affects people and stated: "Music . . . if properly cultivated . . . [can be used to] improve the state of society, to inculcate patriotism, as well as virtue, and generally, to advance us in refinement and civilization." Holcomb predicted that moral problems would arise from empty leisure time, the lack of a sense of place by

Americans, the ability of Americans to make money, and the unbridled ambition of Americans. He argued that music is a suitable leisure activity, that it provides cultural significance in America, that money-makers could patronize the arts, and that the ambitions could be calmed by music. Holcomb based his appeal for universal instruction in voice, piano, and other instruments on these arguments. He did not persuade the Pennsylvania legislature, however, and music was not made compulsory in the curriculum of that state's schools.[33] There were isolated introductions of school music in various parts of Pennsylvania, including Lancaster, but the contrast with New York State is conspicuous. Pennsylvania was atypical in that music was often introduced at the high school level before it was approved for the lower grades.

New Jersey. Newark had many of the components that characterized those communities that were successful in introducing school music in the 1830s. At the turn of the century there were many music teachers. By 1830 three churches had installed organs, and the Harmonic Society had been established. The next year a second, the Newark Handel and Haydn Society, was founded. A third harmonic society, the Mozart Sacred Society, was also established. William B. Bradbury taught a class of young singers at the Presbyterian Church; public concerts by both traveling professionals and Newark residents were commonplace. Something was missing, however, as music was not introduced into the Newark schools until 1846. It was adopted in Morris County in about 1854.[34] Trenton introduced music in 1842, but with a common proviso—music would be taught in the schools without charge to students, but it "was not to interfere with other studies."

Kentucky. Reports of early music teaching around Lexington are probably references to Joseph Neef's use of music in his Pestalozzian institutions. Louisville's connections with New England and its large German population in the first half of the nineteenth century are characteristics similar to those of other western communities that established early school music programs. Louisville had a number of German singing societies in the 1840s. In the mid 1840s, W. C. Van Meter gave some time to teaching in the schools and was thanked by the board of education in 1846. From then on there were regular music teachers on the staff. William Fallen and Luther Whiting Mason were both teaching there by 1852.

Ohio. The first teacher paid to teach music in Ohio was probably the principal of the Female Seminary in Zanesville, which was the capital of the state from 1810 to 1812. That teacher may have been Jesse P. Hatch, who was named principal in 1845 and given the responsibility of teaching music and writing in both the boys' and girls' schools. Whether this was a new appointment or a reappointment after three years is impossible to know because the minutes of the board were burned with all the contents of Board Secretary Uriah Parke's home.

Zanesville was settled by New England Presbyterians and Episcopalians from Loudon County, Virginia. Hatch belonged to the first group that settled in Putnam, on the south side of the Muskingum River. He came from Vermont, where he had attended Captain Partridge's Military Academy at Norwich before 1839. In that year he drilled the Putnam Greys following a riot that resulted from an antislavery meeting in May 1839. Whether he learned music at Norwich is unknown, as is his relationship to Leonard K. Hatch, who attended Lowell Mason's National Music Convention of 1838. Nevertheless, he used *The Sacred Harp* by Lowell and Timothy Mason in his schools.

Cincinnati has a history of music education worthy of recounting in detail for two reasons: first, it most closely replicates what happened in Boston; second, there is much documentary evidence, which is not the case in other communities. The majority of early inhabitants were from New York, New Jersey, and Pennsylvania, but the community leaders were from New England. Many were graduates of Harvard, Yale, and Dartmouth. A medical school and a theological seminary in Cincinnati attracted some of the most eminent men of the day to their faculties. One musical visitor, Nathaniel D. Gould, wrote:

> Cincinnati, sometimes called the Queen City, seems to stand in the same musical relation to the western country as Boston does to the eastern,-that is, the musical and other educational institutions of the respective regions centre in those cities.[35]

Almost exactly one year after the incorporation of the Boston Academy of Music, Cincinnatians formed the Eclectic Academy of Music with the object "in the first place, to aid in promoting the introduction of vocal music as a branch of education throughout this country."[36] Timothy Mason came from Boston to serve as professor of the academy. The famous preacher Lyman Beecher had just come west to head the new Lane Seminary and to be the pastor of the Second Presbyterian Church. Having left Bowdoin Street Church in Boston and Lowell Mason's outstanding choir, it is understandable that the Reverend Beecher wanted Timothy to come to Cincinnati to build a choir.[37]

The Western Literary Institute and College of Professional Teachers of Cincinnati met each October to hear papers on all kinds of educational subjects. William Nixon, who with his wife conducted the "Logerian Musical Institute" on Fourth Street, was the first to plead the case for music education in 1834. Three years later, at the Seventh Annual Meeting, two papers were read that compare in importance for the future of school music to Woodbridge's speech of 1830. One was by Calvin E. Stowe, who had recently returned from Europe. There, he and his bride, the former Harriet Beecher of the well-known Beecher family, had visited schools. His address was entitled the *Course of Instruction in the Schools of Prussia and Wurtemberg*. It read, in part:

> This branch of instruction can be introduced into all our common schools with the greatest advantage, not only to the comfort and discipline of the pupils, but also to their progress in their other studies.
>
> The students are taught from the blackboard. The different sounds are represented by lines of different lengths, by letters, and by musical notes; and the pupils are thoroughly drilled on each successive principle before proceeding to the next.[38]

Stowe broadened the influence of his report when he delivered it before the Ohio legislature. It became one of the most discussed educational documents of its time.

The 1837 meeting held further interest for school music in the form of a committee report by Timothy Mason and Harriet Stowe's brother, Charles Beecher. The two men had been appointed to the committee in 1836. The committee had a tripartite conclusion: (1) all men can learn to sing; (2) vocal music is of physical, intellectual, and moral benefit as a school subject; and (3) to bring about the introduction of music to the schools the "public mind must be made ready to recognize its desirability" and the "teachers must be qualified." The report mentioned the Boston Academy Class-Conventions and said, "Twenty-three gentlemen thus instructed have gone into the various parts of the United States and instructed with success. . . . In this city also, we are aware of two teachers of public schools, who have been successful in introducing the study into their schools." They pointed out that there was no reason why every teacher should not be expected "as a part of his profession to teach both vocal and instrumental music." All that was needed, they argued, was for the educators of the country to encourage men of professional talent to "cast themselves hand and heart into the grand work of education." The college accepted the report and passed the following resolution:

> *Resolved*, as the settled sentiment of this convention, that the capacity for vocal music is common to mankind, and that vocal music may be employed to great advantage as a means of discipline, of health, and of intellectual and moral advancement; and ought to be part of the daily course of instruction, in all our common schools, as well as higher seminaries.[39]

First Music Classes. Music was taught formally for the first time in the Cincinnati schools in 1838. The classes might have been those taught by the two pupils of Timothy Mason mentioned in the Mason and Beecher report, and other teachers may have followed their lead after the College of Professional Teachers approved music instruction in the schools. It is probable that Mason himself went into the schools and conducted classes gratuitously to promote the cause; his brother did so in Boston during the same year.

When the college convened in October 1838 at the Sixth Street Methodist Church, "several select pieces were sung by a large number of pupils of the Common Schools, led by Mr. Mason."[40] The minutes of the college show that the juvenile choir, "composed of pupils of the different City schools," sang on Thursday and Monday. Of even greater significance is the fact that in June "volunteer exercises in singing, by a portion of the pupils" was part of the Annual Procession and Exhibition of the Common Schools of Cincinnati.[41] Thus it is likely that the academic year 1837–1838 witnessed the first recognized instruction in music in the common schools of the city. The annual report also recognizes that "music has been taught and practised in several of the schools— not by any request of the Board of Trustees, but as a means of rational amusement . . . a useful auxiliary in the promotion of good order. They think it has a tendency to render study more easy and pleasant, to produce a greater harmony of voices and a stronger union of hearts."[42]

During the next several years the board debated whether to hire music instructors. Singing continued, led by either the classroom teachers or approved volunteers from the community. The minutes of the board show that William F. Coburn and Elizabeth Thatcher were thanked for giving their services during the 1843–1844 school year.[43] They were hired to begin teaching on August 12, 1844 (the Cincinnati schools were on an eleven-month schedule at that time).[44] Coburn's salary of $45 a month for thirteen and one-half hours a week in the schools indicates that "music professors" were considered specially qualified employees because male principals earned the same amount. Thatcher taught one third as many hours and was paid twelve dollars a month, only three dollars less than the lowest-paid, full-time women teachers.

Charles Aiken became the outstanding figure in public school music in Cincinnati, although he did not join the staff until 1848. He had given his services as an examiner earlier that year, and when Colburn resigned the board asked Aiken to replace him. Aiken was a Dartmouth graduate who had worked his way west conducting singing schools. He came from a musical family in Goffstown, New Hampshire, but nothing is known about his musical education. His brother, John Calvin Aiken, attended Lowell Mason's 1836 convention, and another brother, Henry, was a soloist with the Boston Handel and Haydn Society, but there is no record of Charles Aiken studying with any of the Boston Academy professors. He had gone on to Saint Louis and was persuaded by a Dartmouth friend, Dr. R. D. Mussey, to return to Cincinnati to establish a singing school in the basement of the Sixth Presbyterian Church. Colburn is reported to have studied with him there.

Another attraction of Cincinnati for Aiken was the chance to study

Hebrew at Lane Seminary and to have access to that institution's large collection of church music. He could also learn about European schools from Calvin Stowe in Cincinnati. Aiken had graduated from Lane before he started teaching for the city, but he preached only once or twice.[45]

During his thirty-one years of service to Cincinnati, Aiken was the first music specialist to teach in the primary grades. He was mentor to a staff that produced books for use in the Cincinnati schools (*The Young Singer, The Young Singer's Manual, The Cincinnati Music Readers*), and he was the city's first superintendent of music. He compiled two books of choral music for use in high schools—*The High School Choralist* and *The Choralist's Companion*. These books, which contained music of high quality, belie the accusation that American music education was satisfied with less than the best. Aiken once wrote to his son, then teaching in Hamilton, "If you find that the Hamiltonians don't appreciate that class of music don't give any more concerts, 'Cast not your pearls before swine' is good doctrine."[46]

Music Education in Other Cities. Several larger cities established music programs before the Civil War, although in many the subject did not remain in the curriculum for long periods of time. Unique among these cities is San Francisco. Music was a high school subject there in 1851, before it was adopted as a curricular subject in the grammar schools. Galveston instituted a program in 1847 and San Antonio in 1853. An early example of state funds being used for the teaching of music came about with the establishment of the Texas Institute for the Blind in 1857.[47] Detroit began a music program in the 1850s.[48] Chicago, Memphis, Saint Louis, Terra Haute, Cleveland, and Columbus[49] had music instruction in their schools, although for some of these it was not until after the Civil War that a stable, unified program was in place.

THE NEW MUSIC EDUCATION LITERATURE

The introduction of music into the school curriculum was a glorious event for American education because it opened the way for the development of music education as it is known today. There was, however, one ironic aspect of this milestone in music education history that was somewhat unfavorable to future developments. Lowell Mason and his colleagues struggled to replace the indigenous music of the singing school with a kind of music reminiscent of that produced by the lesser European composers. Britton wrote:

> By 1838, when Lowell Mason succeeded in introducing music to the public schools, music teachers found to be better music the blander and, to modern ears, more insipid music of English and third-rate Continental composers, and such music was gradually adopted . . . to replace the virile

native product of the days of early sovereignty. . . . Music education, although created and nurtured by a popular love of music, has nevertheless always operated at a certain distance from the well-springs of American musical life, both popular and artistic. Music education in the United States has tended to create a world of its own with its own people, music, and thought patterns. . . . Since folk or popular music has been considered to lack gentility, and since the highly artistic forms of European art music have been little understood by the public, the music educator has found himself in the position of trying to find understandable music that could be taken as "classical." The term "polite" is perhaps as good as any other to characterize much of the music utilized in schools from the time of Lowell Mason to the present day.[50]

Britton's analysis of the qualitative problem of music education literature raises the question of why music educators chose to disdain their native music in favor of an insipid, even banal genre for the education of children. One answer lies in the relationship between the young country and the old, the culture of which many Americans considered to be immeasurably better. American colonists of English extraction had always maintained a strong tie to the musical life of the mother country. When English parish church congregations began singing fuging tunes and adorning their singing with graces and ornaments during the Restoration, Americans did the same. Then, in the last half of the eighteenth century, there was a break in the relationship and American singing school masters had the chance to develop their own style. They flourished in isolation, first in an atmosphere of revolution and later in the rural southern and western regions of the new nation. As the ties with England were restored and European musicians reappeared on the scene, Americans once again turned to Old World models. Unfortunately, it was not a period of great English church music. There was no Thomas Tallis or Orlando Gibbons to imitate. The style adopted by Lowell Mason, Thomas Hastings, and others who wrote for both school and church was not vigorous or innovative.

Mason contributed some lasting hymn tunes. "Olivet" ("My Faith Looks Up To Thee"), "Missionary Hymn" ("From Greenland's Icy Mountains"), and "Bethany" ("Nearer My God to Thee") are the best known. He is credited in many hymnals with arranging "Antioch" ("Joy to the World") from Handel, but William Chalmers Covert believes that honor belongs to "Clark of Canterbury."[51] Covert also points out the unlikelihood of Mason incorporating the elements of a fuging tune, as in "Antioch," into one of his hymn tunes. Mason published an anthem entitled "Joy to the World" in the 1827 edition of *The Boston Handel and Haydn Society Collection*. The only musical resemblance to the hymn tune is in separate measures of an accompaniment passage but not in the voice parts.

Another factor must be considered in regard to both the musical and literary material used in nineteenth-century schools. The development of taste in music, prose, or poetry was not uppermost in the minds of those writing the textbooks—moral development was. For that reason, the music textbooks closely paralleled the McGuffey Readers. The quality of music education literature was not of primary importance, and children were expected to learn to read music with inferior musical materials. Their interest would be aroused later, when they had learned to read and could participate in choral performances of European oratorios. Many nineteenth-century music educators expressed the conviction that children should learn to read music before being given the opportunity to sing the choruses.

A different kind of answer lies in the commercialism of Lowell Mason and his colleagues, whose music replaced the authentic and virile Yankee music. As has been documented, Mason had an excellent business sense. By creating a need for new music, he and his colleagues opened a huge market that they themselves satisfied. A great deal of money was made in the process. However, in reflecting on the nature of the literature of American music education since Mason's time, one must wonder what might have been accomplished in American schools if a more musical genre of literature was selected as the foundation for education in music. Perhaps the goal of universal music literacy would have been more readily achievable.

In the publisher's introduction to *The Sacred Harp or Eclectic Harmony*, an explanation was offered of how the works of European classical composers came to be included in American songbooks by compilers such as Lowell Mason:

> Subjects or arrangements from celebrated composers, as Beethoven, Haydn, Mozart and others. These authors never wrote psalm and hymn tunes. The tunes ascribed to them are *themes* from their various works, and arranged in their present form by other composers. In many instances, only the principal ideas contained in the tune, have been derived from the author to whom it has been ascribed. In such cases, more or less of the tune is the composition of the arranger, and it is usual to say, "Subject from Beethoven," "Arranged from Mozart," "Arranged from Gregorian Chant," &c. Many composers have in this way greatly extended the boundaries of Psalmody, and added much to the richness and variety of church music. The Sacred Harp contains a great amount of music of this class arranged by the Editors, and *all* such tunes are claimed as *property*, under the law made and provided for the protection of such property. To arrange psalmody from such peculiar materials with judgment, accuracy, and elegance, as much scientific knowledge and labor are requisite as for composing new tunes. Music of this class was first introduced into this country in the Handel and Haydn Collection, by Lowell Mason, and his arrangements from European subjects in that work have often been inserted in other publications *without permission*.

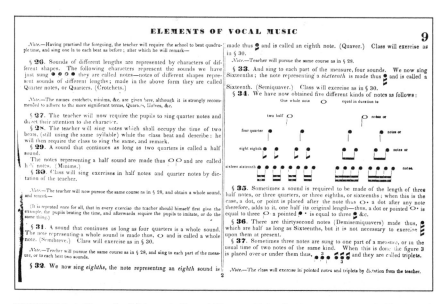

FIGURE 8–1 Page 9 of *Mason's Sacred Harp or Eclectic Harmony: New Collection of Church Music,* by Lowell Mason and Timothy Mason. Cincinnati: Truman and Smith, 1837.

SUMMARY

The common school movement, which gained momentum toward the end of the third decade of the nineteenth century, was germinal to universal instruction in music. Nonmusicians such as William Channning Woodbridge, Horace Mann, Henry Barnard, Calvin Stowe, and Charles Beecher introduced Pestalozzianism to music teachers and helped mount a campaign to make music a regular part of the curriculum. By being adopted early in a few major cities respected for their culture, music was given an opportunity to be a part of the school experience of children in many communities across the land. Before 1860, these tended to be the larger cities, but the fact that a few towns like Palmyra, New York, and Zanesville, Ohio, were able to add music as a regular subject for all children pointed to a brighter future in the years to come.

It should also be noted that two opportunities were missed. The first was the chance to make music instruction in the schools truly Pestalozzian by developing creative individuality in American children. The other was the opportunity to describe the professional teacher as an individual who believed that the development of his artistic (musical) nature was equally important to the mastery of academic knowledge and methodology. Holcomb in Pennsylvania, and Stowe and Beecher in Ohio, presented ideas along these lines. Had they been adopted, they could have influenced not only music education but the entire course of public education in the United States.

The success of the musical citizens of Boston in making music a part of the common school curriculum depended on several factors. There had to be a critical mass of citizens experienced in, or at least appreciative of, singing. Therefore, there had to be enough church choirs and singing schools offered by singing masters, even though some of the masters were self-trained. There also had to be strong public support for the developing common school system. There was the need for musicians who loved children. Finally, there was the need for volunteerism.

Lowell Mason contributed to more than one of the essential elements. He earned a reputation first as one who could improve church music, then he delighted Bostonians by demonstrating the musicality of their children. To make certain that those responsible for the developing common school system understood the musical accomplishments of which schoolchildren were capable, he gave time to teaching in Hawes School in the 1837 school year. Cincinnati went through a similar sequence of events. Boston and Cincinnati provided the pattern for the rest of the country to follow.

NOTES

1. James A. Keene, *A History of Music Education in Vermont 1700–1900* (Macomb, IL: Glenridge Publishing, 1987), p. 95.
2. *Encyclopedia Britannica*, 1958 ed., s.v. "Choral Singing" by Albert Stoessel.
3. Ralph Nading Hill, ed., *The College on the Hill* (Hanover, NH: Dartmouth Publications, 1964), p. 208.
4. Edward Bailey Birge, *History of Public School Music in the United States* (Washington, DC: Music Educators National Conference, 1928), p. 10.
5. Henry M. Brooks, *Olden-Time Music: A Compilation from Newspapers and Books* (Boston: Ticknor, 1888), p. 196.
6. "Handel & Haydn Society," *The Columbian Centinel*, December 23, 1815, in Brooks, *Olden-Time Music*, pp. 190–91.
7. Gerald Lee Gutek, *Joseph Neef, The Americanization of Pestalozzianism* (University, AL: University of Alabama Press, 1978), p. 7.
8. Claude K. Sluder, "Music in New Harmony, Indiana, 1825–65" (Ph.D. dissertation, Indiana University, 1987), p. 141.
9. Ibid., p. 115.
10. Louis C. Elson, *The History of American Music* (New York: Macmillan, 1915), pp. 73–93, in Lloyd F. Sunderman, "The Era of Beginnings in American Music Education (1830–1940)," *Journal of Research in Music Education* 3 (1971): 35.
11. Betty Bandel, *Sing the Lord's Song in a Strange Land* (East Brunswick, NJ: Associated University Presses, 1981), pp. 54–59.

12. Porter Gale Perrin, "Thomas Green Fessenden," *University of Maine Studies* 28 (January 1926): 25.
13. M. Hale, *Annals of the Town of Keene, New Hampshire*, 1859, n.p.
14. School Committee, "Report," *Boston Musical Gazette: Devoted to the Science of Music,* December 5, 12, 1838, p. 123. Report completed in edition of December 26, 1836.
15. Ibid., December 26, 138.
16. Wilson, "A Documentary History of Music in the Public Schools of the City of Boston, 1830–1850," vol. 2. (Ph.D. dissertation, University of Michigan, 1973) pp. 110–31.
17. *Boston Musical Gazette,* July 25, 1838.
18. *Boston Musical Gazette,* May 30, 1838.
19. A. W. Brayley, *The Musician,* November 1905, reported in Edward Bailey Birge, *History of Public School Music in the United States* (Washington, DC: Music Educators National Conference, 1928), p. 53.
20. Birge, *History of Public School Music,* p. 55.
21. Samuel L. Flueckiger, "Why Lowell Mason Left the Boston Schools," *Music Educators Journal* 22 (January–February 1936): 20–21.
22. Wilson, vol. 1, pp. 128–29.
23. Flueckiger, "Why Lowell Mason Left the Boston Schools," pp. 20–21.
24. Pemberton, *Lowell Mason: His Life and Works,* p. 122.
25. Wilson, pp. 119, 132.
26. "Music in Common Schools," *American Annals of Education and Instruction* 1 (July 1831): 330.
27. Clifford V. Buttelman, "A Century of Music in Buffalo Schools," *Music Educators Journal* 39 (September–October 1952): 19.
28. Terese M. Volk, "The Growth and Development of Music Education in the Public Schools of Buffalo, New York, 1843–1988," *Bulletin of Historical Research in Music Education* 9 (July 1988): 91–118.
29. Lloyd F. Sunderman, *Historical Foundations of Music Education in the United States* (Metuchen, NJ: Scarecrow Press, 1971), pp. 111–16.
30. L. Wilder, *Musical Elementary,* pt. 1, 2nd ed. (Baltimore: Robert Neilson, 1844), pp. 4–5.
31. "Mr. Barnard's Labors in Connecticut from 1838 to 1842," *Barnard's American Journal of Education* 1 (1856): 695. In Sunderman, "The Era of Beginnings . . . ," p. 38.
32. "Third Annual Report of the Secretary of the Board of Commissioners of Common Schools," *The Connecticut Common School Journal* 3 (May 1841): 254.
33. J. Terry Gates, "Lowell Mason's America: Social Reconstructionism and Music in the Schools," Unpublished paper presented at the Symposium, Music in American Schools, College Park, MD, 1988.
34. C. H. Kaufman, *Music in New Jersey, 1655–1860* (East Brunswick, NJ: Farleigh Dickinson University Press, 1981).
35. Nathaniel D. Gould, *Church Music in America* (Boston: A. N. Johnson, 1853), p. 138.
36. *Cincinnati Daily Gazette* 7 (April 16, 1834): 2.
37. Gould, *Church Music in America,* p. 139.
38. C. E. Stowe, "Report on the Course of Instruction in the Common Schools of Prussia and Wirtemberg," *Transactions of the Seventh Annual Meeting of the Western Literary Society and College of Professional Teachers* (Cincinnati: James H. Allbach, 1838), p. 217.

39. *Transactions of the Seventh Annual Meeting of the Western Literary Society*, p. 18.
40. *Cincinnati Daily Gazette* 12 (October 3, 1838): 2.
41. *Minutes of the Board of Trustees and Visitors of Common Schools*, Cincinnati, June 18, 1838, vol. 1.
42. *Ninth Annual Report of the Trustees and Visitors of Common Schools for the school year ending June 30, 1838* (Cincinnati: Daily Times Office, 1838), p. 4.
43. *Minutes of the Board and Trustees of Common Schools*, Cincinnati, September 2, 1844, vol. 3.
44. *Appendix to the Common School Report for June 30, 1844*, September 2, 1844 (Cincinnati: Daily Gazette Office, 1844), p. 21.
45. Interview with Carrie Aiken Bagley (daughter of Charles Aiken) by Charles Gary, Cincinnati, April 17, 1950.
46. Letter from Charles Aiken to Walter Aiken, January 21, 1877.
47. David W. Sloan, "History of Texas Public School Music" (Ph.D. dissertation, University of Texas, 1970).
48. Mary E. Teal, "Musical Activities in Detroit from 1701 through 1870" (Ph.D. dissertation, University of Michigan, 1964).
49. Miriam B. Kapfer, "Early Public School Music in Columbus, 1845–1854," *Journal of Research in Music Education* 15 (Fall 1967): 191–200.
50. Allen P. Britton, "Music Education: An American Specialty," in Paul Henry Lang, ed., *One Hundred Years of Music in America* (New York: Schirmer, 1961), pp. 214–15.
51. William Chalmers Covert, ed., *Handbook to the Hymnal* (Chicago: Presbyterian Board of Christian Education, 1946), p. 141.

BIBLIOGRAPHY

Appendix to the Common School Report for June 30, 1844, September 2, 1844. Cincinnati: Daily Gazette Office.

Bandel, Betty, *Sing the Lord's Song in a Strange Land*. East Brunswick, NJ: Associated University Presses, 1981.

Birge, Edward Bailey, *History of Public School Music in the United States*. Washington, DC: Music Educators National Conference, 1928.

"Report," School Committee, *Boston Musical Gazette: Devoted to the Science of Music*, December 5, 12, 1838.

Britton, Allen P. "Music Education: An American Specialty," in Paul Henry Lang, ed., *One Hundred Years of Music in America* (New York: Schirmer, 1961).

Buttelman, Clifford V. "A Century of Music in Buffalo Schools," *Music Educators Journal* 39 (September–October 1952).

Covert, William Chalmers, ed., *Handbook to the Hymnal*. Chicago: Presbyterian Board of Christian Education, 1946.

Ellis, H. "Lowell Mason and the Manual of the Boston Academy of Music." *Journal of Research in Music Education* 3 (Spring 1955).

Elson, Louis C. *The History of American Music*. New York: Macmillan, 1915.

Fisher, James L. "The Origin and Development of Public School Music in Baltimore to 1870." Ed.D. dissertation, University of Maryland, 1970.

Flueckiger, Samuel L. "Why Lowell Mason Left the Boston Schools," *Music Educators Journal* (February 1936).

Gary, Charles L. "A History of Music Education in the Cincinnati Public Schools." *Journal of Research in Music Education* 2 (Spring 1954).

Gates, J. Terry. "Lowell Mason's America: Social Reconstructionism and Music in the Schools." Paper read at the Symposium, Music in American Schools. Edited by Bruce Wilson. College Park, MD: University of Maryland, 1988.

Gould, Nathaniel D. *Church Music in America.* Boston: A. N. Johnson, 1853.

Gutek, Gerald Lee. *Joseph Neef, The Americanization of Pestalozzianism.* University, AL: University of Alabama Press, 1978.

Hale, M. *Annals of the Town of Keene, New Hampshire,* 1859.

Hill, Ralph Nading, ed. *The College on the Hill.* Hanover, NH: Dartmouth Publications, 1964.

Johnson, H. Earle. *Musical Interludes in Boston: 1795-1830.* New York: AMS Press, 1967.

Kapfer, Miriam B. "Early Public School Music in Columbus, 1845-1854." *Journal of Research in Music Education* 15 (Fall 1967).

Kaufman, C. H. *Music in New Jersey, 1655-1860.* East Brunswick, NJ: Farleigh Dickinson University Press, 1981.

Keene, James A. *A History of Music Education in the United States.* Hanover, NH: University Press of New England, 1982.

Mark, Michael L. *Source Readings in Music Education History.* New York: Schirmer, 1982.

Mason, Lowell. *Manual of the Boston Academy of Music for Instruction.* Boston: Carter, Hendee, 1843.

Minutes of the Board of Trustees and Visitors of Common Schools, Cincinnati, June 18, 1838, vol. 1.

Minutes of the Board and Trustees of Common Schools, Cincinnati, September 2, 1844, vol. 3.

"Music in the Common Schools," *American Annals of Education and Instruction* 1 (July 1831).

Ninth Annual Report of the Trustees and Visitors of Common Schools for the School Year Ending June 30, 1838, Cincinnati: Daily Times Office, 1838.

Pemberton, Carol A. "Critical Days for Music in American Schools." *Journal of Research in Music Education* 36 (Summer 1988).

———. "Revisionist Historians: Writers Reflected in Their Writings." *Journal of Research in Music Education* 35 (Winter 1987).

Perrin, Porter Gale. "Thomas Green Fessenden." *University of Maine Studies* 28 (January 1926).

Pestalozzi, Johann Heinrich. *How Gertrude Teaches Her Children.* Translated by Holland and Turner. Syracuse, NY: C. W. Bardeen (original book published 1801).

Sloan, David W. "History of Texas Public School Music." Ph.D. dissertation, University of Texas, 1970.

Sluder, Claude K. "Music in New Harmony, Indiana, 1823-65." Ph.D. dissertation, Indiana University, 1987.

Stowe, Calvin E. "Report on the Course of Instruction in the Common Schools of Prussia and Wurtemberg." *Transactions of the Seventh Annual Meeting of the Western Literary Society and College of Professional Teachers.* Cincinnati: James H. Allbach, 1838.

Sunderman, Lloyd F. "The Era of Beginnings in American Music Education (1830–1840)." *Journal of Research in Music Education* 3 (Spring 1956).

——. *Historical Foundations of Music Education in the United States.* Metuchen, NJ: Scarecrow Press, 1971.

Teal, Mary E. "Musical Activities in Detroit from 1701 through 1870." Ph.D. dissertation, University of Michigan, 1964.

"Third Annual Report of the Secretary of the Board of Commissioners of Common Schools." *The Connecticut Common School Journal* 3 (May 1841).

Transactions of the Seventh Annual Meeting of the Western Literary Institute and College of Professional Teachers. Cincinnati: James H. Allbach, 1988.

Volk, Terese M. "The Growth and Development of Music Education in the Public Schools of Buffalo, New York, 1843–1988." *The Bulletin of Historical Research in Music Education* 9 (July 1988).

Wilder, L, *Musical Elementary,* pt. 1, 2d ed. Baltimore: Robert Neilson, 1844.

Wilson, Bruce. "A Documentary History of Music in the Public Schools of the City of Boston, 1830–1850," 2 vols. Ph.D. dissertation, University of Michigan, 1973.

PART IV

THE GROWTH OF
MUSIC EDUCATION

9

MUSIC EDUCATION IN AN INDUSTRIALIZING AMERICA

William Woodbridge, Lowell Mason, Elam Ives, Calvin Stowe, Charles Aiken, and a few others are credited with establishing a foothold for music in the public schools when the common school curriculum was established in the middle third of the nineteenth century. Recognition must also be given to the those who consolidated the gains during the years following the Civil War. In Boston and Cincinnati, the eastern and western cultural centers, music has continued in the schools from the time of its introduction. This was not the case in other cities such as Buffalo, Philadelphia, Chicago, San Francisco, and Columbus, where the position of music instruction in the schools was vulnerable. Whatever the reason for the discontinuation of music education—budgets disrupted by the frequent financial panics, unavailability of competent teachers, or doubt of the value of music education—the interruption is a reminder that the final thirty-five years of the nineteenth century were a critical period for the development of music education in the United States.

Music in the Primary Grades. The foothold of music in the schools was tenuous at best. For many years programs consisted of instruction by music teachers only in the grammar school grades. In Cincinnati, a Mr. E. Pease taught music in the primary grades of the Eleventh District School during the spring of 1853, nine years after the introduction of music, and his experiment was successful enough to earn him an appointment to teach music in the primary department of the schools.[1] Charles Aiken was teaching in the primary grades in the early part of 1855. During August of that year a six-year course of study was adopted for the city schools. Although full twelve-year music programs were unusual before the Civil War, Aiken had begun teaching in the high schools with the opening of the Hughes and Woodward High Schools in 1852, thus providing the city with music instruction for all public school students. This was only five years after the opening of the first public secondary school in Cincinnati. The title of Tunison's 1888 publication *Presto, From Singing School to the May Festival* (Cincinnati), made it seem easier than it was to have such programs approved.[2]

Post-War America. At the end of the Civil War the United States was emotionally exhausted. In 1865 historian S. L. Mayer called the country a "cultural backwater." But, as Charles Francis Adams observed in 1868 when he returned from seven years as ambassador to Great Britain, there was a "greatly enlarged grasp of enterprise." This, along with the inventions of Alexander Graham Bell, Thomas Edison, George Eastman, and others, would transform an isolated social experiment into a world leader before the end of the century. In the process, America's first philosopher, William James, developed the school of thought eventually known as *pragmatism.*

"Scientific" Music Education. Schoolmen, as they were known at that time, were inclined to be pragmatic. Enjoyment had been one of the many values that the early supporters of school music had mentioned in urging the introduction of the subject. Improved attendance, pupils' affection for their music teachers, and attitudes toward public performances indicate that students found enjoyment in music instruction and activities. Music reading skill remained a goal for early school music classes as it had been for the singing schools before them, but those musicians among the first generation of public school music teachers knew there was more to the art than the mere acquisition of skill. After the war, however, pragmatic administrators were not interested in enjoyment or beauty, and it would be almost a century before aesthetic reasons would be used as a rationale for music in the schools. As the nation began to forge a business society, school boards and administrators began to favor subjects that reflected the new mechanization. They wanted subjects organized scientifically and evaluated accurately. Thomas Lothrop, superintendent of the Buffalo schools, wrote:

> Musical instruction should be systematized and become a part of the graded course, both teachers and pupils being held to a strict account for the amount of their work in this as other studies, by term and annual examinations. By a careful apportionment of the elementary principles

among the different grades the pupils will secure, while learning the sounds and combinations of letters required in reading the language they speak, such a familiarity with music that they can read it as readily as the letters of the alphabet.[3]

Apparently the superintendent found music instruction satisfactory. He reported:

In July last, by direction of the Council, a teacher of Vocal Music was employed for the term of six months. He is required to visit each school twice a week, and devote half an hour to instruction and practice in Singing in each at every visit. The gentleman employed has thus far devoted himself assiduously and faithfully to this business, perambulating the City from District to District, in sunshine and in storm; and it is gratifying to me to be able to state that in most of the Schools he is a welcome visitor, and a valuable coadjutor in the work of education. The progress the children have already made in acquiring a knowledge of music, and the decided testimonials of public approbation have resulted in the re-employment of the Teacher for another term of six months. The experiment of introducing vocal music as a branch of education into our public schools has thus been made, although singing was introduced as a recreation into several of the schools soon after the free school system were established. Whenever the teacher was able to lead in music, he found the children ready to follow; and thus to some extent music was introduced before the present teacher commenced his labours, and many of the children were able to sing before music was taught as an elementary study. The success of the experiment has thus far exceeded the anticipations of its friends, and little doubt now exists of its becoming a permanent branch of juvenile instruction.[4]

The Music Specialist. The elementary schools were created to teach the elements, and a "careful apportionment of the elementary principles," as stated by Superintendent Lothrop, is exactly what many music teachers attempted during this period. Armed with philosopher Herbert Spencer's assurance that the arts could be taught scientifically, music teachers obliged by developing materials and methods that presented information about music in a "scientific" way. Knowledge about music was considered important, and pupils were tested regularly. The approach to reading music at sight was treated similarly, with much reliance on recitation by individual students. The responsibility for imparting information on the elements of music and for developing skills was turned over to the classroom teacher. Music specialists became supervisors who visited the schools on a regular schedule to test the pupils, improve the quality of their singing, and assign new material to be learned. This widely practiced arrangement, which gave rise to granting the title *supervisor* to school music specialists, was begun in some school systems before the Civil War.

MUSIC INSTRUCTIONAL MATERIAL

Many supervisors were involved in the preparation of books, charts, and examinations that would help children learn music. Carefully planned series of exercises or songs on which children were to be drilled, preferably daily, were created. This could be done efficiently only with the involvement of the classroom teacher, an arrangement that influenced the school textbooks of the time. The movable "do" system of solmization had been almost universally adopted by then. School music still meant singing, and much of the song material was created for didactic purposes. The texts were frequently designed to impart secularized lessons drawn from Protestant Christian morality. Supervisors began to emphasize methodology as school music expanded, and it became an important part of the business of textbook publishers.

Graded Music Series. Shortly after the Civil War, the first graded music series began to appear to satisfy the need for materials to help children learn to read music. Lowell Mason and his followers believed in the Pestalozzian concept of the "thing before the sign," which later became known as the rote song method. Others, however, believed that children should learn to read printed music before they sang songs. The differences grew into a pedagogical controversy that lasted for the rest of the century. During this period, numerous graded music series were published to support music teachers on both sides of the controversy. The term "graded music series" was used first by Lowell Mason in reference to his *The Song Garden*, a three-volume set that he began in 1864.

In 1850 Joseph Bird published a pamphlet entitled *To Teachers of Music,* in which he disagreed with Mason's rote method as advocated in the *Manual of the Boston Academy of Music*. Bird wrote in the pamphlet:

> Teach a class by rote and the "Elements" and a few will read, but the greater number give up in despair. . . . We believe the only way by which reading music will become as universal as the reading of our language is by changing the system, and making books and teaching from them in the same way we do from our reading books.

Joseph Bird's two volume set, *Vocal Music Readers,* was designed for primary and grammar grades and published by the Oliver Ditson Company in 1861.

The two methods were described in a letter from Osbourne McConathy to the *Louisville Journal*. McConathy's judgment of the rote method was harsh:

> There are two methods adopted by professors of music in teaching children to sing. To illustrate what I mean, it is a uniform habit with some

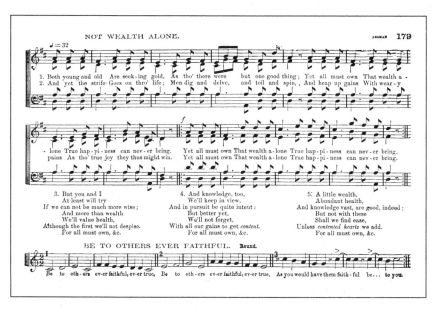

FIGURE 9–1 Page 179 of *The Song-Garden: A Series of School Music Books Progressively Arranged, Each Book Complete in Itself,* 2nd book, by Lowell Mason. Boston: Olive Ditson & Company, 1864.

masters of vocal and instrumental music too, to begin as soon as the children have learned the names of the notes, with very little else, to set them to singing by leading off by the sound of his flute or violin or with his voice, and then require the children to give the same sound by imitating his as best they can. This I call mimicry or teaching to sing by imitation, just as the parrot might catch the air and learn to sing, and to sing tunes readily, and yet not understand anything truly valuable concerning the true principles of music. This method of teaching music lays the foundation in error and hedges up the way to a thorough understanding of this branch of ornamental science. . . . The other method of teaching is directly the reverse of the foregoing, and the master endeavors in the first place to teach the children the principles of music whether vocal or instrumental, and to cause the children to understand them well before he allows them to commence singing. . . . Our children should be thoroughly taught the principles of music, and to such a degree of perfection as to enable them to read off a piece of music with as much ease and readiness as they would read a lesson in prose. . . . A child so taught needs no prompter. He needs no one to lead off upon his flute or fiddle. He makes use of his eyes and not his ears only, and practically employs the intellectual instruction imparted and received, and tunes the voice in varied tones and measures of sweetest melody and enrapturing song.[5]

Most American music educators preferred the moveable *do*; others, the fixed *do* of the French and Italians. Another reading method, "Tonic Sol-fa," which was invented in England around 1840, gained limited acceptance in the United States in the 1880s. Elizabeth Glover developed the system, and John Curwen later improved it. In fact, historical evidence indicates that he simply appropriated Glover's work and represented it as his own.[6] It became the accepted method for teaching music reading in British schools. The system used the movable *do*. The tones of the scale were taught from a tone ladder, or vertical modulator. Notation, using the *sol-fa* syllables, followed the study of the vertical modulator. There was no staff, but the measures were separated by bars. Meter and rhythm were indicated by a system of dots, commas, and dashes. An American version of the system, *The Tonic Sol-Fa Music Course* (Oliver Ditson, 1884), was written by Daniel Batchellor and Thomas Charmbury. The authors wrote in the Introduction:

> The Tonic Sol-fa method has been taught now for fifteen years in the public schools of Great Britain, with such success that it is superseding all other systems of teaching vocal music. It has recently been introduced into several of the public schools of America, and in every instance has won the hearty approval of the teachers.
>
> Without any unnecessary complications, it sets forth in a plain, unmistakable way, the fundamental principles of music. The method is carefully arranged in progressive steps, and is so entirely in accord with true educational principles, that school teachers can and do teach it as successfully as they teach other branches of study.

There was a Tonic Sol-fa Society for a brief period; Theodore Seward of New York City served as president. American teachers finally rejected Tonic Sol-fa because its notation was not traditional and students who learned it would then have to learn standard notation to sing choral music. Tonic Sol-fa is still widely used in Great Britain.

George Loomis. *First Steps in Music* was produced in 1866 by George Loomis, the music supervisor in Indianapolis. This three-book series was distinctive because it introduced music reading by placing notes on or around a single line. The method was similar to that of Guido d'Arezzo as he built on the original red line of the anonymous teacher who sought to assist the monks in approximating the pitches represented by neumes. Staff lines were gradually added until the pupils were reading from a full staff. *First Steps in Music* was in three volumes. The first volume contained exercises on progressively developed staves of from one to five lines, and songs, also on staves of varying numbers of lines. Loomis did not use clefs, meter or key signatures, or accidentals. The second book contained short songs and rounds on five line staves. It too had no clef signs or key signatures, although Loomis indicated the key with a system of his own invention. A number was placed on the staff where the key signature would normally appear. It indicated the degree of the scale for the key of the song. If the number 5 was printed on the

THE

TONIC SOL-FA MUSIC COURSE

FOR SCHOOLS

A SERIES OF EXERCISES AND SONGS IN THE TONIC SOL-FA METHOD, PROGRESSIVELY ARRANGED
IN STEPS; WITH A CORRESPONDING SUPPLEMENTAL COURSE IN THE STAFF NOTATION

BOOK I.

BY

DANIEL BATCHELLOR

AND

THOMAS CHARMBURY.

BOSTON:
OLIVER DITSON COMPANY.
NEW YORK: CHICAGO: PHILA: BOSTON:
C. H. Ditson & Co. Lyon & Healy. J. E. Ditson & Co. John C. Haynes & Co.

FIGURE 9–2a Title page of *The Tonic Sol-Fa Music Course for Schools,* Book 1, by Daniel Batchellor and Thomas Charmbury. Boston: Oliver Ditson & Company, 1894.

third space (C on the G clef), that space was the fifth note of the scale, or C in the key of F. The student simply counted up or down from the indicated line or space. Key signatures were introduced later.

Ivison, Blakeman, Taylor and Company eventually obtained the rights to the series and published it under the title *Progressive Music Lessons.* Two more books were added. The fifth, *The Progressive Glee and Chorus Book,* came out in 1879. In 1898 the American Book Company purchased the publication rights. The series was widely used throughout the midwest during the 1870s and 1880s.[7]

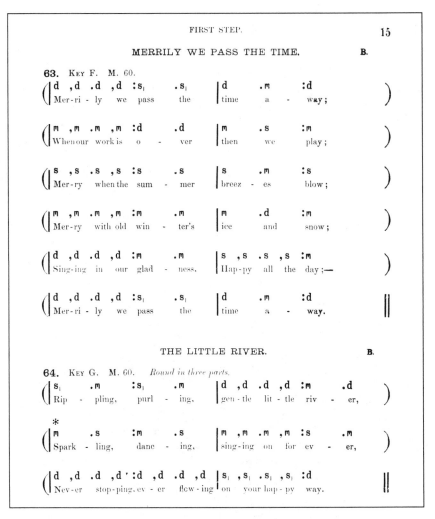

FIGURE 9–2b Page 15 of *The Tonic Sol-Fa Music Course for Schools.*

Luther Whiting Mason. In January 1856 Luther Whiting Mason moved from Louisville to join the Cincinnati music staff. He had been teaching for less than a month when "Mr. Startzman moved that [he] be allowed to teach gratis, the pupils of the 5th and 6th [i.e. the two lowest grades] in the Third District, during the ¾ of an hour that he is not employed teaching the Intermediate School in the same house."[8]

While in Cincinnati, Mason was introduced to the works of Christian Heinrich Hohmann. He used Hohmann's materials in his teaching from that time on. The charts that he prepared from Hohmann were approved by the board of trustees in 1862. With D. H. Baldwin, who later founded the Baldwin Piano Company, Mason was responsible for the "Elements of Music" section of *The Young Singer*, the first of many

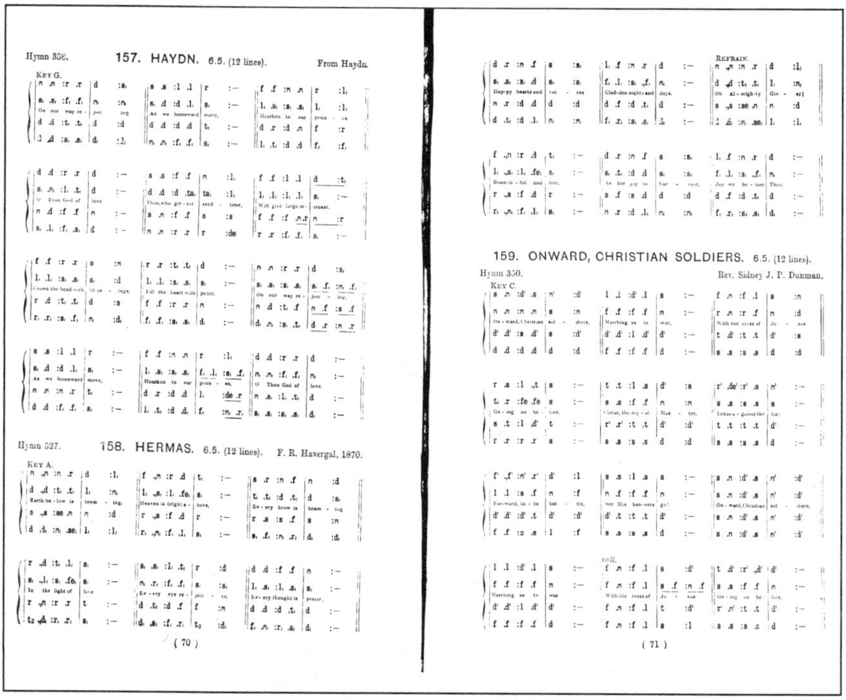

FIGURE 9–3 Page 71 of *The Methodist Sunday-School Tune-Book: A Collection of Tunes for the Hymns and Spiritual Songs Contained in The Methodist Sunday-School Hymn-Book.* London: Wesleyan Methodist Sunday-School Union, n.d.

books prepared by the Cincinnati music staff. In 1864, Mason was lured to Boston to begin lower-grade instruction in music. There he held the title of superintendent of music in the primary schools. He was successful, and H. S. Perkins reported that 14–15 percent of the grammar school pupils could not sing in 1864–1865, but in 1869, after Luther Whiting Mason had been working in the primary grades for four years, the proportion had been reduced to 7 percent.[9] High school music was an even later addition in Boston.

Mason emulated European methods of teaching. He stressed the importance of teaching a body of rote songs from which the elements of music could be drawn for study and understanding. He borrowed the use of charts from Hohmann and is probably responsible for the great popularity they had with publishers and teachers as aids in teaching music. Mason began by using the first five notes of the G major scale, which he taught in a variety of small motives working from one to two measures, to four measures, and finally to a period of eight measures. He employed his own time names, with the rests whispered.[10]

The National Music Course. Mason's devotion to rote singing as the initial experience for children made him an outstanding figure in Ameri-

FIGURE 9–4 Page 7 of the *Practical Course of Instruction in Singing, Prepared on School Principles,* by Christian Heinrich Hohman. Boston: Oliver Ditson, 1856.

can music education. He wrote a pivotal graded series called *The National Music Course,* which was published in 1870 by Ginn Brothers of Boston (soon Ginn and Company). The tremendous popularity of *The National Music Course* helped Ginn and Company achieve financial stability and become a leading publisher of school texts.[11] Also listed as authors on the covers of the books were Julius Eichberg, J. B. Sharland, and H. E. Holt. It quickly became the accepted text from New England to San Francisco. *The National Music Course* was side-bound like most books, rather than end-bound in the style of the singing schools. It was also a model for future graded series.

The National Music Course consisted of seven books—five readers, an intermediate book that included books two and three, and an abridged fourth reader. The series was accompanied by sets of charts to help in music reading. They provided a sequential approach to music reading through all the grades. Much of the song material was based on German folk music.[12] The introduction discussed the philosophy of the authors:

"Singing as it happens," as the celebrated Dr. A. B. Marx terms it, is that which is most common among the people. It is fostered and vigorously perpetuated in our Sunday Schools, and in common schools where no regular instruction in music is given, and where the object is to have the children sing a few simple melodies, without reference to musical culture as such . . .

This kind of singing is not altogether useless, as in many cases there is a freshness and energy about it which serves to awaken a love for singing, and to furnish a basis on which to build a subsequent course of musical instruction.

But there is a wide distinction between this hap-hazard singing and genuine "Rote-Singing." The latter is the *most important* part of instruction, without which in fact there can be no real tuition in vocal music. Genuine rote-singing . . . leads to a discrimination between a musical and unmusical style. . . . We propose in the course of instruction indicated in the series of *National Music Readers and Charts* to do away with all hap-hazard singing. We therefore, start with a regular course of instruction in rote singing, as indicated in the *National Music Teacher* ; and we endeavor to preserve all the freshness and energy of the "singing as it happens" without any of its vicious qualities.[13]

The sequence of instruction had students learn "all the alphabet of music in a practical way." In the second book, rote singing was continued with new songs, but the students began to apply their knowledge of notation to learn two-part songs after hearing them played only once or twice. They were expected to use the song texts by the third time through the songs.

Mason provided detailed lesson plans because the classroom teacher provided most of the music instruction with the assistance of the music supervisors. Lesson I of the *New Second Music Reader* (1888) follows:

LESSON I.

BEATING TWO-PART MEASURE.—POSITION.

Teacher. Attention!

[The pupils give their attention.]

T. Place your hands as I do mine!

[*a.* The teacher places her hands so that the end of the middle finger of the right hand shall rest in the centre of the palm of the left, and draws the elbows well back, bringing the forearms into a horizontal position, quite close to the body. The pupils imitate her with more or less success at first, but finally all do it very well; for it is not very difficult.]

T. You are doing very well indeed. Now watch me, and do as I do!

[*b.* The teacher raises her hand from its horizontal position to a nearly upright one, by a quick motion from the wrist only, and keeps her hand in that position. The pupils imitate her.]

T. [With her hand still in upright position.] When I say, Position for beating time, I wish you to place your hands as you have them now. Watch me again, and do as I do. Attention!

[Teacher drops her hands at her sides. The class imitates her.]

T. Very well. Position for beating time!

[Many of the pupils understand, and take the position promptly; some move indolently, others place the left hand above the right, and so on.]

T. Some of you did quite well. But I want you all to do it well; and to do that, you must be smart, quick, about it.

When I say, Attention, drop your hands at your sides. Attention!

[Teacher drops hands at her sides. The pupils imitate her.]

T. Position for beating time!

[Teacher again takes position, as at *b,* and the pupils imitate her more successfully, as a class, than at first. As this is the first step, it will be better to be quite sure of it before proceeding farther; and it may need several trials to enable all to take the position promptly.]

In Lesson II the pupils learn to actually beat the two-part measure (the above lesson only covers the *position* for beating the two-part measure), Lesson III the three-part measure, and Lesson IV the four-part measure. Similar lessons for melodic notation, rhythm, and meter follow.

The degree to which those who used Mason's books followed his commitment to song material is rendered questionable by such artifacts as the San Francisco Course of Study for the year 1873.[14] It called for learning four songs in the first year of school and four more the second. San Francisco second graders were also to sing scales with syllables and copy notes, rests, staffs, and clefs onto their slates. This approach, used by advocates of the "song method," emphasized the facts of music rather than the music itself. It was probably not very different qualitatively from the note method of those who advocated drill in note read-

THE

NATIONAL MUSIC TEACHER:

A PRACTICAL GUIDE IN TEACHING VOCAL MUSIC
AND SIGHT–SINGING TO THE

YOUNGEST   PUPILS

IN SCHOOLS AND FAMILIES.

DESIGNED TO ACCOMPANY THE NATIONAL MUSIC CHARTS AND MUSIC READERS.

By LUTHER WHITING MASON,

SUPERINTENDENT OF MUSIC IN THE PRIMARY SCHOOLS OF BOSTON, MASS.

BOSTON:
PUBLISHED BY GINN BROTHERS.
1872.

FIGURE 9–5 Title page from *National Music Teacher: A Practical Guide in Teaching Vocal Music and Sight-Singing to the Youngest Pupils in Schools and Families,* by Luther Whiting Mason. Boston: Ginn Brothers, 1872.

ing with progressivley difficult exercises. Both, evidently, felt the need to be ''scientific.''

Mason's books brought him international recognition and respect. The Emperor of Japan, who was anxious to bring Western culture to his country, invited Mason to introduce his method to Japanese music teachers. American baseball was introduced to Japan not much later. Mason spent three years there as a government supervisor introducing ''Mason Song,'' and both American music education and baseball have influenced Japanese culture since the last part of the nineteenth century. Mason's travels later took him to Germany, where again his work was highly esteemed. A letter to his ten-year-old twin grandsons offers an insight to the man:

December 8, 1889
Louis and Luther:
    It is now getting very near to the first of January, 1890 when I must settle up with you. You must remember that for every day, except Sunday, that you neglect to practice 45 minutes, you lose twenty-five cents; and for every page that you can play to your Mama without making a mistake you gain twenty-five cents.

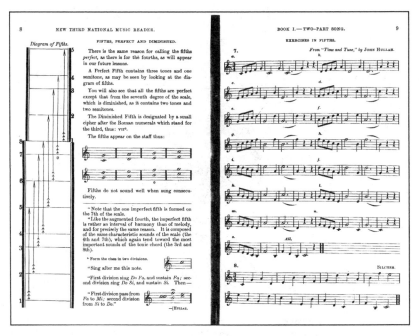

FIGURE 9–6 Pages 8 and 9 of the *National Music Course. The New Third Music Reader,* by Luther Whiting Mason. Boston: Ginn & Company, 1888.

> If this plan works well and you wish to keep it up, I will send your father $100 on the first of January, 1890, so you can go over. I will also allow you twenty-five cents a page for the violin. So your Mama and Papa must examine you and write to me so I can make a settlement with you and begin again. . . .
>
> I shall write you again soon. Your affectionate Grandpa,
>
> Luther Whiting Mason

The importance of daily practice was also the key to classroom vocal music lessons. There were seldom enough music specialists to handle all of the teaching responsibilities, and so the scheme of making the classroom teacher responsible for daily instruction became widespread. Fifteen minutes was the time most often allotted in the daily schedule for music. The music supervisor heard each class once a week, assisted with musical problems, and left the assignment for the next week. The organization of many of the textbooks confirms this pattern. Each book of *The Model Music Course,* for example, had eight chapters, each to be used for a month, and thirty-two lessons, each of a week's duration.

Benjamin Jepson. One of the serious competitors to Mason's work was *The Elementary Music Reader* by Benjamin Jepson (published by A. S. Barnes). Jepson had resigned his commission in the army after losing part of an ear to a Confederate sharpshooter and returned to his home in New Haven in late 1864. He was the son of an oratorio singer, had been a singing school master, and had studied with Gustav Stoeckel, who joined the faculty of Yale University in 1855. On January 3, 1865, Jepson began teaching music to the pupils of Cedar Street School.[15] At the end of the 1865 school year, Jepson staged a "Public School Music Rehearsal" attended by parents, Yale faculty, ministers, and citizens and the mayor of New Haven. The event, which included sight-singing demonstrations and the singing of choruses, ensured the future of vocal music in the New Haven schools. Jepson taught in the city schools for more than forty years.

Early in his schoolteaching career, Jepson constructed a mammoth music chart that he transported from school to school in a wagon. It consisted of over 1,200 square feet of canvas cranked on a frame. The chart soon wore out, and he abandoned it for the blackboard and chalk. Jepson's teaching plan called for children to have fifteen minutes of drill each day. In the library of the Yale School of Music there is a copy of *The Elementary Music Reader*, which Jepson himself published around 1865. The title page described it as "containing a thorough and progressive series of lessons in the elements of music, designed for schools, seminaries, acadamies, and for private instruction." He later wrote that he revised this book seven times.

In 1871 Jepson published the first of three books of the series entitled *The Elementary Music Reader*. It consisted of exercises interspersed with songs. The second and third books were published in 1873. Jepson's goal was the achievement of sight reading skills, and the sight-reading material in the third book was very difficult. In 1888 Jepson wrote a revision of *The Elementary Music Reader* with the new title *Standard Music Reader*. The *Standard Music Reader* consisted of four books for eight grades. His last series was a six-volume set entitled *The New Standard Music Reader* (New Haven, 1904).[16]

Jepson wrote other books as well. One of the most interesting is *Dictation in Music*. It is described as "Exercises to be sung by Teachers and Written by Pupils; All Grades in Schools for Primary to High where music is taught as a regular branch of study." The book is an example of the seriousness with which music "as a regular branch of study" was taken in some school systems. Exercises for the first year were all in quarter notes and incorporated only the neighboring tones of the major scale in $\frac{2}{4}$, $\frac{3}{4}$, and $\frac{4}{4}$ meters. In the second year half notes were introduced, still only with neighboring tones. Rests and slurs, all with neighboring tones within the C scale, were added in the third year. In the fourth year the speed increased and the exercises included eighth notes, and skips of a third in major and minor keys of G, D, F, and B♭. The learning increments were small, and the system depended on daily repetition.

New Haven children dealt with musical problems as musicians do and learned from Jepson, who was a dedicated and engaging personality. William Lyon Phelps discussed Jepson in a little book entitled *Music*. He recalled Jepson's classes and recommended that music be taught to twentieth-century children "as he taught us."

A NEW SCHOOL OF THOUGHT
ABOUT MUSIC INSTRUCTION

The Normal Music Course. By the 1880s concern developed among school personnel that music in the schools had become more of an entertainment than an educational experience. Students did a great deal of singing but apparently did not master music reading well enough to satisfy educators. Music was being adopted in school systems throughout the country, and administrators wanted to be sure that its purpose would be educational. The rationale that worked in the 1830s was used again. Music was adopted by new school systems as a *scientific* subject that provided mental, physical, and moral benefits for pupils. A scientific approach to music instruction required a scientific method, and the new graded series of music texts were based solidly on music reading. The authors of the most significant series of this persuasion were Hosea Holt and John Tufts. Their work, *The Normal Music Course*, was published originally by D. Appleton and Company in 1883. Edgar Silver purchased the rights in 1885 and entered the field of music education publishing with a huge success—*The Normal Music Course*.[17] Silver's company became Silver, Burdett & Company.

Hosea Edson Holt (1836–1898) and John Wheeler Tufts (1825–1908) were the coauthors of *The Normal Music Course*. Holt, from Boston, was a woodturner and singing school master, and served as a bandsman during the Civil War. He was a student of Benjamin Baker and John Tufts and a music teacher at Wheaton Seminary and Bridgewater Normal School. Holt joined the music staff of the Boston schools in 1869 and remained until 1898, the year of his death. He obviously changed his mind about rote teaching, as he was listed as one of the authors of Luther Whiting Mason's *National Music Course*. Tufts had studied piano in Europe with Ignaz Moscheles and theory with Moritz Hauptmann. He later taught in the Boston Music School and was organist at King's Chapel.[18] The *Normal Music Course* presented every possible music-reading problem students might encounter in stages of increasingly difficult steps. Many of the problems were presented in two-part contrapuntal exercises conceived by Tufts.

The Normal Music Course was a series of five books of which sight-singing exercises were the most important part. The part exercises were contrapuntal so that every voice would have a melody to sing, and exercise material was incorporated into the songs. Supplementary music for *The Normal Music Course* was published in a serial pamphlet entitled *The*

Coda, which cost three cents per copy. Like *The National Music Series, The Normal Music Course* was accompanied by large charts.

The authors regarded sight singing as the only means by which students could truly understand music. They wrote:

Sight-reading alone is not the object of the *Normal Music Course.* Through sight-reading a way is opened to the knowledge of music, and the Readers are offered as illustrations and suggestions in harmony and rhythm. This is more easily effected by careful study of the component melodies. Let each melody be carefully sung until it becomes familiar, the various combinations of the parts can then be produced and the resulting harmonies critically examined. It is not intended by this that the student shall become expert in the use of technical terms, but that the education of the ear may be gained by the *production* of these sounds in combination. By this course the ear receives its best training, and the effect will be lasting.[19]

THE

NORMAL MUSIC COURSE

A SERIES OF EXERCISES, STUDIES, AND SONGS, DEFINING AND ILLUSTRATING THE ART OF SIGHT READING, PROGRESSIVELY ARRANGED FROM THE FIRST CONCEPTION AND PRODUCTION OF TONES TO THE MOST ADVANCED CHORAL PRACTICE.

SECOND READER

NEW EDITION. REVISED AND ENLARGED.

BY

JOHN W. TUFTS

AND

H. E. HOLT.

SILVER, BURDETT & CO., Publishers
(Successors to SILVER, ROGERS & Co.),
6 HANCOCK AVENUE, BOSTON.
31 East 17th Street, NEW YORK.   122 and 124 Wabash Avenue, CHICAGO
1891.

FIGURE 9–7a Title page from *The Normal Music Course, Second Reader,* by John W. Tufts and H. E. Holt. Boston: Silver, Burdett & Co., 1891.

FIGURE 9–7b Pages 28 and 29 of *The Normal Music Course, Second Reader.*

By 1893 *The Normal Music Course* had become the standard for school music series. Many subsequent series were based on the note-reading method.[20]

Publishers' Schools. To introduce *The Normal Music Course,* Holt arranged for a summer music school in Lexington, Massachusetts, for teachers of music in the schools. The emphasis on teaching methodology differentiated it from previous summer institutes that covered church music and vocal pedagogy. The success of Holt's summer school led Luther Whiting Mason's publisher, Ginn and Company, to establish a school of its own—the National Summer School of Music—to promote *The National Music Course.*

Silver, Burdett and Ginn extended their competition by opening western sessions in Chicago for *The New National Music Course* and one in Lake Geneva, Wisconsin, for *The Normal Music Course.* Silver's school was moved to Chicago in 1891, where it was incorporated by Silver, Burdett & Company, and renamed the American Institute of Normal Methods. Both schools based their curricula on the school music books of their respective owners, but both also taught music appreciation, theory, melodic interpretation, and conducting.

The National Summer School of Music remained open for more than a quarter of a century. It closed only when public normal schools and colleges took over its function of training school music teachers.

THE AMERICAN INSTITUTE OF NORMAL METHODS

STUDENT'S REGISTRY BLANK

DEPARTMENT OF VOCAL MUSIC

{ Eastern or Western } School, Session of 19

Date,..........................19

Name in full,...

Permanent P. O. Address, Town or City..

Street and Number,...............................County, ...State, ...

P. O. Address *for the coming year,* if not as above,..................................

1. Age.............................. 2. Married or unmarried?...............................

3. What previous sessions of this Institute have you attended?...................................

4. What other advantages and Training in Vocal Music have you had by way of preparation

for teaching it?..

....

5. Have you had experience as a Special Teacher of Music?...................If so, where, and how

many years in each place?..

....

6. Have you done Grade Work in Music?......, ...

Where?.................................In what Grades?.......................................

7. State fully your qualifications and experience, if any, in Teaching Instrumental Music,..............

....

8. State your general educational advantages and training, Outside of Music,........................

....

9. Are you qualified to do High School work, outside of Music?...................................

10. Could you, if necessary, teach Penmanship, Drawing, Physical Training, or Pianoforte in addition to

Vocal Music?..

11. What other branches could you teach?........ ....

....

12. Do you care to teach any of the above, in connection with Vocal Music?............................

13. What experience, if any, have you had in teaching other branches than Music? (Give full particulars.)

....

....

14. What is the compass and quality of your voice?..

15. What experience, if any, have you had as church organist, or singer?...............................

16. Would you like to fill such a position in addition to your teaching?..............................

17. What are your church preferences?...............18. Have you a position for next year?............

19. As a special or as a grade teacher?.................................20. Where?..............

21. At what salary?...... 22. How much of your time does the work occupy?...........................

23. If a position for next year is desired, what location or section of country do you prefer?..............

24. What salary do you desire?.................25. What is the lowest salary you would accept?.........

26. Do you intend to complete the course in this school to graduation?...............................

Give, on the back of this sheet, names of persons to whom you would refer for testimonials as to your ability, experience and training.   File with this blank any testimonials you have with you, and your photograph.

N. B.—It is earnestly desired that every member of the school fill out this blank at the opening of the session. As these records are carefully preserved for the benefit of the pupils, the propriety and advantage of answering each question explicitly are evident. Students are requested to read these questions through carefully before beginning to answer them.

FIGURE 9–8 Student's registry blank from The American Institute of Normal Methods.

Other Series. Orlando Blackman began teaching in Chicago when the city reinstated school music in 1863; he soon became one of the leaders in the profession. In 1873, with his assistant E. E. Whittemore, he published *The Graded School Singer*. This series, like the one discussed next, was widely adopted.

The music teachers in Cincinnati were full-fledged employees of the school board rather than outside contractors like Lowell Mason. They produced for the board *The Young Singer* (1860) and *The Young Singer's Manual* (1866). Later came several *Cincinnati Music Reader*s which were used by schools in many cities. Their last revision was by Gustave Junkermann in 1893. The *Cincinnati Music Readers* demonstrate that the teaching of music reading was taken very seriously in the last third of the nineteenth century. "Part Third" (for Intermediate Schools) of the 1882 edition began with 361 exercises in unison, two, and three parts, followed by 84 three-part songs. It ended with chromatic scales in notes and syllables and two pages of definitions. Curricula were geared to these books on a grade-by-grade basis.

At the 1876 Centennial Exposition in Philadelphia, charts used for oral examinations of Cincinnati schoolchildren and their written examinations formed the content of the city's music exhibit. They were extraordinary enough to be displayed in Paris two years later at the exhibition that featured the Trocadero buildings.

The Public School Music Course (1889), by Charles E. Whiting, used the syllables *ta* and *te* for teaching the reading of rhythms. Letters with sharps and flats next to them were printed below the scale to signify pitch. This system was similar to the one used in *The Normal Music Course*. According to Robert John, it was not successful and "was actually more a handicap than a help."[21] The series consisted of six readers and a supplementary *Book Three*, the *Girls' Edition of Book Six*, and the *Institute Reader and Young People's Song Book*.

The Natural Music Course (American Book Company, 1895), by Thomas Tapper and Frederick Ripley, was the outstanding series published at the end of the last decade of the nineteenth century. Tapper was an authority on music teaching, and Ripley was headmaster of a Boston school. They recognized that so many gimmicks and devices had accumulated in school music series that a straightforward and simple method was needed. *The Natural Music Course* was conspicuous for its uncomplicated approach. It also contained some new and innovative approaches to simplify music instruction. Ripley discussed the series almost twenty years later:

> I concluded that the one vital idea . . . contained in Mr. Holt's repeated assertion [was] that real musicianship was based on the perception of tone relations as a perfectly definite thing. All the rest went by the board. Hav-

THE

CINCINNATI

MUSIC READER.

COMPLETE.

A

COLLECTION OF EXERCISES AND SONGS,

IN ONE & TWO PARTS,

FOR GRADES H, G, F, E AND D.

PREPARED AT THE REQUEST OF THE

BOARD OF EDUCATION

BY THE

TEACHERS OF MUSIC.

—⊶∘⦂⦿⦂∘⊷—

Published by

JOHN CHURCH & CO.,

66 WEST FOURTH ST., CINCINNATI.

FIGURE 9–9 Title page of *The Cincinnati Music Reader* (texts in English and German). Cincinnati: John Church & Co., 1875.

ing reached this conclusion I set myself the task of devising a presentation of music which should be entirely free of technicalities, so called, but which should make the notation as it now exists an actual, vital expression of a real thing to all pupils who beheld it. Definition and theory were entirely eliminated. Number, hand signs, ladders and the like were omitted. Rhythm was joined to melody, and the interval as a study disappeared from elementary work. All representations were musical and complete. . . . I accidentally hit upon the scheme which I found out afterwards was common in France, namely, the rhythm-building scheme. That is, a certain note is adopted as a standard, this note is tied with other notes so as to produce all higher note values used in the exercise. Thus in four-four meter, taking the quarter note as the standard, two quarters tied give the half, three quarters tied give the dotted half, and four quarters tied give the whole note. Thus the child, beating quarters, passes easily from the representation in tied quarters to the presentation in notes of higher values, and also the use of the dot. Proceeding in the same way, but taking the eighth note as a standard, everything above the eighth in value is worked out.[22]

The same authors published the *Harmonic Course in Music* in 1903 and the *Melodic Course in Music* in 1906. It is ironic that books intended to eliminate gimmicks should be named in such a prankish fashion— after the three modes of the minor scale—without revealing whether the series of titles itself was a gimmick. In 1895 J. A. Broekhaven and A. J. Gantvoort published *The Model Music Course,* a series of music readers that used both numbers ("scale names") and syllables ("music names") in the *Primer,* designed to be introduced in the second grade.

William L. Tomlins developed a method in which beautiful singing was the major concern of the teacher. Tomlins, an Englishman, had come to Chicago in 1870. He began as the director of a male chorus of sixty, which he changed to a mixed group that grew to a membership of four hundred. About 1890 he began to work with children's groups and to train teachers for the Chicago board of education. The children's chorus that Tomlins directed at the Columbian Exposition in 1893 was so outstanding that his work became the standard for teaching children to sing. Striving for beautiful song became a method in its own right, taking techniques from both the reading and rote approaches but focusing on tone. At the turn of the century, Tomlins was the editor of C. C. Birchard's *Laurel Series,* originally copyrighted in 1900, which provided folk and composed song literature of high quality.

Twentieth-Century Series. The change in textbooks for the music classroom that began in the nineteenth century with Eleanor Smith, Robert Foresman, John Broekhoven, and A. J. Gantvoort proceeded slowly until the establishment of the Music Supervisors National Conference (MSNC) early in the twentieth century. The Ripley and Tapper *Revised Natural Music Series,* published in 1903, continued a traditional approach to music reading, although it was of more interest to children than many of its competitors. The same was true of Ginn's *The New Educational Music Course* (1906) by James McLaughlin and W. W. Gilchrist. Publishers were cautious. Silver, Burdett & Company, which had taken a step in a new direction with the Smith and Foresman *Modern Music Series,* reversed itself in 1910 by publishing the *Normal Music Course,* a revision of the Holt and Tufts work by Samuel Cole and Leonard B. Marshall. This series continued the subject-centered approach of the original.[23] The American Book Company had asked Smith and Foresman to prepare a new set of books to capitalize on their earlier success. The company produced the *Eleanor Smith Music Course* (appearing in six volumes from 1908 until 1911). It offered some rhythmic experiences but was less forward-looking than her earlier work. In 1914, however, Silver, Burdett followed up on the original gamble they had made with Smith's *Modern Music Series*. The gamble paid off handsomely.

As nineteenth-century educators had used the word "science" to mean modern, so did Silver, Burdett borrow the word "progressive" from Theodore Roosevelt's political party for a new series with three leading MSNC figures as editors. They were Osbourne McConathy, Edward Bailey Birge, and W. Otto Miessner. The *Progressive Music Series* was first published in 1914. Horatio Parker, dean of the Yale School of Music, whose opera *Mona* had just won a Metropolitan Opera prize, was included among the authors. McConathy, who had pioneered with his programs for the schools of Chelsea, Massachusetts, served as senior editor while Birge and Miessner contributed songs related to the musical concepts to be taught. There were no exercises or scales for drill. "Observation Songs" provided opportunity to become familiar with the notation for tonal and rhythmic elements. Songs and singing games with large bodily motions characterized the experiences of the first three years. Themes from compositions by Mozart, Beethoven, Dvořák, and others were printed in the student texts and related to musical elements experienced in the singing. Teacher's manuals were provided to make certain that the sequential nature of the singing (learning) activities would not be missed. The series was widely adopted and other publishers had been challenged.

Yet there was no rush to meet the challenge. The American Book Company had released the first book in the *Hollis Dann Music Course* in 1912. Dann placed primary importance on the "study of tone and rhythm . . . [and] musical dictation."[24] Though the Dann series was carefully planned and included many interesting songs, some by Harvey Worthington Loomis and Arthur E. Johnstone, its primary emphasis was still on learning to read music. The commitment to this project and the Smith books kept the American Book Company from responding with a truly new entry for thirty years. In 1920 the firm of Hinds, Hayden and Eldridge produced *The Universal Music Series*, edited by Karl Gehrkens and George Gartlan. Walter Damrosch provided the glamour in the series, which emphasized development of love for music as its primary objective. Rhythmic activities were stressed, and free rhythmic interpretation allowed the children to be creative. Music history, analysis, and listening were incorporated.

It was 1923 before *Songs of Childhood*, the first book of Ginn and Company's *Music Education Series*, appeared. Once again, MSNC leaders were asked to prepare the books. This time the editors were Will Earhart, T. P. Giddings, and Ralph Baldwin. Like the "progressive"

books, there were no musical exercises, but students were encouraged
to look for motives rather than read from note to note, and eurhythmics
were introduced. Appreciation was a major goal, and a series of phonograph records was keyed to the student books. Melody writing provided
the opportunity to experience the creative joy of music.

In addition to these textbook series, a number of songbooks appeared, some of which provided musical material of exceptionally high
quality. Among them were Alys Bentley's *The Song Series* (A. S. Barnes,
1907, 1910), William L. Tomlins' *The Laurel Song-Reader* (Birchard, 1914),
and *The Foresman Book of Songs* (American Book Company, 1925–1926).
Charles Fullerton's *One Book Course*, with accompanying records, filled
a particular need because it was designed for rural schools: it brought
music to those schools years earlier than might have been otherwise
possible in many areas of the country.

In the 1920s Silver, Burdett published an enlarged edition of some
of the *Progressive* books while Ginn laid plans for a new series to be
known as *The World of Music*. Its principal editor was Mabelle Glenn,
who was assisted by Helen Leavitt, Victor Rebmann, and Earl Baker.
Glenn, having encountered Dalcroze eurhythmics at an international
conference in Lausanne, Switzerland, incorporated similar ideas in her
approach to reading rhythms. She also devised a scheme of keying
twelve common melodic patterns to songs in the second-grade book,
which gave the children a basis for elementary music reading and creating. Two-color illustrations and a few masterpieces of art in four colors
made the books attractive. Harold Rugg of Teachers College helped integrate the songs with other subjects. An outstanding feature of the series
was the teacher's handbook, which provided a means of sequencing the
learning experiences throughout the grades.

Francis E. Howard of Bridgeport, Connecticut, was another teacher
who concentrated on the beauty of the child's voice. He was best known
for his book *The Child's Voice in Singing*, but earlier he had edited the
Novello Music Course. His teaching countered the problems of pupils
who had been drilled excessively with modulators, hand signals, prepared exercises, and so on but could not read a simple beautiful melody
expressively. He taught children to sing new music in a musical manner
and exposed them to as much beautiful music as possible.[25] His methods
were in keeping with some of the new psychological ideas being introduced at the close of the century.

Thaddeus P. Giddings was a midwesterner who also believed in
teaching children to read songs by having them read through as much
music as possible. He described his "Song Method" to his colleagues.
A condensed form of the practice he instituted in Minneapolis, and possibly earlier in Oak Park, Illinois, follows:

First Grade: As many as 100 songs taught by rote. Second Grade: *Two* weeks of reviewing songs known. Assigned good singers to back row so others always had a better tone to which to listen. *Third* week, syllables taught to six or seven familiar songs. *Circa Seventh* week, teacher seated in front of the children who sing a familiar song slowly with syllables. Repeats it, more slowly; and again, more slowly. On the fourth time the teacher stops them on a tone and has them sing the tone several times; then they sing *do*. Then each of the tones of the scale was presented in the song and compared with *do,* then with each other and it sometimes happened, in a room where the attention was good, that all the tones were learned in twenty minutes. . . . When a tone was forgotten, it was not given by the teacher but the school were told to sing the song until they came to that tone. The activity was repeated the next day and by the end of the week individuals were trying the skips. Much individual work followed. *Eighth* week the children are shown the song in the book, following which the teacher, using whole notes, put the notes on a blackboard staff as children sing song. When it is fully displayed children sing tones as teacher points to various notes. Then students drew notes on board as teacher sang. *Ninth* week, books distributed to children.[26]

William A. Hodgdon. Some earlier music teachers had utilized elements of the song method along with other approaches. Among these eclectic educators was William A. Hodgdon, a student of Lowell Mason and George Webb, who taught in Fort Wayne and Saint Louis after the Civil War. His plan of instruction was based on a repertoire of twenty songs, some his own compositions. These songs were taught by rote with the intent of developing love for music. He taught the scale as a tune and then worked with intervals starting with the least difficult. He led a chorus of 3,500 Saint Louis school children that he prepared for the 1903 "National Song Festival of the North American Singing Society" and was selected to be the music organizer of the Saint Louis World's Fair the next year.[27]

Sterrie A. Weaver was a highly respected supervisor in Westfield, Massachusetts, who was also a successful individualist. He ignored the charts, modulators, and specially prepared textbooks that were popular elsewhere and focused the attention of his pupils on the blackboard or on exercise slips that he wrote out as needed. Like many others, he believed that individual recitation in music was the only way to build the confidence of his pupils. Efficiency was the keyword of his teaching, and his "scientific" approach to the subject was what many school administrators were looking for.

HIGH SCHOOL MUSIC

The high school was the last segment of the public school system to be put in place. Common school education in many American communities, especially rural areas and small towns, ended with the eighth grade until well after the Civil War. The 1860 census listed only three hundred public high schools, mostly in northern cities where full twelve-year programs were first developed. When the school systems in the South were finally organized, a full ten years after the war, seven-year common schooling was normal. In time, four year secondary schools were added. The discrepancy between the two regions continued well into the twentieth century. Progress in secondary common schooling was slow. Public high school enrollments in the 1889–1890 school year represented only 3.7 percent of the 14–17-year-old population. The figures began to improve in the twentieth century, but by 1930 the figure passed 50 percent only by including those in private schools.[28]

The high schools were generally comprehensive in nature. Vocal music was part of the high school curriculum from the beginning in most places. The curriculum usually consisted of singing the great choruses of European masters. Charles Aiken's *High School Choralist* (1866) and *The Choralist's Companion* (1872) contained four-part choral works by Handel, Haydn, Mozart, Beethoven, Mendelssohn, Silcher, Barnby, Dr. Calcott, Meyerbeer, Spohr, Rossini, and Mehul. In schools that were large enough, senior classes provided music for their own graduation ceremonies. Underclassmen were undoubtedly called upon to help in smaller schools. In cities such as Worcester and Cincinnati, the high schools became the training ground for community festival choruses that established international reputations. The production of operettas also became an established tradition in some schools by the end of the century. A few schools were even able to present full oratorios, although the supervisors or professional singers sang the major solos.

Early Concerts. In April 1849 the Germania Society Orchestra gave an afternoon concert for Boston children. It was one of the earliest children's concerts in the United States. The orchestra also performed children's concerts during the 1850s, when it was on tour with such artists as Jenny Lind, Henriette Sontag, Ole Bull, Camilla Urso, and Alfred Jaell. The Philharmonic Society of Cincinnati gave a free concert for teachers and students of the intermediate and high schools in March 1857.[29] Walter Aiken wrote that the society played a rehearsal concert the next year for the children and that the program was discussed in school beforehand.[30] The society allowed high school students to attend rehearsals in 1884 for twenty-five cents. An early expression of the purpose of teaching music appreciation came from the annual school report for 1908–1909:

With the reorganization of the Cincinnati Orchestra this year, a remarkable series of concerts has been given. The programs have been obtained in advance, and the various numbers analyzed and discussed with high school classes and their attendance upon the concerts encouraged in order that they might familiarize themselves with classical compositions and be taught to recognize the style of the different composers. The future of music depends as much upon well trained listeners as upon performers.[31]

Instrumental Music. With the interest created by town bands after the Civil War and by tours of such professional organizations as the Theodore Thomas Orchestra and the Patrick Gilmore and Frederick Innes bands, it was inevitable that some extracurricular ensembles would appear in schools. Walter Aiken and Edward Bailey Birge both report playing in school groups in the 1872 and 1883, respectively. The students usually learned to play their instruments at home, from a private teacher, or in a private music academy. The director of the group, when there was one, might have been the music supervisor or any other faculty member. A few school bands were formed in the South before the turn of the century. The most celebrated school instrumental ensemble was the orchestra organized by Will Earhart in Richmond, Indiana in 1898.

TEACHER TRAINING

The earliest American music teachers were the products of the singing schools. Moses Cheney, John Stickney, and their counterparts have left testimony to the encouragement and counsel they received from their music masters.[32] From the singing schools of the years following the Revolutionary War came such early trainers of teachers as Samuel Holyoke, Lucius Chapin, and Samuel Read Hall. Hall's "Lectures for School Keeping" speak of the wisdom of teaching music as language "from their childhood." In a summary paragraph, Charles Hamm refers to Chapin as "teacher of sacred music, patriot, pioneer, poet and composer," omitting teacher trainer after having detailed a school system "whereby certain of his [Chapin's] more talented scholars held schools of their own under his supervision."[33] This was in 1800 or even earlier, several years before Holyoke's vocal and instrumental schools in Salem or Hall's "Lectures for School-Keeping." Even Lowell Mason began to study music at home and in a singing school.

The singing societies, at least two of which (Orpheus in Philadelphia and Saint Cecilia in Charleston, South Carolina) predate the Revolutionary War, provided an important training ground for musicians who taught the teachers of the early nineteenth century. Because they were established by musicians trained in Europe, they eventually changed the nature of music instruction. From these societies grew the conventions, which served to provide tutelage to those who desired to teach music. Robert John suggests that the first of these was held in Concord, New Hampshire, in 1829.[34] Henry E. Moore, the young man who organized the convention with the help of the New Hampshire Central Music Society of Goffstown, planned a two-day meeting for singing school masters, choir directors, and those aspiring to such careers. It set a pattern followed by other musical societies. Lowell Mason made the Boston Academy of Music the center of the convention movement and trained hundreds of future teachers over a period of fourteen years. The establishment of the National Music Convention and the American Music Convention (which moved to New York City), and the encouragement of state conventions is an interesting chapter in the spread of music teacher training, as recounted by John.

Following the Civil War, normal schools, which had begun in Lexington, Massachusetts, in 1839 came into their own and played a major role in making teaching in the common schools a profession.[35] Most of the normal schools were established by the states, but there were many private institutions, and some cities had their own training centers. In Cincinnati a normal school was a permanent part of its school system from 1868. Victor Williams taught the "theory and practice of music" to young ladies preparing to be grade school teachers. J. L. (Daddy) Zeinz replaced him in 1875. Superintendent of Music Junkermann taught from 1882 until 1900, one year before the normal school ceased to function.

Saint Louis also had a normal school that prepared classroom teachers for their role in teaching music. In the first decade of the new century it became the teachers college named after the former superintendent of the city schools, William Torrey Harris. Harris had established the first public kindergarten in the United States and was U.S. commissioner of education from 1889 to 1906.

The grade school teachers who enrolled in most of the normal schools had instruction in vocal music, but music supervisors were not the products of these institutions until Julia Ettie Crane opened Potsdam (New York) Musical Institute in 1884. In connection with the Normal School at Potsdam, she offered her music students actual teaching experience in a model classroom. Her curriculum for the public school offered a compromise in the "rote-note" disagreement as she instructed her students to develop listening skills and musical memory in the younger children and to delay sight reading until the grammar grades. Crane was firmly committed to the importance of musicianship in supervisors, but, understanding the role of pedagogy, she helped initiate the balance that characterized the curriculum of future music educators.

In the 1880s candidates for music specialist positions in public schools were still examined only in music. Even when the theory and practice of teaching was included in the examinations, most of the candidates were products of music schools rather than teacher-training institutions. Joseph Surdo, who began teaching in Cincinnati in 1891 after two years at the College of Music, was told by Junkermann to prepare for the pedagogy part of the examination by visiting the schools to see how school music teaching was done.[36] The tests could not have been very demanding. Elwood Cubberly reported in the *National Society for the Study of Education Yearbook* of 1906 that an eleven-year-old boy received a mark of 98% on a county teacher test.

The same year that Crane opened her institute, Hosea Holt held his summer school to introduce his new *Normal Music Course*. Two dissimilar philosophies were represented by the various means of teacher preparation. Julia Etta Crane, who had graduated from Potsdam Normal School in 1874, was closely tied to the public school movement and the goal of providing music to all Americans. The book company institutes came into being specifically to serve the schools. Colleges and conservatories, on the other hand, were direct descendants of their counterparts in Europe, and many of their faculty members had been trained there. To them, music was an elite art not to be wasted on the untalented. Their graduates could not be expected to be comfortable as school music supervisors. There was an attempt by colleges and universities to limit the normal schools, and their descendant teachers colleges, to training elementary school teachers, leaving the high school subjects to the traditional institutions of higher education. Music specialists who needed to operate at both levels may have contributed to the solution of the problem in favor of the teachers colleges, but vestiges of the differences still remain in music teacher preparation programs.

Summer Schools. Music summer schools such as Holt's, although obviously initiated for commercial reasons, served a real need because music was becoming a regular subject of study in the schools. Neither the colleges nor the normal schools had developed early training programs for music supervisors. The summer schools sponsored by the book companies continued to be the major source of trained supervisors for twenty-five years, however. The American Book Company established the New School of Methods in Chicago with Thomas Tapper as principal. The Emma Thomas School was opened in Detroit. Ginn and Company hired Enos Pearson, a music supervisor in New Hampshire, to head a summer school to be operated in cooperation with Plymouth Normal School. Others were established by conservatories.

An interesting observation can be made about these summer schools. Women attendees outnumbered men by a wide margin, in many instances as much as ten to one. Of 210 students who attended the National Summer School from 1887 to 1903, only 23 were men.[37] A similar enrollment pattern occurred at the western session of the American Institute of Normal Methods. The predominant role of women in music education dates from this period, although there are isolated instances of women teaching music in the schools earlier. Mrs. E. K. Thatcher taught in Cincinnati in 1844, and in 1869 Letitia Arnold became the first black music teacher in the schools of Washington, D. C.[38]

Another observation is the number of twentieth-century music education leaders who were teachers or students in the summer schools.

Osbourne McConathy assisted Luther Whiting Mason with the National Summer School and then took over the leadership role on Mason's death in 1896. Both Hollis Dann and Walter Aiken were on the faculty of the American Book Company New School of Methods under the direction of Thomas Tapper. Ralph Baldwin assisted Sterrie A. Weaver and eventually directed the Institute of Music Pedagogy in Northampton, Massachusetts. C. C. Birchard managed the Emma Thomas School, where Frances E. Clark prepared herself to be a supervisor and Peter Dykema attended as a "boy observer."[39]

CHILD-CENTERED EDUCATION

Given the commitment of school administrators of the period to systematic organization and efficiency, it is not surprising that few in America heard a native voice crying in the wilderness. Among the Transcendentalists of Concord, Massachusetts, was Amos Bronson Alcott, a schoolmaster and philosopher sometimes referred to as the "American Pestalozzi." Like Pestalozzi, Alcott was a visionary who had founded "ideal" schools in Pennsylvania, Connecticut, and Boston. His Temple School, which he fitted out to surround his pupils with comfort and beauty, involved the students in singing, dancing, school newspapers, plays, and dialogues with the master.[40] Elizabeth Peabody taught subjects he was not qualified to teach (and thought unimportant), such as Latin. The school was an apparent success, and its continuance might have influenced the common schools strongly, since Alcott was an associate of many American intellectual leaders. The innocent and always well-meaning Alcott, however, mixed abolitionist politics with business and insisted on enrolling a black girl in Temple School, after which much of his support evaporated. Alcott later spent five years as superintendent of the Concord, Massachusetts, schools. The 2,500 pages of observations of his own children, including Louisa May, presaged the psychology of early childhood. His lecture tours across the Midwest in the 1870s led to the establishment of a summer school for adults five years before Hosea Holt's summer program at Lexington.

Friedrich Wilhelm Froebel. If America had not been ready for the antebellum ideas of Bronson Alcott, it could not long resist the intermittent stream of ideas from Rousseau and Pestalozzi that surfaced in the form of a new kind of school—the kindergarten—invented by one of Pestalozzi's students, Friedrich Froebel. Froebel believed that the teacher did not give the child potential but helped draw it from the child. He accepted Pestalozzi's faculty psychology and the need for exercise to develop the faculties. The teacher's role was to devise ways to help the child voluntarily engage in meaningful activity. Like Rousseau, Froebel believed that each stage in life is built on the previous one. He invented the kindergarten because the early stage of life influenced the rest of the child's life. The kindergarten was expected to provide opportunity for creative self-involvement for children not yet of school age.

The Kindergarten was intended to be a place where children could learn through play. To ensure that play would result in useful, educational outcomes, Froebel developed objects, or "gifts," that would encourage the cultivation of the senses. At the Centennial Exhibition of 1876, eighteen orphans from the Philadelphia Northern Home for Friendless Children demonstrated a model Froebel kindergarten. The presentation helped to popularize the kindergarten. Frank Lloyd Wright credited the Froebel "gifts" his mother brought him from the exhibition with "helping develop his creative powers."[41]

Froebel died in 1852. Mrs. Carl Schurz opened a kindergarten for German speaking children in Wisconsin in 1856, and Elizabeth Peabody founded a private kindergarten in Boston in the 1860s. The first American kindergarten connected with a public school system was established in Saint Louis in 1873. The teacher, Susan Blow, had the support of Superintendent William Torrey Harris, an educator who was influential in changing American education. Ironically, his debates with G. Stanley Hall at the annual meetings of the National Education Association earned him a reputation as a conservative, since he opposed those who sought to diminish the formality of schooling at the turn of the century.[42]

Music played an important role in the growth of the kindergarten movement. The *Kindergarten Songbook* was one of the principal vehicles for the spread of the kindergarten influence.[43] Eleanor Smith dedicated her significant publication, *Songs for Little Children*, "To Chicago Kindergaerteners [sic], and to all lovers of Children Everywhere."[44] The preface to this book raised many questions about the music books of the day, including appropriateness of the texts, song meter, accompaniments, and arrangements of music by famous composers. Alice H. Putnam, principal of the kindergarten department of Cook County Normal School, wrote the preface. She concluded with this statement: "This book is sent out in the hope that it may lead . . . teachers to look more carefully *every where* for the right means to develop a right musical feeling in children."[45]

Colonel Francis W. Parker. The director of Alice Putnam's Normal School was Colonel Francis W. Parker, an innovative educator whose new ideas had proven successful in the Quincy and Boston, Massachusetts, schools. He was invited to work in the Cook County, Illinois, public schools in 1883. Like Froebel and Alcott, he regarded unity to be a fundamental principle. To him, this meant educating the whole child. Also like Froebel, he believed that true learning occurred only through self-generated activity. Parker's interest in the "whole man" led him to the belief that, while music training incorporated intellectual and disciplinary aspects, its true and unique contribution was in the realm of the emotions.

The view of the role of music as trainer of the emotions was not accepted by the majority of music educators until well into the new century. Even then, many thought that teaching children to read music took precedence over any other objective. Practicing the new psychology, however, educational leaders such as Parker reversed the process. The new music teacher sought ways to replace years of joyless drill with deeply moving musical experiences. These experiences were expected to motivate children to develop the skills to continue musical enjoyment for a lifetime.

Parker and John Dewey, the founder of the Laboratory School at the University of Chicago, helped set American education on a new course. John Walquist wrote that "progressive education" dates from the day John Dewey made the rounds of school supply stores for student furniture that would be conducive to work and not just listening. Dewey himself called Parker the "father of progressive education."[46] The opportunities for music education were enhanced by the changes they and others of the time set in motion.

G. Stanley Hall. Dewey's teacher, Granville Stanley Hall, earned a doctorate at Harvard University under William James after studying with Wundt and Helmholtz in Germany. Hall established the first psychological laboratory in the United States at Johns Hopkins University in 1881. Upon becoming the first president of Clark University, he initiated a child development study and edited the *Pedagogical Seminary*, which was a strong voice for the child-study movement. Hall believed that psychology could transform education from a merely efficient activity into a scientific one and that scientific education was the key to progress for mankind.[47] This was in keeping with what Parker and Dewey had been practicing in their schools in Illinois. Women's clubs and individuals familiar with Froebel's writings took up the cause of making schools child-centered. Hall not only changed practices in music education by recognizing that music provided the best access to an individual's emotional world, but he also laid the groundwork for music therapy, a discipline that was to develop much later.

The writings of Hall and the new schools of Parker and Dewey were highlighted by a study by Joseph M. Rice, who wrote after visiting thirty-six cities, "The general educational spirit of the country is progressive."[48] Rice deserves recognition for naming a movement that was a complex assortment of educational trends. He allied these trends with other facets of American society that also believed the great industrial system being developed could be harnessed for the good of all.[49] In 1895 the National Herbart Society was formed and another phase of the movement toward a science of education was entered.

The term "progressive education" became synonymous with the entire movement to change the practices of the traditional school, although no official organization was formed until 1919. By that time John Dewey had developed a philosophy and a theory of education that came to represent "progressivism" in the minds of most people. Hall, who was chosen president of the National Education Association Department of Music Education in 1885, continued his active interest in education and music education until his death in 1924. Unfortunately for the movement, the nondirective nature of progressive education was often misunderstood by the general public because programs appeared to be unstructured. Although many of the changes begun by progressive education are incorporated in current educational practice, opportunities were overlooked. This was especially true in the arts. The Progressive Education Association disbanded in 1955.

THE NEW EDUCATION AND MUSIC

John Dewey moved from Chicago to New York just before the establishment of the Music Supervisors National Conference. By then, he was the accepted leader of what had resulted from the child-study movement that G. Stanley Hall had set in motion. Both were friendly to music and spoke about the role it could play in the school. Music educators were sympathetic to education that required physical demonstrations of what students learned because they had been doing this for seventy-five years. Especially meaningful for music education was Dewey's statement on doing that appeared in *Moral Principles in Education* : "Who can reckon up the loss of moral power that arises from the constant impression that nothing is worth doing in itself, but only as a preparation for something else." Music educators were beginning to increase their emphasis on "doing music" well and were grateful for the support of an esteemed educational figure such as Dewey.

"Progressive education" was the term most often used to describe the changes brought about by the new approach of Hall, Parker, and Dewey. The innovative *Progressive Music Series* became available to the schools five years before the Progressive Education Association was founded in 1919. Experiments stimulated by the new thinking made significant uses of music. One of Dewey's students, William Wirt, had the opportunity to apply the principles to a new school system that he designed for the model city—Gary, Indiana. The platoon system he conceived for the Gary schools called for half of the students to be busy in activities on the playground, in rehearsal halls, and gymnasiums while the other half was engaged in academic pursuits. Melvin E. Snyder taught instrumental music in Gary and was a member of MSNC for many years.

Attempts to transpose the platoon system to New York City failed for political reasons, among others. The failure, however, dramatized the difficulties facing the "new education." It was built on concepts with which Americans had little experience. They were comfortable with learning to read music and singing patriotic songs, but they were suspicious of sensitizing children to beautiful sound and color. Also suspect were teaching methods that spent time motivating children, or worse, allowing them to decide what they would do on a given day. Dewey's pragmatism fit in with the "can do" attitude developed on the frontier, but many of the subtleties of the new relationship between teacher and learner did not. Often the teachers themselves, despite the benefits of workshops, graduate study, and lectures and demonstrations at MSNC and other professional meetings, did not change the atmosphere of their classrooms.[50] Despite notable successes, progressive education did not achieve wide acceptance, although many of its concepts permeated American education. The lack of acceptance of many of the ideas of the new education denied to children musical experiences that they might have had otherwise.

Some of the best examples of what the new education could mean for music were to be found in independent schools. Enlightened parents sometimes founded schools to offer what they considered better curricula. The Park School in Baltimore is an example. Laboratory schools on university campuses provided the atmosphere in which progressive education could flourish. From the laboratory school at Ohio State University came a book by Beatrice Perham (later Mrs. Max Krone) entitled *Music in the New School*. The following phrases quoted from the book describe music education in such schools:

> Much more opportunity for individual learning. Challenging musical environment which causes music learnings to occur many times during the day. Skills taught as they grow out of the needs and problems of the children. Music as a means of child development and creative expression for all, rather than for talented ones only.[51]

There were many practitioners of psychology as a science who were interested in music, and some music educators became so engrossed in the problems of learning music that they became psychologists themselves. The most influential person to do so was James L. Mursell. Two of his books published in the 1930s, *The Psychology of School Music Teaching* (with Kansas City music supervisor Mabelle Glenn) and *Human Values and Music Education*, became standard texts. Mursell and other psychologists will be discussed later.

THE STATE OF MUSIC EDUCATION—TWO SURVEYS

General John Eaton was commissioner of the United States Bureau of Education from 1870 to 1886. His interest in music and encouragement by Theodore Presser, through the Music Teachers National Association, led him to survey the condition of music instruction in American Schools in 1886. The survey requested the following information from public school systems throughout the United States:

> Is music taught? In what grades? By special teacher? By regular teacher? By both regular and special teachers? Number of hours per week? Please state what, if any, instrument is used to lead the singing. Which system is used of the three commonly known as "fixed-*do*," "movable *do*," or "tonic *sol-fa*," or are different ones used in different schools? If different systems are used, which finds most favor? What text-books or charts are used? Are there stated musical examinations, or exhibitions, or both? Is notation required in music books? Please send copy of regulations, if any have been printed. Please state, if possible, whether any established vocal societies (independent of church choirs) are now in active operation in your city; if so, please give names of societies and full addresses of conductors. If music is not taught in your schools, what objections, if any, would probably be urged against the introduction of systematic intruction in it?[52]

The survey, which produced a great deal of information, was discussed frequently in conference presentations. Generally, it revealed that public school music was not yet widely accepted. In fact, only 250 school systems indicated that music was being taught regularly. The fact that the survey was done, however, and especially by the federal government, showed that school music was gathering strength.[53]

The National Education Association. In 1889 the Department of Music Education of the National Education Association approved a resolution to collect data on the condition of music instruction throughout the United States. An appropriation of not more than one hundred dollars was also approved to carry out the study, which was to be done by means of a questionnaire sent to the "State and county superintendents of the respective States, and the superintendents or secretaries of school boards in the leading towns and cities of the United States." One thousand seventy-eight questionnaires were sent and 621 responses returned. The responses indicated that music instruction had increased since the 1886 survey by the U.S. commissioner of education and that the feelings of administrators toward the subject were favorable in all parts of the country. In fact, only four superintendents expressed negative opinions about music instruction. The conclusions of the report stated that music "had withstood the crucial test of experience and critical observation," and that "music should be regularly and systematically taught in the schools."

Of special significance is that the rationale for this statement is the same used by the Boston School Committee fifty-one years earlier—the intellectual, moral, and physical improvement of the pupils. It was that rationale that had supported the introduction of music into school systems across the country and would continue to do so well into the twentieth century. There was also a recommendation to replace recreational music with systematic instruction in those school systems that did not yet have music teachers. The report also recommended that teachers learn to teach music during their teacher-training period and that musicians who wished to be music teachers should study educational methods in order to supervise classroom teachers as they presented music lessons.[54]

SUMMARY

The last third of the nineteenth century was a period of growth and consolidation. The concept of the common school was adopted by the new states as they joined the Union. After ten years of post Civil War carpetbag control, the South began building a system that bore little resemblance to what had existed in the plantation days. The creation of state departments of education began to raise standards, especially in teacher education, and eventually in certification as well.

Music, having established itself as part of the common school curriculum in large cities, became part of the offerings in other communities as the nation developed. As was true of other subjects, instruction became systematized, although not in a unified manner. Textbooks and other teaching aids proliferated. The teaching of music reading continued as a major objective of most programs, but methods differed widely. Luther Whiting Mason had a large body of followers for his rote approach, and Hosea Holt drew many advocates by coauthoring a series with John Tufts designed to teach students to read from the very beginning. Many others devised variations of either the rote or the note approach, and another group concentrated on beautiful singing of good song literature toward the end of the century. The English method, Tonic-Sol-fa, was popular for a brief period.

The demand for music teachers led to the establishment of summer schools operated by the textbook publishers. Toward the end of the century normal schools began to train music teachers, and the colleges and conservatories developed interest in public school music. Throughout the period, high school music generally consisted of compulsory choral singing. The pupils could sing choral works because of the efficiency with which music reading was taught in the lower grades. Particularly in cities with large German populations—Saint Louis, Milwaukee, Cincinnati—the schools played a role in developing a musical culture. Beginning efforts to introduce instrumental music were made, and some were successful enough to convince music educators that growth should continue in the new century. Similarly, a few experiments with music electives in the high school indicated that singing alone would not constitute a full program of public school music in the future. Yet thousands of Americans had been taught to sing, and many were good enough to participate in singing societies that developed parallel to professional orchestras to give the country a balanced musical culture.

The "scientific" educational system of the period, to which music teachers gladly adapted, was confronted with the new science of psychology toward the end of the period. Because psychology dealt with discovering the true nature of man and the stages he went through to achieve his potential, it had more to offer educators who understood Rousseau, Pestalozzi, and Froebel and thus suggested a break in the formal structure that characterized American education for much of the nineteenth century.

NOTES

1. *Minutes of the Board of Trustees and Visitors of Common Schools of Cincinnati, Ohio,* June 27, 1853, vol. 6.
2. F. E. Tunison, *Presto, From the Singing School to the May Festival* (Cincinnati: E. H. Beasley, 1888), p. i.
3. C. V. Buttelman, "A Century of Music in Buffalo Schools," *Music Educators Journal* 23 (March 1937): 80.
4. *Superintendent's Annual Report for 1843, Buffalo Public Schools.* Buffalo, NY, 1843.
5. Osbourne McConathy, "Evolution of Public School Music in the United States," *MTNA Proceedings, 1922,* p. 162, published in *Louisville Journal,* 1854. Reported in Robert John, "Nineteenth Century Graded Vocal Series," *Journal of Research in Music Education* 2 (Fall 1954): 104.
6. Peggy D. Bennett, "Sarah Glover: A Forgotten Pioneer in Music Education," *Journal of Research in Music Education* 32 (Spring 1984): 49–65.
7. Robert John, "Nineteenth Century Graded Vocal Series," *Journal of Research in Music Education* 2 (Fall 1954): 110.
8. *Minutes of the Board of Trustees and Visitors of Common Schools of Cincinnati, Ohio,* January 21, 1856, vol. 7, p. 221.
9. H. S. Perkins, "Reminiscences of Early Days in School Music," *School Music* 9 (May 1908): 5-9.
10. Kenneth Ray Hartley," A Study of the Life and Works of Luther Whiting Mason" (Ed.D. dissertation, Florida State University, 1960).
11. Ibid., p. 111.
12. John, "Nineteenth Century Graded Vocal Series," p. 111.
13. Luther Whiting Mason, *Second Music Reader: A Course of Exercises in the Elements of Vocal Music and Sight-Singing, with Choice Rote Songs for the Use of Schools and Families* (Boston: Ginn Brothers, 1870), pp. iii–iv.
14. Robert M. Fowells, "Public School Music in San Francisco, 1848–1897," *Journal of Research in Music Education* 11 (Spring 1963): 71.
15. *School Music Monthly* 4 (May 1903): 11.
16. John, "Nineteenth Century Graded Vocal Series," p. 112.

17. Ibid., p. 113.
18. Ibid.
19. John Tufts, *Normal Music Course: A Series of Exercises, Studies, and Songs, Defining and Illustrating the Art of Sight Reading; Progressively Arranged from the First Conception and Production of Tones to the Most Advanced Choral Practice,* Introductory Third Reader (Boston: Silver, Burdett & Company, 1894), pp. 3-4.
20. John, "Nineteenth Century Graded Vocal Series," p. 114.
21. Ibid., p. 115.
22. F. H. Ripley, "How to Promote Musical Appreciation without Technical Work," *MTNA Proceedings* 29 (1917): 94-104.
23. Florence Growman, "The Emergence of the Concept of General Music as Reflected in Basal Textbooks 1900-1980," (DMA dissertation, The Catholic University of America, 1985), p. 97.
24. Reven S. DeJarnette, *Hollis Dann: His Life and Contributions to Music Education* (Boston: Birchard, 1940), p. 100.
25. Edward Bailey Birge, *History of Public School Music in the United States* (Washington, DC: Music Educators National Conference, 1928), p. 122.
26. T. P. Giddings, "Song Method," *School Music* 9 (May 1908): 29-30.
27. Hermann C. Suehs, the "Legacy of William Augustus Hodgdon, School Music Teacher" (MA thesis, The Catholic University of America, 1971), pp. 37-8.
28. *Progress of Public Education in the United States of America* (Washington, DC: U.S. Government Printing Office, 1962), p. 48.
29. *Minutes of the Board of Trustees and Visitors of Common Schools,* Cincinnati, March 2, 1857, vol. 7, p. 500.
30. Walter H. Aiken, "Music in the Cincinnati Schools," *Journal of Proceedings of the Seventeenth Annual Meeting of the Music Supervisors National Conference* (Tulsa: Music Supervisors National Conference, 1924), p. 51.
31. *Eightieth Annual Report of the Public Schools of Cincinnati for the School Year Ending August 31, 1909* (Cincinnati, 1909), p. 50.
32. Moses Cheney, "Letter to Friend Mason," *Musical Visitor,* vol. 2 (Dec. 1, 1841): 139; and John Stickney, see Frank J. Metcalf, *American Writers and Compilers of Sacred Music* (New York: Abingdon Press, 1925), p. 41.
33. Charles Hamm, "The Chapins and Sacred Music in the South and West," *Journal of Research in Music Education* 8 (Fall 1960): 91-98.
34. Robert W. John, "Origins of the First Music Educators Convention," *Journal of Research in Music Education* 13 (Winter 1965): 207.
35. Charles A. Harper, *A Century of Public Teacher Education* (Washington, DC: American Association of Teachers Colleges, 1939), p. 128.
36. Interview with Charles L. Gary, Norwood, Ohio, September 3, 1950.
37. *Handbook of the Alumni Association* (Chicago: Alumni Association of the National Summer School, 1903). MENC Archives, University of Maryland.
38. Thomas J. Elward, "A History of Music Education in the District of Columbia Public Schools from 1845 to 1945" (DMA dissertation, The Catholic University of America, 1975): 55.
39. Frances E. Clark, "School Music in 1836, 1886, 1911, and 1936," *Proceedings of the National Education Association for 1924* 62: 603-11.
40. William T. Anderson, "Concord's Man for the Twenty-First Century," *American History Illustrated* 23 (March 1988): 30-37, 48.

41. Robert C. Post, ed., *A Centennial Exhibition* (Washington, DC: Smithsonian Institution, 1976), p. 197.
42. R. R. Rideout, "On Early Applications of Psychology in Music Education," *Journal of Research in Music Education* 30 (Fall 1982): 143.
43. Nina C. Vandewalken, "The History of the Kindergarten Influence in Elementary Education," *Sixth Yearbook* (National Society for the Study of Education, 1907), p.124.
44. Eleanor Smith, *Songs for Little Children* (Springfield, MA: Milton Bradley, 1887), frontispiece.
45. Smith, *Songs for Little Children*, p. v.
46. Lawrence A. Cremin, *The Transformation of the School* (New York: Knopf, 1961), p. 129.
47. Lawrence A. Cremin, *American Education: The Metropolitan Experience, 1870–1980* (New York: Harper & Row, 1988), p. 279.
48. Joseph M. Rice, *The Public-School System of the United States* (New York: Century Company, 1893), p. 320.
49. Keith H. Polakoff, et al., *Generations of Americans: A History of the United States* (New York: Saint Martin's, 1976), p. 524.
50. Larry Cuban, *How Teachers Taught: Constancy and Change in American Classrooms, 1890–1980* (New York: Longman, 1984).
51. Beatrice Perham, *Music in the New School* (Chicago: Neil A. Kjos Music Co., 1937), pp. 7–9.
52. U.S. Bureau of Education, "Education in Music at Home and Abroad," *The Study of Music in the Public Schools*, circular of Information No. 1 for 1886, pp. 51–52, reported in Martin Bergee, "Ringing the Changes: General John Eaton and the 1886 Public School Music Survey," *Journal of Research in Music Education* 35 (Summer 1987): 107.
53. Ibid.
54. Edgar O. Silver, "Special Report on the Condition of Music Instruction in the Public Schools of the United States," *National Education Association Proceedings*, 1889, pp. 684–93.

BIBLIOGRAPHY

Aiken, Walter H. "Music in the Cincinnati Schools." *Journal of Proceedings of the Seventeenth Annual Meeting of the Music Supervisors National Conference*. Tulsa: Music Supervisors National Conference, 1924.

Alvarez, Barbara Jo. "Preschool Music Education and Research on the Musical Development of Preschool Children: 1900 to 1980." Ph.D. dissertation, University of Michigan, 1981.

Anderson, William T. "Concord's Man for the Twenty-First Century." *American History Illustrated* 23 (March 1988).

Bennett, Peggy D. "Sarah Glover: A Forgotten Pioneer in Music Education." *Journal of Research in Music Education* 31 (Spring 1984).

Bergee, Martin J. "Ringing the Changes: General John Eaton and the 1886 Public School Music Survey." *Journal of Research in Music Education* 35 (Summer 1987).

Birge, Edward Bailey. *History of Public School Music in the United States.* Washington, DC: Music Educators National Conference, 1928.

Buttelman, Clifford V. "A Century of Music in Buffalo Schools." *Music Educators Journal* 23 (March 1937).

A Centennial Exhibition, Robert C. Post, ed. Washington, DC: The Smithsonian Institution, 1976.

Cheney, Moses. "Letter to Friend Mason." *Musical Visitor,* vol. 2 (December 1, 1841).

Clark, Frances Elliott. Autobiographical manuscript, "Music Education As I Have Lived It," 1950, in MENC Historical Center, Special Collections in Music, University of Maryland at College Park.

———. "School Music in 1836, 1886, 1911, and 1936." *Proceedings of the National Education Association for 1924* 62.

Cremin, Lawrence A. *American Education: The Metropolitan Experience, 1870–1980.* New York: Harper & Row, 1988.

———. *The Transformation of the School.* New York: Knopf, 1961.

Cuban, Larry. *How Teachers Taught: Constancy and Change in American Classrooms, 1890–1980.* New York: Longman, 1984.

DeJarnette, Reven S. *Hollis Dann: His Life and Contributions to Music Education.* Boston: C. C. Birchard, 1940.

Eightieth Annual Report of the Public Schools of Cincinnati for the School Year Ending August 31, 1909. Cincinnati, 1909.

Elward, Thomas J. "A History of Music Education in the District of Columbia Public Schools from 1845 to 1945." DMA dissertation, The Catholic University of America, 1975.

Fowells, Robert M. "Public School Music in San Francisco, 1848–1897." *Journal of Research in Music Education* 11 (Spring 1963).

Furnas, J. C. *Great Times.* New York: Putnam, 1974.

Giddings, Thaddeus P. "Song Method." *School Music* 9 (May 1908).

Growman, Florence. "The Emergence of the Concept of General Music as Reflected in Basel Textbooks 1900–1980." DMA dissertation, The Catholic University of America, 1985.

Hamm, Charles. "The Chapins and Sacred Music in the South and West." *Journal of Research in Music Education* 8 (Fall 1960).

Handbook of the Alumni Association. Chicago: Alumni Association of the National Summer School, 1903, in MENC Historical Center, Special Collections in Music, University of Maryland at College Park.

Harper, Charles A. *A Century of Public Teacher Education.* Washington, DC: American Association of Teachers Colleges, 1939.

Hartley, Kenneth Ray. "A Study of the Life and Works of Luther Whiting Mason." Ed.D. dissertation, Florida State University, 1960.

John, Robert. "Nineteenth Century Graded Vocal Series." *Journal of Research in Music Education* 2 (Fall 1954).

———. "Origins of the First Music Educators Convention." *Journal of Research in Music Education* 13 (Winter 1965).

Metcalf, Frank J. *American Writers and Compilers of Sacred Music*. New York: Abingdon, 1925.

Minutes of the Board of Trustees and Visitors of Common Schools, Cincinnati, January 21, 1856, vol. 7; June 27, 1853, vol. 6; March 2, 1857, vol. 7.

Perham, Beatrice. *Music in the New School*. Chicago: Neil A. Kjos Co., 1937.

Perkins, H. S. "Reminiscences of Early Days in School Music. *School Music* 9 (May 1908).

Polakoff, Keith H., et al. *Generations of Americans: A History of the United States*. New York: Saint Martin's, 1976.

Progress of Public Education in the United States of America. Washington, DC: U.S. Government Printing Office, 1962.

Rice, Joseph M. *The Public-School System of the United States*. New York: The Century Company, 1893.

Rideout, Roger R. "On Early Applications of Psychology in Music Education." *Journal of Research in Music Education* 30 (Fall 1982).

School Music Monthly 4 (May 1903), 5 (June 1904).

Silver, Edgar O. "Special Report on the Condition of Music Instruction in the Public Schools of the United States." *National Education Association Proceedings*, 1889.

Smith, Eleanor. *Songs for Little Children*. Springfield, MA: Milton Bradley, 1887.

Suehs, Hermann C. "The Legacy of William Augustus Hodgdon, School Music Teacher." DMA dissertation, The Catholic University of America, 1971.

Superintendent's Report for 1843, Buffalo Public Schools.

Tunison, F. E. *Presto, From the Singing School to the May Festival*. Cincinnati: E. H. Beasley and Co., 1888.

Vandewalken, Nina C. "The History of the Kindergarten Influence in Elementary Education." *Sixth Yearbook*. Chicago: National Society for the Study of Education, 1907.

Volk, Terese M. "The Growth and Development of Music Education in the Public Schools of Buffalo, New York, 1843–1988." *The Bulletin of Historical Research in Music Education* 9 (July 1988).

10

THE DEVELOPMENT OF PROFESSIONAL EDUCATIONAL ORGANIZATIONS

Alexis de Tocqueville wrote in *Democracy in America*: "Whenever at the head of some new undertaking you see the government in France or a man of rank in England, in the United States one is certain to find an association." This is as true of American musical and educational undertakings as it is of political, religious, economic, military, and other endeavors.

THE NATIONAL EDUCATION ASSOCIATION

The Society of Associated Teachers of New York City, founded in 1794, was an early, and possibly the first, American association of teachers. Massachusetts singing masters formed the Essex Musical Association to advance the cause of the seven-note syllable system over the prevalent *fa-sol-la*.[1] By the middle of the nineteenth century, three quarters of the states had statewide teacher organizations. Horace Mann was the first president of a group known as the American Association for the Advancement of Education (founded in 1848). In 1857 the presidents of the New York and Massachusetts associations, T. W. Valentine and D. B. Hagar, issued a call for a meeting in Philadelphia to discuss the formation of a national organization of teachers. Forty-three individuals responded, and the National Teachers Association (NTA) was founded. Its purposes were to advance the interests of the teaching profession and to promote the cause of education.

The NTA proved its value early in its existence, when Congressman James A. Garfield of Ohio introduced a bill in 1866 creating the Department of Education. The bill was passed with the assistance of the NTA. This was an early accomplishment for the young organization and one that encouraged it to continue in the direction it had taken. The new department was not given Cabinet rank and was reduced to the status of a bureau after one year, but the NTA had demonstrated its ability to influence the government.

When Horace Mann attended the NTA meeting in Cincinnati the next year, he agreed to a merger between his group and the National Teachers Association. Even with the merger, the membership was not large. Two other organizations appeared soon after, however—the National Association of School Superintendents and the American Normal School Association. Both joined with the National Teachers Association in 1879 to form the National Education Association (NEA).

The National Education Association did not grow much until 1884, when Thomas W. Bicknell, editor of the *Journal of Education*, traveled widely to promote the next annual meeting, to be held in Madison, Wisconsin. He was successful, and over five thousand educators attended. The meeting proved significant for music teaching as well as for the education of Indians and Blacks and for the greater involvement of women in the affairs of NEA. It was at this meeting that Booker T. Washington had his first national audience, and Frances E. Willard was the main speaker for the "Women's Evening."

Curricular Expansion. One of the early functions of the NEA was to advocate positions relative to the limited curriculum of the schools. In 1860 a resolution had been passed in favor of "physical culture." Three years later, in the middle of the Civil War, a similar position was taken with respect to the teaching of history and music.

Many of those who attended the early NEA meetings were superintendents or principals of normal schools, and some had experience with strong music programs. They included A. J. Rickoff, superintendent in Cincinnati and later in Cleveland, and E. E. White, who, after being superintendent in Columbus and Cincinnati, became president of Purdue University. Daniel B. Hagar, head of the Salem (Massachusetts) Normal School, was an early leader of the normal school group that made music an important part of their meeting agendas. At one meeting, Eben Tourjée, of the Conservatory of Music in Boston, gave a major address entitled "A Plea for Vocal Music in the Public Schools." He called for music to be "a strong educational appliance coordinated in rank with the other studies . . . to be pursued as systematically and thoroughly as they." Tourjée presented several reasons to support his position. They included practical, moral, aesthetic, and religious grounds:

> Sculpture, painting and architecture may charm, may elevate, but music softens, thrills, subdues. It quickens the whole range of emotions. For each it has a voice, of each it is the interpreter. Sown in the heart of youth, its influence blesses his whole life.[2]

J. C. Greenough, principal of the State Normal School in Providence, spoke of music in schools as a means of aesthetic culture at the 1872 Boston meeting. J. B. Buchanan of Kentucky delivered a major address entitled "Full-Orbed Education" at the NEA meeting in Minneapolis in 1875. Buchanan discussed the value of music in education and mentioned that Wesleyan president Joseph Cummings had expressed similar thoughts in an earlier meeting. Music education had influential supporters in the early years of the NEA.

The Department of Music Education. At the 1883 meeting, Professor L. S. Thompson of Lafayette, Indiana, was successful in persuading the NEA to approve a department of art. President T. W. Valentine was probably aware of this when he suggested to Luther Whiting Mason and Theodore F. Seward that they encourage vocal music teachers to attend the NEA meeting in Madison, Wisconsin. Daniel Hagar was chairman of the music sessions. Gustavus Junkermann, superintendent of music in Cincinnati, gave an address on method. Seward spoke about the Tonic Sol-fa approach. The important event was the drawing up of a petition to the NEA board of directors to request the creation of a department of vocal music. As a past president of the NEA and one of its founders, Hagar's support was influential. The board suggested one alteration when it granted the petition. The name was changed to the Department of Music Education, a foresighted move in the light of the many changes soon to come.

Hagar was elected the first president of the department, O. S. Wescott (Chicago) vice president, T. A. Brand (Madison) secretary, and Luther Whiting Mason (Boston), N. Coe Stewart (Cleveland), Orlando Blackman (Chicago), and T. F. Seward (New York) directors. It was a distinguished and representative group of officers. The next year the NEA met in Saratoga, New York, and the department chose psychologist G. Stanley Hall as its second president. Other officers were continued from the previous year, and Benjamin Jepson (New Haven) was elected a director after his speech "A Plea for the Elements of Music in Primary Grades."

Discussions of music education and singing demonstrations by school children became regular parts of subsequent NEA meetings. Not only music supervisors were involved. Both Rickoff and White gave addresses on music education at NEA meetings in the late 1880s. Other active members of the NEA Department of Music Education were Nathan Glover (Akron, Ohio), David Kelsey (Saratoga, New York), George Young (Wichita), Philip C. Hayden (Quincy, Illinois), A. J. Gantvoort (Piqua, Ohio), Walter Aiken (Cincinnati), Julia Ettie Crane (Potsdam, New York), Sterrie A. Weaver (Westfield, Massachusetts), Charles Fullerton (Cedar Falls, Iowa), Stanley Osbourne (New Paltz, New York), Samuel W. Cole (Brookline, Massachusetts), Ralph Baldwin (Northampton, Massachusetts), Frances E. Clark (Ottumwa, Iowa), Thomas Tapper (Chicago), Hamlin Cogswell (Indiana, Pennsylvania), Edward B. Birge (Indianapolis), Elsie M. Shaw (St. Paul), Anna Allen (Peoria), and Charles Rice (Worcester, Massachusetts).

Although many of the presentations at the department meetings dealt with aspects of singing, new ideas in education began to be discussed in the context of music education at the turn of the century. Samuel W. Cole said in his speech at the 1903 meeting in Boston:

> What then is the purpose of teaching music in the public schools? I answer: the creation of a musical atmosphere in America; the establishment of a musical environment in every home; the development of a national type of music; . . . In short, the real purpose of teaching music in the schools is to lay the foundation for all that we can hope or wish to realize, musically, in the United States of America. . . . To sum it all up: the real purpose of teaching music in the public schools is not to make expert sight-singers nor individual soloists. I speak from experience. I have done all these things, and I can do them again; but I have learned that, if they become an end and not a means, they hinder rather than help. . . . A much nobler, grander, more inspiring privilege is yours and mine: to get the great mass to singing and to make them love it.[3]

Teacher Welfare. The two initial purposes of the National Education Association caused a rift in the membership. One of the original organizers had spoken at the first meeting about the importance of raising the salaries of teachers. Others felt that promoting the cause of education, rather than teacher welfare, should be the overriding objective of the NEA. John Philbrick emphasized salaries and working conditions in his 1863 address. President Thomas Bicknell carried on the crusade for salary increases in 1884 and added his concern for "equal pay for equal training." By the turn of the century, however, little had been accomplished in terms of improved salaries for elementary teachers, and when commercial employment became more readily available to women, desertions from the classroom began. In 1903 the Chicago Teachers Federation asked the NEA to gather information on salaries, but some NEA officers felt that teacher welfare was not in the province of a professional association.[4] The NEA passed resolutions on teacher welfare, and eventually committees were appointed to address the subject. One of the first tasks of the Department of Research, established in 1922, was to gather data on salaries. Tenure, retirement plans, working conditions, contracts, teacher liability, cooperatives, and credit unions were other matters with which the NEA eventually became involved.

NEA members who were more concerned about educational matters devoted their efforts to curriculum improvement, improved teacher preparation, the establishment of a professional periodical (*The NEA Journal*), and a publications program to produce professional books and pamphlets. The establishment in 1935 of the Educational Policies Commission in conjunction with the Department of Superintendence was an important contribution of the NEA to the cause of education. The distinguished educators who served in these endeavors prepared policy statements on many aspects of education, including "The Structure and Administration of Education in American Democracy" (1938), "Social Service and the Schools" (1939), "Learning the Ways of Democracy" (1940), "Education and the People's Peace" (1943), "America Education and International Tension" (1949), "The Education of the Gifted" (1950), "Strengthening Community Life" (1954), "Mass Communication and Education" (1958), "The Central Purpose of Education" (1961), "Education and the Spirit of Science" (1966), "Universal Opportunity for Early Childhood Education" (1966), "On the Role of the Teacher" (1967), and others.

Cooperative Efforts. Over the years the NEA pulled together many educational associations that represented all aspects of public education. They included school administration at every level, subject-oriented specialists, those dedicated to the improvement of teacher education, curriculum development, educational technology, and various school services. Most of these groups came together in the late 1950s in their new home, the six-million-dollar NEA Building in Washington, DC, built entirely with member contributions. The editor of *The NEA Journal* regularly consulted with those in the NEA Building in Washington to be sure the magazine was in step with all aspects of public education. Specialists from the various departments assisted the NEA by contributing to such endeavors as the Academically Talented Student Project and the Project on Instruction. The NEA Research Department produced *Music and Art in the Schools*, which provided a clear picture of the status of the two disciplines in 1963.

This halcyon state of affairs lasted for a little over ten years. In the 1970s competition for members with the American Federation of Teachers, a trade union of the AFL-CIO, resulted in the decision by NEA to abandon the role of a professional association. It gave up its tax-exempt status as a not-for-profit organization and took on the role of a labor union. Its new status permitted NEA to lobby Congress for the direct welfare of its members. A major casualty of this event was the education "family," which was dismantled. Administrator organizations were told they were now considered "management" and would have to leave the NEA Building. The Music Educators National Conference, part of the NEA family, also left because its purpose was not compatible with that of a labor union, although it might be considered complementary.

Although the NEA gave up its leadership in promoting higher education standards, it was effective in that arena. While striving to improve the working conditions of elementary classroom teachers, the NEA forced school boards throughout the country to hire thousands of special teachers of art, music, and physical education to create preparation time for classroom teachers. This increased the amount of time for music instruction substantially, and school systems that had reduced elementary music programs during the Great Depression and World War II were forced to reinstate them.

THE MUSIC TEACHERS NATIONAL ASSOCIATION

In the summer of 1875, plans were being made for a summer school at the Seminary in East Greenwich, Rhode Island. Eben Tourjée, a former faculty member who had founded and now directed the New England Conservatory of Music, was asked to organize the school. He had tried to establish a national music congress following the World Peace Jubilee but there were only three meetings. Tourjée attracted a number of music teachers from a wide geographical area in the summer of 1875, among them three Ohioans—N. Coe Stewart and William Henry Dana of Akron and Theodore Presser, professor of piano at Ohio Female Seminary, Delaware. These men and G. M. Cole of Richmond, Indiana, fell into conversation about the desirability of an organization for music teachers. Presser agreed to host a convention of teachers in Delaware, Ohio, the following year, thereby preparing the way for the Music Teachers National Association (MTNA), the first permanent association of musicians in the United States.

The first meeting of MTNA attracted sixty-three men and women who spent three days in late December 1876 listening to papers (including two by Tourjée) and coming to agreement on three purposes for the organization: mutual improvement through the exchange of ideas, broadening of musical culture in the United States, and cultivation of fraternal feelings. The MTNA constitution still remains close to the original principles, as did previous revisions in 1883, 1899, 1906, and 1926. The current constitution states:

(1) The object of the Association is the advancement of musical knowledge and education. (2) Activities of the Association are aimed at the promotion of the art of music, advancement of musical knowledge by disseminating the knowledge of educational activities, and the appreciation of music by the people of the nation.

Dana presented a talk, "The Beginnings of the MTNA," at the l914 meeting. He said that some of the original attendees had come for the opportunity to advertise their publications; others anticipated gaining pupils through their participation. Three who had "overstepped the bounds of propriety," including first President Tourjée, never again "identified themselves with MTNA or helped to serve its interest and the cause of music."

Private Music Instruction. Dana's comments also shed light on the condition of private instruction in the United States at that time. He commented particularly on the young women who began to teach piano for "pin money" without having attained true competence. Voice teachers were, "for the most part, charlatans or broken down opera singers." According to Dana, these conditions "called into existence the Music Teachers' National Association." Most who came to the first meeting were private teachers of piano, organ, or voice. School music leaders also attended. They included George F. Root and Luther Whiting Mason from Boston, George Loomis from Indianapolis, N. Coe Stewart from Cleveland, and his former student Nathan Glover from Akron. The other schoolteachers were all from Ohio: M. N. Dane (Toledo), D. T. Davis (Mt. Gilead), George Housel (Akron), J. D. Luse (Norwalk) and A. J. Phillips (Warren). There were attendees from as far away as Georgia and Maine. The host, Theodore Presser, and E. Z. Lorenz of Dayton were destined to go into publishing.

Meeting Formats. The second meeting was held at Chautauqua, New York, in the summer of 1878, but only thirty-eight attended. It featured a full-length recital by William H. Sherwood, a pupil of Liszt and later founder of a school of piano in Chicago. James H. Butterfield of Illinois succeeded Tourjée as president. The choice of the isolated site probably accounted for the low attendance, because 175 people registered at the Cincinnati meeting the following year. Attendance was also helped by having on the program the popular Theodore Thomas Orchestra and two piano recitals, one by Sherwood and the other by Mme. de Roode-Rice. The latter was the wife of the third president of the organization, Rudolph de Roode, from Kentucky.

MTNA continued to expand in size and influence. Adhering to the original high-minded goals, it heard papers on psychology (1880), government patronage of the arts (1881), increased instrumental music in the schools (1883), international pitch of A = 435 (1883), and works of

American composers (1884). The 1882 meeting in Chicago was significant because for the first time the program included performing groups
and soloists who were not paid. This was the beginning of a new practice of music organizations—having their musical programs provided by
members or their students. Attendance approached one thousand in
Boston in 1886 and greatly exceeded it in Chicago two years later.

Certification of Music Teachers. In 1883 at the Providence meeting,
President Edward M. Bowman suggested the formation of a national
college of teachers. The idea was debated and tabled, but it brought to
light the interest of the association in providing a certification process
for private teachers. Certification was first put into practice by state music teacher groups, with Kansas having a functional scheme in place
in the 1890s. The plan developed by the Washington Music Teachers
Association, approved by the state board of education in 1921, was
probably the first. Meanwhile, MTNA appointed study committees to
discuss national certification. Ulrich reports that it was 1974 before the
plan, with its accompanying Board and Certification Handbook, went
into operation.[5]

MTNA Membership. President Henry S. Perkins quoted de Roode
as saying at the 1879 meeting, "there are two antagonistic factions . . .
the thoroughly educated musician and the Do-Re-Mi fraternity." This
feeling of class distinction, a different sort of dichotomy than the one
developing within the NEA, may have driven public school music teachers to the NEA and the eventual establishment of the Department of
Music Education. Though many schoolteachers have continued to be
involved in MTNA activities over the years, the possibility of that organization representing all teachers of music was abandoned early on by
officers who represented private studio instruction.

The Operation of MTNA. The business of the Association was carried on through the voluntary service of the elected officers until 1951,
more than twenty years after the younger Music Educators National
Conference had established an office with a paid executive secretary.
That the organization could continue for seventy-five years in this manner speaks well of the dedication of its members, although there were
times when the work did not get done, according to Perkins. S. Turner
Jones was hired as the first paid executive. He set up a national office
in New York City in August 1951. At the same time, publication of the
Annual Proceedings was halted and a journal, the *American Music Teacher,*
was begun. The office was moved to Cincinnati in the 1960s, when G.
William Fehrer succeeded Jones. Other executive officers since then
have been Albert G. Huetteman, Bud A. Udell, Mariann H. Clinton,
and Robert J. Elias. Among the school music teachers intimately involved with the MTNA over the years were N. Coe Stewart (MTNA

president 1895), A. J. Gantvoort (MTNA president 1900), Rossiter W. Cole (MTNA president 1903, 1909–1910), Charles H. Farnsworth (MTNA president 1913–1914), Osbourne McConathy (MTNA president 1921, MSNC president 1919), Karl W. Gehrkens (MTNA president 1934, MSNC president 1923), and Russell V. Morgan (MTNA president 1947, MSNC president 1932). Many others served on committees, read papers at meetings, or wrote articles for the *American Music Teacher.*

Mutual Interests of Associations. There were many common areas of interest between public school music educators and members of the MTNA. John Crowder wrote about these interests in an early issue of *American Music Teacher.* He defined the role of MENC as teaching the masses and that of MTNA as developing leaders in all musical fields. The two associations have been mutually helpful despite their competition for the same exhibitors and advertisers. They have cooperated occasionally on projects of common interest, including the support of copyright law revision. With the National Association of Schools of Music, the groups updated and distributed thousands of copies of numerous editions of the ''Careers in Music'' pamphlet originally prepared by William R. Sur of Michigan State University. A common interest in raising the level of the training of all kinds of music teachers led them to share ideas and recommend changes in college teacher preparation curricula.

EARLY SCHOOL MUSIC ASSOCIATIONS

The Music Teachers National Association decided early in its existence that public school music was only of minor interest to its members. The Department of Music Education of the National Education Association, although it became a strong rallying point, was never a major component of the NEA. The creation of the Department in 1884, however, influenced school music teachers to form other organizations. State education associations, particularly in New England and the Midwest, sprouted music sections whose programs were much like those of the NEA Department of Music Education but had more teaching demonstrations and performances by children.

The Normal Music Teachers Association. In 1885 two groups were established within one week in Boston. The Normal Music Teachers Association met on Saturday, December 5, in Old South Church on Washington Street to adopt a constitution prepared by a committee that had been appointed in November. Hosea Holt was elected president and Edgar O. Silver corresponding secretary. The organization was probably formed to support Holt's *Normal Method* music texts. The stated purpose, however, was ''to promote the study of music in the public schools and to secure its proper universal recognition as a regular branch of study." In conjunction with the organization, the *School Music Journal* was founded by F. H. Gilson in September 1885 with the following statement:

> Music as a branch of education is coming rapidly to the front. . . . There has been no previous journal devoted to music as a branch of education. Nearly every teacher has methods of his own. This journal advocates music as a branch of education on the broadest basis. It will not support any one system to the exclusion of others.[6]

Gilson was the publisher of *Tonic Sol-Fa Course for Schools* by Daniel Batchellor, and more space was given to that system than to any other method. Nevertheless, Gilson gave coverage to all who had something to say on the subject of school music.

While Holt gave demonstrations and illustrative lessons at almost every subsequent meeting, the programs of the Normal Music Teachers Association also included a variety of speakers, some of whom presented advanced ideas for the time. General Thomas Jefferson Morgan of the Providence Conservatory made a plea for instrumental music at the October 1886 meeting. He also said that children had the right to complain to the state if they were not taught music. "You robbed me; you took me when I was young and shut out music."[7] A. E. Winship told those present on February 12, 1887, that children must learn to sing and to listen early. "I question if you can learn to think in tone after you are 20," he warned.[8]

The Normal Music Teachers Association was a selective organization. An examination committee was appointed at the first meeting and charged with reporting on the fitness of applicants to become instructors of music in the schools. Certificates were to be issued to qualified members. This might have been the first attempt at certification by a school music group. The seven examiners were Samuel Cole of Brookline, Massachusetts, H. M. Walton of Newton, Massachusetts, J. E. Shepherdson of Brockton, Massachusetts, Laura S. Merriam of Fitchburg, Massachusetts, F. L. Dinan of New Bedford, Massachusetts, J. Lovell of Norwich, New York, and N. H. Thompson of Burlington, Vermont.

The New England Public School Music Teachers Association was the other organization formed in 1885. An article by George A. Veazie in the second issue of the *School Music Journal* and a circular distributed by Luther Whiting Mason led to the formation of the association. The first meeting was held on December 12, 1885, one week after the normal group. Mason and Veazie presented "specimen lessons," and many officers were chosen. D. B. Hagar was named the first president (he had also been the first president of the NEA Department a year and a half before). Among the many vice presidents were Seth Richards of Worcester, New Hampshire, N. H. Thompson of Burlington, New

Hampshire, and Benjamin Jepson of New Haven, Connecticut. The purpose of the association was "to inquire into every system of instruction with a view to ascertaining which is the best." Membership was open to music teachers, school superintendents, and others interested in educational music.

The group met at Pilgrim Hall on the following Saturday, adopted a constitution, and agreed to meet on the third Saturday of each month for their regular assembly. At the January 16, 1886, meeting they set the dues for ladies at one dollar and for gentlemen at two dollars.[9] Luther Whiting Mason appeared on many of the programs to discuss "Voice Culture in Germany," "Years in Japan," and his books. Among the regular attendants were W. S. Tilden of Medford, L. B. Marshall of Boston, Samuel Cole, and F. H. Ripley, who was soon to produce a textbook series of his own with Thomas Tapper.

The two organizations demonstrate that school music teachers in the East were interested in organizing themselves for professional development, but an ingredient to assure permanence was lacking. The accounts of the short-lived *School Music Journal* suggest that it may have been because the members were more interested in promoting a method than in the broader purposes declared by both associations. Perhaps the fact that New England citizens were not totally committed to the common schools for the education of all its children was a factor. More likely it was because of all the outstanding names on the rolls of the two associations, there was no one with the foresight or organizational ability to create a permanent group.

An interesting fact is made apparent from reading the accounts of these groups. Each of the music teachers in the Boston schools seem to have been free to use any method he chose in the schools to which he was assigned. This contrasted with such cities as Cleveland, Saint Louis, Cincinnati, Chicago, and Akron, where strong superintendents of music provided direction.

The Society of American School Music Supervisors had two meetings at the end of the nineteenth century. Sterrie Weaver, Julia Ettie Crane, T. L. Roberts, Ralph Baldwin, and J. H. Humphrey were elected officers at the organizational meeting in Utica in 1899. A meeting of the group was hosted by Benjamin Jepson in New Haven the next year. An unprecedented heat wave appears to have taken the starch out of the few that attended, and the group never met again.[10]

THE AMERICAN ASSOCIATION OF SCHOOL ADMINISTRATORS

During the 1865 meeting of the National Teachers Association in Harrisburg, Pennsylvania, a group of state and city superintendents discussed the formation of an organization for administrators. The name National Association of School Superintendents was adopted the following year at the NTA meeting, but it was renamed the Department of School Superintendence of the National Education Association in 1870. The current name, American Association of School Administrators, was adopted in 1932. It was still a department of the NEA at that time.

Among the leaders of the AASA have been many who helped advance the cause of music education. One was Randall J. Condon, who was superintendent of the Cincinnati schools from 1913 to 1929. He addressed the music educators at their 1922 meeting in Nashville[11] and again when they met in Cincinnati in 1924. When he became president of the Department of Superintendence he was responsible for preparing the annual meeting in 1927, scheduled for Dallas.[12] Condon had been impressed by the Richmond, Indiana, Orchestra, directed by Joseph Maddy, at the Nashville convention. He asked his own director of music, Walter Aiken, to arrange for Maddy and the newly created National High School Orchestra to perform for the superintendents in Dallas. The concert was the first exposure that most of the superintendents had to excellent music by students, and they were inspired. They brought their enthusiasm home to school systems all over the country. The Dallas program was filled with singing, bands, and smaller ensembles. Maddy gained the confidence to go forward with the National High School Orchestra Camp, which he and T. P. Giddings founded the next year at Interlochen, Michigan.

Members of the Music Education Research Council joined with superintendents such as Philander P. Claxton of Tulsa, Jesse H. Newlon of Denver, Herbert S. Weet of Rochester, and Thomas Finnegan of Harrisburg to discuss school music. One of the resolutions that came from this meeting was a call to immediately extend music study to all rural schools. Joseph Maddy wrote:

> As the result of this "musical crusade" the convention passed a resolution placing music on an equal basis with the other fundamental subjects in education—the greatest victory for music in the history of the nation.[13]

Two years later the superintendents passed another resolution calling for a study "looking toward re-evaluating the arts with a view to assigning them more fundamental recognition in the programs of high schools and colleges."[14]

Condon continued his close association with the music educators. He said at the 1929 meeting of the Music Supervisors National Conference in Philadelphia:

> First, beauty—music and art and drama—is most fundamental to education and unless we begin to build our education on such things our structure is hardly worth the building; and second, that all children can be

educated, some in one way, some in another, and it is our business to so shape our program that education should result from those things we bring to them. . . . We are pointing the way, we are creating the atmosphere that makes people willing to seek, that they may find. . . . So you and I . . . are engaged in the highest, and I believe, the holiest of all pieces of educational work.[15]

Code of Ethics. Shortly after World War II the AASA and the Music Educators National Conference joined forces with the American Federation of Musicians to deal with a problem that affected all three organizations. By this time, many school performing groups had reached a remarkably high level of proficiency, and there was a danger of their being exploited. Band directors and their students felt complimented when they were asked to provide the music for the opening of new commercial ventures or to entertain at professional athletic events. Professional musicians, on the other hand, sensed that their own children were being asked to take work away from them. School administrators observed that the time away from studies was often not justified by the musical experiences the student musicians had. In 1947 an agreement was concluded between James C. Petrillo, president of the American Federation of Musicians, Luther A. Richman, president of the Music Educators National Conference, and Harold C. Hunt of the American Association of School Administrators.[16] The *Code of Ethics* defined events for which it was appropriate for school organization to provide music and those which should be the domain of professional musicians. School and civic events, educational broadcasts, and benefit performances for charities and not-for-profit and noncommercial enterprises were suitable for student participation. All forms of entertainment, including athletic events and festivals or celebrations, were to be the province of professional musicians. The *Code of Ethics* has been renewed many times since it was created, and administrators have come to regard it as protection against the exploitation of students.

Again, in 1959, the AASA exercised its influence for the benefit of music in the schools. After the Soviet Union launched Sputnik I in 1957 and became the first country in space, there was intense pressure to increase the amount of mathematics and science required of American schoolchildren. In doing so, some school systems upset the balance of the curriculum in favor of those subjects. The problem was called to the attention of AASA by Vannet Lawler, executive secretary of the Music Educators National Conference, and the AASA built its 1959 convention on a creative arts theme. Once again, excellent school music groups performed, and this time poets, artists, and dancers were part of the program. Joseph Maddy, founder of the National Music Camp and MENC president from 1938 to 1939, received the prestigious American Education Award. The meeting and the resolution it produced appreciably improved the climate for education in the arts.

The AASA again answered MENC's call for assistance in the 1970s by passing a resolution at a meeting in Atlantic City, New Jersey, that stated: "When cuts in the curriculum become necessary, they should be made across the board rather than categorically."

THE NATIONAL SOCIETY FOR THE STUDY
OF EDUCATION (NSSE)

The National Education Association held its 1895 meeting in Denver. At the meeting, a group of educators interested in furthering the serious study of education formed the National Herbart Society, named in recognition of the contribution made by the German philosopher Johann Friedrich Herbart to the "science of education." The executive council selected a topic for study and appointed a team to write a report to be mailed to all members before the meeting, where it would be discussed. The first report dealt with the teaching of history. Five yearbooks were produced before a reorganization in 1901 changed the name to the National Society for the Scientific Study of Education. It was later shortened to the National Society for the Study of Education.[18] The same publication and discussion plan has been maintained over the years, and the range of topics broadened. Music education was not a central topic of discussion for some time, although it was often mentioned in association with other topics. Yearbook 25 (1926), devoted to extracurricular activities, was significant because it recognized that all music experiences should be considered curricular, though it acknowledged that "there is a natural tendency for it to carry over into extra-curricular activity." This was considered desirable "if the extra-curricular phases grow out of the curricular activity . . . and return to it and enrich it." Herbart's recognition of the importance of interest to learning was recognized in this statement.

NSSE discussed a yearbook devoted to music, and Dean Uhl of the University of Washington College of Education was asked to chair a team of music educators and administrators to develop the first such NSSE report. The report was issued in 1936.[19] James L. Mursell, who had recently joined the Teachers College faculty at Columbia University, prepared the opening chapter, "Principles of Music Education." Peter W. Dykema of the same faculty contributed an essay on the relationship of music to other subjects, and John Beattie, dean of the Northwestern University School of Music, wrote of selecting and training teachers. Other members of the committee were Francis L. Bacon, principal of Evanston Township (Illinois) High School; Russell Morgan, supervisor of music in Cleveland, and Anne E. Pierce of Iowa State University.

Associate contributors included Joseph E. Maddy, Louis E. Curtis, Will Earhart, Edgar B. Gordon, Lillian Baldwin, and Marguerite Hood. Nine past or future MENC presidents were represented in this list.

In 1958 the NSSE again focused on music education. Thurber Madison of Indiana University was asked to head another distinguished group to prepare *Basic Concepts in Music Education.* This landmark publication is discussed in a later chapter.

PRINCIPALS' ASSOCIATIONS

The National Association of Secondary School Principals (NASSP). Seventy-eight high school principals from neighboring states met in Chicago in 1916 to establish a professional organization, the National Association of Secondary School Principals.[20] NASSP conducted the usual business for professional associations—a journal called the *Bulletin,* annual conventions, a publications program to disseminate the products of its committees and commissions, and eventually a headquarters office and staff. NASSP made distinctive contributions to American education, including the National Honor Society, the National Junior Honor Society, the National Association of Student Councils, and a program to promote international understanding between its members and their counterparts in other countries.

Music education has benefited from the existence of NASSP. Several issues of the NASSP *Bulletin* have been devoted to music education. They include issues entitled "The Function of Music in the Secondary Schools" (November 1952), "Music—A Vital Force in Today's Secondary Schools" (March 1959), and "Music Education: Its Place in Secondary Schools" (October 1975). "The Arts in the Comprehensive High School" was another influential issue of the *Bulletin* prepared by a committee of NASSP.

The NASSP Contest and Activities Committee has provided guidance to music educators by evaluating the educational value of various events across the country and approving those considered beneficial to students and education. The MENC and NASSP worked cooperatively with the North Central Association of Colleges and Secondary Schools in preparing and disseminating "Guiding Principles for School Music Group Activities."[21] Visitors are occasionally invited to appear on NASSP in service programs or are consulted by members of commissions with an assignment that has ramifications for music education.

The National Association of Elementary School Principals (NAESP). An organization similar to NASSP, but serving administrators at the elementary level, the National Association of Elementary School Principals was established as the result of a discussion in a school administration class at the University of Chicago during the summer of

1920.[22] At the NEA Department of Superintendence meeting the following year, fifty-one principals organized the National Association of Elementary School Principals. Music educators have promoted music for younger school children by relating to this organization as they have to NASSP. They have written articles for the *National Elementary School Principal*, appeared on NAESP convention programs, and served on joint committees of MENC and NAESP. Entire issues of the *Principal* have been devoted to music—for example, February 1951 and December 1959. MENC reproduced the issues for distribution to its own members.

ACCREDITING AGENCIES

Teacher-training institutions were locally controlled by the states for many years. The first normal school for training music teachers was established by Julia Ettie Crane in 1884, but it was not until the 1920s that a four-year degree program was developed at Oberlin Conservatory by Karl W. Gehrkens. At about the same time, Burnett Tuthill of the Cincinnati Conservatory of Music suggested the formation of an association of music schools. The National Association of Schools of Music (NASM) was created in 1924 with the accreditation of all music degree programs as one of its major purposes. For some time thereafter, music teacher–training programs were approved by NASM and by the various state accrediting offices. Leaders in the field of "public school music" provided guidance to NASM, which tended to be controlled at first by conservatory people with a more European orientation. In time, some conservatory people such as Earl Moore of the University of Michigan and Roy Underwood at Michigan State University became strong supporters of the cause to which their music education faculties were so committed. The growth of school music programs created a demand for licensed music teachers. This in turn increased the size of college faculties, making possible not only adequate programs of teacher education but also stronger offerings in general. Some of the great music schools of the nation, particularly at state universities, were thus made viable.

In 1952 the American Association of Colleges of Teacher Education, which had begun its own accreditation process in 1927, joined with the Council of Chief State School Officers, the National Association of State Directors of Teacher Education and Certification, the National School Boards Association, and the TEPS Commission of the NEA to form the National Council for the Accreditation of Teacher Education (NCATE).[23] In 1970 this organization was named the "sole agency for the accreditation of teachers, educational administrators, and school service personnel" by the National Commission on Accrediting. Eventual reciprocity in certification is, of course, a goal of NCATE, NASM, and the MENC. NASM has continued to accredit programs in music education of its member institutions, and because its standards and those of MENC tend to be more demanding in music than are NCATE's, the result has been a very heavy credit load for undergraduate music education majors. In February 1988, NCATE and NASM ratified a policy that makes it possible for an institution to avoid the duplication of effort that would be required to meet the needs of both organizations.[24]

NOTES

1. Alan C. Buechner, letter to Michael Mark, January 5, 1987.
2. Henry Barnard and C. W. Bardeen, *Proceedings of the National Teachers Association from its Foundation in 1857 to the Sessions of 1879* (Syracuse, NY: National Education Association, 1909), pp. 799–813.
3. *Journal of Proceedings and Addresses of the 42nd Annual Meeting of the National Education Association* (Winona, MN: National Education Association, 1903), pp. 695–99.
4. Edgar P. Wesley, *NEA: The First Hundred Years* (New York: Harper & Brothers, 1957), pp. 334–41.
5. Homer Ulrich, *A Centennial History of the Music Teachers National Association* (Cincinnati: Music Teachers National Association, 1976), p. 161.
6. *School Music Journal* 1 (September 1885): 1.
7. *School Music Journal* 2 (October 1886): 46.
8. *School Music Journal* 2 (February 1887): 93.
9. *School Music Journal* 1 (January 1886): 78.
10. *School Music Monthly* 2 (January 1901): 1.
11. Randall J. Condon, "A Supervisor as Seen by Superintendent," *Journal of Proceedings of the Fifteenth Annual Meeting of the Music Supervisors National Conference* (Ann Arbor, MI: Ann Arbor Press, 1922), pp. 34–37.
12. Letter from Walter H. Aiken to N. R. Crozier, Superintendent of Dallas Schools, dated May 14, 1926 (family files).
13. Joseph E. Maddy, "The Introduction and Development of Instrumental Music," *Volume of Proceedings of the Music Teachers National Association*, Twenty-Third Series (Hartford: The Association, 1929), p. 203.
14. *Journal of Proceedings of the Music Supervisors National Conference*, Twenty-Second Year (Ithaca, NY: The Conference, 1929), p. 57.
15. *Journal of Proceedings of the Music Supervisors National Conference*, Twenty-Second Year (Ithaca, NY: The Conference, 1929), pp. 165–72.
16. *For Understanding and Cooperation Between School and Professional Musicians*, A Code Adopted by the AF of M, MENC, and AASA (Chicago, September 22, 1947).
17. American Association of School Administrators, *Official Report, 1958–1959* (Washington, DC: American Association of School Administrators, 1959), pp. 495–96.
18. *The Encyclopedia of Education*, vol. 6 (New York: Macmillan and Free Press, 1971), pp. 562–63.
19. *Music Education*, Thirty-Fifth Yearbook of the National Society for the Study of Education (Chicago: The Society, 1936).
20. *The Encyclopedia of Education*, vol. 6, pp. 449–501.

21. *The NIMAC Manual* (Washington, DC: Music Educators National Conference, 1963), pp. 134–38.
22. *The Encyclopedia of Education,* vol. 6, pp. 531–33.
23. Ibid., pp. 513–16.
24. Charles Gary interview with Samuel Hope, Executive Director of the National association of Schools of Music, February 2, 1990.

BIBLIOGRAPHY

American Association of School Administrators. *Official Report, 1958–1959.* Washington, DC: American Association of School Administrators, 1959.

The Arts in the Comprehensive High School. Washington, DC: National Association of Secondary School Principals, 1962.

Barnard, Henry, and Bardeen, C. W. *Proceedings of the National Teachers Association from Its Foundation in 1857 to the Sessions of 1870.* Syracuse, NY: National Education Association, 1909.

Basic Concepts in Music Education, Yearbook 57, pt. 2. Chicago: National Society for the Study of Education, 1958.

Encyclopedia of Associations, 22nd edition. Detroit: Gale Research, 1988.

Encyclopedia of Education. New York: Macmillan and Free Press, 1971.

Extra-Curricular Activities, Yearbook 25. Chicago: National Society for the Study of Education, 1926.

Fenner, Mildred Sandison. *National Education Association History.* Washington, DC: National Education Association, 1945.

Fiftieth Anniversary Volume, 1857–1906. Winona, MN: National Education Association, 1907.

Journal of Proceedings and Addresses of the National Education Association, Madison, WI. Boston: Ferneel, 1884.

——, Saratoga Springs, NY. New York: J. J. Little, 1995.

——, Topeka, KS. Salem, OH: The Association, 1886.

——, Boston, MA. Winona, MN: The Association, 1903.

——, Philadelphia. Washington, D.C.: The Association, 1926.

——, Seattle, WA. Washington, D.C.: The Association, 1927.

Journal of Proceedings of the Fifteenth Annual Meeting of the Music Supervisors National Conference. Ann Arbor, MI: The Conference, 1922.

Journal of Proceedings of the Music Supervisors National Conference, Twenty-Second Year. Ithaca, NY: The Conference, 1929.

The Kindergarten and Its Relation to Elementary Education, Yearbook 6. Chicago: National Society for the Study of Education, 1907.

Music Education, Yearbook 35. Chicago: National Society for the Study of Education, 1936.

Perkins, Henry S. *Historical Handbook of the Music Teachers National Association,* 1876–1893, Chicago, n.d.

Ulrich, Homer. *A Centennial History of the Music Teachers National Association.* Cincinnati: The Association, 1976.

Volume of Proceedings of the Music Teachers National Association, Twenty-Third Series. Hartford: The Association, 1929.

Wesley, Edgar P. *NEA: The First Hundred Years.* New York: Harper & Brothers, 1957.

11

THE BEGINNING OF THE MUSIC EDUCATORS NATIONAL CONFERENCE

American teachers and administrators had attained recognition for their professionalism by the second half of the nineteenth century. Music supervisors, however, had not yet received such recognition. Even by 1900 the time was not right, and no leader had yet appeared to bring it about. The reason for lack of professional recognition was the dual nature of the duties of music supervisors. They were expected to be both musicians and teachers. Their time and energy were spent on unusual demands. Unlike high school principals and school superintendents, music supervisors were usually without normal school training. Some were self-taught and had not graduated from high school. Yet they had to learn to be educators as well as musicians. Their unique contribution to the community was recognized, and their salaries were frequently on the level of principals, somewhat higher than that of the teachers they supervised. Some developed methods of teaching music that served their purposes well, and they felt no strong need to pursue professional development with their colleagues.

It was some time before there was a critical mass of music supervisors with a common purpose, but by the beginning of the twentieth century a group of professional leaders emerged. Their efforts brought social, musical, educational, and organizational development to the music education profession.

THE MUSIC SUPERVISORS NATIONAL CONFERENCE

Philip Cady Hayden, the primary force in the founding of the Music Supervisors National Conference (later Music Educators National Conference), was affectionately called "Papa" Hayden by many of the early leaders of the MSNC. The honorific was a reference to his role in founding the conference, as well as to the name of the composer of *The Creation*, the work most often performed by high school choruses at that time.

The beginning of the Music Supervisors National Conference was an invitation by Hayden to thirty music supervisors to come together in Keokuk, Iowa, to observe his work there. The invitation resulted from the cancellation of the 1906 meeting of the National Education Association because of the San Francisco earthquake and the scheduling of the 1907 meeting in Los Angeles. Hayden predicted that few Midwestern music supervisors would attend the west coast meeting of the NEA Department of Music Education.[1] They would have to wait three years for the meeting to be held in a more convenient location. Hayden did not intend to compete with the Department of Music Education of the National Education Association and made it clear in his "call to Keokuk" that his meeting was to be held with the blessings of the NEA officers.

Hayden depicted himself as the staunchest supporter of the Department of Music Education and used the magazine he founded in 1900, *School Music Monthly*, to promote the NEA meetings. He once remarked that he had attended more NEA sessions than any other active supervisor. The Keokuk meeting might have been more premeditated than he implied, however. His biographer, Chester A. Channon, states that Hayden knew he could not make a success of his magazine without a body of subscribers, such as the membership of a professional organization. To promote his magazine, he attended his first Department of Music Education meeting in 1892 and read a paper.[2] He became an active and regular participant and was elected vice president in 1896 and president in 1899. Of considerable significance was his motion in 1897 to create "The National Federation of School Music Teachers," a strategy to enroll all public school music teachers as members at a fee of fifty cents. As members, they would receive the papers and proceedings of the annual meeting. Birge called this the first association of school music people to incorporate the word "national" in its title. It was of little significance, though, as the National Federation was short-lived and had little impact.

School Music Monthly. By 1900 Hayden was ready to start his journal. His experience prepared him well for the venture. He had been broadly educated at New York University and Oberlin, served as a part-time reporter for the *Quincy Daily Journal*, and had business experience. He had worked earlier in his father's dry goods business in New York and run his own music studio in Quincy, Illinois, before a supervisory position was created there for him. As a result of his experience and meticulous planning, *School Music Monthly* succeeded, although it was never actually issued every month. It merged with Helen Place's *Journal of School Music* in 1903 and continued as *School Music* until publication ceased in 1936.

The National Federation ceased to exist with the establishment of the *School Music Monthly,* and in 1901 Hayden began publishing the papers read at the NEA Department meetings in his September issues. He also sent the September issues free to all school music teachers, both as a subscription list builder and as a way of announcing the positions taken at the NEA music meetings. By 1902, however, Hayden's editorials changed in tone. In May of that year he praised the work of the NEA "as a whole" but said that the Department of Music Education meetings "have been merely disconnected conventions, each almost wholly independent of those preceding and following, without any relation to a consistent and abiding aim."[3]

At about that time he began referring to the *School Music Monthly* as the organ of the NEA Department, though it did not officially become that until the 1904 meeting in Saint Louis. That meeting, which he had promoted in *School Music,* suffered from disruptions of the plans to take advantage of the concurrent World's Fair, also held in Saint Louis. Hayden called the atmosphere disorganized, "like all NEA meetings."[4] He complained about the two or three sessions that were generally scattered through the week, disparaged the single activity of reading papers, and asked for time for discussion and committee reports. For the first time, he advanced his idea of what would be an ideal meeting for music supervisors: six sessions—two for paper reading, two for committee reports, and two for "discussion of such questions as might be brought up by supervisors attending."

In the November 1904 issue he called the NEA meetings "too barren of features . . . to travel halfway across the United States to hear six or eight papers which, a little later, they could read in their own homes."[5] He also took credit for the two extra "adjourned meetings" that had been held in Boston in 1903. Again he described his ideal meeting of six sessions and said, "from such a meeting, great good could be derived." In March 1905 he wrote about the NEA convention scheduled for Asbury Park, New Jersey, and commended the department president, William Wetzell of Salt Lake City, for planning meetings every morning and afternoon to accommodate all business and discussion. His enthusiasm continued in the May issue, and he was pleased that the Asbury Park meeting would have a music headquarters where the supervisors could meet.

The Call. When the 1906 NEA meeting was canceled because of the San Francisco earthquake, Hayden waited until it was certain that the NEA would meet on the west coast in 1907. Then he sent his letter to thirty supervisors in the Midwest on November 27, 1906, asking if they would come to Keokuk to observe "my work in school-music in rhythm." He proposed that the convention last "two days, comprising six lessons with a regular program, my work in ear training in rhythm forms to take up two or three of these sessions, the rest of the meeting to be given up to problems of general interest, to papers and discussions."[6]

Edward Bailey Birge, who helped Hayden with the final program, wrote that the letter makes clear his friend was not proposing a "national affair."[7] When a strong majority of those originally invited responded positively, though, a "Call" was issued in the January (1907) issue of *School Music*. NEA Department of Music Education president Hamlin E. Cogswell and Vice President Frances E. Clark signed the "Call" along with P. C. Hayden, secretary. Whether or not Hayden anticipated the formation of a new organization, he would at last have the meeting he had wanted, and with the blessings of the NEA Department. He may have been confident that having experienced the type of meeting he had been advocating, the supervisors would demand changes and thus take a step toward the professionalism for which he and his journal stood. Subsequently, he was careful to avoid appearing to have undermined the NEA Department. When discussing whether to have a

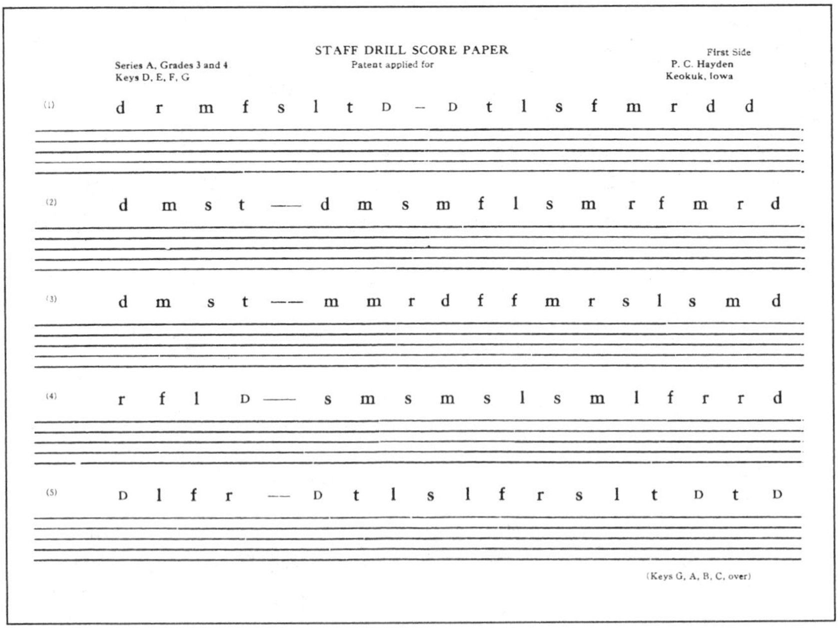

FIGURE 11-1 Staff Drill Score Paper, by P. C. Hayden, Keokuk, Iowa.

"conference"[8] meeting in 1908, he wrote that he and "this journal could not think of promoting a meeting that would have any tendency of interfering with the highest success of the Cleveland [NEA] meeting."[9]

The second meeting of the new group was held in Indianapolis in 1909, but a constitution was not adopted until 1910 in Cincinnati, where the group officially became the Music Supervisors National Conference. Hayden finally had the independent professional organization he had worked so long and hard to establish. It was probably inevitable that such an organization would have developed at some time. Its appearance, when it could contribute to the remarkable expansion of American society in the second and third decades of the twentieth century, might well have been due to the foresight of P. C. Hayden.

THE MEETING AT KEOKUK

About one-third of the meeting in Keokuk was dedicated to Hayden's rhythm-form demonstrations, but there was still ample time for discussion of other matters and for entertainment. Molnar points out that the meeting format contained many features that have characterized subsequent meetings of the organization.[10] Presentation of papers are a sine qua non for any professional assembly, but demonstrations of teaching strategies with children from the local schools has also been important for music teachers. Such demonstrations had been a part of NEA Department meetings, and they were a major part of the Keokuk conference. Students from all grades of the city schools appeared in connection with Hayden's work. In the opening sessions, Alys Bentley of Washington, DC, had a group of first-graders imitate the sounds of nature as preparation for singing. Girls glee clubs from Keokuk and Carthage High Schools provided musical breaks in the afternoons.

Musical presentations by students also tend to determine another special characteristic of the organization's gatherings. The scheduling of the meetings in the spring, when children have had ample time to prepare for musical presentations before critical audiences, is still a normal practice. The performance of Jessie Gaynor's children's operetta, *The House That Jack Built,* on the final evening was the forerunner of many "Host Nights" that American children have prepared for music supervisors. The attendees also made music themselves, as they have done at table or in hotel lobbies ever since.

Molnar refers to the music publishers present in Keokuk with samples of their materials. Publishers and other suppliers offered substantive financial support from the begining. C. C. Birchard, who had been closely associated with school music since the early days of the summer schools sponsored by book companies, was among them. He had advocated an independent professional association for some time and was an ardent supporter of the new organization. He remained so for almost forty years. Robert Foresman, another publisher, presented a paper on the value of written work in school music. He cautioned the educators that undue attention to organization of the study of music could result in something that was not music at all but mere thinking of sounds in certain relations—that is, the form of music without the spirit.[11] Foresman's comment was a unique instance of the new thinking in education that was expressed at Keokuk, although a year later at the NEA meeting in Cleveland Frances E. Clark welcomed the passing of the "day of factionalism of petty differences, of quibbling over tweedledum and tweedledee."[12]

The banquet at Keokuk established the tradition of eating together. As schedules became more crowded, breakfasts replaced banquets, and by the 1960s the organization was too large to make conference-wide meal functions feasible.

The attendance in Keokuk must have been gratifying to Hayden. A few who had expressed an initial interest, however, including Will Earhart, could not come because of church responsibilities at Easter when the original March dates were postponed until April. One hundred four registered for some or all of the three-day meeting. When Herman Owen (Madison, Wisconsin) made the report for his committee and recommended the formation of a new independent organization, sixty-nine of those attending indicated a desire to be charter members. The list was representative of turn-of-the-century America. There was a preponderance of representation from small towns. As Molnar observes, there was a decided Midwestern cast to the membership.[13] Only three locations had more than one representative. Forty-four women and twenty-five men were among the founders. Many were the only music supervisors in their towns.

Relatively few of the names are recognized today, but among them, in addition to P. C. Hayden and Frances E. Clark, were many leaders in the profession, including C. A. Fullerton (Cedar Falls, Iowa), Thaddeus P. Giddings (Oak Park, Illinois), Charles H. Miller (Omaha), C. H. Congdon (New York City), E. L. Coburn (Saint Louis), Jessie L. Clark (Wichita), Stella R. Root (Springfield, Illinois), and Birdie Alexander (Dallas). NEA Vice President Clark presided when illness prevented Cogswell from attending. The founders included

Alexander, Birdie (Dallas)

Allen, Anna M. (Peoria)

Arnold, Fannie (Omaha)

Ball, Cora A. (Fairfield, Iowa)

Ball, Edith (Princeton, Illinois)

Bassett, Irene (Bloomington, Indiana)

Bentley, Alys E. (Washington, DC)

Birchard, C. C. (Boston)
Birge, Edward Bailey (Indianapolis)
Black, J. M. (Washington, DC)
Boals, M. M. (Alton, Illinois)
Boyle, Charles A. (Emporia, Kansas)
Brooker, Lena (Mt. Pleasant, Iowa)
Bryan, Florence N. (Parkersburg, West Virginia)
Bushong, Melvin S. (Olathe, Kansas)
Butz, Louise M. (Grand Rapids, Missouri)
Carmichael, Elizabeth (Charles City, Iowa)
Caron, Emma (Canton, Illinois)
Christy, W. P. (Iowa City)
Clark, Frances Elliott (Milwaukee)
Clark, Jessie L. (Wichita, Kansas)
Coburn, E. L. (Saint Louis)
Congdon, C. H. (New York City)
Davis, Elizabeth L. (Fort Madison, Iowa)
Dysart, Jeanette (Superior, Nebraska)
Early, William T. (Independence, Kansas)
Field, Charlotte (Findlay, Ohio)
Fink, Ella (Mankato, Minnesota)
Foresman, Robert (New York City)
Freeburg, J. E. (Jewell, Iowa)
Fullerton, C. A. (Cedar Falls, Iowa)
Gantvoort, A. J. (Cincinnati)
Giddings, T. P. (Oak Park, Illinois)
Goembel, Lela (Centerville, Iowa)
Graham, Laura (Boone, Iowa)
Gray, Florence (Kansas City, Kansas)
Harrington, Grace (Kewanee, Illinois)
Hayden, P. C. (Keokuk, Iowa)
Hazelrigg, Mildred (Topeka, Kansas)
Henry, Arthur (New York City)
Inskeep, Alice (Cedar Rapids, Iowa)
Johnson, M. Edwin (East Saint Louis, Illinois)
King, Florence J. (Marshalltown, Iowa)
Kinnear, W. B. (Minneapolis)
Leedy, H. E. (Bellville, Ohio)
Lyon, Mary (Owosso, Michigan)

Marsh, Alice (Augusta, Illinois)
Mason, Arthur (Columbus, Indiana)
McDonald, Theo (Canon City, Colorado)
McNair, Elizabeth (Mattoon, Illinois)
Miller, C. H. (Lincoln, Nebraska)
Owen, H. E. (Madison, Wisconsin)
Philbrook, E. L. (Rock Island, Illinois)
Pierce, Mary R. (Chicago)
Pollock, Cora A. (Beloit, Wisconsin)
Pratt, Elizabeth (Quincy, Illinois)
Roger, Alice (Clinton, Iowa)
Root, Stella R. (Springfield, Illinois)
Scott, Martha (Carthage, Missouri)
Selleck, E. Evelyn (Pueblo, Colorado)
Stabler, W. J. (Noblesville, Indiana)
Stenwall, Hulda M. (Monmouth, Illinois)
Stonaker, Mabel (Pueblo, Colorado)
Thomas, Mary S. (Waterville, Kansas)
Treat, Ella (Decorah, Iowa)
Wallace, J. A. (Mendota, Illinois)
Westhoff, F. W. (Normal, Illinois)
Winkler, Theo (Sheboygan, Wisconsin)
Woodson, Myrtle F. (Greenfield, Indiana)

The sense of dedication and mission that these people felt about their profession was responsible for the desire to continue meeting in subsequent years. This meeting was different from the NEA Department gatherings, where musicians were a small minority of the large association. The opportunity to spend several days with others who shared the same interests and problems has given the Conference special meaning from the beginning. The festive meal prepared by the ladies of the Westminster Presbyterian Church where they met, and the following period of levity and wit with Giddings as toastmaster, provided the leaven of sociability that seemed to make the Conference a family affair.

A CONSTITUTION AND A NAME

The Conference did not meet in 1908 because the NEA convened in a Midwestern city, Cleveland. With the NEA in Denver the following year, however, the second meeting of the new group was planned for

Indianapolis, with Birge as host.[14] He had trained a chorus of school-children to sing the cantata *Into the World* by the Flemish composer and educator Pierre Benoit. The Theodore Thomas Orchestra provided the instrumental accompaniment, and the performance was intended to stress the seriousness of purpose of the new organization.

Many who attended had played leadership roles in the NEA Department of Music Education and in the school music section of the Music Teachers National Association. Ralph Baldwin had presented a committee report on "Music in the Public Schools" at the MTNA meeting in Washington the previous December,[15] and it was natural for a discussion of this report to have a central spot on the Indianapolis program. The concern that Frances Clark had expressed in Cleveland over the differences resulting from the many approaches to sight-reading in the nineteenth century prompted discussion, and a ten-member committee was appointed to study the possibility of standardization. Elsie Shawe of Saint Paul was appointed to chair a committee charged with the responsibility to prepare a report before the next meeting. Frances Clark's prophecy of the end of factionalism began to be realized.

The 1909 meeting was advertised in *School Music*, but there was little other publicity, and only ninety-three people registered. Yet this was growth, and the enthusiasm generated at the meeting resulted in the appointment of a committee to consider organizational structure. The committee was also to report at the next meeting, which was to be held in Cincinnati. Supervisors who lived farther west raised some opposition to meeting in the "Queen City," but Walter Aiken's mention of the world-famous May Festival, in which schoolchildren had been participating since 1873, was persuasive. The 1910 site proved to be a wise choice because it attracted many new members from the South and East.[16] Approximately 150 music educators from 23 of the 46 states registered.

Music Supervisors National Conference. The attendees approved a constitution and adopted the name Music Supervisors National Conference. By 1910 there was no longer any thought of the conference as an occasional assembly that would meet in the Midwest when the NEA was scheduled to convene on either coast. The broad geographical representation emboldened the group, and any previous trepidation about claiming to represent the entire country vanished. A twofold purpose— "mutual helpfulness and the promotion of good music through the instrumentality of the public schools"—was declared. With the approval for publication of a yearbook of proceedings, most of the features of a truly professional association were in place.

Children representing fifteen city elementary schools sang in the May Festival performance of Gabriel Pierne's *The Children's Crusade.*[17] Arrangements were made for the attendees to visit music classes in the city's schools, the beginning of a tradition that continued for over thirty years. Old business at Cincinnati was dealt with in the form of a report from Elsie Shawe's committee on the standardization of sight singing.[18] Having just added the word "national" to the official name of the organization, the group evidently did not feel sufficiently recognized to make pronouncements of great importance, and no action was taken on the report.

The belief of P. C. Hayden, Herman Owen, Frances E. Clark, Stella Root, C. C. Birchard, and others who thought such an organization was needed was corroborated. The meeting that president E. L. Coburn had planned for Cincinnati, with the help of host supervisor Walter Aiken, was enough to convince any who might have still been skeptical.

The Educational Council. As the organization grew, the practice of making decisions on conference positions through a committee of the whole became cumbersome. An educational council was created in 1918 at the Evansville meeting, with Will Earhart as chairman. Other members were Hollis Dann, Peter W. Dykema, Charles H. Farnsworth, Karl W. Gehrkens, Thaddeus P. Giddings, Alice Inskeep, Osbourn McConathy, W. Otto Miessner, and Charles H. Miller. Three of the group had already been presidents of the Conference, and four more would serve in that capacity within six years. The council served as a "brain trust" to respond to requests for information on music education. It offered a vehicle for deliberation on significant matters before positions were presented to the membership. Most important, it provided the organization with a means of establishing direction and priorities beyond the interests of the presidents, who at that time served only a one-year term.

Council Bulletins. With the establishment of the Educational Council, Karl Gehrkens and Hollis Dann were assigned the task of making recommendations for a collegiate course of study to prepare supervisors. The acceptance of the report on April 8, 1921, and its subsequent publication with the Standard Course in Music for the Elementary Grades was a momentous event in conference history. They comprised *Bulletin No. 1.* The 1921 report of the Education Council contained a statement about the position of school music that prepared the way for action taken by school administrators in 1927:

> Music has proven itself worthy to be classed as a major subject, coordinate with reading, writing and arithmetic, and must no longer be considered an adjunct more or less superfluous and unrelated to educational processes. Therefore the music supervisors voice the demand of musicians, music teachers, musical organizations and intelligent lovers of music as well as the progressive educators of the country for such readjustment of the school curriculum as will make possible the proper and adequate teaching and use of music as an integral part of the regular school work.

Bulletin No. 1 was the first of a series of publications on many topics that have reappeared in many publications, conferences, and other forums since that time. During the early years the productions were priced modestly (ten cents). The titles of the first thirteen *Bulletins* indicate the ways in which the Conference attempted to serve its membership and advance the cause of music education.

1921 No. 1: *Standard Course in Music for the Elementary Grades* and *Four-Year Course for Training Music Supervisors*

1922 No. 2: *High School Credits for Applied Music Study*

No. 3: *Report on the Study of Music Instruction in the Public School of the U.S.*

1925 No. 4: *Junior High School Music*

No. 5: *Standard Course of Training in Music for Grade Teachers*

No. 2: *High School Credits for Applied Music Study*

No. 3: *Report on the Study of Music Instruction.*

No. 4: *Junior High School Music*

1926 No. 6: *Report on Music in the One-Teacher Rural School*

No. 7: *Survey on Tests and Measurements in Music Education*

No. 8: *College Entrance Credits and College Course in Music*

No. 9: *Standards of Attainment for Sight-Singing at the End of the Sixth Grade*

No. 10: *High School Music Credit Course*

No. 11: *The Accrediting of Music Teachers*

No. 12: *Contests, Competitions and Festival Meets*

No. 13: *Newer Practices and Tendencies in Music Education*

Music for Every Man. At the meeting in Pittsburgh in 1915, Willis P. Kent, teacher at the Ethical Culture School in New York, gave a speech entitled "Music for Every Man."[19] The following year Kent's former colleague at the New York school, Peter W. Dykema, spoke about community music to the American Academy of Political and Social Science. He used the phrase "music for the people, music by the people, and music of the people," an indication that he was relating his work, and that of his colleagues, to the future of the nation. When Osbourne McConathy was planning his meeting for Saint Louis in 1919, he announced his theme to be "Every child should be educated in music in accordance with his capacities, at public expense and his musical development should function in the life of the community." Later he wrote:

> I have twisted and turned this statement in innumerable ways in an endeavor to abbreviate it until it might serve as slogan, but all my efforts in this direction have been unavailing. I have not been able to find words with which to state the proposition more briefly."[20]

One of his colleagues may have subconsciously taken this as a challenge.

"What is the place for music in the new educational democracy?" asked Otto Miessner in a speech entitled "Music Democratized." Arguing that the supervisors had too narrow a vision, he made a plea "to democratize music by teaching it in all branches, instrumental as well as vocal, in classes like other subjects and at public expense. Let us give music, the best we have, to all of the people."[21] Reflecting the belief of the Progressive Education Association that was organized that same year, Miessner urged that the schools treat children as individuals and not force all children to sing if they showed an aptitude for instrumental music. He went on to share his confident belief that a community would be a better place to live if it became truly musical.

A Standard Course of Study in music for the first six grades at the elementary school had not yet been developed in 1919. This was the first task the council had set for itself. Ever since the Civil War, the subject matter taught in the schools had been determined by the book adopted for the class and the particular method that accompanied it. At the Saint Joseph meeting (1921) the council reported on the standards it had set. They were described in terms of expected competencies, a concept that was ahead of its time. Each statement began with, "Every child shall. . . ." The council was pointing out to the profession its responsibility to the young citizens of the democracy.

Nashville. In 1922 the Conference was held in Nashville, Tennessee, at the request of members from the South who recognized that music education in their region was behind that in other sections of the country. President Frank Beach developed a creed that was somewhat reminiscent of McConathy's theme of 1919. It started: "Every boy and every girl in every section of our country has the right to efficient daily instruction in music in the public schools." The creed was long, so Beach also made use of a slogan, "More Music in Education: More Education in Music." At that time the president of the conference was elected at the annual meeting. Karl W. Gehrkens was selected to be the 1923 president and to plan the Cleveland meeting. Remembering his awe at having such responsibility thrust upon him, Gehrkens wrote in 1936 of standing in the back of the auditorium of the Social-Religious Building of George Peabody College when the slogan that McConathy had searched for earlier suddenly came to him—"Music for Every Child, Every Child for Music." The motto expressed the democratic feeling that so many had been speaking and writing about for years. Gehrkens made it the theme for his meeting, and the conference has used it in many ways since 1923. Karl W. Gehrkens is especially remembered for that particular contribution among many that he made during his long life.

A PUBLICATIONS PROGRAM

A Periodical. At the Minneapolis meeting in 1914 there was a discussion of how to extend the influence of the Conference. T. P. Giddings suggested that instead of issuing an annual book of proceedings, the Conference consider issuing it in four installments to every known supervisor at no charge. Frances Elliott Clark made an impassioned speech against the idea on the grounds that a yearbook was essential to the organization. The matter was left in the hands of the board of directors, who scheduled a special meeting to consider the matter. Their solution was the publication of a journal, which would be sent free to supervisors but would not replace the *Proceedings.*

The Bulletin. Peter W. Dykema, then at the University of Wisconsin, was appointed editor of *The Bulletin.* It was a modest seven inches by ten inches' paper with a self cover. Even so, it was an expensive undertaking for the young organization, whose annual membership dues were only one dollar after paying two dollars for the initial year of membership. Advertising by publishers helped support the cost of the magazine.[22] The masthead announced that the periodical "was published four times a year and sent free to all interested in school music by the National Conference of Music Supervisors." Editor Dykema, who was not at Keokuk and had not attended a conference gathering until 1913, nevertheless wrote about the "group consciousness" discovered in 1907. He saw the periodical as an extension of that feeling of comradeship.

In its early years the *Music Supervisors Bulletin* was more of a house organ than the refereed journal it was to become. The editor decided which professional papers were to be published. At first, many of the articles were speeches made at meetings; in time members and others began to submit material written especially for its pages. The name of the periodical was changed to *Music Supervisors Journal* with the September 1915 issue. In that issue, C. A. Farnsworth recommended that a permanent editor be hired in view of the rapid expansion the Conference was undergoing.[23] No action was taken by the board of directors, and the *Journal* and the *Proceedings* continued to be prepared gratis by appointed members for another fifteen years.

A mailing list of 6,000 names developed from those maintained by publishers grew to 8,000 by 1919. A fifth annual issue was added that year so reports of the spring conference could be made available before the September issue, as had been the practice. Though the dues had risen to $1.50, Dykema felt it necessary to ask the members for contributions to help bear the expenses of the additional issue and an enlarged mailing list. Contributions from members were recognized in print— $.25 Edna Lane, Hopkinson, Iowa; $.25 Alice Eddy, Marion, Illinois;

$.35, Public Library, Kansas City, Missouri; $1.00 Letha McLure, Seattle, Washington; and so on.

Peter Dykema. The volunteer efforts of the editors and their successors, the chairmen of the editorial board, have made unusual contributions to the strength and the professionalism of the organization. This is especially true of Peter Dykema. He utilized the magazine to build the Conference with great effect. Though his name is one of the most revered in the history of the Conference, he may deserve even more recognition for the development of the association and its magazine than he has received. Peter Dykema used the periodical adroitly to advance the Conference during a crucial period in its development.

Dykema had been active in the Music Teachers National Association and the NEA Department of Music Education, but he had not participated in conference activities until President Henrietta Baker Low of Baltimore included him on her Rochester meeting program in 1913. There he read a paper entitled "The Effect of the Festival and Pageant Revival on the Teaching of Music." He suggested at the meeting that the Conference might best promote singing if it would select a small number of songs on which teachers could agree to concentrate their attention. Dykema found himself the head of a committee of three charged with the responsibility to develop a list of not more than twelve songs appropriate for group singing. This action, taken over a year before the assassination at Sarajevo that triggered World War I, proved auspicious for the Conference and the country. At the meeting in 1914 the committee was ready to announce the final ten or twelve songs they had chosen from the eighteen selected for the supervisors' reaction. A pamphlet containing the eighteen songs had been prepared by Birchard's company and was available at the Minneapolis meeting. It sold for five cents, or four dollars a hundred.[24]

Possibly it was Dykema's swift action on his first assignment for the organization that caused the board to appoint him second vice president with the responsibility of editing the magazine. As he later observed, the board did not hamper the editor "with any funds for carrying on the work." Nevertheless, with the help of the publishers Dykema produced four issues and mailed out a total of 25,000 copies. He ended the year with a balance of less than one hundred dollars, which the Conference used to help with the publication of the *Proceedings.*

At the time of the Rochester meeting Dykema was still the head of the music program at the Ethical Culture School in New York, a post he had held since 1901. Previously, he had been principal of an Indianapolis junior high school. Dykema had been invited to New York by Frank Addison Manny, a friend he had made while directing a church choir in Ann Arbor during college days.[25] His remarkable talent for getting a group to sing had already been demonstrated while a student at the University of Michigan. Although his first jobs had been as a teacher of

English and German, and as administrator, he had also directed singing.

Dykema's outlook on life must have been influenced by his twelve years at Felix Adler's Ethical Culture School. He sympathized with the concept of the Ethical Culture Society, an organization independent of religious institutions that was dedicated to proper behavior. Coming from a strongly religious family but satiated with church attendance as a youth, he himself provided religious instruction for his own children. The Sunday evenings spent singing hymns with his parents and eight brothers and sisters were echoed in the family musicals he encouraged. He obviously believed in the power of communal music-making as did the Ethical Culture Society. Its promotion of music is attested to by its People's Choral Union, directed by Frank Damrosch from 1892 until 1909. It is possible also that Dykema was influenced by Adler's friend, Josiah Royce, the editor of the *International Journal of Ethics*. Royce espoused voluntary loyalty to the group as the road to freedom that Americans were seeking.

Community Singing. The early leaders of the Conference were loyal and voluntary. It is likely that Dykema melded these attributes to his strong faith in music and was prompted to promote community singing as a worthy endeavor for the organization. He used the *Journal* to promote the idea. In the first issue he ran a report by Edgar B. Gordon, a member of Dykema's song committee and a supervisor in Winfield, Kansas. Gordon described the community program in Winfield where his father, Louis, had built an early orchestra with schoolchildren. By the time of the 1915 meeting in Pittsburgh, community music had become a topic of considerable interest.[26] Dykema contributed an article on producing a "Community Christmas" and also published a piece by Eva Hegy of California, Missouri, on the value of twice-weekly sings involving all students and faculty of her school. Successful community sings in various parts of the country were reported. Promotional ideas were advanced in a feature Dykema called "For Your Local Papers."

Dykema was actually operating a one-man public relations program for the Conference. In 1917, as he was about to finish his one-year term as president, he was appointed chairman of publicity. He used the magazine to provide a running account of the activities of the Community Music Committee. By request, the members expanded the song list from eighteen to fifty-five. With America's entry into World War I came the Liberty Edition and eventually the *Twice 55* series. Other publishers recognized the interest that had been created and produced such collections as Hall and McCreary's *Golden Book of Favorite Songs*.

Following the publication of an article entitled the "Faith That Is in You," an advisory council was created with a representative for each state. Its purpose was to enable the Conference to become "better known as an educational force" by seeing that music is represented at other educational meetings. "The Faith That Is in You" was represented to be a contributed article, but no author had been identified. Because of this, and also because the editor had suggested in another part of the journal the manner in which the membership of the advisory council should be selected, it is possible that Dykema exercised his editorial privilege to build a stronger association by writing the article himself. The national character of the organization was furthered as members of the advisory council were able to carry the conference message to the state teachers' associations. Dykema's paper, "Music in Democracy: The Spread of the Community Music Movement," prepared for the American Academy of Political and Social Science, was presented again but read for Dykema by Henrietta Baker Low at the NEA meeting. As proof of the effectiveness of the conference activities, the *Journal* quoted a "prominent musician in our city" to a member:

> I have been reading the last issue of the *Music Educators Journal* which a friend thrust into my hand on a train. I must say . . . you are a wide awake lot. In fact, you seem to be the only well-organized and earnest bunch in the business. I wonder if your claims are not going to come true, namely, that you are the dominating power in music in this country. I believe this is true and will be increasingly so in proportion as you realize your importance and the opportunity you have.[27]

The opportunity increased as the United States became more nationalistic with the progress of the war in Europe. Community sings flourished across the country, and Dykema continued to tell the supervisors that they must be involved. From Kansas, Gordon reported that all the state colleges, and many denominational ones, were promoting community music. Birchard made the Committee's *55 Songs and Choruses* available just before the 1917 meeting in Grand Rapids, which was planned by President Dykema. In the *Journal*, Dykema wrote of the new songbook:

> Every time the book is used, the claims of public school music—from which the book arose—are strengthened. As the people sing more they appreciate better the claims of music for a larger place in our educational system.

55 Songs appeared just in time for the declaration of war against Germany in April. Patriotic rallies became even more popular. Thanks to the Conference, the country was prepared to sing the traditional songs of the nation as well as the outpourings of George M. Cohan and Irving Berlin. Dykema published Washington supervisor Hamlin Cogswell's account of conducting a "chorus" of thirty-two thousand citizens in a carol sing in front of the Treasury Building in Washington, DC, during the week before Christmas in 1917. Some music educators disagreed with the promotion of popular music in community sings. They thought of the sings as another way to make America seriously musical. Dykema, who recognized the value of some popular music, published letters from song leaders John Beattie and Duncan McKenzie, then in France. They attested to the value of what their colleagues might call trivial music because they had seen what such songs could do for the men in uniform.[28]

Community singing was an important part of the World War I effort, as patriotism was stirred in the civilian population by community singing of appropriate songs. Morale in the military was maintained by community singing as well, and many musicians were trained to be military song leaders. Bartholomew and Lawrence wrote:

> Aided by the splendid spirit of patriotism which swept the country after the declaration of war, and realizing the great need of music to help build morale, wonders were accomplished in incredibly short periods of time. . . . A proof of the popularity of this singing program may be found in the fact that in the contonments of the United States during the second year of the war (1918), there was an attendance of thirty-seven millions at soldier gatherings in Y.M.C.A. huts at which the main attraction, frequently the only one, was mass singing. More than thirty thousand soldier song leaders were trained. Everywhere the army went they sang. The result in fighting spirit has been testified to by military leaders the country over.
>
> The people at home began to sing also. War Camp Community Service, The Commission on Training Camp Activities, and the Y.M.C.A. engaged a number of excellent professional song leaders and many hundred volunteers undertook similar service independently at various local points. Trained song leaders were sent into the war industries and men and women in factories were taught to sing at noon hours and rest periods.[29]

Industrial settings for community sings were common, and time was set aside each week in thousands of factories and other work settings for community singing. A normal part of the movie experience for Americans was community singing ("Follow the bouncing ball") as one of the short features, along with the cartoons and serials.

The National Anthem. One and a half million copies of the *55 Songs* were sold in the first year and a half, and the Liberty Edition was in preparation in the summer of 1918. It promised more patriotic songs and a new, more singable version of the national anthem. The supervisors working on the new version learned that another group was doing the same thing for inclusion in the *Army Songbook,* which would be distributed to the troops. Commercial publishers did not know which version to print. At the suggestion of the Conference, a joint committee was formed and the service version was created.[30] The story of conference

FIGURE 11-2 Class of Y.M.C.A. song leaders being trained at Camp Kearny, California (position of "Cut-off"). From *Music for Everybody: Organization and Leadership of Community Music Activities,* by Marshall Bartholomew and Robert Lawrence. New York: Abingdon Press, 1920.

involvement in this project was described by Clifford V. Buttelman, the first executive secretary of the association, in a pamphlet entitled "The Music Educators National Conference and the Star-Spangled Banner." Dykema is clearly the hero of the piece, although Francis Scott Key is not forgotten.

Reflecting on this period, Frances Elliott Clark[31] said that the action in Rochester in 1913 was taken because the route to making America musical through the schools was too slow. By offering singing opportunities to all adults in their communities, the supervisors hoped to share the joy of experiencing uplifting song. Whatever the reason that Dykema's suggestion was implemented, it could not have been more timely. Not only did the community music movement serve the country, it also helped the Conference gain acceptance as an educational force to be acknowledged and utilized.

Increasing Membership. Dykema recounted every triumph in the *Journal*, which was being sent free to every music educator for whom an address could be found. He and his successors George Oscar Bowen (1921–1926) and Paul J. Weaver (1926–1930) made believers, if not always members, of the thousands of musicians who were answering the call for help with the rapidly expanding music curriculum in the schools. Giddings and President Elizabeth Casterton had wanted visibility for the conference, and Dykema gave it to them. Conference membership remained relatively stable during the first seven years. At the Minneapolis meeting the active membership was 182, although some nonmembers paid to attend the meetings. After the first four issues of the *Journal* there was a 72 percent increase in active membership at the Pittsburgh meeting in 1915. The next year in Lincoln many attendees joined the association, and the total membership rose to 503, although many never attended meetings again. After the war the active membership more than doubled. By the time Dykema passed the editorship to Bowen, the number of members stood at 1,481.

George Oscar Bowen. George Oscar Bowen, head of the department of public school music at the University of Michigan, succeeded Dykema as editor in 1921. Bowen continued the support of the community music movement, having himself been responsible for the development of one of the most significant experiments in the social uses of music while at Flint, Michigan.

His first action as editor was to move the publication date of the first issue of volume 8 to October 1921. During that year he promoted the idea of holding the 1922 meeting in Nashville. He provided President Beach with the "President's Corner" to build the concept that the Conference must give as well as get. "Are we a dress parade or a fighting battalion?" asked Beach, who stressed the "every section of the country" part of his Nashville creed.[32] This missionary attitude of Bowen and Beach became characteristic of conference thinking as it entered a period that eventually found six regional conferences integrated into the national organization.

George Bowen was the first national president to organize a biennial convention and hold office for a two-year period. His comments in the *Journal* indicate that he was not pleased with the board's decision, but he wrote: "Let us all work for the success [of the biennial plan] whether we believe in it or not."[33] The *Journal*, he said, was the one agency that must hold us together and bring about a large and successful meeting in 1928. He was unhappy about giving up the editorship of his "beloved *Journal*," but he planned a historic gathering for Chicago's mammoth Stevens Hotel (now the Conrad Hilton). He chose to emphasize choral music. The first national high school chorus, directed by Hollis Dann, was the centerpiece. The appearance of the Flint High School A Cappella Choir began a new era of unaccompanied singing in American schools.[34] Both musically and organizationally the meeting was one of the most significant in conference history.

Regional Organizations. The major common characteristic of the forty-nine members of President Dykema's advisory council in 1917 was enthusiasm for the association as a professional organization. There were some who felt differently, however. Although the Grand Rapids meeting showed more diversity of interests than any previous program, problems of a regional character were difficult to deal with at a national meeting. There was some dissatisfaction with the Midwestern domination of the Conference. The 1913 meeting in Rochester, New York, was the only one to have been scheduled in that part of the country, and the majority of the presidents were from the Midwest.

The Eastern Division. A few delegates from the Eastern states and some members from the Boston Pulse Club laid the groundwork for the first of the conference divisions on the train trip home from Grand Rapids. At the instigation of Frederick Archibald of Waltham, Massachusetts, and Howard Davis of Chelsea, Massachusetts, organizational meetings were held that year, and in May 1918 the Eastern Music Supervisors met in Boston with about four hundred in attendance. Albert E. Brown was elected president. A publication, eventually known as the *Eastern School Music Herald*, was begun that same year. Among the leaders of that group during the almost ten years of independent existence were Ralph Baldwin, Laura Bryant, Samuel Cole, Walter Butterfield, and Richard Grant. The group met annually through 1927. There was danger of a rift with the MSNC, but the leaders of both the national and regional organizations felt that the regional must be subordinate to prevent a split. The point was made, however, that the country was very large and more local contact needed to be established with the supervisors throughout the United States.

The Southern Division. When the MSNC members in the South asked the Conference to help them by meeting in Nashville in 1922, they set the stage for another regional organization. During the Nashville meeting a group of over one hundred southerners met to form the Southern Music Supervisors Conference, and Paul Weaver was elected president. D. B. Gebhart and Paul Weaver played important roles in laying the groundwork for the new organization at the Nashville meeting. A convention was held in Atlanta in the fall, and the new conference set out to develop a course of study in music for southern high schools. The southern group took a leadership role in dropping the word "supervisor" from its title. It adopted the name "Southern Conference for Music Education."

Some changes have been made in the boundary between the eastern and southern divisions over the years. The District of Columbia was originally in the southern group and West Virginia in the eastern. Both have changed to the other group.

A Biennial Meeting Plan. While the southern group always considered itself a branch of the the MSNC, there was some jealousy and rivalry among the easterners. What both groups did was double the number of meetings for those who wanted to be active both regionally and nationally. When the MSNC met in Detroit in 1926, a biennial meeting plan was approved. Regional groups would meet on odd-numbered years and the national on the even ones. The 1928 MSNC meeting was scheduled for Chicago, and new divisions were created to join the eastern and southern and hold meetings in 1927. This necessitated the establishment of other divisional groups by 1927, and four divisional meetings were held that year—the eastern in Worcester, Massachusetts; the southern in Richmond; the north central in Springfield, Illinois; and the southwestern in Tulsa.

The Southwestern Division. Mabelle Glenn, who was named president of the southwestern division, planned the meeting in Tulsa. Oklahoma, Arkansas, and Texas were divorced from the southern division, and with Colorado, Kansas, Missouri, and New Mexico make up the balance of the southwestern division.

The North Central Division. The north central division elected Anton Embs of Oak Park, Illinois, president. It met in Springfield, Illinois, a central location in the vast expanse of the ten states that stretch from the Dakotas to the Ohio River and from the North Platte in Nebraska to the shores of Lake Huron in Michigan.

The Northwest Division. The National Education Association met in Seattle in 1927. Following it, a number of music supervisors met to form the northwest division. The first conference of that division was held in

Spokane in 1929 with Letha McClure, director of music in Seattle, as the first president.

The Western Division. What is now known as the western division began as the California division. It became the California-Western division when it incorporated only four states, with Utah having been transferred from the southwestern division. The first meeting was held in Los Angeles in 1931 with Herman Trutner as president. For demographic reasons it was fourteen years before a western division meeting was planned outside of California. Since those early years the western division has also incorporated Hawaii and Guam.

When the headquarters office opened in Chicago, the MSNC had just completed its successful second biennial meeting and the division organizational scheme was in place. The scene was set for the development of state associations that would make possible the further penetration of professional music organizations into small towns and villages.

Paul Weaver. As the new editor of the *Journal*, Paul Weaver of the University of North Carolina did much to see that the transition to the biennial schedule was smooth. He also managed to ensure that the magazine would be the official journal of the Conference and of the southern, north central, and southwestern divisions. The eastern group, having created its own periodical, did not agree at first to an arrangement similar to that planned for other divisions. By the time of Weaver's first issue (October 1926), however, it was agreed that the eastern division would try the scheme of having a department for each of the divisions. Each had its own contributing editor, who supplied Weaver with regional information. The *Journal* flourished during the four years of Weaver's editorship. Before he left Chapel Hill for Cornell University in 1929, the magazine had grown to over one hundred pages in length, and Weaver had begun to publish an index of advertisers. This was a helpful device in a magazine whose readers constantly searched for new ideas and materials. The March 1930 issue (published in Ithaca) was one hundred sixteen pages in length. Weaver had recruited a dozen Cornell students for part-time jobs under the efficient management of his wife, Hazel. The growing list of names of members and subscribers was put on the addressograph system that served the *Journal* until it transferred to computers in the 1970s.

During his first two years as editor, Weaver sent the magazine to all music educators for whom he could get addresses, as had Dykema and Bowen. In 1928 the policy was changed, and teachers had to request the magazine. This resulted in a temporary decline in the print run, but the recovery to the old level was swift—an indication of how indispensable the three editors had made the *Journal* to members of the profession. Because the practice of sending free copies was continued, however, Weaver could not get a second-class mailing privilege for the magazine. In his last issue (May 1930), Weaver announced the policy that was to take effect with the establishment of the headquarters office. Subscriptions were to be one dollar for nonmembers, and that amount of each members' dues was to be allocated to the official magazine. This would produce a paid list that would meet the requirements of the United States Post Office. The second-class privilege secured in 1930 has been carefully guarded since.

Edward Bailey Birge. Under the new organizational scheme, Executive Secretary Clifford V. Buttelman was to be the managing editor and Edward Bailey Birge the chairman of the editorial board. Dykema, Bowen, and Weaver were members of the board, as were John Beattie, Anne Landsbury Beck, Max Krone, and Will Earhart. Buttelman's experience in business and printing allowed the music educators to concentrate on content, although both the managing editor and his wife, Eulalia, who was a professional pianist, contributed interesting commentary and column fillers. The new page size selected by the managing editor was 8 ½ inches by 11 ½ inches, giving the *Journal* an extra half inch of depth to its page without disturbing advertising plates designed for other "normal" magazines. Vanett Lawler, the first employee hired by Buttelman, proved to be exceptionally gifted in working with the music industry, and the magazine thrived.

When the Conference recognized the change in the profession by modifying its name from Music Supervisors National Conference to Music Educators National Conference in 1934, the periodical followed suit and became the *Music Educators Journal*. Birge was chairman of the editorial board for fifteen years. He originated the "MEJ Clubs" on college campuses that made possible the student memberships that Osbourne McConathy had suggested in 1926. Through the clubs, the *Journal* was used in classes with prospective teachers. This greatly increased the circulation of the magazine. In recognition of his long service to the *Journal* and to the Conference from the days when he helped P. C. Hayden plan for the Keokuk meeting, the MENC board of directors named him chairman emeritus. His close friend and associate, Will Earhart, wrote: "His dry wit, his sometimes acid humor, his never-failing crusade for brevity and crispness not only have made working with him a delight, but have born fruit in establishing sound editorial standards for the *Journal*."[35] Birge is also remembered for writing the first history of American music education, the rights to which the Oliver Ditson Company gave to the Conference in 1966. It is still available from the Music Educators National Conference.

Committee Reports. With the opening of the headquarters office in Chicago, reports of some of the official conference committees were also made available. The first, that of the committee on vocal affairs, was released in 1930. The second was "A Course of Study in Music Appreciation for the First Six Grades." For years, some of the committee reports were produced by mimeograph for distribution at sessions of the organization's meetings, or they could be obtained by members on request. This service provided assistance to the members and carried forward the idea of mutual helpfulness as expressed in the constitutional purpose of the organization.

Russell Morgan, whose term as president began just before the opening of the headquarters office, expanded committee activity within the organization. He recognized that the Conference had grown too large to permit the intimate involvement that had characterized the experiences of the founders and their immediate successors. To remedy the problem, Morgan found ways to provide expanded opportunities for any member who wished to contribute his services for the good of the profession. In a letter to a colleague written in 1930 he wrote:

> In an organization such as ours, each member has the same right to derive benefits and make contributions if he so wishes, as was the case when there were less than one hundred members. . . . Committees for busy-work cannot justify the organization that tolerates them. . . . Whether or not the achievements are complete does not matter if through group work our members have the opportunity to think and work constructively. . . . The total power of our group is enhanced by the growth of the individuals who wholeheartedly or even causally take part in these cooperative assignments and projects, even although nothing ever appears in print to record their efforts and contributions.[36]

Much has appeared in print as the result of the voluntary work of the membership since that time. The list of bulletins continued to increase rapidly. Seven revisions of *Bulletin No. 17* (*Music Buildings, Rooms, and Equipment*) have appeared, the last in 1987. The various editions of this bulletin have been widely used by architects throughout the country and have helped make possible the construction of the unique educational environments for music that exist in the United States.

THE CONFERENCE HEADQUARTERS

The decision to open a permanent MSNC headquarters office was a major one, especially for a voluntary organization. When the music supervisors met in Chicago during the week of March 23, 1930, they heard a report from C. C. Birchard, who had been appointed chairman of the committee on business management. The constitutional changes suggested by the committee were approved unanimously.[37] The time had come for the Conference to have an office and a permanent staff to carry on its business. The future could hardly have looked brighter. Music education had just completed a decade of growth during which instrumental music was added to the curriculum, thereby greatly increasing the potential membership. The phenomenal success of Joseph Maddy's

National High School Orchestra at the meeting of the Department of Superintendence had resulted in that prestigious body calling for music to be given equal consideration with other subjects in the high schools. No one, with the possible exception of the prescient W. Otto Miessner, who had liquidated his piano-manufacturing company, was wary of the changes to be brought by the disastrous economic conditions of the Great Depression.

The office was opened in the Lyon & Healy Building in Suite 820, 64 E. Jackson Boulevard in Chicago, almost a year after the October 1929 Wall Street crash. Even then, the country did not feel the effects of the depression. The collapse of Samuel Insull's widespread utility enterprises in Chicago and the surrounding areas was nearly two years in the future. With an executive secretary experienced in advertising, printing, and the music business, the future of the MSNC looked bright. Had Clifford Buttelman, the executive secretary, been able to see what was ahead for the country he might have decided to remain in Boston. Had the board delayed its decision until the twenty-fifth anniversary meeting in Cleveland, it is possible that there would have been no office or permanent staff until after World War II. The accomplishments of the organization over that sixteen-year period suggest that such a postponement would have been tragic for American music education.

The MSNC members must have been pleased with the first evidence they were to see as a result of the change—the new *Music Supervisors Journal*. It compared favorably with *Childhood Education*, the *NEA Journal*, and the federal government bureau of education publication *School Life*. The larger, more professional-looking magazine symbolized the vigor of the MSNC. Buttelman was a man of infinite patience with a love for the printed page that led him to spend hours pushing around a line of type until he had it just right. Fortunately, he was a big, virile man who could get by on four hours of sleep a night. Also fortunate was his selection of Vanett Lawler as his first employee. She was the desired complement to her supervisor. They worked together as a team for twenty-six years, and when the board selected her to succeed Buttelman, he stayed on for a few years to produce the *Journal*.

The Great Depression eventually affected the headquarters office, as it did every school system. At times there were no funds to pay the staff, and local merchants had to carry the employees "on the tab" until the membership dues arrived at the beginning of the school year. At one time it was necessary for Lawler to be loaned to the Pan-American Union in Washington to ease the burden on the the MENC budget. Her close association there with Charles Seeger was fortuitous. Seeger, a distinguished leader among American musicologists, as well as a composer, folklorist, and philosopher, gave Lawler a broadened view of music and society, thus preparing her for leadership of the conference. It was also fortunate for the Latin American countries, as she made several flying trips in DC-3s to teach music educators there how to organize into associations that could lead toward improved music education in their schools. Her Washington experience also gave her the chance to help the MENC prepare for the move to the National Education Association Center for Education in the nation's capital.

The first two executive secretaries built a structure for a national organization that in time had a federated unit in each state, auxiliary organizations that included the Music Exhibitors Association (created in 1926), and a collection of associated groups that represented the special interests of members of the profession. Their philosophy was to ''keep everybody together so that we can work together'' for the advancement of music education. This was a difficult task, and they were not always successful, but the current listing of the MENC associated groups attests to the wisdom and diplomacy exercised over the years.

In addition to the successful management of the *Journal,* the new office also ran the national and divisional meetings on a more business-like basis. The meetings had grown to such an extent that there were only a few cities in the country that had facilities to handle the conferences. The Stevens Hotel in Chicago hosted 5,003 attendees out of a membership of 7,505 in 1930. It has served as an MENC convention site six more times after becoming the Conrad Hilton, the last in 1984. The headquarters office relieved the presidents of the many tasks associated with organizing meetings of such size and complexity. The host supervisors and staffs continued to do much of the groundwork at the site and to supply musical equipment for the visiting performing groups. The members of the recently established auxiliary group, the Music Exhibitors Association, assisted with arranging for displays of instruments and music, but it was the office staff that planned for the exhibits, advertised the space, and sold the display booths. The displays became an increasingly important part of the meetings and contributed to the work of the Conference both financially and educationally by keeping the membership abreast of the latest in materials and equipment.

The permanent executive staff also provided continuity to the organization. As they gained experience, especially with the meetings, they were able to guide the presidents away from practices that had been unsuccessful, to point out needs of the membership that might have been overlooked, and to make the contacts with other educational leaders and major speakers from outside the world of music education. The team of Buttelman and Lawler, with such excellent helpers as Helen Peterson, Helen Hatter, and Edna Pierce, soon became expert at handling all of the meeting responsibilities. Buttelman later referred to himself as an ''organization engineer.''

SUMMARY

The first third of the twentieth century was an exciting time for music educators as it was for most Americans. As the supervisors of music pursued the goal of universal music education they had inherited from generations of public school teachers, the country experienced enormous development. In the process of adjusting to this and to other societal modifications resulting from the vigor and mutability of early twentieth-century America, school music was bursting from the limited confines of vocal music into music education that involved instruments, listening skills, theoretical studies, and a timid experimentation with creativity. At the same time, music was expected to serve the interest of general education, patriotism, and to a lesser extent than before, religion.

In the process of coping with so much growth and development, it was critical that music educators talk to each other, share their ideals, help solve common problems, and build self esteem to sustain them in a profession that demanded art, discipline, and limitless energy. To make this possible, an enduring professional organization was created. The leaders who founded it and guided its course in the first years proved notably qualified to establish a democratic institution structured in such a way that the resources of thousands of dedicated teachers could be utilized for the benefit of children and music. The Music Educators National Conference became an embodiment of the spirit that had sustained the school music teachers of the preceding century.

NOTES

1. Seventy-five music educators attended the Los Angeles meeting, compared to the 104 who came to Keokuk.
2. Chester N. Channon, "The Contributions of Philip Cady Hayden to Music Education in the United States" (Ed.D. dissertation, University of Michigan, 1959), p. 109.
3. *School Music Monthly* 10 (May 1902): 17.
4. *School Music* 21 (September 1904): 8.
5. *School Music* 22 (November 1904): 10.
6. Channon, "The Contributions," p. 62.
7. Edward Bailey Birge, *History of Public School Music in the United States* (Washington, DC: Music Educators National Conference, 1966, reprint), p. 241.
8. The word "conference" was Hayden's choice, according to Birge. See *Proceedings of the Music Supervisors National Conference 21st Yearbook* (Chapel Hill, NC: MSNC, 1928), p. 166.
9. *School Music* 9 (January 1908): 20.
10. John W. Molnar, "The Establishment of the Music Supervisors National Conference 1907–1910," *Journal of Research in Music Education* 3 (Spring 1955): 42.
11. *School Music* 8 (May 1907): 35.
12. Frances E. Clark, "Presidential Address: Department of Music Education," *Journal of the Proceedings of the Forty-Sixth Annual Meeting of the National Education Association* (Cleveland: The Association, 1908), p. 13.

13. Molnar, "The Establishment," p. 44.

14. Ibid., p. 46.

15. Homer Ulrich, *A Centennial History of the Music Teachers National Convention Association* (Cincinnati: MTNA, 1976), p. 251.

16. Harry M. Kauffman, "A History of the Music Educators National Conference" (Ed.D. dissertation, George Peabody College for Teachers, 1942), pp. 46–47.

17. Charles L. Gary, "History of Music Education in the Cincinnati Public Schools" (Ed.D. dissertation, University of Cincinnati, 1951), p. 222.

18. Elsie M. Shaw, "Standardization of Sight-Reading," *Journal of the Proceedings of the Third Annual Meeting of the Music Supervisors National Conference* (Cincinnati: The Association, 1910), pp. 37–52.

19. *Music Educators Journal* 2 (May 1915): 28–30.

20. Osbourne McConathy, "The Place of Public School Music in the Educational Program," *Proceedings of the Music Supervisors National Conference*, (Saint Louis: The Conference, 1919), pp. 24–25.

21. *Music Supervisors Journal* 6 (September 1919): 10.

22. Especially to be remembered in that regard was Clarence C. Birchard, a strong advocate of an independent music education association. The Birchard Company and its successor, Summy-Birchard, had the advertisement on the back page, and later on cover four, for fifty-two years, from Volume 1, Number 1, until Volume 52, Number 9 (1966).

23. *Music Supervisors Journal* 2 (September 1915): 10.

24. The songs were "America," "Star-Spangled Banner," "Come Thou Almighty King," "Swanee River," "O How Lovely Is the Evening," "The Ash Grove," "Auld Lang Syne," "Dixie," "Annie Laurie," "My Old Kentucky Home," "How Can I Leave Thee," "Flow Gently Sweet Afton," "O Tannenbaum" (translated), "Nancy Lee," "O Who Will O'er the Downs," "Minstrel Boy," "A Capital Ship," and "Row, Row, Row the Boat."

25. Henry E. Eisenkramer, "Peter W. Dykema, His Life and Contributions to Music Education" (Ed.D. dissertation, Teachers College, Columbia University, 1963), p. 67.

26. *Music Educators Journal* 2 (September 1915): 15.

27. *Music Supervisors Journal* 2 (March 1916): 3.

28. *Music Supervisors Journal* 5 (September 1918): 5.

29. Marshall Bartholomew and Robert Lawrence, *Music for Everybody: Organization and Leadership of Community Music Activities* (New York: Abingdon Press, 1920), pp. 16–17.

30. The joint committee was composed of John Alden Carpenter, Frederick S. Converse, Wallace Goodrich, Walter Spalding, Hollis Dann, Peter W. Dykema (chairman), Osbourne McConathy, Clarence C. Birchard, Carl Engel, William Arms Fisher, Arthur E. Johnstone, and Elbridge W. Newton.

31. Frances E. Clark, "Speech" to the General Federation of Women's Clubs meeting in Hot Springs, Arkansas, May 18, 1918. *Music Educators Journal* 5 (September 1918): 14.

32. *Music Supervisors Journal* 8 (September 1921): 8.

33. *Music Supervisors Journal* 12 (May 1926): 6.

34. Richard Kegerris, "Flint Central Launches the High School A Cappella Movement," *Journal of Research in Music Education* 14 (Winter 1966): 254–65.

35. Will Earhart, "A Tribute to a Colleague," *Music Educators Journal* 30 (May–

June 1944): 13, 59. Earhart quoted a few typical Birge comments on manuscripts under review, including one that read: "Number 1 is too long and
rambling. It ought to be boiled down to the sugaring off point, if it is to be
used."
36. Clifford V. Buttelman, "Dedication," *Music in American Education* (Chicago:
Music Educators National Conference, 1955), p. xi.
37. *Music Supervisors Journal* 16 (May 1930): 5.

BIBLIOGRAPHY

Bartholomew, Marshall, and Lawrence, Robert. *Music for Everybody: Organization and Leadership of Community Music Activities.* New York: Abingdon Press, 1920.

Birge, Edward Bailey. *History of Public School Music in the United States.* Washington, DC: Music Educators National Conference, 1966.

Channon, Chester N. "The Contributions of Philip Cady Hayden to Music Education in the United States." Ed.D. dissertation, University of Michigan, 1959.

Clark, Frances E. "Presidential Address: Department of Music Education." *Journal of Proceedings of the Forty-Sixth Annual Meeting of the National Education Association,* Winona, Minnesota. Cleveland: 1908.

———. "Speech" to the General Federation of Women's Clubs meeting in Hot Springs, Arkansas, May 18, 1918. *Music Educators Journal* 5 (September 1918).

Earhart, Will. *Music Supervisors Journal* 7 (December 1921).

———. "A Tribute to a Colleague." *Music Educators Journal* 30 (May–June 1944).

Eisenkramer, Henry E. "Peter W. Dykema: His Life and Contributions to Music Education." Ed.D. dissertation, Teachers College, Columbia University, 1963.

Gary, Charles L. "History of Music Education in the Cincinnati Public Schools." Ed.D. dissertation, University of Cincinnati, 1951.

Journal of Proceedings and Addresses of the Forty-Seventh Annual Meeting of the National Education Association. Denver, 1909.

Journal of Proceedings of the Eighth Meeting of the Music Supervisors National Conference. Pittsburgh, 1915.

Journal of Proceedings of the Second Biennial Meeting of the Music Supervisors National Conference. Chicago, 1930.

Kauffman, Harry M. "A History of the Music Educators National Conference." Ed.D. dissertation, George Peabody College for Teachers, 1942.

Kegerris, Richard. "Flint Central Launches the High School A Cappella Movement." *Journal of Research in Music Education* 14 (Winter 1966).

Lendrim, Frank T. "Music for Every Child: The Story of Karl Wilson Gehrken." Ed.D. dissertation, University of Michigan, 1962.

Molnar, John W. "The Establishment of the Music Supervisors National Conference 1907–1910." *Journal of Research in Music Education* 3 (Spring 1955).

———. "The Organization and Development of the Sectional Conferences." *Journal of Research in Music Education* 1 (Fall 1953).

Morgan, Hazel Nohavec. *Music in American Education.* Chicago: Music Educators National Conference, 1955.

Music Supervisors Journal 2 (September 1915, March 1916), 3 (November 1916), 5 (September 1918), 6 (September 1919), 8 (September 1921), 9 (October 1922), 9 (February 1923), 12 (May 1926), 16 (May 1930).

Platt, Melvin C., Jr. "Osbourne McConathy: American Music Educator." Ph.D. dissertation, University of Michigan, 1971.

School Music (September 1904, October 1904, January 1908).

Schwartz, Charles Frederick, Jr. "Edward Bailey Birge: His Life and Contributions to Music Education." Ph.D. dissertation, Indiana University, 1966.

Shaw, Elsie M. "Standardization of Sight-Reading." *Journal of Proceedings of the Third Annual Meeting of the Music Supervisors National Conference*, 1910.

Stoddard, E. M. "Frances Elliott Clark: Her Life and Contributions to Music Education." Ed.D. dissertation, Brigham Young University, 1968.

Ulrich, Homer. *A Centennial History of the Music Teachers National Convention Association.* Cincinnati: Music Teachers National Association, 1976.

Warren, Frederich Anthony. "History of the Music Education Research Council and the *Journal of Research in Music Education*." Ed.D. dissertation, University of Michigan, 1966.

12

THE BROADENING
MUSIC CURRICULUM

DEMOCRACY IN MUSIC EDUCATION

In 1907, the same year that the supervisors met to form what would become the Music Supervisors National Conference, Henry Ford announced his intention to mass-produce a family car and provide an automobile for everyone. This action was followed by the liberalization of work hours and the doubling of wage scales so that his workers might become potential customers and have time to enjoy the beauties of their country. Ford changed American society. His concern for the man in the street, whether generated by altruism or business acumen, was in step with the thinking of many Americans who were buoyed by optimistic humanism at the beginning of the new century. As it had been America's "Manifest Destiny" to subdue the wilderness all the way to the Pacific, so was it now the challenge to create an egalitarian social order.

Twentieth-century music supervisors, many of whose predecessors had found a mission in sharing music for moral or religious reasons, were characterized by an earnestness that was commented upon by people such as A. E. Winship, editor of the *Journal of Education*. They were comfortable with the thesis of advertising executive Bruce Barton that "service is worship," and they saw their service as that of providing their country with a musical culture. The avenue for accomplishing this was to be the one element of society shared by both American-born and immigrants—that is, the public school system, which was the basis upon which a democratic nation would be built. Just as Henry Ford planned to give everyone the means to enjoy leisure and travel, music supervisors would see that no American was deprived of the opportunity to experience the pleasure of music. Many of the early members of the Conference expressed this commitment over a period of years. Their thinking, writing, and speaking about music education as an expression of a true democracy in the early days of the conference gave the organization a special quality.

The High School became part of America's "common schooling" late in the nineteenth century, and music educators made four-part choral singing the music activity for the high schools. Other experiences—listening lessons, instrumental performing groups, music history, and theory—began to appear in isolated places near the turn of the century. These offerings were extracurricular at first, but later they evolved into curricular subjects.

Leo Lewis of Tufts College made an informal report to the NEA Department of Music Education on the work planned by the music committee of the New England Education League. The committee was composed of professors from several New England colleges and A. T. Manchester, president of the Music Teachers National Association. Three NEA representatives (Benjamin Jepson, C. A. Fullerton, and Julia Ettie Crane) were named to cooperate with the league in its endeavor to develop a high school course of study in music. Jepson reported at the Saint Louis meeting of the NEA, and the framework for a four-year course of study was distributed. It included one hour of music study four days each week in addition to the usual one hour per week of required choral music. That would have put the music program on a par with other disciplines in the high school curriculum.[1]

Academic Credit for Music. When Superintendent of Schools F. B. Dyer welcomed the MSNC convention to Cincinnati in 1910, he asked for advice on the introduction of music appreciation classes into the high school, as well as what to do about the secondary school students who wanted to study music at either of the two conservatories in the city or with members of the Cincinnati Symphony Orchestra.[2] Osbourne McConathy, one of the first to organize a four-year high school music course, had described his Chelsea, Massachusetts, program at an NEA meeting and in *School Music*. Aiken, and probably Dyer as well, knew of this and also knew that Chelsea was awarding high school credit for music study with an outside teacher. Charles Farnsworth of Columbia University had also reported on the status of acceptance of music credit by colleges, both for admission and for degree credit.[3] Superintendent Dyer's request, a first for the Conference,[4] resulted in the appointment of a committee to develop a high school music course—that is, a major in music. The working group consisted of some of the leading music

FIGURE 12–1 Pages 126 and 127 of *The High School Music Reader for the Use of Mixed and Boys' High Schools,* by Julius Eichberg. Boston: Ginn and Heath, 1880.

educators of the time—Will Earhart, Hollis Dann, Walter Aiken, Edward B. Birge, and Karl Gehrkens.

The NEA Department of Music had had committees studying "Terminology" and "National Songs," but these topics were not closely related to the problems associated with the high school, an institution undergoing a restructuring of its function. The neophyte conference took advantage of Dyer's request to enhance its professional stature and its ability to involve scholars and supervisors with national reputations.

The 1911 MSNC meeting in Detroit was presided over by President Birge. Earhart gave a preliminary report on the deliberations of the high school committee. At the St. Louis meeting in 1912, credit was recommended for music study in high school. The practice of granting full credit for music courses requiring homework and half credit for rehearsals originated at that time. The Saint Louis conference also witnessed the first serious attention to the contribution that the science of psychology might make to music education. G. Stanley Hall had made a number of addresses to the NEA Department meeting, but at the Saint Louis convention Carl E. Seashore, in presenting his concept of testing for musical aptitude, offered a practical application that caught the interest of many in attendance.

Electives. Charles W. Eliot, president of Harvard University, was influential in instituting the elective system to broaden college study. Eliot was chairman of the National Education Association Committee of Ten and later the first president of the Progressive Education Association. He also helped break the stranglehold of the rigid classical curriculum on the nineteenth-century high school. Eliot's early comments about the inefficiencies of instruction in grades seven and eight of the public schools were among the factors that led to the attempt at liberalization represented by the junior high school movement. He acknowledged his debt to Herbert Spencer.[5] Fortunately for music educators, he was the son of Samuel Atkins Eliot, mayor of Boston, first president of the Boston Academy of Music, and a member of the School Committee that approved music as a curricular subject in 1838. Music electives were important to Charles Eliot.

Music Electives. American schools finally achieved universal music education when the idea that all children could sing was accepted. Because they could sing they should be educated in music, and so music education was expanded to include primary grade children and those in high school. After that came the liberalizing trend that would free school music from the formalized practices developed in the nineteenth century. The trend provided opportunities for more creative music experiences. The elective movement came at the same time, and the consequences for music education were significant. In the matter of a few years many high schools reduced the music requirement from four years to one. High school music came to mean experience in performing groups on an elective or selective basis, with other courses available for those who wished to concentrate in music. In time, high school music became an activity of a minority of the student body, a matter the conference was not to deal with seriously until the 1960s.

The move from required vocal music in high school to a largely elective program, which came with the broadening of the curriculum in the early twentieth century, reflected a change in purpose for American music education. Music educators devoted themselves to defining their purposes and organizing programs to bring them about. In doing this for the elective offerings, however, they neglected the needs of many teenage students. Ironically, this happened at the same time that conference members were earnestly fashioning a democratic philosophy for music education.

The problems created by elective music courses did not escape the notice of the MSNC Educational Council. In explaining why his 1921 program at Saint Joseph, Missouri, devoted an entire day to discussion of problems raised by the council, President John Beattie noted that "Music of the 7th and 8th grades is becoming optional in the majority of cities where the Junior High school plan is working." He recognized that there was a crisis because administrators were making it difficult or impossible for children to elect music. He observed that music in these grades in other cities with the old 8–4 plan was also being affected. This discussion did not result in action by the Conference or cause any abatement in the practice.

MUSIC APPRECIATION

Before the turn of the century, Frances Elliott Clark spent ten minutes of her chorus rehearsals with her Ottumwa, Iowa, students telling them about composers or helping them recognize the stylistic features of the work that made it possible to place it in its correct historical context. Will Earhart was doing much the same thing with his orchestra members in Richmond, Indiana, where they concentrated on sixteen composers. George Oscar Bowen, while at Northampton, Massachusetts, had established an appreciation course for credit. Teachers like Mary Regal in Massachusetts, who were good pianists and had a decent instrument at school, were able to perform works for the students to study. When American engineer Edwin Votey patented a mechanical piano in 1897, another means of presenting music became available to the schools.[6] Charles Rice in Worcester, Massachusetts, Ada Fleming in Chicago, and Frank Beach in Emporia, Kansas, were early supervisors who made use of the new instrument. Beach was concerned about the possibility of the mechanical piano being used solely for entertainment rather than as a means of presenting organized music lessons.

Frances Elliott Clark. Shortly thereafter, the phonograph added new opportunities for students to listen to music. Frances Elliott Clark, who by 1903 had moved to Milwaukee, told of her introduction to the potential of Edison's invention. She heard the voice of Welsh singer Evan Williams coming from a phonograph in a music store. He was singing "All Through the Night," the very song she had been teaching her elementary students that week. She realized the difference it could make to her students if they could hear Williams sing it. Her principal agreed and approved the purchase of a machine for the schools. Beach and Alice Clement of Rochester, New York, were also among the earliest to use the phonograph in their teaching.

Clark made herself an authority on the use of the phonograph to teach music to children and in 1910 spoke to the Wisconsin Teachers Association on "Victrolas in the Schools." President Birge invited her to present this subject at his MSNC program in Detroit. Within a year she had moved to Camden, New Jersey, where she established an educational department for the Victor Talking Machine Company. She supervised the preparation of recordings designed for use in the classroom. Recordings were also developed to correlate music with English and American literature. Among other responsibilities, Clark assisted record and Victrola dealers in setting up educational displays to help music educators learn the benefits of the phonograph.

Victor issued a number of instructional booklets prepared by Clark and assistants such as Ruth Shaw Faulkner and Franklin Dunham. Clark wrote:

> Music should be the concomitant of every day's experience in a child's life at home and in school,—not only the music period, but permeating every phase of his activity and development. The need is great, and the material offered with the Victrola and Victor records is rich in volume, usefulness, and adaptability. If we have pointed out the road for millions of American children, and if we have led the way to a new field of the child's fairyland which shall grow with him to manhood's most beautiful *playground of the soul,* our highest hopes will have been fulfilled.[7]

Clark remained with Victor for the rest of her professional career but kept up with the times in the 1920s, when she promoted the radio as an avenue to music appreciation.

The Radio. Alice Keith of the Cleveland schools and D. C. Boyle of the Ohio School of the Air also pioneered the use of radio for teaching music. Keith wrote *Listening in on the Masters*, a music appreciation course to be used with radio and records.[8] She collaborated in this effort with Arthur Shepherd, director of young people's concerts for the Cleveland Orchestra. Edgar B. Gordon, a president of MSNC, used the radio for a statewide music program after he moved from Kansas to Wisconsin in 1917. He was instrumental in devising materials and techniques for effective music teaching via radio.[9] When Walter Damrosch took to the air in 1928, he introduced millions of schoolchildren across the country to *In the Hall of the Mountain King, The Sorcerer's Apprentice, Omphale's Spinning Wheel, The Flying Dutchman,* and many other other pieces of symphonic music. Some adults still remember affectionately his Friday morning greeting to his "Yunk Frenz." Birge credits him with being the first to organize Young People's Concerts with his New York Symphony Society Orchestra, while Grove's *New Dictionary of American Music* credits Theodore Thomas with this achievement.[10] Elizabeth Beach gave a series of Christmas carol festivals on the CBS Radio Network beginning in 1931. She utilized thousands from the elementary schools, high schools, and normal school of Syracuse. There were forty boys in the chorus in 1931, and seven hundred boys by the end of the decade.[11]

Young People's Concerts. Frank Damrosch had inaugurated a series of Symphony Concerts for Young People in 1898 during his second year as supervisor of the New York City schools. He conducted six of them himself. His brother Walter had done the same earlier but with music "of a light character without any explanation."[12] Walter's purpose was to make children like music, while Frank's was to instruct. His youth concerts were a means of training Damrosch's teachers, who escorted the pupils to them.

Will Earhart became director of music for the Pittsburgh schools in 1912. Children's concerts were performed there too. Birge helped Earhart prepare four books in a series entitled *Master Musicians* (the Richmond course), which C. C. Birchard began publishing in 1909. Both men had been intensely interested in appreciation as early as the turn of the century.

In addition to the many helpful publications that Frances Clark issued from the Victor Company, numerous other books also appeared on the market to help students, teachers, and the general public become better listeners. Some of the best were prepared by Lillian Baldwin in connection with her radio broadcasts and the children's concerts of the Cleveland Orchestra, which began in 1929. In time, student textbooks began to include appreciation material.

Music Appreciation as Part of Progressive Education. Many of the early music appreciation books were structured according to principles of progressive education, especially in terms of stages of child development. The three stages of development, as defined by educational psychologists of the time (and still recognized by many), were the Sensory Period (grades 1–3), the Associative Period (grades 4–6), and the Adolescent Period (grades 7, 8, and high school). Books such as Agnes Moore Fryberger's *Listening Lessons in Music: Graded for Schools*[13] were divided into sections that corresponded to the three periods. Frances Elliott Clark's book *Music Appreciation for Little Children* (quoted above) was "designed to meet the needs of the child mind during the sensory period of development."

INSTRUMENTAL MUSIC

Theodore Thomas (1825–1905). The roots of instrumental music in the public schools extend back to the middle of the nineteenth century, when the American public was introduced to touring orchestras and bands. One of the most important figures in American instrumental music was Theodore Thomas, a violinist who was born in Germany and emigrated to America with his parents when he was ten years old. He was a professional violinist who organized his own orchestra. He recognized that the only way to build an American orchestra of similar quality to European orchestras, and to hire and retain the best musicians, was to provide it with steady activity. The best way to keep the orchestra continually busy was by touring. The tours took the Theodore Thomas Orchestra to almost every community of any size. For countless Americans, their first exposure to a good orchestra playing the finest orchestral literature was the Theodore Thomas Orchestra. He directed the Cincinnati May Festival from 1873 to 1905 and was the first president of the College of Music of Cincinnati. Thomas later became conductor of the New York Philharmonic Society, and then he traveled to Chicago, where he founded the Chicago Symphony Orchestra. He conducted the Chicago Symphony until 1905, the year of his death.

Concert Bands. Unlike the early American orchestras, bands were not modeled after European examples. The concert bands met a different need than did the orchestras, which had to conform to European models to perform the orchestral repertoire. The bands, especially those of Patrick Gilmore and John Philip Sousa, sought to entertain their audiences, and with their superb showmanship, they did so with remarkable success. The bands met the popular needs of the people, and the orchestras maintained the traditions of the Old World.

Patrick Sarsfield Gilmore (1829–1892) was a virtuoso cornetist, conductor, and showman who knew how to please an audience. He was born in Ireland, traveled to Canada with a British band, and later settled in Boston, where he formed a band called Ordway's Eolians. He conducted several bands under his own name and the bands of several military units.

The Peace Jubilees. Gilmore had a gift for the spectacular. To celebrate the end of the Civil War, he arranged the National Peace Jubilee in Boston in 1869. There was an orchestra of one thousand and a chorus of ten thousand. The concertmaster was virtuoso violinist Ole Bull. Adding to the production were effects by cannon fired by electricity and the simultaneous ringing of every church bell in Boston. Gilmore unashamedly stated that the "hand of God was on his creation." President Ulysses S. Grant and his entire Cabinet attended, Oliver Wendell Holmes wrote a poem in commemoration of the event, and orator Edward Everett Hale delivered the opening blessing. John Sullivan Dwight, who viewed himself as the arbiter of all things musical in nineteenth-century America, comments at length on the festival. Of the large chorus, he noted that "all large bodies are hard to move," and while the chorales from *St. Paul* were well rendered, the "elephant could not dance." Yet he thought the Europeans would think the event appropriate to the vastness of the United States and recognize that the nation of "mechanical inventions and the all-mighty dollar" had a musical future. "When the chorus of 10,000 withdrew," wrote Dwight, "there were still 10,000 children to take their place and sing almost as well as their elders." Chauvinist that he was, Dwight maintained this was all possible only because Boston and its environs led the country in education and culture.[14]

In 1872 Gilmore created the eighteen-day International Peace Jubilee, again in Boston, to celebrate the end of the Franco-Prussian War. President Grant was sufficiently interested to send Gilmore to Europe to promote the jubilee. There he managed to persuade several musicians and ensembles to participate. They included the Band of the Grenadier Guards, the Garde Republicaine, the Kaiser Franz Regiment, an Irish band, and Emperor William's Household Cornet Quartette. For this jubilee, the orchestra numbered two thousand and the chorus twenty-thousand. A coliseum was erected especially for the International Peace Jubilee at a cost of $500,000. Ole Bull was concertmaster again, and Johann Strauss, who thought American beer to be poor, conducted the "Blue Danube Waltz."[15] The Fisk Jubilee Singers were also on the program. The "Anvil Chorus" was performed again (as in 1869), with orchestra ("better than the last," said Dwight), full chorus, organ, military bands, drum corps, over a hundred anvils, and all of the city bells. Once was enough, though, and the public was not as supportive of the second jubilee as it was of the first. Often there were three times as many people on the stage as in the audience.

Gilmore became bandmaster of the Twenty-second Regiment in New York, to be succeeded by Victor Herbert. He arranged another jubilee for the Centennial Exposition in Philadelphia in 1876, but it was relatively small. He died on a concert tour while his band was booked at the Saint Louis Exposition.

John Philip Sousa (1854–1932) carried on Gilmore's work and furthered it by touring not only throughout the country but around the world as well. He composed and played his famous marches while on tour. Sousa influenced American instrumental music education because he was at the height of his popularity when schools began to establish bands; his band served as the model for most American bands, including those composed of students. Toward the end of his career he would invite school and college musicians to join his band during rehearsals. He was a close friend of Albert Austin Harding, the founder of the department of bands at the University of Illinois. Their friendship resulted in Sousa's decision to give his extensive library of printed and manuscript band music to the University of Illinois.

Other Bands. Numerous concert bands crossed the country over and over in their concert tours, sometimes traveling to Europe as well. They also traveled to Cuba, Canada, and Mexico, and bands from those countries traveled throughout the United States. Some of the other important American bands were those of Allen Dodworth, Allessandro Liberati, Frederick Innes, Thomas Brooke, Preston Patrick Conway, Giuseppe Creatore, Arthur Pryor, and Edwin Franko Goldman.

The Concerts. The bands often played at the the hundreds of amusement parks and beaches with concert pavilions, almost always with financial success. Most of the amusement parks were owned by public and private traction companies. Those under other ownership were dependent on the transportation companies, whose electric and steam railroads and ferry steamers brought the public to them. Each visitor paid a fare to reach the park, bought a general admission ticket, and sometimes paid an extra fee to hear the concert. Usually, though, the concert was included in the general admission fee.

The Decline and Legacy of the Concert Bands. The amusement parks were popular before the automobile became a commonly owned item. People were dependent on public transportation for their weekend entertainment, and the transportation took them to the parks. When Americans could buy automobiles, they could go anyplace they wished, and the amusement parks and beaches began to decline in popularity, as did the concert bands.[16] The commercialization of radio, which brought live concerts broadcast by the New York Philharmonic, was another blow to the bands because people could hear fine music in their own homes.[17] Jazz also hastened the end of the bands. One of the functions of the concert bands was to play for dancing. They played the polka, schottische, waltz, and two-step. The new dances, however, which included the fox trot, Charleston, shag, rag, and black bottom, were best played by jazz bands.[18]

American professional concert bands virtually disappeared by 1930. They left their impression on the American public, however and numerous communities throughout the country still have their own community bands that perform in parks and at various community functions each summer. American musical taste was formed, to a large extent, by the professional bands that frequently emphasized entertainment and virtuosity rather than a highly musical repertoire. The legacy of the professional bands remains in community, school, and military bands. The symphony orchestra has continually increased in stature in American society but has been secondary to bands in American education since the 1930s. It is one of the ironies of history that the professional band, now a thing of the past, is re-created and emulated in the schools, while the symphony orchestra, which is held in esteem by society, is not as prevalent in the schools. The adage that the schools are a mirror of society does not hold up in this case.

School Orchestras. There was much interest in instrumental music in the schools at the turn of the century. The violin was a popular instrument at that time, and when enough students in a school had studied it privately, it was not uncommon for a school orchestra to be formed. A grammar school orchestra existed at Nathan Hale School in New London, Connecticut, as early as 1896. There were also elementary orchestras in New Britain and several Hartford schools.[19]

The orchestra that Will Earhart built at the high school in Richmond, Indiana, beginning in 1898 was important, not only because it was an early school orchestra with symphonic instrumentation but also because of its high standards. Those standards were maintained by Joseph Maddy after Earhart left. It was the seminal group in a series of events that led to the creation of both the National High School Orchestra and the National Music Camp at Interlochen, Michigan. Other orchestras were well developed before the Richmond High School orchestra played at the 1922 MSNC program in Nashville, but that appearance inspired many musicians to establish new high school orchestras.

Joseph Maddy, who had been a violist with the Minneapolis Symphony Orchestra, became the "first supervisor of instrumental music" in America in 1918 in Rochester, New York. He was an excellent teacher and promoter, and at the age of twenty-seven he persuaded Rochester's most famous industrialist, George Eastman, to give ten thousand dollars' worth of instruments to the Rochester schools. The school instrumental program was so successful that Eastman continued to grant money to the schools for new instruments. These were Eastman's first philanthropic ventures, and he was so enthusiastic about school music that it became one of his strongest interests after the photographic industry that he founded. Also in 1918, he discussed founding a school of music in Rochester. In 1921 the Eastman School of Music opened, thanks to the benefaction of George Eastman.

In 1926 Maddy formed the first National High School Orchestra to perform for the Detroit meeting of the Music Supervisors National Conference. The orchestra consisted of 236 high school musicians from 30 states, chosen from eight hundred applicants. Maddy organized the Second National High School Orchestra in 1927 to perform for the Department of Superintendence of the National Education Association in Dallas. There were two full orchestral concerts and several by small ensembles. The superintendents were so impressed by what they heard that they voted to "adopt a resolution recommending that music and art be given everywhere equal consideration and support with other basic subjects."

The following year Maddy organized the National High School Orchestra for the third time, this time for the Chicago MSNC meeting. Many of the musicians performed with the orchestra for the third time that year. They were so enthusiastic about their experience that Maddy, with his close associate Thaddeus P. Giddings, decided to search for a summer home for the orchestra. With assistance from many musicians, educators, philanthropists, and educational foundations, Maddy and Giddings founded the National High School Orchestra and Band Camp at Interlochen, Michigan. Its beginnings were humble, but it has grown to a prestigious year-round arts academy that attracts faculty and students from many countries.

As early as 1898 the Rock Island, Illinois, schools established the practice of giving credit toward graduation for instrumental music.[20] Other early examples of credit for orchestral participation include Richmond, Indiana (1912), Cincinnati (1914), and Parsons, Kansas (1920).

CLASS INSTRUMENTAL INSTRUCTION

Another significant event in the history of instrumental music was the introduction of class instruction. Group instruction for singing was the norm, and it fit easily into the structure of the American common schools; it was as yet unknown for instrumental music, however. The academies and female seminaries of the nineteenth century frequently advertised the availability of instruction in instrumental music as a way of attracting students.[21] Outside teachers of piano (and sometimes violin) would come to the school to give lessons, for which the pupil's parents paid a fee. The teaching was done on an individual basis, as had been the usual practice for centuries. The regular faculty of the public schools was hired initially to teach vocal music. Music theory and appreciation were added at the turn of the century, but instrumental music was more apt to be extracurricular.

Charles H. Farnsworth of Columbia University spent 1908, his sabbatical year, in Europe studying various aspects of music education in Germany, Switzerland, France, and England. His comments on the "advantages of everyone knowing 20 or 30 songs or chorals," a practice he found in Germany, could have influenced Peter Dykema, who suggested the practice to the music supervisors at the 1913 Rochester convention.[22] Farnsworth's recognition of the educational value of Émile Jaques-Dalcroze's use of improvisation, which he observed in Geneva, opened another path for American music education. His description of the Maidstone movement in England, sponsored by the London violin dealer Murdoch and Company, was the key to the explosion of instrumental music in American public schools.[23] (The Maidstone movement is described in detail by Deverich.[24]) Unfortunately, the identity of the creative individual who originated class instrumental instruction in Maidstone is unknown. The curate of the parish church in Maidstone formed the first violin class with children from the village school around 1905.

Albert G. Mitchell, a teacher in the Boston public schools, asked for a leave of absence in 1910 to study the class method pioneered at Maidstone. He had arrived in America some twenty years before, having earned the doctor of music degree from Oxford. He was a friend of Hans von Bülow, Sir John Stainer, and Sir Arthur Sullivan, and was the orchestrator of *The Mikado*. After serving as an organist in Watertown, Massachusetts, Rochester, and Buffalo, he moved to Boston to become organist at Saint John's Episcopal church. Mandolin clubs were popular then, and his sons played in them. He wrote a series of contrapuntal melodies for Sousa's marches for mandolinists, with the composer's blessing. For a period the *New York American* published one of his songs every week. Hearing of a vacancy in the Boston schools, Mitchell took a civil service examination and was hired to continue the work of the illustrious public school music teachers who preceded him in Boston.

When Mitchell returned from England in 1911, he organized five classes of violin students with sixteen to twenty students in each class. The lessons, which were free, were held from four to five o'clock after school. He was so successful in this experiment that after two years he was relieved of his high school teaching duties to become a full-time teacher of instrumental music. After using English books for several years he wrote *Violin Class Method* (Oliver Ditson, 1924). He later wrote class methods for cello, cornet, trombone, and clarinet. Mitchell's first class method was preceded by Stuber's *Instrumental Class Course* (E. T. Root & Sons, 1923). Mitchell pioneered the use of the metal E string, and with Paul Stoeving of New York and some members of the Boston Symphony, he developed a shoulder rest for violinists. He addressed the music supervisors at their Philadelphia meeting in 1920 and assured them that the purpose of violin class instruction was not to turn out a finished violin player but simply to open the door to music and to "educate the sense of touch, sight and hearing."[25] After leaving the Boston schools, Mitchell instructed many string teachers in summer classes at New York University.

Heterogeneous Class Teaching. Joshua Collins advertised in the Annapolis, Maryland, *Gazette* in 1773 that he would hold an evening class to teach "German flute, hautboy, clarionet, and bassoon." Such mixed instrumental classes did not become popular immediately. Twentieth-century teachers who wanted to build bands and orchestras did not have enough time to give class instruction on separate instruments, and some developed techniques to teach several instruments in one class. A memorable heterogeneous class method was published in 1923. It was *The Universal Teacher* by Joseph E. Maddy and Thaddeus P. Giddings (Conn Limited, Elkhart, Indiana). All of the instruments were given equal importance in this work, and all had melodies to play. This was a change from previous heterogeneous methods, in which instrumentalists who normally did not play the melody in a band or orchestra would learn to play only accompaniment figures limited to simple rhythms and limited range. *The Universal Teacher* was adopted widely and enabled more children than ever to study instruments in school.

Homogeneous Class Teaching. Other method books were developed to teach groups of similar instruments (trumpet, baritone, horn) in one class. Still other teachers resorted to microteaching—weekly short lessons with each student. When Otto Miessner began a band at Connersville, Indiana, in 1906 he gave all of the instruction to beginners himself. He provided individual instruction, allotting each boy fifteen minutes a week.

Resistance to class instrumental instruction prompted Will Earhart to come to its defense at the MSNC 1921 meeting in Saint Joseph, Missouri. There he quoted Pittsburgh principals who mentioned, among other things, the improvement in personal appearance, regular attendance, and attitude toward other studies that they had observed in pupils in the instrumental classes. Earhart made clear that the school's job was not "[to] fit the pupil into a musical life, but to fit music into the pupil's life."[26]

Professional touring band director Frederick Innes credited the Boy Scout band that he took to London with fueling interest in school bands and class instrumental instruction. He said "I believe in class teaching. It brings about a spirit of emulation." In 1924 he wrote:

> The playing of the Denver Boy Scouts Band in London, England some few years back is responsible for much of the present-day band movement. This band won the first place in the band tournament which featured the international Boy Scouts Jamboree over there. The methods used were of interest. The boys were playing on the streets sixty days after they got instruments. They played a concert at the Empress Theater in Denver within ninety days of organization, and within eight and a half months they went to London.[27]

Elementary School Orchestras frequently followed the establishment of successful high school orchestras. In Cincinnati, for example, there were eight orchestras in lower schools in 1913, three years after the official recognition of high school orchestra as part of the curriculum. In the early 1920s, all-city orchestras drawn from as many as eleven elementary schools played for conventions of the Federation of Mothers Clubs and the Western Arts Association. Among the selections played were Tchaikowsky's "Chanson Triste" and the "Minuet" from Mozart's Symphony in E.[28] Gladys A. Brown's report on instrumental music in 1916 implied that elementary school instruction in instruments was valuable in keeping boys in school beyond the "grades." Sixty-six orchestras and 12 bands were included in the survey of 72 schools.[29] John Beattie reported eight elementary orchestras in Grand Rapids in 1916.[30]

The contest movement (later, this chapter) and a skillfully devised advertising campaign by instrument manufacturers supported the growth of instrumental music in the schools. "Gee, Dad! It's a Wurlitzer" became a part of the language and eventually an essential gag line for comedians and cartoonists.

Class Piano Instruction in the schools followed class violin by only a few years, although its legacy was older. Johann Bernard Logier had advocated the teaching of beginning students in groups in Ireland and in London during the second decade of the nineteenth century.[31] William Nixon, who made the first plea for school music before the 1834 meeting of the Western Literary Institute, was, with his wife, operating a Logieran Musical Seminary on Fourth Street in Cincinnati at that time.[32] It is not clear whether his instruction included keyboard classes or whether his studio was so named because he had adopted the chiroplast, a frame for holding the hands that Logier had invented. Calvin Cady, professor of piano and harmony at Oberlin from 1874 to 1879, the first director of music at the University of Michigan (1879–1888), and teacher at many other institutions from coast to coast, used small groups of students at the keyboard in teaching music fundamentals.[33] There were other reports of class piano instruction in ladies' seminaries in the South after the Civil War. Blanche E. K. Evans experimented with class piano teaching in 1913 in Hamilton, Ohio, when Superintendent Condon called her for the introduction of such work at Woodward High School in Cincinnati.[34]

Inez Field Damon, supervisor of music in Schenectady, New York, observed that it did not take the schoolchildren long to ask, "We have violin classes in school, why can't we have piano classes, too?" The earliest classes were offered to high school girls, but school systems soon made arrangements for younger students as well. Sometimes an outside teacher came to the school to give group instruction for a minimal fee from each child. Elsewhere, instruction was given by school personnel. T. P. Giddings soon wrote a text on the subject, and Otto Miessner not only had his own specially designed school piano, which he manufactured, but used his "Melody Way" for marketing and as an instructional device. Dummy keyboards were developed for classrooms with only one piano. Mirrors mounted on upright pianos enabled the teacher to check hand positions from any point in the room. Inez Field Damon related the entire phenomenon to the community music movement of the early 1920s.[35] Olga Prigge, a student of Blanche E. K. Evans at Woodward High School, had so many students from Hyde Park Elementary School in Cincinnati that one of her colleagues jokingly accused her of running a conservatory in the 1920s.

By the end of the 1920s, instrumental music had assumed an importance equal to that of vocal music and might have overshadowed it if not for the popularity of the a cappella choir, following the Flint (Michigan) High School triumph at the first biennial MSNC meeting in 1928. School music now embraced instrumental instruction along with vocal music and music appreciation.

The Marching Band. The marching band originated in the military but began to appear in schools around the turn of the century. The most important figure in the movement was Austin A. Harding, who became director of the University of Illinois Band in 1905. At Illinois he founded the department of bands because he did not want his bands to be under the music department, which would impose budgetary and policy authority on him.

Previously, high school and college marching bands were ragged, untrained aggregations of instrumentalists. Harding said:

> When we first began to form letters and words . . . we had never seen or heard of a college band which formed words while marching and playing. It has always been the policy of the Illinois Band to avoid copying any feature from any other band.''[36]

His innovations, however, were copied extensively. The University of Illinois Marching Band, which was imitated throughout the country, was the most important force in the development of high school marching bands. It should be noted that Harding's excellent work with the concert band was similarly influential.

The marching band eventually became an important public relations tool for the schools. As such, it was incumbent on band directors to promote the marching band as a part of the music education program that, like the concert band, developed musicianship and appreciation. Mark Hindsley wrote in 1940:

> [The band teacher] must seek to elevate the standards of music appreciation and at the same time popularize his performances so that his music will belong to all. His job cannot begin and end in the classroom. He and his work must merit the attention of the general public, if it is to succeed in full measure. . . . A by-product of music education is the marching band. Marching is a legitimate and essential part of every band's training, and it is necessary that every band teacher be qualified to handle this part of the program.[37]

This was a toned-down version of his 1932 rationale for the marching band:

> The value of the marching band to music education in general lies in its advertising power. It provides a strong incentive to all youth to study music so as to participate in band activities. Parents are quick to realize the worth of such an organization in a disciplinary way and as an outlet for some of the child's leisure time and surplus energy, and accept it also as providing an entrance to further musical culture, in which they are at the time probably more interested than the child himself.[38]

New Instrumental Music Teachers. A new supply of teachers, especially band directors, helped elevate school bands above orchestras, which had held the primary role in school music during most of the first three decades of the twentieth century. As men returned from the World War I with military band experience, many found employment as musicians for symphony orchestras, theaters, vaudeville houses, and silent movies. Some had been trained by the Damrosch brothers while in the service. Many of these former bandsmen became instrumental music teachers. They returned to school to learn to teach and to meet certification requirements.

Another boost was given to the teacher supply by changes in American entertainment. Thousands of musicians in communities of all sizes throughout the country had been employed in vaudeville house orchestras and movie theaters, which needed an orchestra and an organist to accompany silent films. When the talking film was invented, thousands of musicians were suddenly thrown out of work. That, in addition to the Great Depression of 1929, left many musicians with nothing to do, and many chose to use the time to further their educations. A large number went to teachers colleges and eventually began to fill instrumental music positions in the school. As the number of music teaching positions grew, teacher employment agencies prospered.

CONTESTS

The competitive American characteristic that prompted New England singing master Justin Morgan to pit his horse Figure against all comers in races and sled pulls remained in frontier society as the West was settled. Spruill quotes an advertisement in the *Virginia Gazette* of 1737 for "contests in playing violin and singing" as part of a holiday celebration.[39] In the next century Welsh miners brought with them their Eisteddfod tradition. In the nineteenth century small towns were serious about wanting better brass bands than their neighboring communities. At least part of the funds with which some communities support municipal bands today were left by earlier citizens for that purpose. Karl King recognized public support of the movement by naming one of his marches after the passage of the Iowa Band Law. As early as 1915, Austin A. Harding, director of bands at the University of Illinois and pioneer in the symphonic and marching band movements, could tell the MTNA that there were more bands than towns in his state.[40]

Musical Instrument Manufacturers. In such an environment it was natural for competitions to develop when school bands began to proliferate after World War I. State and county fairs had offered early venues for band comparisons. Kansas was an early state with school music contests. Mark Fonder credits William V. Arvold, a history teacher in Reedsburg, Wisconsin, with organizing the high school band in 1919 and planning a tournament involving three other bands the following year.[41] The involvement of the Holton Band Instrument Company of Elkhorn, Wisconsin, the next year was an economic factor that firmly established the Wisconsin contest. American music instrument manufacturers had become large and prosperous during the time when professional bands, such as those of Sousa and Gilmore, toured every part of the country and helped town bands flourish. World War I was a golden opportunity for band instrument manufacturers, who were called on to supply instruments for a multitude of army bands that played for the troops and toured the country to help raise money for the war effort.

By the early 1920s, however, many professional bands had ceased to function because of changing life-styles caused by the automobile, moving pictures, the phonograph, the radio, the player piano, and the disruption of World War I. The end of the war abruptly stopped the sale of instruments to the military. With instrument sales off, a new market was needed. Several companies joined Holton in donating instruments as prizes for the 1921 contest at Elkhorn.

School Bands. The MSNC had given little attention to school bands, although several of its leaders had spoken about them. Miessner and Russell Morgan were especially positive about bands as a way of keeping young boys in music during their awkward period. Cities such as Oakland, California, and Rochester, New York, had begun to offer wind instrument instruction before the United States entered the war. Louis Aiken, a violinist himself, organized the first high school band in Cincinnati in 1919 at Hughes High School.

Joseph Maddy's performance at the 1922 MSNC meeting with his Richmond High School Orchestra (discussed later in this chapter) prompted the conference to appoint members to the Committee on Instrumental Affairs. Jay W. Fay of Rochester was named chairman, and Russell Morgan, acting director of music in Cleveland, Victor Rebmann, B. F. Stuber, and Eugene Hahnel were members.

The committee was sorely needed. In October 1922 the *Journal* reported 14 bands in Los Angeles high schools, 10 high school orchestras in Detroit, and 800 instrumental students in Pittsburgh, 440 in Indianapolis, 1,350 in Seattle, and 1,871 in Oakland. Everett Allyn Moses, supervisor in Grand Forks, North Dakota, had an orchestra of 45 and a band of 60, both of which were state contest winners.[42] It was another ten years before a Texas state superintendent, L. A. Woods of Waco, was finally able to eliminate the independent school districts, and introduce county school music supervisors who promoted school music.

The Tournament. Emil Holz described the organization of a "tournament" in connection with the Chicago convention of the music trades in the summer of 1923.[43] The tournament was held in Grant Park across from the Congress Hotel. C. D. Greenleaf, then president of the Band Instrument Manufacturers Association as well as of C. G. Conn, played a key role in planning the event. Thirty bands (twenty-six high school and four elementary ensembles) participated in the early part of June 1923. Each unit was allowed to select its own pieces. The announced marching competition was cancelled, but this being what has become known as a media event, the parade and massed band concert were held. Lieutenant William H. Santelmann, director of the United States

Marine Corps Band, was the lone judge, a fact that disturbed some of the directors who had performed for a panel of judges in their own state contests. The Fostoria (Ohio) High School Band, directed by John W. Wainwright, was awarded the first place ribbon and one thousand dollars.

The Instrumental Affairs Committee. Instrument manufacturers were just becoming aware of the rapid growth in instrumental music in the schools of the United States. At the tournament, C. M. Tremaine of the National Bureau for the Advancement of Music, an organization funded by piano manufacturers, knew of the MSNC committee and suggested to Greenleaf that future contests be handled by educators. The acceptance of Tremaine's suggestion prevented the further commercialization of the contest. The Committee on Instrumental Affairs of the MSNC, taking control, prepared a repertoire list containing better musical literature than the average band was apt to play in 1924; contest selections had to be chosen from the list. A requirement for the selection of regional winners chosen from state winners was instituted, and the judging procedure was improved. The problems of putting the changes in place delayed the first national contest, which was held in Fostoria, Ohio, until 1926. The winner was A. R. McAllister's band from Joliet (Illinois) Township High School.

In promoting the event, the bureau commented that a "good school band can add more than perhaps anything else to the prestige of its school and town," thereby initiating a public relations concept with which music educators have struggled since. Bands and other school music organizations have since played an important role in advancing the cause of music in the schools. Lowell Mason and others used public performance of schoolchildren to win a place for music in the schools. With bands, however, came the danger of exploiting the students by using them for other than civic or educational purposes. Professional education organizations, particularly the National Association of Secondary School Principals, the North Central Association of Colleges and Secondary Schools, and the MENC have established guidelines to avoid exploitation of students, but individual schools have often been pressured to ignore them.

The contests led to the standardization of band instrumentation, the practice of publishing full band scores, increased emphasis on instrumental music in teacher-training programs, and a phenomenal growth in enrollment for school bands. In time, contests for orchestras and choirs became part of the movement. Associations were formed to take over the administration of the competitions. The first national contest for orchestras was held in Iowa City in 1929, and the National School Band Association expanded to become the National School Band and Orchestra Association and then changed again to become the National School Band, Orchestra and Vocal Association. In 1932 the organization divided into two groups, and in 1936 the National School Vocal Association was formed. By then there were three groups—band, orchestral, and vocal—all of which became separate auxiliaries of the Music Educators National Conference (recently renamed from the Music Supervisors National Conference). As auxiliary organizations, they had complete charge of the National School Music Competition-Festivals. Because of the necessity for schools to qualify for the national competitions through state and district levels, boards of control were established at all levels. They gave impetus to the establishment of state music education associations.

During ten years of contests there were differences of opinion about their value. Marguerite Hood, then supervisor for the state of Montana, observed that contests had prompted the most heated debate among music educators since the days of the rote-note disagreement.[44] From 1921 to 1931, Montana had held Interscholastic music meets of several days duration with both instrumental and vocal contests for large and small ensembles. Growth forced the abandonment of the contests because towns were unable to host them. Smaller local festivals immediately sprouted to satisfy the desire for interscholastic events.

School administrators became concerned about events in which there was one winner and many losers. Overstimulation and overspecialization were also cited as undesirable results of contests. They acknowledged that competitive events frequently resulted in higher levels of musical performance than noncompetitive events, but there was strong feeling that modification was necessary. Joseph Maddy, Hollis Dann, Walter Butterfield, Elbridge Pitcher, George Waln, and Robert Milton were among the many music educators who expressed themselves on the matter. Frank A. Beach served as chairman of the MENC Standing Committee on Contests. Max Krone of Northwestern University called attention to the festival pattern in New England and under the sponsorship of the Michigan Vocal Association.[45] In 1933 the ranking system was replaced by one of rating the participants.[46] World War II caused the suspension of national contests, which were never resumed. Before the war there had been ten contest regions, but with the establishment of NIMAC in 1952, the regional system was eliminated.[47] At that time the states became the highest level of interscholastic events sponsored by the MENC or its affiliated groups. A system of grading performances that used required music and "Selected Lists" replaced ranking of the groups and helped raise musical standards.

MUSIC MEMORY CONTESTS

In 1923 Julia D. Owen, chairman of the Public School Music Committee of the Texas Federation of Music Clubs, conducted a survey in her state.[48] She summarized the responses she received from 55 schools in response to a questionnaire sent to 700 Texas schools. Only 35 reported having a music supervisor, and only 24 required students to have some music instruction. Fifty-four, however, had a prohibition against jazz. The responses to Julia Owen's Texas school questionnaire may have identified only 35 music supervisors, but it also revealed that students in 34 schools had been drilled for the music memory contests. The contests, which reflected the desire for universal music education in the United States, involved as many students as teachers wished to have participate. The movement was similar to one in England that had existed for several years.

Music listening as a worthwhile endeavor for students had been introduced by a few teachers before the turn of the century. A school memory contest, possibly the first, was conducted in 1916 by Mabel Bray in Westfield, New Jersey.[49] It may have been instigated by Tremaine of the Bureau for the Advancement of Music, who had tried it with his family. He spoke about it to the Conference at the 1918 Evansville meeting. The General Federation of Women's Clubs sponsored a national contest, and local groups, such as the MSNC-affiliated In-and-About Chicago Club, ran their own. Once the idea caught on it swept the country. Perhaps its popularity can be explained by its resemblance to something that parents remembered from their own schooling—the spelling bee. Parents drilled their children to help them prepare. No other aspect of music education appears to have involved the family as did the music memory contests.

It was not only the students and their families who were interested in contests. The newspapers published lists of works to be used in the contests. Theater organists and theater orchestras, still accompanying silent films in 1926, played the contest music between film showings to give their young patrons one more chance to familiarize themselves with the melodies. Fifty radio stations played the music on the National Contest List.[50] Mr. and Mrs. Marx Oberndorfer, both pianists, broadcast the music for the Chicago contest. The Victor Talking Machine Company offered to send a free booklet to anyone conducting a contest. The booklet listed 250 standard selections that might be used in conducting a contest. This activity coincided with the community music movement and reinforced the positive feelings of the public toward school music and the conference goal of making America musical. By the late 1920s most homes had a radio, the movies were singing, and the memory contest craze was a thing of the past. Despite its educational purpose, it was a short-lived fad.

Musical Discrimination Contests. In the early 1930s the Conference upgraded the memory contest to a contest of musical discrimination. Walter Damrosch played ten musical selections over the National Broadcasting Company network, and NBC offered three scholarships to the winners. For each composition, students were asked to identify the style of the music and suggest a possible composer. They were also asked questions about form and the solo instruments, and to give an appropriate name to a piece of program music. The fact that fifty-four of the seventy-five best papers came from members of the National High School Orchestra and the National High School Chorus suggests that what later came to be known as comprehensive musicianship was being taught to student musicians before World War II.

PSYCHOLOGY AND MUSIC EDUCATION

The insights into the child mind and its development that were first set forth by Jean Jacques Rousseau during the Enlightenment of the eighteenth century did not lead to a science of psychology. It was not until the rise of science in the nineteenth century that the empirical study of the mental processes began to be separated from the discipline of philosophy. After displacing the earlier ideas of special faculties of the mind advocated by Pestalozzi and many others, the pioneers in the new science began collecting data about the mind that they thought was necessary to understand how people learn.

Connectionism. One of the early influential schools of thought was connectionism (also known as associationism). One of the leading connectionists was Edward L. Thorndike, who held that learning does not result from strengthening the faculties by conquering difficult challenges but rather from establishing bonds between specific stimuli and responses.[51] Thorndike's laws of learning included the law of effect, the law of exercise, and the law of readiness. The law of effect stated that learning bonds would be stronger if the effect of the response was pleasant rather than disappointing. This principle worked well for certain small bits of learning and became the basis for the "teaching machines" of S. L. Pressey, and later, of computer-assisted instruction. John B. Watson of Johns Hopkins University and B. F. Skinner of Harvard University were leaders in what became known as the behaviorist school, which appealed strongly to music educators.

Testing. Carl E. Seashore's *Measures of Musical Talents*, first published in 1919, was atomistic in nature. The *Measures* evaluated responses to five aspects of musical tone, only one of which involved more than an isolated musical element. The interest in aptitude testing remained strong for at least seventy years after the first Seashore tests appeared. Seashore revised the *Measures* in 1938 and used a composite score rather than evaluating responses separately for each musical element, but he did not change the basic structure of the tests. European tests, such as those by Herbert Wing, tended to be less atomistic and dealt more with musical content.

Psychoanalysis. G. Stanley Hall invited Sigmund Freud to speak at Clark University in 1909. Some of the ideas of psychoanalysis, such as motivation, related to the changes being made in American education. Freud's approach, however, was almost entirely biological and over-looked cultural influences. For this reason, it was not of great interest to music education leaders of the early decades of the twentieth century.

Field Theory. When an English translation of Kurt Koffka's *Growth of the Mind* appeared in 1924, Americans were introduced to another view of psychology that was better matched to the ideas of progressive education. In Germany, Koffka, Max Wertheimer, and Wolfgang Koehler developed Gestalt psychology, based on the prediliction of the mind for wholes rather than fragments. The emphasis that the theory put on insight, problem solving, and the natural spontaneous interest of children put it closer to the new American educational thought. Some leaders in the progressive education movement were ready to accept such support.

James L. Mursell carried the Gestalt message to music education. Mursell was born in England and earned a B.A. from the University of Queensland in Australia and a Ph.D. in philosophy with Josiah Royce from Harvard University. His first academic post was at Lake Erie College, where he taught psychology and education courses. He later taught at Lawrence College and then joined the remarkable assembly of educational thinkers that James E. Russell had brought together at Teachers College of Columbia University. From that post, and from his positions on the MSNC Research Council and the editorial board of the *Music Supervisors Journal,* as well as from his voluminous writings in books and periodicals, he guided the thinking of many music educators throughout the middle third of the twentieth century. He was a dramatic speaker who inspired MENC audiences at both divisional and national meetings for many years.

Metz discussed the influence of Mursell on two of the leading contemporary (1968) publications in music education.[52] He found positive relationships between Mursell's writings and *Foundations and Principles of Music Education* by Charles Leonhard and Robert House. Leonhard was Mursell's student, and, in the minds of some colleagues, his successor as an intellectual leader of the profession. The same is true for the MENC publication *Music in General Education.* Some of the committee members who worked on the book had been Mursell's students at Columbia, and others had used his materials in their teacher-training courses.

Other Psychologists. Robert Gagne, though an active undergraduate musician at Yale University, never concentrated specifically on the problems associated with learning music, although his eight-step hierarchy of learning proved useful to music educators. Edwin Gordon, a music educator who created the *Music Aptitude Profile*, studied most of the other tests of musical aptitude and achievement. He discovered the importance of real musical experience during the preschool years as a means of raising potential musical aptitude, which he claimed to be unchangeable after about the age of ten.

Following World War II, a group who referred to themselves as humanistic psychologists studied the nature of successful people. Among them was Abraham Maslow, who assured teachers that music and dance were two of the most important experiences the schools could provide young children. He said: "Aesthetic perceiving and creating . . . are seen to be a central aspect of human life and of psychology and education rather than a peripheral one."[53] Maslow attracted many music educators to his view. Carl Rogers is another psychologist whose views are compatible with those who teach music for human development rather than simply to develop musical facility.

TEACHER EDUCATION

At the 1902 meeting of the NEA Department of Music Education in Minneapolis, Hollis Dann, George Krinbill, and a Miss Brant were appointed to suggest names of members to serve on a committee to formulate a plan of study for teachers of music in the public schools. Thomas Tapper of Boston, A. J. Gantvoort of Cincinnati, and O. T. Corson of Columbus were suggested by Dann's committee and approved by the assembly.[54] The following year at Boston Gantvoort explained that, because of Corson's illness and the extended absence of Tapper in Europe, the committee was unable to report. At the suggestion of P. C. Hayden, two additional members were named to the committee—Samuel W. Cole and George Krinbill. In 1904 in Saint Louis, Tapper read a report accompanied by a letter from Samuel Cole and by verbal comments by Krinbill and Gantvoort. Hayden moved the approval of all this as "a report in progress," and the motion carried. Finally, in 1905 Tapper's report was accepted and he was directed to publish and circulate it to the supervisors of the country.[55] The report set in place elements that have existed in teacher-training programs since: (1) literary qualification at least equal to those of high school graduates (suggesting possibly that many professional musicians who had tired of touring with opera companies or circuses sought school supervisory positions); (2) musical qualification to include proficiency on an instrument or as a singer, knowledge of theory, music history, and conducting; and (3) familiarity with school music textbooks and courses of study.

Few colleges offered "public school music" courses at that time. *The Etude* carried advertisements in 1906 for such programs at the Crane Normal Institute, Northwestern University, and the Detroit Conservatory. The American Conservatory in Chicago offered some lectures on the subject. Many were available at teachers colleges. Gantvoort had been active in the NEA Department of Music and introduced a teacher's course at the College of Music of Cincinnati in 1894. The institution had been connected with the schools through the May Festival since its founding by the orchestra conductor Theodore Thomas. The Cincinnati Conservatory, however, did not offer a summer course in school music until 1905 and made it part of its winter curriculum only in 1909.

When the Music Supervisors National Conference was established, teacher training was not uppermost in the minds of most of the original members. It was several years before the conference planned sessions for teacher educators at its meetings. Concern for the quality of teacher preparation was exhibited in many states, however, and a competition was developing between the normal schools that were changing to teachers colleges and the traditional colleges and universities.

The first issue of the *Music Supervisors Journal,* published in September 1914, reported that several of the Midwestern states were formulating regulations governing those who taught music either in the schools or privately. Walter Van Dyke Bingham, head of the department of teacher training at the Carnegie Institute, presented a major address at the 1916 MSNC meeting in Lincoln. The same year, Frank Beach of Kansas State Teachers College at Emporia reported that many states required two years of college for school music supervisors and that ''it may not be long before the states will require four years for music, as for other studies.''[56]

In the spring of 1907, Karl W. Gehrkens was teaching German and algebra and directing the choir at Oberlin (Ohio) High School. The next year he returned to his alma mater to establish the public school music program at Oberlin Conservatory. Gehrkens was intimately involved with the growth of teacher training. At the 1915 MTNA meeting he spoke on ''Training the Music Supervisor,'' and in 1918 at the Evansville MSNC meeting he chaired a panel (with Frank Beach and Alice Inskeep of Grand Rapids) on ''Normal Schools and Other Training Schools.''

Education Council. The *Music Supervisors Journal,* meanwhile, was running a series entitled ''Selected Bibliography,'' assembled by Vivian Gray Little and expanded by Peter Dykema. It must have had considerable influence in convincing doubtful professors as to the existence of extensive literature on a broad series of topics, including school music history, pedagogy, music appreciation, teacher and supervisor training, general courses, music in colleges, books for supervisors, and general references. It is not surprising, then, that when the Conference created the Educational Council, the first committee assignment made by the council was to a group charged with the task of developing a course for the training of supervisors of music. Nor is it surprising that Gehrkens was appointed to the committee, along with Hollis Dann, who had built a reputation for his summer course at Cornell University. Gehrkens, who had already extended the Oberlin curriculum to three years, recounted Dann's reluctance to serve.[57] Lendrim suggested that his reluctance might have been due to the desire to avoid competition with his summer course.[58]

At the Saint Louis meeting (1919) where the committee was created, A. J. Gantvoort, who by this time had had over twenty years of experience with a training program for music supervisors, presented a talk in which he discussed general education, general music education, professional education, and natural ability and adaptability. His talk closely paralleled the 1905 suggestions of the NEA department. Gehrkens had sought information from over three hundred colleges and discovered that of the hundred schools reporting some form of training for music supervisors, approximately half offered two year courses. Twelve granted the bachelor of science and five the bachelor of music degree at the completion of a four-year program.[59] Gehrkens, having prepared a four-year program for his school, made it the basis of the committee report he presented in 1921 at Saint Joseph (Missouri). It was printed, and along with the Standard Course in Music for the Elementary Grades, was distributed by the Educational Council as *Bulletin No. 1*. Gehrkens's report has, to a large extent, determined the nature of the teacher preparation program in music to the present. Once he had the sanction of the Conference, he returned to Oberlin and threatened to resign if his four-year program was not begun immediately. In June 1922, three students were awarded the bachelor of science in music education degree by Oberlin.

The Curriculum for preparing music teachers consisted of three major areas of study—general education, professional education, and music. One-quarter of the program of study was assigned to each of the first two. The other half was taken up by applied and theoretical music. The council decided to leave the specifics of academic work and the proportion of theoretical and applied music to the individual institutions, although Gehrkens stressed applied music. The basic plan, including the relative share given to musical experiences, general culture, and professional training, has been altered only slightly over the years.

The balance has been maintained because those who believed in the importance of one area or another began jockeying immediately for a better position. Individual state education department requirements often dictated the balance. In 1928 the recently formed National Association of Schools of Music began to accredit collegiate programs in music, and served as an effective protector of the musicianship segment of the program. Additions to the curriculum of many one- and two-credit courses in music specialties, in addition to mandated courses in subjects such as state history, soon began to balloon the requirements for undergraduate music education majors. In some institutions, the number of credit hours for a degree rose as much as 15 percent higher than for other undergraduate programs, giving rise to the student boast that their program was the most difficult in the university with the exception of the "premeds."

Tuition differed as well. A 1930 study by a master's degree candidate, who went on to be president of the MENC, concluded that the "average cost of the college music curriculum is 111% greater than the average cost of academic curricula."[60] Conservatories, liberal arts colleges, and teachers colleges all had the same differential, except for Harris Teachers College, which charged no tuition. The higher cost of education was no longer offset by the traditionally higher salaries of music teachers, who were beginning to be paid at the same level as other teachers. Saint Louis had a salary scale in 1910 that began an assistant music supervisor at $1,100 and a classroom teacher at $560. By 1930 that difference had virtually disappeared.

In 1937, a study by Edna McEarchen indicated that many schools were accepting high school graduates with insufficient background to become competent music teachers in four years. Suggesting that the "vicious circle" had to be broken, she urged three screening points— before entrance, before practice teaching, and before graduation. This was not out of line with the procedures then being established in the respected schools of education. By 1940 a major issue was mastery of content, and a few institutions, including Cornell University, were already planning a five-year program in music education.

Teacher Preparation Materials. After the first decade of the twentieth century, many new manuals were published as music teacher education texts. They were usually small and claimed to be complete. An example is Hamlin E. Cogswell's *How to Teach Music in Public Schools: A Complete Outline. Graded, Un-Graded, High and Normal Schools* (Walker & Watson Publishers, Indiana, Pennsylvania, 1910). This sixty-page manual covers the goals and methods for eight grades, normal schools, music theory, instrumental music, and other topics. By comparison, *The Teachers' Manual MUSIC: Newly Revised and Enlarged Edition* (probably written by H. W. Fairbank, published by H. W. Fairbank Publishing Company, Jackson, Michigan, 1924), only forty pages long, covered the teaching of music from the first through the eighth grades. Like most manuals of this type, both of the above were intended to be used with any of the graded series then available. Issues that teachers deal with now also confronted earlier teachers. The problem of the monotone, for example, was covered in both manuals. Cogswell wrote in 1910:

> Monotones, **must not** be permitted to sing **with** the class. **Encourage— never tell a child he is a monotone,** this is a serious mistake. Never cease trying to help the non-singing pupil. Often the change comes suddenly.

He then goes on to suggest ways to help the monotone students. Fairbank took a more proactive view of working with monotones:

ELIMINATION OF MONOTONES

Clear the front one or two rows of seats, and place therein all of the children who can not hum the pitches given. Do not fear that it will make them self-conscious and do not begrudge the time it takes to make the change each day. The children who have taken the tones given, correctly, are to be seated immediately back of the monotone rows, and may be called "Bluebirds." The monotones may be called the "Robins." This distinction enables the teacher to stop the monotones from singing without mentioning them individually.[61]

Like Cogswell, Fairbank then presented exercises to cure the monotone.

Thomas Tapper, author of several graded series mentioned earlier, was a highly respected trainer of teachers. He taught at New York University and Cornell University Summer School, and was a lecturer at the Institute of Musical Art of the City of New York; he also wrote several books, including *The Music Life, Efficiency, First Studies in Music Biography*, and several others on musical subjects for young students. Tapper's book, *The Education of the Music Teacher* (Philadelphia: Theodore Presser Company, 1914) was more characteristic of the large literature on music teacher training that was to follow and with which we are familiar today. This 223-page book covered numerous topics in twenty-five chapters, some of which were entitled "Music Teaching as Service," "Music Teaching as Profession," "Equipment and Success," "Pedagogy," "Musical Theory," "Music in the Home," "Mechanical Musical Instruments," "Community Music," "Public School Music," "Music in Social Settlement Work," and "Examinations in Music."

SUMMARY

The new ideas in education were accepted rather slowly by music educators with certain notable exceptions. Chief among these was Osbourne McConathy, who had moved from being a rigid disciplinarian as young man in Louisville to a follower of Luther Whiting Mason's approach. From that position he matured to lead the profession into progressivism. He was one of the most influential persons in music education during his lifetime. Others of truly outstanding caliber included W. Otto Miessner, Will Earhart, P. C. Hayden, Frances Elliott Clark, Joseph Maddy, John Philip Sousa, Albert G. Mitchell, Karl W. Gehrkens, Austin Harding, Thaddeus P. Giddings, and Peter Dykema. By the end of the professional lives of these people and others, music education had changed from the "vocal music" for which music educators had sought recognition from the NEA to a new "music education," as supported by the Music Supervisors National Conference.

NOTES

1. *Journal of the Proceedings and Addresses of the Forty-Third Annual Meeting of the National Education Association* (Winona, MN: The Association, 1904), pp. 702–707.

2. Corwin Taylor shed light on this demand for serious study by the city's high school musicians (*Triad*, November 1982; December–January 1982–1983; and February–March 1983). According to Taylor, there was considerable employment for musicians in the hotels and cafés, in ten theater orchestras, and in the professional bands that had become community institutions. John C. Weber's group was known as the Prize Band of America, having won first place at the 1904 Saint Louis World's Fair, where attendees had been told they could hear three bands daily. Cincinnati has Local 1 of the American Federation of Musicians because of Weber, who was the president of the union from 1900 to 1940.

3. *Journal of Proceedings and Addresses of the Forty-Seventh Annual Meeting of the National Education Association* (Denver: The Association 1909), pp. 681–87.

4. John W. Molnar, "The History of the Music Educators National Conference," *Journal or Research in Music Education* 3 (Spring 1955): 87.

5. Charles W. Eliot, introduction to *Essays on Education and Kindred Subjects* by Herbert Spencer (New York: Dutton, 1910), p. xviii.

6. Eric Blom, ed. *Grove's Dictionary of Music and Musicians*, 5th ed., vol. 6 (New York: St. Martin's Press, 1955), p. 251.

7. Frances Elliott Clark, *Music Appreciation for Little Children: In the Home, Kindergarten, and Primary Schools* (Camden, NJ: Victor Talking Machine Company, 1920), p. 11.

8. Alice Keith and Arthur Shepherd, *Listening in on the Masters: A Course in Music Appreciation for Home, School and Club with Radio and Record Illustrations* (Boston: C. C. Birchard, 1926), n.p.

9. Anthony L. Barresi, "Edgar B. Gordon: A Pioneer in Media Music Education," *Journal of Research in Music Education* 35 (Winter 1987): 259.

10. "New York, 5," *The New Grove Dictionary of American Music* III, ed. H. Wiley Hitchcock and Stanley Sadie (New York: Macmillan, 1986), p. 357.

11. Family records of Elizabeth Beach, now in the MENC Historical Center, University of Maryland at College Park.

12. Lucy B. and Richard Stebbins, *Frank Damrosch: Let the People Sing* (Durham, NC: Duke University Press, 1945), p. 181.

13. Agnes Moore Fryberger, *Listening Lessons in Music: Graded for Schools* (Boston: Silver, Burdett, 1916).

14. *Dwight's Journal of Music* 9 (July 3, 1869): 59.

15. *Dwight's Journal of Music* 9 (July 27, 1872): 276.

16. Frederick Fennell, *Time and the Winds: A Short History of the Use of Wind Instruments in the Orchestra, Band, and the Wind Ensemble* (Kenosha, WI: Leblanc Publications, 1954), pp. 39–40.

17. Richard Franko Goldman, "Band Music in America," in Paul Henry Lang, ed., *One Hundred Years of Music in America* (New York: Schirmer, 1961), p. 135.
18. Fennell, *Time and the Winds*, p. 40.
19. W. D. Monnier, "Grammar School Orchestras," *School Music* 5 (January 1904): 24.
20. Gladys A. Brown, "Report of Survey on Instrumental Music in Our Schools, *Music Supervisors Journal* 3 (November 1916): 12.
21. James A. Keene, *Music and Education in Vermont* (Glenbridge, IL: Glenbridge Publishing, 1987), p. 77.
22. London interview reprinted from the *Musical Herald* in *School Music* 10 (January 1909): 5–9.
23. Edward B. Birge, *A History of Public School Music in the United States* (Chicago: Music Educators National Conference, 1937), p. 189.
24. Robin K. Deverich, "The Maidstone Movement—Influential British Precursor of American Public School Instrumental Classes," *Journal of Research in Music Education* 35 (Spring 1987): 39–55.
25. William G. Mitchell, *Journal of Proceedings of the Thirteenth Annual Meeting of the Music Supervisors National Conference* (Madison: The Conference, 1920).
26. Will Earhart, *Music Supervisors Journal* 8 (December 1921): 37.
27. Frederick Innes, "The Music Possibilities of the Wind Band," *Music Supervisors Journal* 10 (May 1924): 43.
28. *School Index* (Cincinnati), 8 (April 28, 1922): 270.
29. Gladys A. Brown, "Instrumental Music in Our Public Schools," *Music Supervisors Journal* 3 (November 1916): 12; and 3 (January 1917): 24, 26.
30. *Music Supervisors Journal* 3 (January 1917): 7.
31. John Love Norman, "A Historical Sketch of the Changes in Attitude toward the Teaching of Piano Technique from 1800 to the Present Time," (Ph.D. dissertation, Michigan State University, 1968), p. 19.
32. *Cincinnati Daily Gazette* 7 (July 1, 1834): 1.
33. William Richards, "How Group Teaching Started," *Clavier* (January–February 1965): 39–41.
34. Cincinnati Public Schools, *Eighty-Fourth Annual Report for the School Year Ending August 31, 1913* (Cincinnati, 1914), p. 61.
35. Inez Field Damon, "Public School Piano Classes As I Have Known Them," *Journal of Proceedings of the Thirteenth Annual Meeting of the Music Supervisors National Conference* (Oberlin, OH: The Conference, 1920), pp. 69–72.
36. Cary Clive Burford, "Band Formations and Pageantry at Football Games," *We're Loyal to You, Illinois* (Danville, IL: Interstate Printers, 1952), p. 373.
37. Mark Hindsley, *School Band and Orchestra Administration* (Lynbrook, NY: Boosey & Hawkes, 1940), pp. 7–8.
38. Mark H. Hindsley, *Band—At-ten-tion! A Manual for the Marching Band* (Chicago: Gamble Hinged Music, 1932), p. 9.
30. Julia Cherry Spruill, *Women's Life & Work in the Southern Colonies* (New York: Norton, 1972), p. 110.
40. Austin A. Harding, "The Band as a Community Asset," *Proceedings of the 37th Annual Meeting of the Music Teachers National Association*, Buffalo (Hartford: The Association, 1915), p. 189.
41. Mark Fonder, "The Wisconsin School Music Association and Its Contests: The Early Years," *Journal of Research in Music Education* 37 (Summer 1989): 112–31.

42. *Music Supervisors Journal* 9 (October 1922): 32–35.
43. Emil A. Holz, "The School Band Contest of America," *Journal of Research in Music Education* 10 (Spring 1962): 3–12.
44. Marguerite Hood, "Can Festivals Take the Place of Contests?," *Music Educators Journal* 22 (October 1936): 27.
45. Max Krone, "Do Festival-Clinics Solve the Problem?," *Music Educators Journal* (March 1939): 22.
46. Noreen D. Burdette, "The High School Music Contest Movement in the United States" (Mus.Ed. dissertation, Boston University, 1985), p. 106.
47. Ibid.
48. *Music Supervisors Journal* 9 (February 1923): 40.
49. Birge, *A History of Public School Music,* p. 210.
50. William Arms Fisher, "The Radio and Music," *Music Supervisors Journal* 9 (February 1926): 8–16.
51. Edward L. Thorndike, "The Nature, Purposes and General Methods of Measurement of Educational Products," in *Seventeenth Yearbook,* National Society for the Study of Education, pt. 2 (Bloomington, IL: Public School Publishing, 1918), p. 16.
52. Donald E. Metz. "A Critical Analysis of Selected Aspects of the Thought of James L. Mursell" (Ph.D. dissertation, Case Western Reserve University, 1968) pp. 125–153.
53. Judith Murphy and George Sullivan, *Music in American Society* (Washington, DC: Music Educators National Conference, 1968), p. 27.
54. *Journal of Proceedings and Addresses of the Forty-First Annual Meeting of the National Education Association* (Chicago: The Association, 1902), p. 616.
55. *Journal of Proceedings and Addresses of the Forty-Fourth Meeting of the National Education Association* (Winona, MN: The Association, 1905), p. 629.
56. At that time, Illinois issued three classes of certificates to music teachers— licentiate, associate, and fellow. Examinations in music history and theory were given for teachers of voice, piano, organ, violin, and public school music. In the same year, Will Earhart did a study for the U.S. Bureau of Education that indicated that of the 164 colleges preparing teachers, forty-three had programs for music supervisors.
57. *Music Supervisors Journal* 3 (November 1916): 3.
58. Frank T. Lendrim, "Music for Every Child: The Story of Karl Wilson Gehrkens" (Ed.D. dissertation, University of Michigan, 1962), p. 96.
59. Frederick Anthony Warren, "History of the Music Education Research Council and the *Journal of Research in Music Education* " (Ed.D. dissertation, University of Michigan, 1966), p. 17.
60. Luther Anton Richman, "The Cost to the Student of a Four-Year Course in Public School Music on the Collegiate Level" (M.A. thesis in Education, University of Cincinnati, 1931), p. 37.
61. H. W. Fairbank, *The Teacher's Manual MUSIC: Newly Revised and Enlarged Edition* (H. W. Fairbank Publishing Company, Jackson, MI, 1924).

BIBLIOGRAPHY

Barresi, Anthony L. "Edgar B. Gordon: A Pioneer in Media Music Education." *Journal of Research in Music Education* 35 (Spring 1987).

Beach, Elizabeth. Family records in the Music Educators National Conference Historical Center, University of Maryland at College Park.

Birge, Edward Bailey. *A History of Public School Music in the United States.* Chicago: Music Educators National Conference, 1937.

Brown, Gladys A. "Report of Survey on Instrumental Music in Our Schools." *Music Supervisors Journal* 3 (November 1916, January 1917).

Bryant, Carolyn. *And the Band Played On: 1776–1976.* Washington, DC: Smithsonian Institution Press, 1975.

Burdette, Noreen Diamond. "The High School Music Contest Movement in the United States." Mus.Ed. dissertation, Boston University, 1985.

Burford, Cary Clive. "Band Formations and Pageantry at Football Games." *We're Loyal to You, Illinois.* Danville, IL: Interstate Printers, 1952.

Clark, Frances Elliott. *Music Appreciation for Little Children.* Camden, NJ: Victor Talking Machine Company, 1920.

——. *Music Appreciation with the Victrola for Children.* Camden, NJ: Victor Talking Machine Company, 1926.

Cuban, Larry. *How Teachers Taught: Constancy and Change in American Classrooms, 1890–1980.* New York: Longman, 1984.

Damon, Inez Field. "Public School Piano Classes As I Have Known Them." *Journal of Proceedings of the Thirteenth Annual Meeting of the Music Supervisors National Conference.* Oberlin, OH: Music Supervisors National Conference, 1920.

Deverich, Robin K. "The Maidstone Movement—Influential British Precursor of American Public School Instrumental Classes." *Journal of Research in Music Education* 35 (Spring 1987).

Dvorak, Raymond Francis. *The Band on Parade.* New York: Carl Fischer, 1937.

Dwight's Journal of Music 29 (July 3, 1869); 32 (July 27, 1872).

Earhart, Will. *Music Supervisors Journal* 8 (December 1921).

Eliot, Charles W. Introduction to *Essays on Education and Kindred Subjects* by Herbert Spencer. New York: Dutton, 1910.

Fennell, Frederick. *Time and the Winds: A Short History of the Use of Wind Instruments in the Orchestra, Band, and the Wind Ensemble.* Kenosha, WI: G. Leblanc, 1954.

Fisher, William Arms. "The Radio and Music." *Music Supervisors Journal* 11 (February 1926).

Fonder, Mark. "The Wisconsin School Music Association and Its Contests: The Early Years." *Journal of Research in Music Education* 37 (Summer 1989).

Fryberger, Agnes Moore. *Listening Lessons in Music: Graded for Schools.* Boston: Silver, Burdett, 1916.

Goldman, Richard Franko. "Band Music in America," in Paul Henry Lang, ed., *One Hundred Years of Music in America.* New York: Schirmer, 1961.

Grove's Dictionary of Music and Musicians, 5th ed., ed. E. Blom. New York: St. Martin's Press, 1955.

Harding, Austin A. "The Band As a Community Asset." *Proceedings of the 38th Annual Meeting of the Music Teachers National Association.* Hartford: Music Teachers National Association, 1915.

Hindsley, Mark H. *Band—At-ten-tion! A Manual for the Marching Band*. Chicago: Gamble Hinged Music, 1932.

——. *School Band and Orchestra Administration*. Lynbrook, NY: Boosey & Hawkes, 1940.

Holz, Emil A. "The School Band Contest of America." *Journal of Research in Music Education* 10 (Spring 1962).

Hood, Marguerite. "Can Festivals Take the Place of Contests?" *Music Educators Journal* 23 (October 1936).

Journals of 41st, 42nd, 43rd, and 44th Annual Meetings of the National Education Association, 1902, 1903, 1904, 1905.

Journal of Proceedings and Addresses of the Forty-Seventh Annual Meeting of the National Education Association. Denver: National Education Association, 1909.

Keene, James A. *Music and Education in Vermont*. Glenbridge, IL: Glenbridge Publishing, 1987.

Keith, Alice, and Shepherd, Arthur. *Listening in on the Masters*. Boston: C. C. Birchard, 1926.

Krone, Max. "Do Festival-Clinics Solve the Problem?" *Music Educators Journal* 36 (March 1939).

Lahee, Henry C. *The Orchestra*. Boston: Boston Musical and Educational Bureau, 1925.

Lendrim, Frank T. "Music for Every Child: The Story of Karl Wilson Gehrkens." Ed.D. dissertation, University of Michigan, 1962.

Metz, Donald E. "A Critical Analysis of Selected Aspects of the Thought of James L. Mursell." Ph.D. dissertation, Case Western Reserve University, 1968.

Mitchell, William G. *Journal of Proceedings of the Thirteenth Annual Meeting of the Music Supervisors National Conference*. Madison: Music Supervisors National Conference, 1920.

Molnar, John W. "The History of the Music Educators National Conference." *Journal of Research in Music Education* 3 (Spring 1955).

Monnier, W.D. "Grammar School Orchestras." *School Music* 5 (1904).

Murphy, Judith and George Sullivan. *Music in American Society*. Washington, DC: Music Educators National Conference, 1968.

Mursell, James L. *The Psychology of School Music Teaching*. New York: Silver, Burdett, 1938.

Music Supervisors Journal 3 (November 1916), 9 (October 1922, February 1923).

"New York, 5." *The New Grove Dictionary of American Music* 3, ed. H. Wiley Hitchcock and Stanley Sadie. New York: Macmillan, 1986.

Richman, Luther Anton. "The Cost to the Student of a Four-Year Course in Public School Music on the Collegiate Level." M.A. thesis in Education, University of Cincinnati, 1931.

Schwartz, H.W. *Bands of America*. Garden City, NY: Doubleday, 1957.

School Index (Cincinnati), 8 (April 28, 1922).

Seashore, Carl E. "Measurement of Musical Talent." *Music Supervisors Journal* 6 (September 1919).

Spruill, Julia Cherry. *Women's Life & Work in the Southern Colonies.* New York: Norton, 1972.

Stebbins, Lucy B. and Richard. *Frank Damrosch: Let the People Sing.* Durham, NC: Duke University Press, 1945.

Tapper, Thomas. *The Education of the Music Teacher.* Philadelphia: Theodore Presser, 1914.

Thorndike, Edward L. "The Nature, Purposes and General Methods of Measurement of Educational Products." *Seventeenth Yearbook,* Part II, National Society for the Study of Education. Bloomington, IL: Public School Publishing, 1918.

Warren, Frederick Anthony. "History of the Music Education Research Council and the *Journal of Research in Music Education.*" Ed.D. dissertation, University of Michigan, 1966.

Wassell, Albert W. "Albert Gore Mitchell: A Pioneer Class Instrumental Music Instructor in America." *Music Educators Journal* 60 (April–May 1954).

13

THE MUSIC EDUCATORS NATIONAL CONFERENCE MATURES

By the time the Music Supervisors National Conference changed its name to Music Educators National Conference in 1934, it was apparent that the Department of Music Education of the National Educational Association had been superseded as the focus of leadership in music education. Even so, in that year NEA reinstated a Department of Music meeting after having allowed its meetings to lapse for six years. The program of the meeting included descriptions of statewide music developments in Vermont and Texas, and a group was selected to appoint new officers. The Music Department met in each of the next three years and then lapsed again. In 1939 NEA announced that a reorganization plan was under way. The plan was finalized when the MENC adopted a new constitution at its 1940 meeting in Los Angeles. It contained articles that defined the relationship between the two organizations. The MENC became a department of NEA, and it absorbed the fifty-six-year-old Department of Music Education.

The MENC leadership at that time included Fowler Smith of Detroit as president; Louis Curtis of Los Angeles and Richard Grant of State College, Pennsylvania, as vice presidents; and Frank Biddle of Cincinnati, Hayden Morgan of Newtonville, Massachusetts, Lilla Belle Pitts of Columbia Teachers College, and Lorraine E. Watters of Des Moines as members of the Executive Committee. All were part of an enlarged board of directors, which now numbered nineteen and included the six division presidents, four auxiliary presidents, and six members at large. In conjunction with the NEA meeting in Milwaukee a few months later, a joint "Conference on Organizational Activities and Relationships in the Field of Music Education" was held.[1] Among the resolutions was a call for recognition of the importance of placing more emphasis on state music organizations, the need for attention to rural schools, and the desirability of controlling travel in interscholastic activities. The alliance was confirmed by the NEA at its meeting.

THE 1940 CONSTITUTION

Although the biennial convention arrangement with six regional divisions had been in operation for over ten years, there had never been a universal understanding of the exact relationship between the national and regional organizations. The new constitution remedied this situation, making it clear that there was one organization with a central headquarters. Richard Grant, chairman of the Revision Committee, characterized it as one conference, operating a biennial national meeting with six alternate year national meetings in the geographical divisions.[2] All meetings, and even the makeup of the divisions, were under the jurisdiction of the National Board of Directors. It is significant that the chairman of the committee that prepared these revisions was from an eastern state because the Eastern Division was the most autonomous of the six. It had accumulated some funds in a separate account that were transferred to the MENC books and became part of what Grant called a centralized business procedure.

The new constitution also made clear that the affiliated state units were an important part of the design. This concept of a totally unified organization working at national, divisional, and state levels was the critical element in the new document.

State Music Education Associations. The Conference leadership agreed with the National Education Association idea of extending service on behalf of music education through activities at the state level. The Ohio Music Education Association had sought an affiliated relationship with the Conference in 1933. Louisiana followed shortly after, possibly because Samuel Burns was familiar with the affiliated relationship, having moved from Medina, Ohio, to become the Louisiana state supervisor of music. Edith M. Keller of Ohio was the first state supervisor of music. As state units of a national organization, the recognition, authority, and usefulness to music education of the state groups were enhanced.

The first state organizations grew out of associations of instrumental music teachers who needed to solve problems associated with statewide contests and festivals. A unified state and national dues structure helped many state units because the MENC membership was nation-wide, and unification required all members to pay dues to a state organization. As the state units developed local activities that attracted members, the benefit proved reciprocal because members could take their groups to state-sponsored events only if they held at least partial membership in the national organization. This category of membership, which required full membership in the state organization and a subscription to the *Music Educators Journal,* was instituted specifically to build state units and a fully unified national organization.

There were eleven affiliated state units in 1940 when Grant wrote a piece for the *Music Educators Journal* alerting members to the vote on the new constitution at the upcoming Los Angeles meeting. By the time the results of the April balloting were reported, there were thirteen; others affiliated in the fall of that year. One was the department of music of the Delaware State Teachers Association. Although some affiliated groups were inherited from the NEA with the merger, more were the result of the organizational activity of music educators in the individual states. At the end of 1940 there were nineteen state units. World War II slowed the process, but by April 1945 the number of fully affiliated state organizations had grown to thirty-two.

When Arkansas affiliated in 1958, the Conference announced that it was fully unified with the states. On face value this appeared to be true, but the MENC board of directors was unaware that, in order to add Texas to the roster, Executive Secretary Buttelman had made a compromise with Texas Secretary D. D. ("Prof") Wiley. Wiley was convinced that he could not get the majority of his band directors, who constituted the greater part of the membership, to agree to pay even partial membership dues to the MENC. He asked for time to educate them to the advantages of knowing what was going on outside of Texas and of attending the MENC national and divisional conventions. Believing that Wiley would follow through and the affiliation would soon be constitutional, Buttelman agreed to the proposition. Nothing happened for several years, and a change in the national constitution in 1958 eliminated the partial membership category.[3] This made true affiliation even more difficult to promote in Texas.

A major controversy arose in the late 1960s. When other states learned that members of the Texas Music Educators Association were not required to be members of the MENC, some states, especially Illinois and New York, began inquiring about similar arrangements. When members of the board of directors were told of the situation, there was strong feeling that the Texas Music Educators Association should be expelled. Native Texan Wiley Housewright, MENC president from 1968 to 1970, hoped to solve the problem by attending a Texas executive board meeting. He even considered moving the 1970 convention to Texas after the intended host city, Chicago, alienated many Americans when its police force brutally beat young demonstrators before television cameras outside of Democratic National Convention headquarters. Rather than an inducement, however, a national meeting in Texas proved to be one of the fears of the Texans. They counted on income from their own very large and successful meeting for funding of their numerous activities and were suspicious of the MENC motives. Representatives of the MENC went to Texas to try to improve the situation. Texas Executive Secretary Bill Cormack and President J. R. King came to MENC headquarters to seek a solution. One member of the MENC group observed, ''At least I now understand Texas better and realize that they think differently than other Americans because they can't forget that Texas was once a country itself.''

All efforts led to nothing, and eventually the Texas Music Educators Association was replaced as the MENC-affiliated unit by a new organization, the Texas Music Educators Conference. TMEC was developed mainly by music educators at the college level, led by David G. McGuire and Hugo Marple. Since then the Texas Music Educators Conference has provided a means for Texas college students to join the MENC, for representation at the State Presidents National Assembly, and for cooperative efforts within the Southwestern Division. During the administration of national President Mary Hoffman a joint meeting of the three groups—MENC, TMEA, and TMEC—was held in San Antonio in 1982.

State associations have made substantive contributions to the national program. The Ohio Music Education Association, followed by the New York State School Music Association, developed codes dealing with proper relationships between music educators and various other organizations. The *Code of Ethics with Professional Musicians*, which the MENC, the American Association of School Administrators, and the American Federation of Musicians first signed in 1947, and have kept in force with regular renewals, is essentially the one prepared by the Ohio affiliate. The California Music Educators Association contributed the ''Student Code of Conduct,'' which provides guidance in respect to interscholastic music activities.[4]

Resolutions. The Council of Past Presidents of the MENC had been given the responsibility of preparing any appropriate resolutions in advance of biennial meetings, where they would be presented to the membership for approval. In 1940 the past presidents were concerned that conference programs varied too little from one year to the next and from one state and one region to another. They felt there was too much emphasis on public performance by highly trained groups on the secondary level. The past presidents suggested that choirs sing more than just unaccompanied serious and religious music and that there be a nationwide attempt ''to revive interest in string instruments.'' They felt that progressive philosophies had resulted in lack of stress on the acquisition of musical skills in the elementary schools, and they recommended definite time allotments for music study under the guidance of expert musicians. The presidents also recommended higher standards for those admitted to music teacher–training programs.[5]

OUTLINE OF A PROGRAM

The historical significance of the year 1940 was further heightened because of the preparation and distribution of a pamphlet known as "Outline of a Program for Music Education." The outline had been prepared by the Music Education Research Council and was adopted by the MENC at the Los Angeles meeting. Five "Basic Music Activities" were described for four different levels of the elementary school. The categories were singing, rhythmics, listening, playing, and creating. Appropriate activities for each category were described in short phrases for each of the four levels—preschool, kindergarten, and first grade; grades two and three; grades four and five; and grade six. The minimum daily amount of time suggested for music activities at the various levels were 20 minutes for K–3 and 25–30 minutes for grades 4–6. Five types of courses, or activities, that should be offered at the junior high school level were also listed and briefly described. Similar recommendations were made for grades ten, eleven, and twelve. Experiences recommended for students at all levels included assembly programs, concerts and recitals by student performers, educational concerts, music clubs, and community music programs. The significance of the pamphlet was that it presented a model for local school systems by which local programs could be measured. The model was designed by a professional organization of stature, a member of the family of the National Education Association, with which the professional groups of principals and superintendents were also allied. The Conference distributed the outline to interested persons across the country. Music educators posted them on school bulletin boards and used the recommendations to strengthen their programs. Conference sessions were keyed to the outline. The outline brought some stability to music education because it symbolized nationwide agreement on music instruction and helped create a degree of uniformity in the profession. The outline was updated in 1951 and continued to be used for many years.

1940 YEARBOOK

The Conference had been producing yearbooks since 1910; volume 30 was the last. It is an informative relic that demonstrates how complex music education, as represented by the MENC, had become in thirty-three years. The substantive portion of the 1940 yearbook encompassed 460 pages in eight sections:

  I. Music in Education and Life (philosophy and sociology)

 II. Special Phases and Applications (research)

III. Current Trends in Music Education (curriculum and regional problems)

IV. Instrumental Music

 V. Piano Class Instruction

VI. Vocal Music

VII. Music in Colleges and Universities

VIII. Teacher Training

Another 150 pages covered indices and "Organizational Miscellany." The size and diversity of the MENC at the age of thirty-three is illustrated in this yearbook. The practice of listing the names of all members was abandoned as the association grew, but it included 550 names of members who held office in the national, division, and state associations or in the structure developed to carry on the contest and festival programs. Officers of auxiliary organizations, such as the Music Exhibitors Association, were listed, as were those providing leadership in a unique cluster of members who belonged to In-and-About Clubs.

In-And-About Clubs. American society in the first half of the twentieth century was becoming increasingly urbanized. Only one-third of the population lived in cities in 1890, but one-half had moved to cities by 1920 and two-thirds by 1950. The invention of electric streetcars, elevators, telephones, and eventually trucks and buses contributed to urbanization. The phenomenon required the development of large, well-managed school systems to serve the cities. Suburbia became an integral part of the metropolitan scene. The suburbs usually had schools of equal, and sometimes superior, quality to those of the cities. By 1910 the Census Bureau identified twenty-five metropolitan areas with central city populations of at least 200,000.

Such concentrations meant there were many music educators within a short distance of each other, although they could still feel isolated because there was usually only one in each school. Following World War I, MSNC members in metropolitan areas began to meet in what became known as "In-and About" Clubs. Before the establishment of the state associations, these clubs were a vehicle for sharing professional ideas and for providing social contact among music educators. Meetings were usually held in a central location during the late afternoon or evening, sometimes in conjunction with a meal. A short musical program was generally given. Thirty-one In-and-About Clubs existed in 1940, but the number decreased rapidly after World War II as state associations became more active.

Big Cities. The role of music education in big cities during the period between the wars is worthy of special mention. The largest cities had individuals who served as city supervisor (later director of music) to coordinate the many aspects of the K–12 program. The best of them saw to it that there was (1) a unified philosophy of music education, (2) an articulated sequence of music learnings from grade to grade, (3) an opportunity for children to experience all the avenues to music that the schools could offer, (4) a high standard of musical performance, and (5) a program of staff development that would keep teachers current.

Among the outstanding city music program and their directors during the period between the Wars were:

Atlanta: Anne Grace O'Callahan

Buffalo: William Breach

Cedar Rapids: Alice Inskeep

Chicago: Helen Howe

Cleveland: Russell V. Morgan

Dallas: Marion Flagg

Des Moines: Lorrain E. Watters

Kansas City, Missouri: Mabelle Glenn

Los Angeles: Louis Woodson Curtis

Milwaukee: Herman Smith

Minneapolis: Thaddeus P. Giddings

Pittsburgh: Will Earhart

San Francisco: Charles M. Dennis

Tulsa: George Oscar Bowen

Rural Schools. Although the outstanding music education programs before World War II were in the large city school systems and in some small towns, the profession was also concerned about children in one- or two-room schoolhouses. Research Council Bulletin #6 (1926) sparked interest in rural music education. In that year, Edith M. Keller spoke on the responsibility of the state music supervisor in this regard. In the next few years, other states created similar supervisory positions that influenced rural music education in states such as Louisiana, Virginia, Missouri, California, and Montana. Marguerite Hood, who became Montana's first state music supervisor in 1930, wrote and spoke about the special problems of the rural school, as did Samuel Burns, Lloyd Funchess, Charles Fullerton, and Luther Richman. Over four thousand rural children from Missouri sang at the 1938 MENC convention to demonstrate the results of that state's first year of experience with a statewide program. Thomas Annett reported in 1939 that nine states had appointed supervisors of music and seventeen other state directors of education recognized the need for such a position.[6]

Texas delayed its rural music program until the many district schools could be consolidated, which they were under Superintendent Woods in 1937. In Tennesssee, the lack of roads hampered the development of statewide programs until Governor Austin Peay built highways that made the schools accessible to traveling specialists. Some states reported cooperative efforts with Four-H Clubs to provide music experiences for rural children; others made use of musicians from the Music Project of the federal Works Progress Administration.

Rural education efforts, including special subjects such as music, art, and physical education, were overshadowed by the entrance of the United States into World War II. Eight years after the conclusion of the war, Annett made another report for the Conference.[7] He recognized that in the 1952–1953 school year there were still over 45,000 one-room schools and over 11,000 two-room schools still in operation. Increased consolidation, more states with state supervisors of music, radios, phonographs, and more appropriate texts improved the situation in most sections of the country, although providing instrumental music instruction to all children in smaller schools remained a problem needing special attention.

THE WAR YEARS

There is little evidence of concern with the events in Europe visible in the records of the MENC April 1940 meeting in Los Angeles, but in two months the French Army had been defeated and the British driven off the mainland of Europe. By the time school started in the fall, the United States was experiencing its first peacetime draft and had loaned ninety-nine destroyers to Great Britain. The Conference had strong leadership from its elected officers during the war. Louis Woodson Curtis, Fowler Smith, and Lilla Belle Pitts all worked closely with Executive Secretary Buttelman to provide MENC support for all aspects of the war effort.

Music educators were encouraged by President Franklin D. Roosevelt's call for "more bands, more parades, more flag waving" to build national spirit.[8] At a board of directors meeting in Chicago from October 18 to 20, 1940, the theme "American Unity Through Music" was adopted. The MENC participated in the war effort in four programs: conducting classes for training community song leaders, coordinating efforts with various agencies, including the Civilian Defense Organization, the Policies Commission of the National Education Association, the U.S. Army Morale Division, and the National Recreation Association.[9] Once again, as in World War I, patriotic song lists were prepared.[10] As Congress was passing the lend-lease law in early 1941, the MENC was preparing an eight-page section for the March–April issue of the *Music Educators Journal*, which emphasized "Music in Our Democracy."[11] It listed four areas for attention by music educators: singing national songs, developing respect for music of the various heritages and races in the United States, singing folk and pioneer songs, and giving attention to meritorious compositions of American composers. There was also a Latin American component labeled "Music for Uniting the Americas," intended to familiarize North Americans with music of South and Central America and making North American music available to Pan-Americans. Harold Spivacke of the Music Division of the Library of Congress offered help in selecting folk songs for use in schools, and the newly established music division of the Pan American Union announced that it was preparing lists of songs.

Another presentation in *Music Educators Journal* was captioned "Music as a Restorative Force." It announced that "our institutions, our very way of life, our form of government are being attacked by organized propaganda." Howard Hanson warned:

> As we go into the program of national defense which is occupying so much of our thought, we must see to it that the emphasis upon material defense does not leave us spiritually bankrupt. . . . We must fight the good fight against materialism to the end that the world not be deprived of beauty. In saving our bodies we must not lose our souls.[12]

Problems During the War. The war years delayed many MENC activities to advance music education. It resulted in some changes in the schools that caused irreparable, though unintended, harm to music programs. The worst was the change from the seven- or eight-period school day to a five- or six-period day in the attempt to create longer periods in which students would have time to do their homework. That saved electricity in the evening by reducing home study. Many school systems forgot to change back after the war, and students, busy with college preparation courses, often found it impossible to schedule choir or orchestra, let alone both as their older brothers and sisters might have done.

There were inconveniences during the war. For example, the government levied an excise tax on musical instruments, as it did on many other items. Instruments were hard to purchase in any event, as the military organizations were taking almost everything the domestic industry could produce. Travel restrictions eliminated the regional and national competitive events. Music educators decided it was probably for the best, and contests beyond state boundaries have not had the sanction of the profession since that time.

Many teachers went off to war, but retired music educators and women who had left the classroom for marriage returned to provide the leadership in music that the communities had come to expect of their schools. Yet, there were schools that could not find music teachers.

Community Music became important again. Augustus Zanzig wrote an article on the effectiveness of community festivals carried out by the Texas Department of Music. Zanzig became a music consultant to the Treasury Department and served as a workshop leader at the 1943 division meetings, which were billed as "Institutes on Music Education in Wartime." The Radio Branch of the Bureau of Public Relations of the War Department prepared a brochure entitled "Music in the National War Effort." When the MENC offered copies to the membership, the 100,000-book edition was quickly exhausted. Marshall Bartholomew, director of the Yale Glee Club, who had been trapped in Europe by World War I when he was a student of Engelbert Humperdinck, wrote a piece for the *Journal* in which he told his colleagues, "our job is to blow the trumpet, beat the drum and keep singing."[13]

Conventions. The MENC continued to hold its divisional and national conventions during the early part of the war, but the six 1945 divisional general assemblies were cancelled and the scheduled elections conducted by mail. Even so, the membership increased by over 8 percent that year. The Office of Defense Transportation had set limits on attendance at meetings that required extensive travel, and only fifty members from each division were invited to attend what became known as the "Six-Fifties." The groups met between March 8 and April 22. Gratia Boyle of Witchita observed that the limited number of delegates had the responsibility of representing the members who were prevented from attending. She said she felt some of the missionary spirit of earlier times. This reaction was common among attendees, and led to "Planning Meetings" in the fall before divisional conventions once they were reinstated. Many members came to feel that the planning sessions, in which they guided the division presidents in building their convention programs, were more stimulating than the conventions themselves.

The "Six-Fifties" reports of the 1945 War Emergency Councils were printed in the May–June issue of the *Journal* and provided coverage of enough topics to invite comparison with the earlier yearbooks. It was made clear that these were not official positions of the Conference, but many forward-looking ideas were presented. The status of music education after the war was obviously on the minds of many participants. One concern was the completion of the unified state and national configuration of the organization.[14] There were thirty-two state units at that time. Other concerns were adding more periods to the school day, creative music activities, and scientific examination of music education problems. These suggestions were addressed by the profession after the war.

AFTER WORLD WAR II

The end of world conflict in 1945 brought about great societal changes, some of the most significant of which were in higher education. The percentage of the population enrolled in schools had declined in comparison to ten years earlier, especially at the secondary level. The G.I. Bill, however, and the expanded horizons of millions of ex-servicemen and women created a new surge of college enrollment. Some of the increase was in programs that prepared teachers who would be needed when the children of the veterans, the "baby boom," reached school age.

Another significant event in 1945 was the publication of the Harvard Committee report *General Education in a Free Society*. Its message was that democracies had to protect themselves by providing a common education for all citizens. Coming at the end of a period in which totalitarian states had created havoc for the rest of the world, the message was well received by Americans. The warning about the dangers of overspecialization was more welcome by the colleges than by the secondary schools. Study of the heritage of Western civilization was the most accepted means of providing a unified purpose for college students. Many new humanities texts were published, and new courses were established to integrate history, art, and literature. Some experience with the art of music characterized most of the general education core of studies that colleges put in place. Even when music courses were only one of a number of choices to meet the core requirement, enrollments were heavy. Thus music, for the first time, became part of the "common schooling" of those who went on to college.

Graduate Students. Many veterans eligible for educational assistance under the G.I. Bill pursued graduate degrees, which led to music education programs in the universities being strengthened. The MENC produced its "Outline of the Course in Music Education Leading to the Master's Degree."[15] Thesis requirements in many master's degree programs began to reflect increased research expectations. Doctoral programs carried research efforts even further, and a cadre of serious scholars in various areas of music education began to develop.

The Journal of Research in Music Education. As graduate programs in music education developed, it became apparent to university music educators that a vehicle was needed to report research results. While visiting Marguerite Hood at the University of Michigan during her MENC presidency, Warren Freeman, dean of the Boston University School of Music, observed that the Conference should provide such a scholarly outlet.[16] Allen P. Britton, a member of the University of Michigan faculty, participated in the discussion. He too felt the need for a scholarly journal, and it was agreed that Freeman and Britton would prepare a proposal to establish one. Britton reports that without the insistence of President Hood, the MENC board of directors probably would not have agreed to accept the proposal that was reworked after an open meeting at the 1952 Philadelphia convention. The proposal was supported strongly by Theodore F. Norman and Ralph Rush, both of whom were directors of graduate programs, but the *Journal of Research in Music Education* is largely a monument to the commitment of Allen Britton, who served as its first editor and guardian of its style and integrity. The initial issue of volume 1 appeared in Spring 1953. It became a quarterly with volume 12 in 1964. Before its twentieth anniversary it had become one of the largest scholarly journals, with a circulation of over 4,000.[17]

The Music Education Research Council. When the *JRME* became a quarterly, it was advantageous to secure a second-class mailing permit for it. It did not go to all MENC members, however, and so failed to meet the U.S. Postal Service requirement for a second-class permit. Buttelmen therefore created the Society for Research in Music Education, to which all *JRME* subscribers would automatically belong. The Music Education Research Council was made the governing body of the society. The society invigorated the council, which had been relatively inactive after the war. The purpose of the society is the "encouragement and advancement of research in those areas pertinent to music education." One of its activities is the sponsorship of research sessions at the MENC biennial meetings.

RESEARCH ACTIVITIES SEPARATE
FROM THE MENC

The Council for Research in Music Education. The increased interest in research spawned initiatives not directly connected to the MENC. The Council for Research in Music Education was founded in 1963 by the University of Illinois and the Illinois Office of the Superintendent of Public Instruction. The CRME *Bulletin* is published by the University of Illinois. CRME also publishes indices of music education doctoral dissertations in progress and of recently completed dissertations.

Other Music Education Research Journals include *The Missouri Journal of Research in Music Education* (Missouri State Department of Education, founded 1962), *The Bulletin of Research* (Pennsylvania Music Educators Association, founded 1963), *Contributions to Music Education* (Ohio Music Educators Association, founded 1972), *The Bulletin of Historical Re-*

search in Music Education (University of Kansas, founded 1980), and *Update: The Applications of Research in Music Education* (University of South Carolina, founded 1982). In 1988 *Update* became an MENC publication. Volume I, no. 1, of the *Southeastern Journal of Music Education* was published in 1989 by the University of Georgia.

Special Research Interest Groups (SRIG) were formed at the 1978 MENC national meeting. The SRIGs, under the governance of the MERC, are vehicles to serve music educators with similar research interests, such as creativity, learning and development, measurement and evaluation, affective response, history, philosophy, instructional strategies, perception, and early childhood. Several SRIGs have developed their own newsletters, hold sessions at the biennial meetings of the Conference, and sponsor special workshops.

Research Symposia have been presented for the benefit of music education researchers. The Theodore Presser Foundation made possible a series of meetings, cosponsored by the MENC and the University of Michigan, held at Ann Arbor between 1978 and 1982, known as the Ann Arbor Symposium. These gatherings provided the opportunity for music educators to meet with leading psychologists and learning theorists. The Music Educators National Conference cooperated with the School of Music and the University of Michigan Center for Research on Learning and Teaching in planning and presenting the meetings. Wilbert J. McKeachie of the center was a special consultant to the project and Paul R. Lehman of the School of Music the director. The first two meetings were devoted to the applications of psychology to the teaching and learning of music.[18] The third meeting concentrated on motivation and creativity.[19]

The Wesleyan Symposium on the Application of Social Anthropology to the Teaching and Learning of Music, sponsored by the MENC, Wesleyan University, and the Theodore Presser Foundation, was held in 1984 to examine the relationship between social anthropology and music education. It was directed by David McAllester, who had first become associated with the MENC as a speaker at the Tanglewood Symposium. "One Hundred-Fifty Years of Music in American Schools" was a 1988 historical symposium at the University of Maryland at College Park, sponsored by the MENC and the University of Maryland in celebration of the sesquicentennial of music in American schools. It was the first major symposium dedicated to historical research in music education, and was directed by Michael Mark.

THE MENC LEADERSHIP

Early in 1942, President Lilla Belle Pitts developed a comprehensive committee organization plan which she named "Widening Horizons for

Music Education." Five hundred thirty-one members of thirty-eight committees began to work on reports that constituted the framework for the 1944 Saint Louis convention. The "Six-Fifties" (1945) of the divisions added considerable input to the reports. The Cleveland convention (under President John Kendal) shortly after the war had demonstrations, clinical observation opportunities, and lectures in accord with the grand design of "Widening Horizons for Music Education." Kendal promoted the relationship between the national, divisional, and state organizations by having interlocking committees in his Advancement Program, which was carried forward by Luther Richman and Charles Dennis.

A Newly Stated Purpose for the MENC. At the 1950 meeting, planned by President Charles Dennis, a constitutional revision was approved to define the purpose of the MENC simply as the "advancement of music education." After forty-three years the hint of self-advantage to the membership was eliminated as the MENC became a voluntary, educational association whose activities were for the benefit of society at large rather than for the members. This was to become increasingly important as tax structures changed because it enabled the organization to take advantage of Internal Revenue 501(c)3 status, which shelters not-for-profit organizations from certain tax obligations. Without such status, few voluntary professional organizations could survive.

During the 1930s and 1940s, while the profession as a whole was more concerned with the functional aspects of music education, including the fad of correlation of subject matter, a few voices continued to stress the importance of experiencing beauty through music. Two of the leaders in this were Frances Elliott Clark and Will Earhart.[20] They were the forerunners of the aesthetic education movement that began in the late 1950s. Earhart said:

> And after we have come to love the true aesthetic element, rather than revel in worldly experience, there is another love we must learn. That is love for the best that is in the souls of man and in the souls of little children. If we can discern the beautiful soul of Music, through all her disguises, and discern the beautiful thing that is the soul of Childhood, under all its complex appearances, and if we can then unite the two, we will have performed what we believe is a worthy task, and one that is full of promise for man and for music as a valuable element in the life of man.[21]

Source Books. The materials developed by the MENC commissions since 1942 resulted in the *Music Education Source Book* (1947), a significant compendium of information on music education. The book was edited by Hazel Nohavek Morgan. Buttelman said it was called a "source book" not because it was the source of answers to many questions about American music education but because the book contained ideas that had welled up from the source of such information, the almost two thousand members working in the field who had been involved in the five-year project.[22] It captures the essence of American music education in the 1940s.

Eight years later another source book appeared, this one entitled *Music in American Education*. It too was edited by Hazel Morgan. The committee structure to develop the book had been set in place by President Marguerite Hood (1950–1952) and was carried on by her successor, Ralph Rush. Many of the reports were given at the 1954 Chicago convention, and others appeared in professional journals. Of great importance was Russell Morgan's statement about the understanding of modern education as it applied to associations, published in the dedication:

> It is vital to our kind of organization to utilize in the most effective way the resources of our membership in order to accomplish the things we agree need to be done. . . . If these things are done through groups working together, it is good. Whether or not the achievements are complete does not matter if through group work our members have opportunity to think and work constructively. . . . The total power of our group is enhanced by the growth of the individuals who wholeheartedly or even casually take part in these cooperative assignments and projects, even though nothing ever appears in print to record their efforts and contributions.[23]

Music in American Education was published in 1955, by which time President Robert A. Choate had a new organizational scheme in place that he called "Music in American Life." Its ten commissions were:

> Basic Concepts in Music Education
> Standards of Musical Literature and Performance
> Music in General School Administration
> Music in Preschool, Kindergarten, Elementary School
> Music in Junior High School
> Music in Senior High School
> Music in Higher Education
> Music in the Community
> Music in Media of Mass Communication
> Accreditation and Certification

In addition to the commissions, there were four standing committees established to deal with music for exceptional children, music in international relations, and organ and piano instruction in the schools.

BASIC Concepts in Music Education. The changing societal conditions of the 1950s created many questions for music education leaders.

They had to find a way to address the significant issues with which they were faced. Thurber Madison, chairman of the Basic Concepts Commission of Robert Choate's Music in American Life program, arranged to have the final report published as Part II of the National Society for the Study of Education 1958 yearbook.

Less noted was *Music in the Senior High School*, produced by a commission centered in the northwest division and chaired by Wayne S. Hertz. It addressed a new subject—comprehensive musicianship in the band rehearsal.

Presidential Preparation. There was a period following Edward Bailey Birge's retirement as chairman of the editorial board of the *Music Educators Journal* when that post seems to have served as a training ground for the presidency. The progression from editor to president provided assurance that the individual would be familiar with the many concerns of the membership.

Charles Dennis succeeded Birge in mid-1944, when the Conference was operating under wartime restrictions. Freed of the paper shortage after the war, the magazine had a rebirth. It recognized the new interest in the application of American technology that had been so vital to victory and was now equally vital to education. Many articles on using the radio for education were published, and "audiovisual" came to mean more than showing a movie. The first *MEJ* article about television, by Westervelt Romain, appeared in the November–December 1947 issue.

When Dennis was elected president and chose to "show the flag" by appearing at all six division conventions during his first year in office, he turned the chairmanship of the editorial board over to Marguerite Hood in January 1949. She was familiar with the magazine, having contributed her first article in 1931. The only woman to have chaired the board, she presided over only nine issues before being elected president of the conference for the 1950–1952 biennium.

Robert Choate, one of the most influential music educators of the midcentury, served as chairman of the editorial board from 1950 until 1954. His wide experience in the schools of Iowa, Illinois, Washington, and California and at Northwestern and Boston Universities gave him an especially valuable perspective to evaluate the concerns of the profession in the 1950s. His background, and the advantages provided by being chairman, gave him a fortunate position from which to plan the MENC Golden Anniversary celebration in Saint Louis in 1956. He turned the chairmanship of the editorial board over to Karl Ernst in 1954. The magazine took on a new look during Ernst's tenure, with color becoming a more important factor. Ernst gave up the chairmanship when he took office as president in 1958.

The last member, to date, to be prepared for the presidency by serving as editorial board chairman was Wiley L. Housewright. Housewright spent eight years as chairman, a position described by the MENC staff as the most onerous of the tasks that the Conference offered. Housewright's tenure was made more difficult because it came during a period of increasing educational ferment.

A Larger Music Educators Journal. It was during this period that the size of the *Journal* increased dramatically, with one issue over two hundred pages. This prompted the MENC board of directors to examine the feasibility of moving from six to nine issues each year. When Managing Editor Charles B. Fowler replied that the staff would make the necessary adjustments, and Housewright indicated that the editorial board could cope with handling additional manuscripts, the decision was made. Housewright did not have to deal with the increased workload, however, as he was elected president for the 1968–1970 biennium. He was succeeded by one of the elder statesmen of the Conference, William C. Hartshorn, supervisor of music for the Los Angeles Schools.

Vanett Lawler. Clifford Buttelman served as executive secretary until 1955, when he was succeeded by Vanett Lawler. Buttelman remained on the staff for several more years to guide the *Music Educators Journal* and the rapidly developing publications program. Not only did Lawler bring twenty-five years of experience with the organization to the position, but she had also been a consultant to the Pan American Union and for six months acting head of the Arts and Letters Section of the United Nations Educational, Social, and Cultural Organization (UNESCO) in Paris. Her travels in fourteen Latin American countries made her an authority on the manner in which American music education might be helpful to other nations. Her work at the Pan American Union and as liaison to the NEA and to federal agencies during the war had made her familiar with the educational scene in the nation's capital.

Buttelman made pertinent comments to the MENC executive committee at the time of Lawler's loan to UNESCO:

> Miss Lawler's assignment is specifically concerned with foundation organization and project planning, for which she is especially qualified. It is of no little significance that the field of music education is drawn upon for assistance in the planning and organization of projects in international relationships to be inaugurated by UNESCO. There is also involved a noteworthy tribute to the MENC, as well as to the Associate Executive Secretary who has so successfully represented our organization in national and international affairs.[24]

The MENC Moves to Washington. In the 1950s the National Education Association built an education center in Washington, DC, and offered free space to its departments. Lawler's first task was to oversee the move to Washington and build a new staff. She hired Geraldine Ivie as bookkeeper and sent her to the headquarters office, still in Chicago, to become familiar with the complicated system of interlocking memberships. Lawler employed Gene Morlan, supervisor of music in Shenandoah County, Virginia, as assistant secretary and charged him with moving the eighteen tons of material and equipment from Chicago to Washington. With Dorothy Regardie and Ruth Hughes, who had worked with her in the MENC branch office in the old NEA headquarters, Lawler began to build a staff of clerks, typists, addressograph operators, and copyreaders. Later she invited Charles L. Gary, head of the music department at Austin Peay State College in Tennessee, to assist Buttelman with publications. She trained Ivie, Morlan, and Gary to plan and produce the professional meetings in cooperation with the elected officials.

Lawler's thirteen years as staff leader were productive for the Conference and for education. Not only did the MENC membership grow rapidly, but Lawler's careful management of financial matters built reserves to guarantee permanence and support new activities. The presence in the NEA Building of all the major educational organizations, both administrative and subject-oriented, made cooperative ventures possible, and Lawler took advantage of the situation for the betterment of music education. Her inventive mind and strong intuitive sense earned her and the Conference respect throughout the NEA community. Among her particular triumphs were the "Creative Arts" convention of the American Association of School Administrators; the Contemporary Music Project, underwritten by the Ford Foundation; and the success of the International Society for Music Education, which she helped establish and for which she served as mentor and treasurer.

THE CONFERENCE FAMILY

The postwar period saw remarkable growth not only in the membership of the MENC but also in the number of associated groups. For some years there were only two groups designated as "Auxiliaries" because their activities were limited to particular aspects of the Conference enterprise.

The Music Industry Council. The 1920 convention in Philadelphia appears to have been the first in which there was a concerted effort by exhibitors to help defray the expenses of the meeting.[25] By 1926 the book publishers, instrument manufacturers, and equipment suppliers who had regularly shown their wares at the MSNC meetings formed a new organization—the Music Education Exhibitors Association. At that time exhibits were not elaborate. They were often all in one room or had their displays on narrow tables on either sides of the hallways leading to the meeting rooms. Association members were interested in making the exhibits as attractive as the site allowed. The association controlled such matters as the nature of signs, depth of displays, and what was legitimate material to be given away. In 1954 the group adopted a new constitution and changed the name to the Music Industry Council (MIC).

By this time, the MENC meetings were being held in convention centers or in hotels with large exhibit areas. Members of the MIC became concerned about the spot in the hall to which they were assigned, and the MENC staff gladly turned this matter over to the MIC officers. They devised a plan to mail exhibit information (with floor plans) on a Friday so all exhibitors could expect to receive their packet on Monday morning. Exhibitors indicated their three preferred choices of booth spaces and returned the forms promptly. The forms were time-stamped as they were received back in the MENC headquarters office. The MIC officers would then meet and assign spaces.

In recent years the MIC has had raffles of donated music or equipment on the last day that the exhibits are open in order to attract attendees late in the convention. MIC officers still police the exhibits to prevent booths from closing early. The MIC has contributed to the quality of the displays which serve an important educational function by keeping music educators up to date.

The MIC has also provided other educational services to the MENC membership. For many years it published a handbook that provided valuable information on ordering music merchandise. Beginning in the early 1970s, many of the firms have provided clinicians to give demonstrations in Music Industry Showcase sessions.

The Conference and the music industry have a symbiotic relationship. This has been recognized by the educators, who agreed to make the president of the Music Industry Council an ex-officio member of the board of directors without voting privileges except for matters that concern meeting and exhibit schedules.

Music Publishing and the Copyright Law. In the field of music publishing mutual interest has resulted in a separate and distinct industry. Many small American publishing firms came into existence specifically to serve the school market. Although they are dependent on the business of music educators, without their products the teachers could not carry on such activities as class instruction in instruments, folk music study, or barbershop quartet singing. It was this interdependence that permitted music educators and music publishers to set an example to other teachers and textbook publishers in copyright law revision discussions during the early 1970s. Compromises by the musicians led others to realize that it was possible to agree on fair-use provisions and supporting guidelines to serve both users of protected material and the copyright owners. This realization made the 1976 law possible.

The National Interscholastic Music Activities Commission (NIMAC). The other original auxiliary of the Conference represented the contest and festival movement. The original National High School Band Association and the National High School Orchestra Association were created to administer the national contests before World War II. They were joined by the National School Vocal Association in 1936, and the three groups merged into a new organization—the National School Band, Orchestra, and Vocal Association (NSBOVA). In 1952 these groups were restructured and became the National Interscholastic Music Activities Commission, an auxiliary with a place on the board of directors. They continued to publish selected lists of music that could be used in the state festivals, prepared adjudication forms, and in 1963 published the *NIMAC Manual*, a guide for those engaged in interschool music activity. This auxiliary was dissolved in 1968, since interscholastic activity had become limited to state boundaries or was controlled by regional groups such as the North Central Association of Colleges and Secondary Schools.

Associated Organizations. By 1940 music education had become a complex field with many specialties. Much as P. C. Hayden had become dissatisfied with the meetings of the National Education Association at the turn of the century, specialists within the Conference felt it necessary to band together to achieve the kind of attention they desired on Conference programs.

The first were the college band directors, who organized in 1938 as the MENC Committee on College Bands and became the College Band Directors National Conference in 1940. Nine years later a constitution was written, with a change in name from "Conference" to "Association," and CBDNA was accepted as an associated organization of the MENC. An even more specialized group, the National Association of College Wind and Percussion Instructors (NACWAPI), became associated in 1954. In 1959 the American String Teachers Association began a relationship that led to associated status. The following year the MENC assisted a group of choral teachers in holding a one-day meeting in conjunction with the Atlantic City MENC convention of president Karl Ernst. From this grew another associated group, the American Choral Directors Association. The National School Orchestra Association became associated the same year and the National Band Association in 1962.

In 1988 there were nine associated organizations—the National Jazz Educators Association, the National Black Music Caucus, the Organization of American Kodály Educators, and those discussed above. There is a difference in closeness to the Conference among these associated groups. Some have their own separate meetings, and others meet during the MENC conventions. Some music educators relate more closely to associated organizations. Others may be members of two or three associated groups but hold their strongest allegiance to the Conference itself.

Outside Organizations. The MENC maintained a close relationship with a number of other music organizations. The National Association of Schools of Music (NASM) is one. Many of the school representatives at NASM meetings are the MENC leaders. The actions of the MENC in regard to teacher education are closely related to NASM policies. For many years the two organizations cooperated with the Music Teachers National Association in updating information and producing and distributing the Careers in Music pamphlet.

The Society for the Encouragement and Preservation of Barbershop Quartet Singing in America (SEPBQSA) is another group that has maintained a close relationship with the Conference. In the early 1970s the Young Men in Harmony program was developed jointly and promoted to help high school vocal teachers interest boys in singing. Robert Johnson was instrumental in developing that program and its musical material. Both he and Joe Liles, executive director of the Society, made possible the inclusion of prizewinning barbershop choruses and quartets in the MENC programs.

THE MENC BOARD OF DIRECTORS

The 1940 constitutional change created a large board of directors that included the three national officers (president and two vice presidents), six division presidents, the presidents of the two auxiliary organizations, and six members-at-large. Three of the at-large members were to be elected for four-year terms at the time the national officers were elected. The board had grown so large that a smaller executive committee was needed, especially at that time, when air travel was not easily available. The board of directors elected five of its members to serve with the national officers as the executive committee, which was ''responsible for the business management and operation of the organization.'' This did not please the board members who were not members of the executive committee, and when air travel became commonplace, there was agitation for abolishing the smaller group and having all decisions made by the full board. During Paul Van Bodegraven's presidency (1964–1966) a special study committee held a meeting in the NEA Building to discuss the matter. This group recommended, against the advice of the executive staff, a smaller board of directors without members-at-large. The board of directors later approved the suggested smaller national executive board that could meet more frequently if, without members-at-large, less intelligently. It was part of the constitutional revision approved by the membership in 1968.

National Executive Board (NEB). The result was a body in which the six division presidents could outvote the three national officers (and the MIC president if it happened to be a convention matter). The arrangement is similar to that of the U.S. House of Representatives, in which pork barrel projects tend to proliferate. Division presidents have been known to put the concerns of the divisions before the interests of the national organization. For example, in 1972 the National Commission on Organizational Development determined that it was time to phase out the division meetings and return to annual national conventions. Business conditions made it difficult for exhibitors to support six division presentations in a period of a few months. Other roles were suggested for the divisions. However, the divisions prevailed, and except for 1981, when a national meeting was held in Minneapolis on an odd year, divisional meetings continued to be held. Some divisions now meet and others do not, and a new role for the divisions had not been devised.

THE NATIONAL ASSEMBLY

At the 1954 biennial meeting in Chicago, the presidents of the federated state units convened as the State Presidents National Assembly one day before the meeting of the membership. Information was profitably exchanged between the national officers and staff and the state officers. The assembly was continued in Saint Louis in 1956 and still exists.

The majority of the state presidents served a two-year term in office, although some states changed their leadership every year. In either situation, a state president could not profit greatly from the experience of attending the National Assembly unless he or she accompanied an incumbent president while serving as president-elect. Few states had a president-elect system in 1956, and so most state officers attended only one assembly. In some cases it came near the end of the term of office. When the presidents met again in Los Angeles in 1958 there was considerable sentiment in favor of holding meetings of the state presidents in the first year of a new national administration as well as at the biennial convention. This idea was approved by the national board of directors.

Interim Meetings. The first Interim Meeting of the State Presidents National Assembly was held at Interlochen, Michigan, in August 1959. Meeting for a longer number of days in an isolated location helped the presidents accomplish much and made them feel an integral part of the national organization. The meeting also gave them an opportunity to discuss the problems they were encountering in their own parts of the country. One common concern, dissatisfaction with the way general music courses were being taught, prompted a request for action by the MENC. The board approved the creation of a commission to consider the matter (see Publications, this chapter).

Two years later the interim meeting was in Washington, DC, where it has continued to be held in alternate years. The meeting has been expanded to incorporate the representatives of the auxiliary and associated organizations and the state supervisors of music, and thus represents all facets of the music education field. The State Presidents National Assembly was then renamed the National Assembly. The meetings have provided the delegates with opportunities to improve their understanding of public relations principles, the National Arts Endowment, the Alliance for Arts Education, the U.S. Department of Education, and the means of improving communication with the membership.

TANGLEWOOD

Shortly after Louis Wersen was elected president of the Conference, Edwin E. Stein, dean of the School of Music of Boston University, was in Philadelphia to visit his son. While there, he called on Wersen to remind him that Boston University had a summer program in conjunction with the famous Tanglewood Music Center in western Massachusetts. He suggested that he would like to offer the summer facility for a cooperative project if it would benefit MENC during Wersen's administration. From this meeting came the plan for a symposium that would allow the Conference to use the vast experience of its membership to counter the insinuations of the Yale Seminar, which Wersen and many other music educators felt were made unfairly by people who had little familiarity with public school music. He persuaded the MENC board to budget funds for a symposium, secured a grant from the Theodore Presser Foundation, and asked Robert Choate to serve as director of the project. Wersen wrote in the foreword of the interpretive report of the Tanglewood project:

> Tanglewood represents the unique situation of an organization taking stock of itself and its place in society. With no prompting from without, with no requirement for self-study as periodically befalls certain other institutions such as school systems or governmental agencies, the MENC arranged to have its leaders and a group of distinquished outsiders turn appraising eyes on itself and the profession it represents. Recognizing complacency as a real danger for a successful organization, those who planned the Tanglewood Symposium chose to ask "How can we better serve?", and "What do we need to do to make music education more useful to the American society of today and tomorrow?"[26]

At the six division meetings in the spring of 1967, members were invited to attend sessions to discuss the following questions: "What are the characteristics and desirable ideologies for an emerging post-industrial society?" "What are the values and unique functions of music and others arts for individuals and communities in such a society?"

"How may these potentials be attained?" The discussions of these questions were the basis of Tanglewood Symposium sessions moderated by Max Kaplan, Wiley L. Housewright, Allen P. Britton, David P. McAllester, and Karl D. Ernst.

Alvin C. Eurich, past president of the Aspen Institute for Humanistic Studies, assisted Robert Choate and Charles Gary in planning the schedule for the two weeks and in identifying many of those invited from the disciplines of sociology, philosophy, history, psychology, labor, and media. Eurich himself spoke on "The Quest for Quality" and reinforced the concept of a unique role for music education in creating a democratic culture.

The guests departed at the end of the first week, and the music educators and consultants wrestled with the implications of a week of discussions. After more discussion and preliminary agreement on the meaning of what had taken place, Allen Britton, Arnold Broido, and Charles Gary were charged with preparing a declaration to summarize the symposium and provide guiding principles for the music education profession in a time of change. The Tanglewood Declaration follows:

> The intensive evaluation of the role of music in American society and education provided by the Tanglewood Symposium of philosophers, educators, scientists, labor leaders, philanthropists, social scientists, theologians, industrialists, representatives of government and foundations, music educators, and other musicians led to this declaration:
>
> We believe that education must have as major goals the art of living, the building of personal identity, and nurturing creativity. Since the study of music can contribute much to these ends, WE NOW CALL FOR MUSIC TO BE PLACED IN THE CORE OF THE SCHOOL CURRICULUM.
>
> The arts afford a continuity with the aesthetic tradition in man's history. Music and other fine arts, largely nonverbal in nature, reach close to the social, psychological, and physiological roots of man in his search for identity and self-realization.
>
> Educators must accept the responsibility for developing opportunities which meet man's individual needs and the needs of a society plagued by the consequences of changing values, alienation, hostility between generations, racial and international tensions, and the challenges of a new leisure.

Music educators at Tanglewood agreed that:

1. Music serves best when its integrity as an art is maintained.
2. Music of all periods, styles, forms, and cultures belong in the curriculum. The musical repertory should be expanded to involve music of our time in its rich variety, including currently popular teen age music and avant-garde music, American folk music, and the music of other cultures.
3. Schools and colleges should provide adequate time for music in pro-

grams ranging from preschool through adult or continuing education.

4. Instruction in the arts should be a general and important part of education in the senior high school.

5. Developments in educational technology, educational television, programed instruction, and computer-assisted instruction should be applied to music study and research.

6. Greater emphasis should be placed on helping the individual student to fulfill his needs, goals, and potentials.

7. The music education profession must contribute its skills, proficiencies, and insights toward assisting in the solution of urgent social problems as in the "inner city" or other areas with culturally deprived individuals.

8. Programs of teacher education must be expanded and improved to provide music teachers who are specially equipped to teach high school courses in the history and literature of music, courses in the humanities and related arts, and music teachers equipped to work with the very young, with adults, with the disadvantaged, and with the emotionally disturbed.[27]

The Goals and Objectives Project (Go Project). An extensive project known as GO (Goals and Objectives) was begun in 1969 to implement the recommendations of the Tanglewood Symposium at the suggestion of president-elect Andrews. After contacting hundreds of members throughout the country, the project, led by Paul Lehman, developed four major goals and thirty-five specific objectives.

The goals were to carry out comprehensive music programs in all schools, involve persons of all ages in learning music, support the quality preparation of teachers, and use the most effective techniques and resources in music instruction.

The National Executive Board marked eight of the objectives for immediate attention. They were:

1. Lead efforts to develop programs of music instruction challenging to all students, whatever their sociocultural condition in a pluralistic society.

2. Lead the development of programs of study that correlate performing, creating, and listening to music and encompasses a diversity of musical behaviors.

3. Assist teachers in the identification of musical behaviors relevant to the needs of their students.

4. Advance the teaching of music of all periods, styles, forms, and cultures.

5. Develop standards to ensure that all music instruction is provided by teachers well prepared in music.
6. Expand its [MENC] programs to secure greater involvement and commitment of student members.
7. Assume leadership in the application of significant new developments in curriculum, teaching-learning patterns, evaluation, and related topics, to every area and level of music teaching.
8. Lead in efforts to ensure that every school system allocates sufficient staff, time, and funds to support a comprehensive and excellent music program.

Charles Fowler coined the phrase a "vital musical culture and an enlightened musical public," which Lowell Mason, Hosea Holt, P. C. Hayden, Will Earhart, Peter Dykema, and James Mursell, among others, would probably find compatible with their views of music education. The goals would not be strange to these men either, although twentieth-century comprehensiveness might astound Mason and Holt.

THE MENC COMMISSIONS

Despite Russell Morgan's comments about the value of the members working together on worthwhile projects regardless of the product, the Conference has made an impact on American music education through meaningful publications that resulted from group efforts. Source Books I and II involved thousands. *Music in General Education* is an example of a small group of experienced educators from across the country pooling their ideas. *The Study of Music in the Elementary School: A Conceptual Approach* represented a different configuration in which members from several different school systems in a geographical area (Southern California) shared the responsibilities of the assignment.

When Wiley Housewright became president in July 1968, he appointed a commission to write a report on teacher education. The Teacher Education Commission, chaired by Robert Klotman, took a competency-based approach to teacher education. The final report, *Teacher Education in Music,* was published in 1972. Charles Ball headed a committee that issued a report on graduate programs in music education in 1980, and in 1987 a committee chaired by Gerald Olson prepared *Music Teacher Education: Partnership and Process.*

Two New Commissions. Two commissions were appointed after the Go Project recommendations had been considered. The MENC Commission on Organizational Development was to prepare the way for recommended changes in the organization, structure, and function of the Conference, including all of its federated and affiliated units. One of the findings had to do with the nature of the meeting structure in the 1970s, when some state associations that did not exist when the divisions were created had annual meetings that were larger than division meetings. Improvements in travel made a different function advisable for the divisions.

The National Commission on Instruction was created to monitor the way music was being taught in the schools. Its first study resulted in an important publication, *The School Music Program: Description and Standards,* which enabled communities to evaluate all aspects of their music programs. It was revised by the commission in 1986. The publication had tangible results, as school systems throughout the country made efforts to reach at least the basic level described in the report.

A bicentennial commission under the leadership of Don Robinson of Atlanta was appointed to suggest ways that music education might contribute to the nation's two-hundredth birthday. The group prepared many materials to assist music teachers celebrate the occasion, including a large calendar of historical events. The J. C. Penney Corporation published a collection of American music, some of which it had commissioned for the occasion. It then gave the collection to schools in communities in which it had stores.

The National Education Association celebrated its centennial anniversary in 1957. As part of the celebration, the NEA commissioned Howard Hanson to create a work for the occasion. Hanson was director of the Eastman School of Music and the only well-known composer to serve on the MENC board of directors. His "Song of Democracy," set to a Walt Whitman text, was premiered by the National Symphony Orchestra under conductor Howard Mitchell with the Howard University chorus directed by Warner Lawson, who later became president of the MENC Eastern Division. A community-sing version of "Song of Democracy" was published in a small songbook and distributed by the MENC and NEA.

PUBLICATIONS

After the MENC headquarters moved to Washington in 1956, there was a significant increase in the number the books and pamphlets published. The North Central Association of Colleges and Secondary Schools adopted and helped distribute "Guiding Principles for School Music Group Activities," which had been prepared by the MENC in cooperation with the National Association of Secondary School Principals. The first of a series of string instruction books prepared under the guidance of Paul Rolland of the University of Illinois appeared shortly thereafter.

During the 1960s the MENC published books on music at all levels

K–12 and continued its regular issue of service items such as *Film Guide for Music Educators* (edited by Donald Shetler), *A Career in Music Education, Approaches to Public Relations for the Music Educator,* and the Selected Music Lists for band, orchestra, choruses, and ensembles. It reprinted Birge's *History of Public School Music in the United States,* and William Hartshorn wrote *Music for the Academically Talented* as a part of the NEA project on gifted students. The request of the state presidents for help with general music issues resulted in *Music in General Education,* a committee report that recommended the subject be treated as a responsibility of all levels of elementary and secondary schools rather than merely of the junior high school. The report stated:

> General education is "common schooling," that quantity of schooling which at any particular time is normally regarded as necessary for all and made available to all. . . . One function of the "common" school in the United States is to prepare young people for life in a free, democratic society in which they will have to make choices. The type of choices they make in aesthetic matters will determine the culture they build for America. The schools cannot afford to send them ill-prepared into this responsible role.[28]

The book recommended desirable musical attributes that school systems should strive to develop in their students.

The publications program had grown so much that in 1964 the MENC established a publications planning committee. It was chaired in its early years by Robert Choate, Theodore F. Norman, and Robert Bays. Significant books continued to appear during the 1960s. Among them were *A Steadfast Philosophy,* a collection of the writings of Will Earhart edited by C. V. Buttelman; *Perspectives in Music Education (Source Book III);* a new edition of *Music Buildings, Rooms and Equipment, Talent Education and Suzuki, Aesthetics: Dimensions for Music Education* by Abraham Schwadron, *The Study of Music in the Elementary School: A Conceptual Approach,* and the two works from the Tanglewood Symposium—*Music in American Society* by Judith Murphy and George Sullivan and *Documentary Report of the Tanglewood Symposium.*

When Charles Gary was promoted from director of publications to executive secretary in 1968, the National Executive Board did not appoint a new director of publications but asked him to carry on in that capacity. Production slowed, however, and a new director, Charles Fowler, was named in 1971. Fowler was followed by Beth Landis.

Additional publications were released in the 1970s. They included *Toward an Aesthetic Education,* produced in cooperation with the Central Midwestern Regional Laboratory (CEMREL); the *Final Report of the Teacher Education Commission; The Eclectic Curriculum in American Music Education; Source Book of African and Afro-American Materials for Music Educators; Music in Early Childhood,* the Contemporary Music Project series, *The School Music Program: Description and Standards* (report of the first

National Commission on Instruction), and *Planning and Equipping Facilities*. The Music Education Research Council did a series entitled "From Research to the Music Classroom," including *Musical Characteristics of Children* by Marilyn P. Zimmerman, *Teaching Performing Groups* by Charles H. Benner, and *Teaching Instrumental Music* by George L. Duerksen. In addition, the conference reprinted some of the special single-topic issues of the *Music Educators Journal*.

Audio-Visual Materials. The MENC began offering publications in nonprint forms with some filmstrips in the late 1960s. During the next decade it produced a multiscreen promotional program on the Motiva system and three motion pictures. *Music's Generation,* produced in cooperation with National Educational Television, was telecast in May 1972 before being made available to members for showings to community and school audiences. It won a Golden Eagle award from the Council on International Nontheatrical Events. The MENC produced *A Band Is . . .* with the cooperation of Coca-Cola USA and its dealers. The Contemporary Music Project issued *What Is Music* to illustrate the comprehensive musicianship approach to the study of music. Gene Morlan, director of professional programs, arranged to have many of the biennial and division meeting sessions available on cassette.

The 1980s saw numerous additions to the list of publications, including the *Documentary Report of the Ann Arbor Symposium: Applications of Psychology to the Teaching and Learning of Music, Motivation and Creativity,* David McAllester's *Becoming Human Through Music,* a revision of *The School Music Program: Description and Standards, Multicultural Perspectives in Music Education, Promising Practices: High School General Music, Promising Practices: Kindergarten Music Education, What Works: Instructional Strategies for Music Education, Readings in General Music,* and *Certification Practices and Trends in Music Education.* The latter, as well as two recent videotapes by Tim Lautzenheiser, *You Make the Difference* and *Canadian Brass Master Class,* have been released on floppy disk.

THE MENC HISTORICAL CENTER

President Paul Van Bodegraven suggested that the MENC should preserve historical material and collect oral histories of older conference members. After negotiations with several institutions, an agreement was made between the MENC and the University of Maryland with the help of Homer Ulrich, Rose Marie Grentzer Spivacke, and Director of University Libraries Harold Rovelstad. Official papers of the MENC are stored there, along with many documents, textbooks, and photographs of historical interest. Curator Bruce C. Wilson has collected a great deal of oral history on tape.

Other archival collections have gravitated to this library, and together with the MENC archives, constitute the Special Collections in Music. The other organizations represented are the International Society for Music Education, American Bandmasters Association, National Association of College Wind and Percussion Instructors, College Band Directors National Association, Mid-West International Band and Orchestra Clinic, Society for Ethnomusicology, International Clarinet Society, American String Teachers Association, Association for Recorded Sound Collectors, Music Library Association, International Association of Music Libraries, Archives, and Documentation Centers—U.S. Branch, Music OCLC Users Group, and the Irving and Margery Lowens collection, which emphasizes American music scholarship. The International Piano Archives are also housed in the University of Maryland College Park Library, but are not part of the Special Collections in Music.

PUBLIC RELATIONS

Louis Wersen had already established himself as an extraordinary salesman when he became director of music for the city of Philadelphia. If any MENC members still questioned his ability when he hosted the biennial meeting in 1964 (he had convinced many when he did the same in 1952), they were persuaded by the final session of the meeting, when he filled the floor of the auditorium with students playing the Saint-Saëns Organ Concerto on thirty organs. The huge neon sign reading ''MENC'' that suddenly burst into view at the end of concert convinced members that they had a Barnum among them.

From the beginning, American music educators have mixed show business with their arguments to promote the place of music in the curriculum. In fact, music educators frequently complained that administrators looked to the music department to build good will for the entire school. The Conference had also used its activities to build support for music in the schools. By the mid-1960s there was a feeling among the membership that the MENC should be doing more, and because advertising had become such an important factor in American life, it was imperative that the MENC promotion of music education be done in a highly professional manner. The dues increase that the membership was asked to approve in 1966 was closely tied to the need for a staff public relations expert.

When the dues were increased from six to ten dollars a year, the MENC was able to hire Joan Gaines for the newly created position of director of public relations. Gaines was a public relations professional with empathy for the purpose of the MENC. After putting in place the standard information sheets and advising officers and staff on how to be better advocates, she enlisted national leaders from all walks of life to record statements in support of music education to be used as public service radio spots. The spots were distributed to stations nationwide.

The testimonies were from Anna Moffo, Richard Rodgers, Leopold Stokowski, Billy Taylor, Clark Terry, Richard Tucker, and Andy Williams.

Gaines arrived at the MENC in time to help the Tanglewood Symposium succeed. She served as an adviser for almost every MENC project undertaken after she joined the staff. In 1971 she coordinated the "Sounds of Music" program prepared for the White House Conference on Children and conducted workshops on "Building Community Support" at all six division conventions in 1971. The next year she offered community relations workshops at four sites across the country, arranged press conferences for the MENC officers, coordinated film projects, and prepared a special issue of the *Music Educators Journal* in 1972. That same year she orchestrated a successful campaign in Chicago to counter an attempt to eliminate the music program.

Gaines produced a wide variety of public relations materials for the Conference, including a taped workshop on crisis prevention. She created Music in Our Schools Day, an activity that the MENC continues each year, having added the "World's Largest Concert" on television as a means of having all the children of the nation sing together. She produced *Music Power*, a quarterly newsletter to share helpful promotional ideas that had worked for members.

The National Catholic Music Educators Association (NCMEA).

Music had been a part of the curriculum in Catholic schools in the nineteenth century. Near the turn of the century, Catholic editions of standard music texts were published. In 1916, Bishop Schrembs of Toledo prepared a Catholic edition of the forward-looking *Progressive Music Series*.[29] A special method for parochial schools was developed by Justine Ward at the request of Thomas Shields, head of the Department of Education at the Catholic University of America. Ward studied chant under Dom Mocquereau at Solesmes, France, and was dedicated to the use of this great body of music in the education of young children. Her method focused on developing the child voice through daily instruction by the classroom teacher under the guidance of a music professional. Her series *That All May Sing* was widely adopted by Catholic schools in the United States and in Catholic countries around the world.

As the Music Supervisors National Conference grew in size and influence, Catholic music educators became interested in the *Music Educators Journal* and the professional development aspect of the meetings. Catholic nuns began attending the meetings, and the MSNC officers accommodated them with special sessions dealing with parochial concerns. There were five such sessions at the third biennial meeting in Cleveland in 1932. Subsequent division meetings during the 1930s also offered programs on liturgical music and the nature of music programs for parochial schools. During his presidency of the Conference (1934–1936), Herman Smith attempted to involve more parochial teachers through the National Catholic Education Association; Glenn Gildersleeve, Pennsylvania state supervisor, did the same a few years later during his period of leadership of the eastern division.[30] By 1940 there was a Catholic Music Education Association in Chicago. Because each diocese developed its own curriculum, however, and because many of the teaching sisters were not competent to teach music, the subject was neglected in many American parochial schools.

When the Conference held its national convention in Milwaukee in 1942, the Very Reverend Monsignor Edmund J. Goebel, superintendent of schools of the Milwaukee diocese, called a meeting of music educators in Catholic schools to consider the advisability of organizing an association. A subsequent meeting was held in August at Marygrove College in Detroit. There, the National Catholic Music Educators Association was established. Harry Seitz, director of music for the schools of the archdiocese of Detroit, was elected president. Only one officer and member of the board of directors was from outside the confines of the MENC north central division. The objectives established for the group were

1. To promote a general interest in good music, liturgical and secular, in Catholic schools;
2. To encourage a spirit of cooperation and mutual helpfulness among Catholic music educators; and
3. To provide a standard whereby Catholic schools may be enabled to evaluate their progress in both liturgical and secular music.

The NCMEA had 215 members during its first official year (1943), 184 of whom were from Illinois, Michigan, and Wisconsin. The first national meeting was held in conjuction with the MENC meeting in Saint Louis in 1944. The group continued to meet with the Conference until 1953, when it held its own meeting in Atlanta. Communication with the membership began with a mimeographed *Bulletin* in 1943. It became a quarterly newsletter, then a quarterly magazine, and eventually developed into a journal entitled *MUSART,* a name suggested by Sister Mary Letitia, S.B.S., of Rock Castle, Virginia.

The 1950s were a period of growth and expansion for NCMEA. In 1953 the first of many summer workshops was held on the campus of The Catholic University of America. Research conferences began at Rosary College in the summer of 1957. By the end of the decade, the national meetings were attracting over three thousand and the membership surpassed four thousand. The publications program was expanded. A catalog of college and high school choral music appeared in 1953. In 1955 Richard Werder of Catholic University prepared an outline for a one-year general music program. A booklet prepared for the 1956 convention contained four masses, communion psalms, and English and Latin hymns. Higher standards for liturgical music became a priority for the association. In 1957 NCMEA published *Criteria for the Evaluation of Music Education in Catholic Elementary Schools.*

The following decade saw emphasis on instrumental music in Catholic schools. Workshops were held at St. Joseph's College in Renssalaer, Indiana, at Duquesne University, and at Immaculata and Misericordia colleges in Pennsylvania. Piano instruction, which had been a part of Catholic school music as early as the nineteenth century, was expanded to a broad instrumental music program in comprehensive secondary schools.[31]

A special issue of *MUSART* in the summer of 1976 was devoted to "Looking Back on Thirty-Five Years."[32] It was the last issue of the NCMEA periodical. The organization had been swept aside by the events of the Second Vatican Council and the pressures developed by the Vietnam War. Lawrence Cremin described the situation:

> The whole enterprise of parochial elementary and secondary schools and of Catholic colleges and universities and of separate Catholic intellectual and cultural organizations began to be challenged—explicit in debates over their necessity, as well as implicitly in the failure of the system to attract financial support, the teaching personnel (underpaid nuns and brothers had supported it for years with the contributions of their time and effort), and the clientele it required.[33]

NCMEA disbanded in 1976, paid what debts it could, and ceased to exist.[34] Its library and subscriptions to *MUSART* were transferred to the *Pastoral Musician*, the newly created periodical of the National Association of Pastoral Musicians.

THE MENC HEADQUARTERS BUILDING

After the Conference had been in the NEA Center for Education for about ten years, the National Education Association found itself in a confrontation with the American Federation of Teachers over which group would represent teachers in bargaining with school boards. NEA building representatives were encouraged to seek one-hundred-percent membership in their schools. When they pressured the MENC members to pay NEA dues, they were frequently shown an MENC membership card with the phrase "A Department of the NEA." This did not help in the count to determine who would represent the teachers at the bargaining table, however, and ill will began to develop between NEA and those departments that had separate dues structures. The MENC had not been delinquent in any way, since NEA membership was encouraged when the MENC membership promotional materials were distributed. The MENC officers had always joined the NEA regardless of whether they had been members before.

Vanett Lawler said, "They invited us in and they'll have to invite us to leave." That did not occur before she retired, but shortly thereafter the situation deteriorated further. The school administrators and the principals were asked to leave the building because they represented management, and NEA now considered itself a labor union rather than a professional association. The MENC changed its relationship from a department to an affiliate in 1969, as did many other associations. These organizations hired a consultant group to help them plan for the future because requests for additional space in the NEA building were unanswered. MENC membership had grown to 60,000, and its activities continued to expand. Consultants recommended the creation of an educational park in the suburbs, and a group of executive officers immediately began to look at large parcels of land in Columbia, Maryland; Tysons Corner, Virginia; and Reston, Virginia.

An interesting sequence of events determined the final location. The Federal Aviation Agency had barred all flights of over five hundred miles from Washington National Airport and forced them to land at Dulles Airport in Chantilly, Virginia. When that happened the Sheraton Corporation built a hotel in Reston only a few hundred yards from Sunset Valley Drive, one of the three sites still being considered. On hearing this, Owen Kiernan, director of the National Association of Secondary School Principals (NASSP), announced that his association would relocate in Reston because there was a suitable hotel to house their many guests. Most of the groups wanted to be near the NASSP headquarters, and so the twenty-six acre parcel was purchased. Within six months members of Congress persuaded the FAA to lift its restriction on National Airport, but the educational organizations were committed to Reston by that time.

The Conference put together a National Building Fund Campaign and hired Marts and Lundy of New York, a firm frequently employed by college fund-raisers, for advice. Louis Wersen was named national chairman and Paul Van Bodegraven, who had served as the conference financial chairman for many years, agreed to head a board of overseers. A former president of the Ohio Music Education Association, Richard Davis, joined the staff to organize the state campaigns. He was assisted by George Christopher of New York. Charles Moody, a member of the MENC staff, also played a major role in this far-flung effort. William F. Ludwig was a fortunate selection as the person to solicit the members of music industry. Many of the firms in the MIC made substantial gifts, as did hundreds of members. It was initially agreed to follow the advice of Van Bodegraven and not break ground until the money was in the bank for the new building, which was planned by Jansons Roberts Taylor Associates. A sudden inflationary move in construction prices and a possible limit on sewer connections, however, led the architect to advise a change in plan. It proved to be a fortunate decision as inflation continued.

The headquarters office was moved to temporary quarters in Tysons Corner, Virginia, in early 1974 and the building, despite one contractor who went bankrupt, was finished in the summer of 1975. The staff moved in one week before the interim meeting was held in the nearby Sheraton Hotel, and the delegates paraded to the Center for Educational Associations on a hot August afternoon to dedicate the first MENC home of its own. At the interim meeting twelve years later many of those who had made the building possible through their work on the Building Fund Campaign were present to burn the mortgage.

The Society for General Music. Certification practices in music education have tended to divide the profession into instrumental teachers and vocal teachers, although the Conference has continued to support the concept of complete music educators. The requirements of the curriculum, especially as developed in the junior high school, demanded teachers for what became known as "general music" classes. The term was probably taken from the general science and general math classes offered at that level. Few music educators have been happy with the name, but no acceptable substitute has been found. Committed band directors and choral conductors have seldom been pleased to be assigned general music classes, although that is where the traditional concern for "Music for Every Child" is to be found in secondary schools, if at all.

During the late 1970s a group of teachers led by Charles Leonhard dedicated themselves to improving instruction in general music, incorporating ideas for some or all of the imported music curricula, and being notably inventive themselves. A Society for General Music was formed and was recognized by the MENC in 1981. Since that time, it has been a productive and forward-looking organization that generates publications and workshops.

NOTES

1. *Proceedings of the 78th Annual Meeting of the National Education Association* (Washington, DC: National Education Association, 1940), pp. 505–512.
2. Richard Grant, "The New Constitution," *Yearbook of the Music Educators National Conference* 30 (Chicago: Music Educators National Conference, 1940), pp. 462–64.
3. Some states never had provision for a partial membership in their constitutions. At a discussion of the matter at the meeting of the State Presidents National Assembly in Los Angeles in 1958, the president of the Tennessee Music Educators spoke in favor of the elimination of partial memberships after noting proudly that the Volunteer State had never provided for it. Later that year he joined the MENC staff in Washington and while being intro-

duced to the office layout his own membership record was pulled from the addressograph file. It showed that Charles L. Gary was first affiliated with MENC as a partial member in Ohio in order to take his high school choir to a festival at Miami University.

4. "Student's Code of Conduct," *The NIMAC Manual* (Washington, DC: MENC, 1963), pp. 125–26.

5. *Journal of Proceedings of the Music Educators National Conference*, vol. 30 (Chicago: The Conference, 1940), p. 476.

6. Thomas Annett, "State Supervisors of Public School Music," *Music Educators Journal* 26 (December 1939): 24.

7. Thomas Annett, "The Status of Rural School Music—A Survey," *Music in American Education* (Chicago: Music Educators National Conference, 1955), pp. 83–85.

8. Michael L. Mark, "The Music Educators National Conference and World War II Home Front Programs," *Bulletin of Historical Research in Music Education* 1 (July 1980): 3.

9. Report of interorganizational meeting, representing officers of affiliated and cooperating organizations, held at the biennial convention, March 29, 1942. The report was approved by the MENC Board of Directors on April 2, 1942.

10. *Music Educators Journal* 27 (October–November 1940): 15.

11. *Music Educators Journal* 28 (March–April 1942): 34.

12. *Music Educators Journal* 27 (March–April 1941): 14.

13. *Music Educators Journal* 28 (May–June 1942): 55.

14. *Music Educators Journal* 31 (May–June 1945): 37, 76–77.

15. *Music Education Source Book* (Chicago: Music Educators National Conference, 1947), p. 44.

16. Allen P. Britton, "Founding *JRME*: A Personal View," *Journal of Research in Music Education* 32 (Winter 1984): 233.

17. Fred Anthony Warren, "A History of the *Journal of Research in Music Education*, 1953–1965," *Journal of Research in Music Education* 33 (Winter 1984): 224–25.

18. Judith Murphy, "Conflict, Consensus, and Communication: An Interpretive Report," *Music Educators Journal* 66 (March 1980): 47–78.

19. John B. Cox, "Ann Arbor III: A Meeting of Minds on Motivation and Creativity," *Music Educators Journal* 69 (March 1983): 57–58.

20. Frances Elliott Clark, "Music Appreciation and the New Day," *Music Educators Journal* 19 (February 1933): 11–14, 20. Will Earhart, "A Philosophical Basis for Aesthetic Values in Education," *Music Educators Journal* 37 (November–December 1950): 15–17.

21. Will Earhart, from his "Response for the Conference" to the welcome address at the Thirteenth Meeting of the Music Supervisors National Conference in Philadelphia, March 1920.

22. *Music Education Source Book I* (Chicago: MENC, 1947), p. 44.

23. C. V. Buttelman, "Dedication," *Music in American Education: Source Book II* (Washington, DC: Music Educators National Conference, 1955), p. xi.

24. MENC Minutes, Meeting of the Executive Committee, August 29, 1947. MENC Historical Center, University of Maryland at College Park.

25. *Journal of Proceedings of the Eleventh Annual Meeting of the Music Supervisors National Conference* (Madison: The Conference, 1920), p. 212.

26. Judith Murphy and George Sullivan, *Music in American Society* (Washington, DC: MENC, 1967), p ii.

27. Robert A. Choate, ed., *Documentary Report of the Tanglewood Symposium* (Washington, DC: Music Educators National Conference, 1968), p. 139.

28. Karl D. Ernst and Charles L. Gary, eds., *Music in General Education* (Washington, DC: Music Educators National Conference, 1965), p. 1.

29. John E. Lamek, "Music Instruction in Catholic Elementary Schools" (Ph.D. dissertation, The Catholic University of America, 1933), p. 26.

30. Rose Anne Murphy, "A Historical Survey of the National Catholic Music Educators Association" (M.A. thesis, The Catholic University of America, 1959), pp.15–16.

31. Ibid., pp. 17–20.

32. *MUSART* 28 (Summer 1976): 3.

33. Lawrence A. Cremin, *American Education: The Metropolitan Experience, 1876–1980* (New York: Harper & Row, 1988), p. 137.

34. Charles Gary interviews with Michael Cordovana and Vincent Walter, The Catholic University of America, February 10, 1990.

BIBLIOGRAPHY

Annett, Thomas. "The Status of Rural School Music: A Survey." *Music in American Education*. Chicago: Music Educators National Conference, 1955.

Britton, Allen P. "Founding *JRME*: A Personal View." *Journal of Research in Music Education* 32 (Winter 1984).

Buttelman, Clifford V. "Dedication." *Music in American Education*. Washington, DC: Music Educators National Conference, 1955.

———, ed. *Will Earhart: A Steadfast Philosophy*. Washington, DC: Music Educators National Conference, 1962.

Choate, Robert A., ed. *Documentary Report of the Tanglewood Symposium*. Washington, DC: Music Educators National Conference, 1968.

Clark, Frances Elliott. "Music Appreciation and the New Day." *Music Educators Journal* 19 (February 1933).

Cremin, Lawrence A. *American Education: The Metropolitan Experience, 1876–1980.* New York: Harper & Row, 1988.

Earhart, Will. "A Philosophical Basis for Aesthetic Values in Education." *Music Educators Journal* 37 (November–December 1950).

Ernst, Karl D., and Charles L. Gary, eds. *Music in General Education.* Washington, DC: Music Educators National Conference, 1965.

Grant, Richard. "The New Constitution." *Yearbook of the Music Educators National Conference* 30. Chicago: Music Educators National Conference, 1940.

"Handbook of the Society for Research in Music Education." *Journal of Research in Music Education* 19 (Summer 1971).

Journal of Proceedings of the Eleventh Annual Meeting of the Music Supervisors National Conference. Madison: Music Supervisors National Conference, 1920.

Journal of Proceedings of the Music Educators National Conference, vol. 30. Chicago: Music Educators National Conference, 1940.

Lamek, John E. "Music Instruction in Catholic Elementary Schools." Ph.D. dissertation, The Catholic University of America, 1933.

Mark, Michael L. "The MENC and World War II Home Front Programs." *Bulletin of Historical Research in Music Education* 1 (July 1980).

McConathy, Osbourne; Miessner, W. Otto; Birge, Edward Bailey; and Bray, Mabel E. *Music in Rural Education.* New York: Silver, Burdett, 1933.

"MENC Forms Two Commissions." *Music Educators Journal* 57 (April 1971).

MENC Minutes, Meeting of the Executive Committee, August 29, 1947. MENC Historical Center, University of Maryland at College Park.

Murphy, Rose Anne. "A Historical Survey of the National Catholic Music Educators Association." M.A. thesis, The Catholic University of America, 1959.

MUSART 28 (Summer 1976).

Music Education Source Book. Chicago: Music Educators National Conference, 1947.

Music Educators Journal 27 (October–November 1940, March–April 1941), 28 (May–June 1942), 31 (May–June 1945).

Proceedings of the 78th Annual Meeting of the National Education Association. Washington: National Education Association, 1940.

Roberts, John T. "MENC's Associated Organizations: NAJE." *Music Educators Journal* 55 (March 1969).

"Student's Code of Conduct." *The NIMAC Manual.* Washington, DC: MENC, 1936.

Warren, Fred Anthony. "A History of the *Journal of Research in Music Education,* 1953–1965." *Journal of Research in Music Education* 33 (Winter 1984).

Wilson, Bruce, and Gary, Charles L. "Music in Our Schools: The First 150 Years." *Music Educators Journal* 74 (February 1988).

PART V

MUSIC EDUCATION FROM THE MIDDLE OF THE TWENTIETH CENTURY

14

THE UNITED STATES AFTER 1950

AMERICAN EDUCATION AT THE MIDDLE OF THE TWENTIETH CENTURY

The United States emerged from World War II as the strongest military, economic, and industrial world force and most other Western countries looked to it for leadership. The United States was the chief agent in helping other nations rebuild and regenerate themselves after the war while at the same time continuing to develop itself. This dual role generated a strong economy and the best in American creative genius as the nation began to transform itself from an industrial society into an early technological society.

The new age brought prosperity, but with it came new tension and anxiety. The conclusion of the war saw the Western world divided between capitalism and communism. The schism spread to Asia as China became a communist country, and to the Western hemisphere, where the revolution in Cuba brought about a new communist state. The Cold War and the Korean conflict brought both new demands on the United States and internal division. World and national conditions fluctuated as the political tension increased and the threat of war reappeared throughout the 1950s.

At the same time the American economy continued to prosper, bringing an ever higher standard of living for most citizens. Throughout the 1950s technology that changed the way most people lived was developed, and it became apparent that the postindustrial society would soon evolve into a technological society. One of the most pronounced characteristics of this time was change. Never before had society changed so radically and so rapidly. Information technology helped fuel a dazzling increase in information and knowledge, which in turn led to new developments that changed American life. Prior to this time, people expected the conditions that shaped their lives to remain static, as had been the case until the industrial revolution of the nineteenth century, or to change slowly, as during the industrial age. Now, suddenly, change came so fast and steadily that it disoriented many people who could not adjust to a new way of life. As a principal characteristic of American life from the 1950s on, change has dominated thought and action by making people realize they could no longer prepare themselves for a certain future. In the past, people had a reasonably accurate view of the conditions that would shape their lives in the future, at least the near future; that was no longer the case.

The Educational Policies Commission issued a book in 1944 entitled *Education for All American Youth*.[1] It called on Americans to think about the kind of school system they wanted when peace came. The book began: "Educational change is bound to come, and to come swiftly. Only the nature and direction of change may be controlled." It then described the kinds of schools the nation could have five years after the end of the war. A current reading of the book, which recommended "preparation for a useful occupation," "education for citizenship," and "personal development for every boy and girl," makes painfully obvious the fact that the commission had no real idea of how swiftly the changes were to come or of their nature. In fact, nobody could have predicted the fundamental changes to come in American society.

The ever-increasing pace of change has required schools geared for teaching well-planned subject matter to prepare children for useful occupations that might have suddenly ceased to exist. Inertia prevented the educational establishment from making the rapid adjustments required by changing societal conditions, and this led to tension between the schools and society. The schools were attacked by critics, most of whom charged the educational establishment with anti-intellectualism. Throughout the 1950s industrial, military, and political leaders became increasingly alarmed as they realized the implications of a weak educational system. In October 1957 the Soviet Union launched Sputnik I and established itself as the leader in space technology. Until then, the American people had thought the United States was ahead of its chief Cold War rival. Americans feared that Soviet technological dominance would lead to another war, and a sense of urgency overtook the United States. An improved educational system quickly became a national priority as the United States struggled to regain technological leadership.

A Reform Movement developed to improve the educational system. One of the most vocal leaders of the movement was Admiral Hyman Rickover, who had directed the development of the United States Navy atomic submarine program. As a highly respected and much admired military leader who depended on an educated population to support his program, his was an influential voice. He said:

> Russia has built an educational system in record time which produces exactly the sort of trained men and women her rulers need to achieve technical supremacy. . . . Russia has no substandard teachers . . . students are studious, polite, well-disciplined, and earnest. . . . [Students] have no competing attractions, no comfortable homes, no playrooms, no jukeboxes, no senior proms, no dating, hardly any radio or TV, and no hot rods.[2]

Rickover was well aware that Americans had a much higher standard of living than Soviet citizens and that the lack of intellectual freedom in the Soviet Union brought with it second-rate art, literature, and theater. He thought it more important, however, to produce scientists and engineers who could support the scientific programs needed to maintain world leadership; Americans had become soft and undisciplined.

Comparing American education with that of other European countries, Rickover found the American system lacking. He felt that European education provided the necessary intellectual, cultural, and physical requirements. Students who could not meet the highest standards were given vocational training. The American system, by attempting to educate all of its children equally, wasted precious resources rather than differentiating between students of high ability and the others. Rickover strongly recommended that more money be spent on education, that science and math offerings be strengthened, and that frills be eliminated from the curriculum. Rickover was a strident reformer whose understanding of the basic purposes of American education was sadly misinformed. His concern was only with the most able students. This was in direct opposition to the principles of democratic education.

Another leader of the educational reform movement was Dr. James Bryant Conant, former president of Harvard University, who also stressed stronger academic preparation. Unlike Rickover, Conant recommended that students study the arts as well as mathematics and science in his book on the American high school.[3] Rickover, Conant, and others helped elevate public awareness of the problems faced by American education. They especially directed public attention to the weakness of academic programs in mathematics, science, foreign languages, and reading. These came to be considered the basic subjects by the public, and other areas, such as music, were often thought to be frills. National attention to education continued to grow when the prestigious Commission on National Goals, appointed by President Dwight D. Eisenhower, issued a report entitled "National Goals in Education" in 1960. In 1961, President John F. Kennedy established the White House Panel on Educational Research and Development as an advisory board to the U.S.

Office of Education, the National Science Foundation, and his own science adviser to help improve American education. As the federal government became more involved in education, the general public became more aware of the importance of its schools in maintaining and improving the quality of American life and the leadership role of the United States.

Another important event, the Woods Hole Conference, took place in 1959 at Woods Hole, Massachusetts. The purpose of the conference was to discuss the problems of science education and recommend solutions. Convened by the Education Committee of the National Academy of Sciences, it was supported by the academy, the U.S. Office of Education, the air force, and the Rand Corporation. It was attended by educators, historians, physicists, biologists, psychologists, and mathematicians. The Woods Hole Conference was the beginning of a new trend—the unified efforts of distinguished people from related fields addressing themselves to the general improvement of education. Many curriculum studies were generated by the conference. In 1962 there were ten projects in science, eleven in mathematics, one in language arts, two in foreign languages, and four in social studies. Similar conferences were held later to discuss music education (see Chapter 15).

For the first time, the federal government became deeply involved in education. The Cooperative Research Branch of the United States Office of Education distributed $10 million a year from 1956 to 1961 for 407 research projects. The National Science Foundation awarded $159 million in 1960, of which $34 million went to teacher improvement institutes that served 31,000 teachers. In 1961 more than half of the funds granted by large foundations went to educational enterprises.[4]

The late 1950s and early 1960s saw vast amounts of resources dedicated to the improvement of curricular areas directly related to the perceived needs of American society. The arts were not excluded from the new wave of funding, but neither did they receive significant amounts of support from it. Still distrustful of the dominance of the Soviet Union in space technology, the American people were concerned about improvement in what was known as the basic subjects. The curriculum in many schools became heavily weighted in favor of those subjects and away from music and the other arts.

The Unbalanced Curriculum was viewed as a dangerous matter by public education leaders, who considered the arts a necessary part of American education. The American Association of School Administrators issued the following statement in 1959:

> We believe in a well-balanced school curriculum in which music, drama, painting, poetry, sculpture, architecture and the like are included side by side with other important subjects such as mathematics, history, and science. It is important that pupils, as a part of general education, learn to

appreciate, to understand, to create, and to criticize with discrimination those products of the mind, the voice, the hand, and the body which give dignity to the person and exalt the spirit of man.[5]

The Project on Instruction, sponsored by the National Education Association, also supported the arts in the curriculum. The project report stated:

> Priorities for the schools are the teaching of skills in reading, composition, listening, speaking (native and foreign languages), and computation . . . ways of creative and disciplined thinking . . . competence in self-instruction and independent thinking . . . fundamental understanding of the humanities and the arts, the social sciences and the natural sciences, and in literature, music, and the visual arts.[6]

Scientists also voiced alarm at the unbalanced curriculum. The Panel on Educational Research and Development, an advisory body of nongovernmental experts, recommended action to the National Science Foundation, the U.S. Office of Education, and the President's Office of Science and Technology:

> Certain members of the Panel were convinced that there was a degree of correlation between excellence in scientific achievement and the breadth of an individual's human experience. The best scientists, it was thought, were not necessarily those who had devoted themselves singlemindedly to their own field; somehow, familiarity with the arts and humanities sharpened a good scientist's vision.[7]

The 1960s saw significant changes in education. Because of the increased attention given to the "basic" subjects, Scholastic Achievement Tests (SAT) scores increased. At the same time, the support given the arts by scientists, school administrators, and other influential people helped music retain a fairly strong place in the curriculum. The economy was prosperous, and the "baby boom" after World War II brought heavy enrollments to schools, thus increasing the need for additional teachers and facilities.

The shortage of teachers to staff the newly expanded schools, and the hurried attempt to recruit and educate large numbers of new teachers, lowered academic standards. The quality of teacher education suffered because the colleges were not prepared to handle the huge influx of new teacher education students, many of whom were not of the highest ability. Those with the potential to be excellent teachers were often discouraged from entering the profession by the traditionally low salaries and by the inferior quality of American education.

By the end of the 1960s the educational decline had become even more highly visible. The SAT scores had begun to drop, and the curricular trend away from the traditional subjects was reluctantly accepted by the public because of the new emphasis on satisfying the needs of the individual student. While teachers and administrators attempted to make schools more humanistic, they eased requirements in subjects that required hard work and discipline. The youth movement of the 1960s had resulted in more influence over educational policy-making by young people, which led to an enlargement of the curriculum. Educators made the curriculum more responsive to student desires by infusing it with experiences that would allow them to "get in touch with their feelings" and "discover themselves." Many of the new courses offered in elementary, junior high, and high schools were in "soft" areas such as decision-making, attitudinal developments, and surveys of subjects of personal interest to students. These studies were not always based on recognized scholastic disciplines. While the new courses, often related to individual interests, gained popularity, enrollments declined in such traditional curricular areas as math, science, English, foreign languages, classical studies, and the arts. Even in traditional disciplines, new approaches to teaching often exposed students to a subject without presenting much content in the vague hope that they would develop appreciation for it.

The increasing problems of juvenile crime and drug abuse were also factors in the decline. The behavioral problems that became prominent during the 1960s were ascribed in some cases to the dehumanized technological society. The schools were expected to be a positive balance to the negative aspects of society, but that was not a realistic expectation. By the end of the 1960s, educational standards continued downward.

American Education in the 1970s continued to decline academically but had the added burden of being underfunded because of world economic conditions. Oil prices increased greatly, and the ensuing inflation forced school districts to provide a lower level of funding than had been possible in the affluent 1960s. The federal government, which had begun to provide economic support to education was faced with new problems in social policy, foreign affairs, and economics. Education no longer claimed as large a share of the federal government's interest or attention. The baby boom that had overflowed the schools in the 1960s was spent by the mid-1970s, and enrollments declined drastically. The earlier large enrollments had resulted in expanded faculties and numerous new buildings. Now, fewer teachers and buildings were needed. The number of music positions throughout the country began to decline. In many locations, schools were closed and the student bodies were combined with those of a nearby school that remained open. This was still another cause of the reduced number of music teaching positions.

By the end of the decade, educational quality had been severely hampered not only by the decline that had continued from the 1960s but also by the severe lack of resources throughout the 1970s. Education had sunk to such a low level that again, like twenty years earlier, the nation was alarmed. In 1980 the average math SAT score had dropped to the all-time low of 466. Juvenile crime, drugs, and other social problems had worsened, and the schools were unable to deal with them. Public confidence in education was at a low ebb.

An Accountability Movement was begun in the early 1970s to help improve the situation. Numerous accountability plans were implemented in school districts across the country. They did not solve the problem, but the movement helped clarify the goals and objectives of education and provided a needed tool to measure the educational growth of individuals and the effectiveness of the educational system. The movement was specific in demanding higher standards of students and teachers. The tone of the reformers and their actions were similar to those of the late 1950s, which in turn were similar to those of other times in American educational history. Even the concern for national security that had been raised by the launch of Sputnik in 1957 was mirrored in the title of a report by a major panel charged with examining the educational system and making recommendations to improve the schools. The report was *A Nation at Risk: The Imperative for Educational Reform.*

Education in the 1980s was again in the national spotlight as the public became vocal about the need for better schools. To clarify the problems, a number of commissions and task forces were appointed, and each issued a report that received national coverage. The most influential was *A Nation at Risk: The Imperative for Educational Reform*, issued by the National Commission on Excellence in Education. *A Nation at Risk* listed numerous defects in the educational system, making the point that the quality of education had declined precipitously The current level of mediocrity was unlikely to produce an educated adult population capable of living productive and satisfying lives in the increasingly technological world community. As other nations overtook the United States in education, it would fall behind economically, thus diminishing the quality of life that its citizens had come to enjoy and expect. The commission reported on problems in curriculum, time in class, teaching, and subject matter content. Other reports, similar to that of the National Commission on Excellence in Education, were issued by the twentieth Century Fund Task Force on Federal Elementary and Secondary Education Policy, the National Task Force on Education for Economic Growth, the National Science Board Commission on Precollege Education in Mathematics, Science and Technology, the College Board, and the Carnegie Foundation for the Advancement of Teaching.

The reports issued by prestigious organizations to the American public received much publicity. The nation was again made aware of the problems with its schools and the given myriad suggestions for improving them. As the 1980s progressed, some improvements were made, but it became even more apparent that many of the problems were caused by societal ills that were beyond the capacity of the schools to cure. Some of the educational weaknesses that could be dealt with by the education establishment did show gains. For example, teacher salaries began to improve, which had the effect of encouraging better candidates to enter the field of teaching.

Many of the reports agreed on the importance of the mastery of language, and that all students should be required to complete a core curriculum. They disagreed, though, about the nature and meaning of core curriculum. Some groups considered the core to be courses that should be required, and others to be a common set of concepts, principals, skills, and ways of knowing. Some reports, based on research and reflection rather than on emotional reaction to the national situation, supported arts education. The major report, *A Nation at Risk*, disappointed arts educators because although it supported arts education, music and the other arts were not identified as part of the basic curriculum.

SUMMARY

Since midcentury, American education has gone through an extended introspection of its strengths and weaknesses. An important aspect of the reform movement of the late 1950s was that its leaders were, for the most part, from outside of the education establishment. Most curriculum developers were professors in the various disciplines. Also, financial support came from private foundations and the federal government rather than through the usual channels by which schools are funded.

The federal government became more involved in public education than ever before, as did private foundations. Huge amounts of money and other resources were directed at education, and the 1960s saw a rich, but brief, period in which experimentation and innovation were valued for their potential to improve education. The various measure of educational success measured improvement at times, but by the end of the 1970s the schools were still failing to prepare students to maintain the United States at the level it had achieved. The flurry of reports of the early 1980s constituted the beginning of another reform movement similar to that which followed the launch of Sputnik in 1957.

One of the important lessons learned from earlier reform movements was that there is no panacea for problems so complex and deeply rooted. Studies have demonstrated that there is little relationship between the amount of money spent for education and improvement in the quality of education. This was demonstrated in the 1960s by the events in American education.

Once in the early 1960s and again in the 1980s music educators faced the problem of having to compete with subjects that are considered by many to be of greater importance. All of the events and movements described in this chapter affected music education. The responses of the music education profession are described in the next chapter.

NOTES

1. *Education for All American Youth* (Washington, DC: National Education Association, 1944), p. 1.
2. "Rickover, in Book, Attacks Schools," *New York Times*, January 30, 1959, p. 10.
3. James B. Conant, *The American High School Today* (New York: McGraw-Hill, 1959), p. 48.
4. Matthew B. Miles, "Educational Innovation: The Nature of the Problem," in *Innovation in Education*, ed. Matthew B. Miles (New York: Bureau of Publications, Columbia University Teachers College, 1964), p. 8.
5. American Association of School Administrators, *Official Report for the Year 1959*; including a record of the Annual Meeting and Work Conference on "Education and the Creative Arts" (Washington, DC: American Association of School Administrators, 1959), pp. 248–49.
6. Ole Sand, "Current Trends in Curriculum Planning," *Music Educators Journal* 50 (September 1963): 101.
7. Irving Lowens, "MUSIC: Juilliard Repertory Project and the Schools," *The Evening Star*, Washington, DC, May 30, 1971, p. E4. This is a report of the Yale seminar working group on "Repertory in Its Historical and Geographical Contexts."

BIBLIOGRAPHY

American Association of School Administrators. *Official Report for the Year 1958*; including a Record of the Annual Meeting and Work conference on "Education and the Creative Arts." Washington, DC: American Association of School Administrators, 1959.

Conant, James B. *The American High School Today.* New York: McGraw-Hill, 1959.

Education for All American Youth. Washington, DC: National Education Association, 1944.

Lowens, Irving. "MUSIC: Juilliard Repertory Project and the Schools." *The Evening Star,* Washington, DC, May 30, 1971.

Mark, Michael L. *Contemporary Music Education.* Second edition. New York: Schirmer, 1986.

Miles, Matthew B. "Educational Innovation: The Nature of the Problem," in

Innovation in Education, ed. Matthew B. Miles. New York: Bureau of Publications, Columbia University Teachers College, 1964.

Sand, Ole. "Current Trends in Curriculum Planning." *Music Educators Journal* 50 (September 1963).

15

GOVERNMENT AND FOUNDATION SUPPORT FOR ARTS EDUCATION

After midcentury, the conditions of public education led many Americans to the conclusion that the problems could not be solved by local and state governments. The federal government first became involved with education with the Northwest Ordinance of 1787, which provided federal land grants for the establishment of educational institutions. From then until the 1950s, federal aid to education was provided infrequently because educational funding was a function of state and local government. From the nineteenth century to the 1950s, federal aid had been provided for such purposes as vocational and agricultural education programs and facilities, rehabilitation and training of war veterans, school lunch programs, and health service education. Federal aid to public education had been viewed with suspicion because of the possibility of government interference in state and local matters. Attitudes changed, however, when the growing discontent with public education in the late 1950s was increased by the success of Sputnik. Even before Sputnik, though, the federal government had begun to take an interest in public education. The National Advisory Committee on Education Act of 1954 established a committee charged with the responsibility of recommending areas of national concern that might be addressed by the U.S. Office of Education (USOE), which was then part of the Department of Health, Education, and Welfare. Music was identified as a "critical subject" of national concern and was thus eligible to receive support from the National Defense Education Act (NDEA) of 1958. The Higher Education Facilities Act of 1963 provided grants and loans for new educational facilities, including electronic music studios.

The United States Office of Education was originally a bureau in 1867 and became an office in the Department of the Interior in 1869. Its chief function for years was the gathering of statistics. It was transferred to the Federal Security Agency, which became the Department of Health, Education, and Welfare in 1953. Under continuing pressure from the National Education Association, it became the Department of Education under President James Earl Carter. It has long had many bureaus, including Elementary and Secondary Education, Adult, Vocational and Library Programs, and Education for the Handicapped. During President John F. Kennedy's administration the arts and humanities branch was instituted, but it seldom controlled substantial amounts of money. The arts education authorities assembled by Kathryn Bloom worked closely with the schools and professional arts organizations. Harold Arberg, formerly of Hofstra College, was the music specialist.

The money made available for educational research was significant. The U.S. Office of Education Bureau of Research was replaced by the National Center for Educational Development, which was succeeded by the National Institute of Education (NIE). The dissemination of educational research results were handled by the Educational Resources Information Center (ERIC). ERIC maintains clearinghouses at universities and other institutions throughout the country. Each is responsible for a specific area of education. Music topics were assigned to the center responsible for social studies research.

The Elementary and Secondary Education Act of 1965 (ESEA, P.L. 89-10) was a significant piece of legislation for American education. The law authorized more than $1.3 billion to be channeled into classrooms to achieve several education goals. It provided support specifically for music education. The section most significant to music education was Title I, which was prefaced as follows: "An ACT to strengthen and improve educational quality and educational opportunities in the Nation's elementary and secondary schools." Until 1973, under the terms of Title I, school districts all over the country received funds (matching funds, in most cases) with which to establish programs to equalize educational opportunities for children of low-income families. Many school districts hired music teachers and purchased instruments and equipment for schools in low-income areas, which were identified by means of well-defined guidelines. Title I enabled many children to participate in music and the other arts. During fiscal 1966, approximately one-third of the 8.3 million children participating in the program were involved in music or art.[1] In 1973 USOE revised the terms of Title I to provide greater support for the development of basic skills, especially in reading and mathematics. Most state education departments interpreted this to mean remedial aid in those areas. Music and art were usually approved for Title I funding in most states if they related somehow to the development of reading, writing, or mathematics skills. The effect of the new interpretation was a greatly reduced involvement of music and art in Title I programs.

ESEA Title II authorized funds for supplementary educational centers and services. Under Title III, funds were made available for a number of arts programs. ESEA Title IV amended the Cooperative Research Act of 1954. It authorized $100 million over a five-year period for national and regional research facilities, expansion of existing research and development programs, and a training program for educational researchers. It funded some music projects, including the Special Training Project in Research in Music Education of the Music Education Research Council (MERC), a component of MENC. The program was held in March 1968 in Seattle preceding the MENC national convention. Title IV also created regional laboratories to develop and implement research data. Two of the laboratories, the Central Atlantic Regional Educational Laboratory (CAREL) in Washington, DC, and the Central Midwestern Regional Educational Laboratory (CEMREL) in Saint Louis, Missouri, were especially concerned with aesthetic education.

ESEA sponsored many other arts projects in addition to the ones discussed above. In 1966 the USOE Arts and Humanities Program sponsored 48 research projects in music, 46 in art, 18 in theater and dance, 4 in the arts in general, and 11 in the humanities.[2] Some of the projects sponsored in music included the Yale Seminar, the Juilliard Repertory Project, and the Manhattanville Music Curriculum Program.

The International Education Act of 1966 (P.L. 89-698) provided grants to institutions of higher education to establish and operate centers for research and training in international studies. Under it, several colleges and universities founded institutes for comparative music education.

The Education Professions Development Act of 1967 (P.L. 90-35) was important for music education. It amended and extended Title V of the higher Education Act of 1965. The EPDA was intended to improve the quality of teaching and to help overcome the shortage of adequately trained teachers by implementing training and retraining programs. The act had the effect, among other things, of attracting top quality people capable of improving education during short- and long-term assignments in the profession. Through the Teacher Retraining Authorization of the EPDA the Interdisciplinary Model Programs in the Arts for Children and Teachers (IMPACT) was established in 1970. The concept of IMPACT was in keeping with the third paragraph of the Tanglewood Declaration, which states:

> The arts afford a continuity with the aesthetic tradition in man's history. Music and other fine arts, largely non-verbal in nature, reach close to the social, psychological, and physiological roots of man in his search for identity and self-realization.

Four arts education associations—MENC, the National Art Education Association, the American Theater Association, and the Dance Division of the American Association for Health, Physical Education, and Recreation—established a plan of operation for IMPACT. Some sites funded under the project demonstrated that core activities in the arts can transform the traditional school curriculum positively.[3]

The Public Broadcasting Act of 1967 (P.L. 90-129) created a corporation for public broadcasting responsible for funding noncommercial radio and television stations, program production groups, educational television networks, and construction of educational radio and television facilities.

The National Foundation on the Arts and the Humanities was created in 1965 by P.L. 89–209 as an independent federal agency in the executive branch. Congress declared:

> The practice of art and the study of the humanities requires constant dedication and devotion and . . . while no government can call a great artist or scholar into existence, it is necessary and appropriate for the Federal Government to help create and sustain not only a climate encouraging freedom of thought, imagination, and inquiry, but also the material conditions facilitating the release of this creative talent.

The National Endowment for the Arts (NEA) and the National Endowment for the Humanities (NEH) are components of the National Foundation on the Arts and the Humanities. They are advised by the National Council on the Arts and the National Council on the Humanities. The NEA has provided little funding for music education. The most visible NEA program concerned with music education is Artists-in-Schools. It has provided funds for artists to work in thousands of schools. Nancy Hanks, the first director of the NEA, felt that the USOE should provide funds for school arts. NEA often referred to the Artists-in-Schools program as its major educational activity when asked to become more involved in arts education. However, arts educators traditionally distinguish between educational activities in which children create art and those for which they serve as audiences. Many arts educators consider Artists-in-Schools to be more for the employment of professional artists than for the education of children.

In 1983 Frank Hodsell, chairman of NEA, stated in a speech to arts education leaders that he wanted to explore the feasibility of having NEA become more involved with arts education. The next year (1984), in cooperation with the National Assembly of State Arts Agencies, NEA held a series of five regional meetings "to help identify and disseminate techniques, strategies and resources for promoting arts education from kindergarten through 12th grade."

> The goal is to find exemplary efforts that improve and promote arts education in schools all across the country. These efforts might be at the state, local or classroom level, and might relate to programs, school board policies or legislative mandates. Using specific examples, the Endowment plans to publish the results of the meetings' findings to serve as a practical guide for encouraging the increasing quality arts programs for all young people.[4]

THE NATIONAL ALLIANCE FOR ARTS EDUCATION

The National Alliance for Arts Education (AAE) was established in 1973 by the John F. Kennedy Center for the Performing Arts and the USOE under the leadership of Sidney Marland in cooperation with the DAMT (Dance, Art, Music, Theater) group. The alliance was created in response to the congressional mandate that the Kennedy Center, as a national symbol of excellence in the arts, become a vehicle and focal point for strengthening the arts in education at all levels. The purposes of AAE are to give young people access to the Kennedy Center as performers and as audience members, to make the center's performances and services available to people all over the country, and to help the center become a vehicle for strengthening the arts in education at the national, state, and local levels.

One of the ways in which the alliance carries out the congressional mandate is by encouraging representative leaders in the arts in each state to establish individual state Alliance for Arts Education committees. The broad goal of the state committees is to promote arts education within each state in order to make the arts an integral part of public elementary and secondary education.

FEDERALLY FUNDED MUSIC EDUCATION PROJECTS

A Catalyst for Change in Music Education was a series of projects and symposia designed to influence educational practices. Since changes on a national scale were difficult to implement, it was necessary to design projects and formulate recommendations that appealed to music educators. Change would be effected through individual music educators.

The Yale Seminar on Music Education took place at Yale University June 17–28, 1963. Its purpose was to consider the problems facing music education and to propose possible solutions. The initial impetus of the seminar was in the National Science Foundation (NSF), which had sponsored science curriculum development in the late 1950s, when the United States fell behind the Soviet Union in space technology. The success of NSF in science education was one of the factors that led President Kennedy to appoint the Panel on Educational Research and Development. Some of the panel members expressed reservations about the heavy emphasis on the sciences in the emerging school curriculum. They felt that a serious study of the arts and humanities would enhance excellence in science, and that students would be stronger in science if they were exposed to the view of human experience as seen through the arts. They believed this because so many successful scientists were also accomplished musicians. The panel recommended that the music curriculum from kindergarten through the twelfth grade be examined to discover why public school music programs had not produced a musically literate and active public. The panel's recommendations led to an award to Yale University by the U.S. Office of Education Cooperative Research Program for a seminar on music education. Claude V. Palisca, professor of musicology at Yale University, was director of the Yale Seminar. The participants included thirty-one musicians, scholars, and teachers who were concerned with the improvement of music education. They examined two areas of music education—music materials and musical performance—and made recommendations for improvement in both.

The Yale Seminar was highly critical of the quality of music used in school music programs and the lack of use of many kinds of music normally considered excellent. While recognizing the accomplishments of the music education profession in the area of performance, the seminar participants were also critical because performance skill development was too often used only for showmanship and other superficial musical experiences rather than for the aesthetic impact of great music. In general, the seminar participants found that the school music program had not kept pace with twentieth-century musical developments. Although many changes occurred after the Yale Seminar, it is unlikely that the seminar had major influence on music education practices. One reason for this is that few music educators participated in the seminar. The great majority of participants were musicologists and educators not involved with music education in the public schools. The value of the seminar was its contribution to a climate conducive to change, in which the music education profession could be free of the restraints of the traditional curriculum so serious consideration could be given to other modes of teaching.

The Juilliard Repertory Project was one of the tangible results of the Yale Seminar. Shortly after the conclusion of the seminar, Dean Gideon Waldrop of the Juilliard School of Music applied to the U.S. Office of Education for a grant to enable Juilliard to develop a large body of authentic and meaningful music to augment and enrich the repertory available to music teachers in the early grades. The grant was awarded and the project established in July 1964 under the direction of the composer Vittorio Giannini. Typical of the kind of bureaucratic decisions made by government agencies was the one to award this project to the Juilliard School of Music (one of the two music schools known to the president's science adviser who made the decision) shortly after the school had abandoned its program for the education of school music teachers.

The purpose of the project was to research and collect music of the highest quality that could be used for teaching music from kindergarten through sixth grade. The project planners kept in mind the Yale Seminar criticism of the quality of music literature used in music education. The repertory was compiled by three groups—research consultants (musicologists and ethnomusicologists), educational consultants (music educators), and testing consultants (public school elementary music teachers). Eminent musicologists and music educators participated in the project. The musicologists included Gustave Reese, Noah Greenberg, Claude Palisca, Paul Henry Lang, Alfred Wallenstein, Norman Dello Joio, and Nicholas England. The distinguished music educators involved were Allen P. Britton, Sally Monsour, Mary Ruth McCulley, and Louis G. Wersen.

Seven categories of music were recognized: pre-Renaissance, Renaissance, Baroque, classical, romantic, contemporary, and folk. More than four hundred compositions were field-tested in selected school systems in different parts of the country, and 230 vocal and instrumental works were included in the Juilliard Repertory Library. It was published by Canyon Press of Cincinnati.

The Juilliard Repertory Project satisfied the Yale Seminar requirement for high quality and authentic music for school music programs. Also in accordance with the seminar recommendations, it brought together scholars and teachers to upgrade music education. Despite the excellence of the music in the Juilliard Repertory Library and the availability of the collection, it did not find widespread acceptance among music educators. Possibly, this indicated that music educators were not searching for authentic music of high quality that represented various periods and genres for their programs. Had the project been done at a university or conservatory with a strong music education program, the collection might have become better known.

The Conference on Educational Media (1964) was another out-growth of the Yale Seminar. It was a cooperative venture with the Music Educators National Conference and the U.S. Office of Education. One delegate from each state and state supervisors of music were invited. The director was Edward Maltzman, and the USOE representative was Harold Arberg.

STATE POLICY ISSUES IN ARTS EDUCATION

Events in several states have adversely impacted arts education and led to "taxpayer revolts." The most well known of such events is the 1978 passage of Proposition 13 in California. California is one of many states that permit laws to be passed by public referendum. Proposition 13, authored by Howard Jarvis and Paul Genn, tied government spending to economic growth. Taxes had imposed such a heavy burden on California residents that they welcomed the opportunity, in the form of Proposition 13, to vote for an initiative that promised economic relief. Proposition 13 reduced property taxes, but it also drastically reduced the financial resources available to the state, county, and local governments. A result of Proposition 13 was the inability to maintain previous levels of such government services as police and fire protection, street and highway maintenance, parks and recreation, libraries, and education. The fiscal problem imposed in 1978 was felt in school districts throughout the state. Arts education, as well as other curricular areas, suffered. Teaching positions were eliminated, equipment could not be maintained and replaced as needed, and morale among educators plummeted.

Proposition 13 was followed by similar initiatives in at least twenty-five other states. The most severe for educators was Proposition 2 ½ in Massachusetts (1980). In 1979 Massachusetts imposed a property tax on its homeowners at nearly twice the national average. Proposition 2 ½ mandated that property taxes be limited to 2.5 percent of the assessed valuation of communities and that increases be limited to 2.5 percent thereafter. Communities could no longer afford to provide public services at the same level as before, and public works suffered. In the first year, 17,263 municipal employees were laid off across the state. The schools suffered even more than other public agencies because local school boards lost fiscal autonomy. They had previously been able to set their own budgets and impose the necessary tax levies to support their budgets, but Proposition 2 ½ gave municipal governments control of school budgets. School employees were laid off in great numbers throughout the state. At least seven hundred music teaching positions were eliminated, and in some communities, entire school music programs were lost. By the 1981–1982 school year, more than one out of five music teaching positions were gone. By the second year of Proposition

2 ½ more than 90 percent of the schools responding to a survey had made cuts in their music programs and 70 percent of the departments had been forced to reduce or eliminate some programs in the music curriculum.

Many of the losses suffered by music education programs across the country have been partially or completely restored, but it became obvious to educators that their programs are at the mercy of the economic system and the condition of the economy. In California, public concern for the quality of education led to the passage of the Hughes-Hart Educational Reform Act of 1983, which was probably the most massive piece of educational reform legislation ever created in the United States. Its purpose was to restore the resources to education necessary for the schools to provide education of high quality.

SOME RESPONSES TO DECLINING SUPPORT OF MUSIC EDUCATION

Alternative Sources of Funds have been sought by arts educators since it became apparent that traditional government support could no longer be relied upon. In California more than one hundred foundations raise money for public schools. A small part of the money is for arts education. Parents have raised money for their local school districts, and occasionally partnerships with business and industry have benefited arts programs, although the greatest part of such funds has gone to other uses in school systems.

Advocacy is another form of response to economic exigency. Advocacy is the means by which the needs of a specific cause (music education, in this case) are made known to the legislators who create laws affecting the cause, the government administrators who create policies to implement the laws, public boards that control education, and the electorate, which has ultimate control over public policy by means of the vote.

In 1966 the MENC established a public relations program under the direction of Joan Gaines. In the early 1970s the program was also directed toward advocacy. For a long time the MENC has provided to Congress information by means of testimony and other means about such matters as taxing musical instruments and copyright law. It has helped its members analyze public policy issues, and trained government relations leaders at the state level. The MENC state-affiliated units have become active in advocacy at the state level, and many have had significant success in maintaining or improving the condition of music programs.

An early example of advocacy for music education was in the form of crisis intervention. In 1972 the superintendent of schools in Chicago proposed to eliminate the music, art, and physical education programs because of funding problems. A strong advocacy campaign was put together with the help of Joan Gaines to retain music in the schools. It involved the Chicago Musicians Union, the area music dealers, the National Association of Music Merchants, the American Music Conference, the Chicago Orchestral Association, and *Down Beat* magazine. The campaign, called Save Our Music Education Citizens' Committee, was successful, and the music program was saved. A similar campaign was mounted in Memphis, Tennessee, when the entire elementary music program and orchestra program were threatened. Sixty percent of the elementary music program was saved, as was all of the orchestra program. Other crisis intervention campaigns have also met with success, but some have not.

Following the passage of Proposition 13, music education administrators in several parts of California joined together to strengthen the position of arts education in the state. They succeeded in having a fine arts requirement added to the secondary curriculum in many school districts and in persuading the University of California to recognize high school arts credits for admission. These successes strengthened the music programs in California schools.

The organizations of the DAMT group cooperated with the U.S. Office of Education and the Alliance for Arts Education of the Kennedy Center to conduct an ARTS ADVOCACY project in the spring of 1976. Leaders from five educational administration associations, including the Chief State School Officers and the National School Boards Association, were brought to the center, each for a weekend of performances and discussion.[5] Subsequently, the DAMT organizations cooperated to oversee an evaluation of all projects in the arts that had been granted any type of federal funding. The report, which appeared in 1979, was entitled *Try a New Face.*[6]

Arts for the Handicapped. The Joseph P. Kennedy Jr. Foundation supported a conference on arts education for the handicapped in 1974. From that meeting grew the National Committee for Arts for the Handicapped, of which Wendy Perks was the first director.

THE ROLE OF PRIVATE FOUNDATIONS

The Contemporary Music Project was a major project undertaken to help the music education profession modernize itself to serve contemporary societal needs. Through its publications and convention sessions, the MENC had been trying, without much success, to interest its members in using more twentieth-century music. At a dinner in New York, composer Norman Dello Joio and Vanett Lawler discussed the difficulty young composers had in having their works performed. Together they developed a plan to use the schools in this capacity. Since 1957 the

Ford Foundation had expressed interest in the relationship between the arts and American society, and Dello Joio was successful in getting the project funded by the foundation. In 1959 the foundation sponsored the Young Composers Project, which for five years was administered by the National Music Council. The purpose of the project was to place young composers (not over thirty-five years of age) in public school systems to serve as composers-in-residence for students. Twelve composers were placed during the first year of the project. By 1962, thirty-one composers had participated. The success of the project made obvious the benefits for composers and music students. Teachers and students who gained firsthand experience with contemporary music from their composers-in-residence were more receptive to new music, and the composers had a better understanding of the peculiarly American market for their work that the schools represented.

The success of the project persuaded the Ford Foundation to elevate its status from a pilot program to one of its ten major projects. The Music Educators National Conference wanted the project expanded so it could influence more music educators and submitted a proposal for it to include seminars and workshops on contemporary music in the schools and for pilot programs in public schools. In 1963 the Ford Foundation awarded a grant of $1.38 million to MENC to organize what was named the Contemporary Music Project for Creativity in Music Education (CMP). The Young Composers Project was continued as part of the CMP under the title Composers in Public Schools. By 1968, forty-six more composers had been placed in public school systems. The purposes of the CMP, as stated in the proposal accepted by the Ford Foundation, were to (1) increase the emphasis on the creative aspect of music in the public schools; (2) create a solid foundation or environment in the music education profession for the acceptance, through understanding, of the contemporary music idiom; (3) reduce the compartmentalization between the profession of music composition and music education for the benefit of composers and music educators alike; (4) cultivate taste and discrimination on the part of music educators and students regarding the quality of contemporary music used in schools; and (5) discover, when possible, creative talent among students.[7]

The CMP sponsored sixteen workshops and seminars at various colleges throughout the country to help teachers better understand contemporary music through analysis, performance, and pedagogy. There were also six pilot projects in elementary and secondary schools to provide authentic situations for the teaching of contemporary music. In 1965 the Seminar on Comprehensive Musicianship was held at Northwestern University to develop and implement ways to improve the education of music teachers, which was one of the most important functions of the CMP. The movement, known as *comprehensive musicianship*, developed from the seminar. The basic principles of comprehensive musicianship were established by the seminar, but methodology and materials remained to be developed. This was done at six regional Institutes for Music in Contemporary Education that conducted experimental programs in 36 educational institutions. Bernard Fitzgerald, Grant Beglarian, and Robert Werner served as directors of the project over the ten year period.

In 1968 the Ford Foundation granted the Music Educators National Conference $1.34 million to administer the Contemporary Music Project for five more years. MENC contributed $50,000 each year. From 1968 to 1973 the CMP consisted of three programs: Professionals-in-Residence to Communities, the Teaching of Comprehensive Musicianship, and Complementary Activities.

When the Comprehensive Music Project ended in 1973, its purpose, which was "to provide a synthesis, a focus, for disparate activities in music, in order to give them a cohesion and relevance in our society, to its cultural and educational institutions and organizations," had been largely fulfilled. The CMP had given direction, provided challenges, developed methodology and materials, and had made the music education profession more receptive to change and innovation.[8]

NOTES

1. Paul R. Lehman, "Federal Programs in Support of Music," *Music Educators Journal* 55 (September 1968): 53.
2. John Goodlad, et al., *The Changing School Curriculum* (New York: Fund for the Advancement of Education, 1966), p. 84.
3. IMPACT brought the arts education associations together in an unstructured organization referred to as DAMT (Dance, Art, Music, Theater).
4. Joe N. Prince (Artists in Education Program, NEA), and Geoffrey Platt, Jr. (National Assembly of State Arts agencies), memorandum to members of Alliance for Arts Education, April 18, 1984.
5. Alliance for Arts Education, *Arts Education Advocacy*. Contract No. 300–75–0133. John Mahlmann, Director.
6. *Try a New Face* (Washington: U.S. Office of Education, 1979).
7. "CMP in Perspective," *Music Educators Journal* 59 (May 1973): 34.
8. Michael L. Mark, *Contemporary Music Education*, 2d ed. (New York: Schirmer, 1986), pp. 35–40.

BIBLIOGRAPHY

Alliance for Arts Education. *Arts Education Advocacy*. USOE Contract No. 300-75-0133. John Mahlmann, Director.

Arts and Humanities Staff, USOE. *Try A New Face*. Charles L. Gary, Project Coordinator. Washington, DC: U.S. Government Printing Office, 1979.

The Arts Education for Americans Panel. *Coming to Our Senses*. New York: Mc-Graw-Hill, 1977.

Boyle, J. David, and Lathrop, Robert. "The IMPACT Experience: An Evaluation." *Music Educators Journal* 59 (January 1973).

Britton, Allen P. "Music: A New Start." *Britannica Review of American Education*, vol. 1. Chicago: Encyclopedia Britannica, 1969.

Eddy, Junius. *The Music Came from Deep Inside: A Story of Artists and Severely Handicapped Children*. New York: McGraw-Hill, 1982.

Fowler, Charles. *Can We Rescue the Arts for America's Children? Coming to Our Senses Ten Years Later*. New York: American Council on the Arts, 1988.

Goodlad, John, et al. *The Changing School Curriculum*. New York: The Fund for the Advancement of Education, 1966.

Lehman, Paul R. "Federal Programs in Support of Music." *Music Educators Journal* 60 (September 1968).

Mark, Michael L. *Contemporary Music Education*. Second edition. New York: Schirmer, 1986.

Prince, Joe N., and Platt, Geoffrey. Memorandum to members of Alliance for Arts Education, April 18, 1964.

Try a New Face. Washington, DC: U.S. Office of Education, 1979.

16

MUSIC EDUCATION SINCE MIDCENTURY

Music Education in the 1950s was quite similar to music education in the 1930s in content and method. Music had been an integral part of the school curriculum during the progressive education era. When progressive education ceased to be an organized movement in the 1950s, however, music, like the other curricular disciplines, lost a philosophical basis of support. Progressive education was not replaced by a new comprehensive philosophy, and so all of the disciplines found themselves with curricula partially suited to progressive education, whose philosophy was under question. Without the guidance of a comprehensive philosophy for American education, there was no new direction indicated for curriculum planners. Music education remained static, as did other disciplines. Society was evolving, and as change became more influential, it was critical that the school curriculum keep up. This could not be done, and the public began to lose confidence in the schools. Music educators, aware that they could not offer a 1930s curriculum in a time of fast and radical societal change, began to seek ways to modernize their offerings.

Without a comprehensive philosophy of education, curricular change affected each discipline differently. The various subject matter specialists developed their areas as they saw fit. The growth in various disciplines was uneven, as it was within disciplines. This was a step backward from the holistic approach to curriculum development of the progressive education movement, which perceived the entire curriculum as a single entity and each subject area an integral part of an overall educational pattern. It was natural that the problem of implementing immediate educational reform on a national scale would be approached by means of the subject matter itself rather than by the organizational structure of the educational system. It was impossible to consider meaningful reform on the national level because education is controlled at the state and local levels. National reform would require the consent and cooperation of thousands of educational decision making bodies. Instead, change was approached through curriculum development, which did not disturb the organizational framework of school systems.

The problems resulting from the fragmented approach to curriculum structure of the late 1950s and 1960s were apparent and pressing. The emerging technological society needed an educational system that could develop in young people the ability to perceive relationships, rather than absorb isolated fragments of knowledge if they were to cope with the almost overwhelming developments in all fields of knowledge. John Goodlad wrote:

> The curriculum and the students of tomorrow may be better served by subjects and subject combinations other than those deemed important today. But curriculum planning takes place in such a piecemeal fashion that across-the-board examination of the total school experience of children and youth is not likely to occur. In all probability, new accretions and formulations will occur in the traditional school subjects if the curriculum revision procedures of the past decade continue. But ongoing inquiry in fields not now firmly established in the curriculum is likely to go unnoticed unless we concentrate on the aims of schooling rather than on the organization of specific subjects.[1]

The conceptual approach to learning found favor among curriculum developers. The older method of imparting a body of facts to children no longer sufficed in an era of change, when the amount and kind of knowledge expanded at an ever-increasing pace. Now, it was virtually impossible to choose the data that would be meaningful to students in either the near or distant future. Instead, curriculum was organized by concepts, principles and modes of inquiry, thus making it possible for students to know how to learn what would be important for their individual needs. The ability to think inductively to resolve unfamiliar problems became the goal of curriculum planners for students.

The core curriculum, which had existed for some time, was emphasized in the late 1950s in response to the need. Language arts, social studies, and some areas of the humanities were treated as one subject, known as *core*. The core curriculum was widely adopted throughout the United States during the late 1950s, but by the middle of the 1960s it too had declined because of its many problems, especially the inadequate supply of teachers capable of mastering and synthesizing several subjects. Disciplinary autonomy has become firmly ingrained, and American education has continued to develop in a fragmented manner to the present.

Music Education developed and evolved during this period, but such activity was usually in individual music programs because there was no effective way to broaden the impact of innovation, when it appeared, on a small scale. The lack of a central philosophy of music education restricted the development of the profession. The history of music education since midcentury parallels that of other subjects, and it is only against the background of developments in general education that change in music education can be understood, measured, and evaluated.

Attitudes toward Music Education changed radically during the 1960s and 1970s. In 1975 the Council on Basic Education (CBE), an organization dedicated to the improvement of public education in those subjects it identifies as basic, finally added the arts to the list of subjects that it supports. The acceptance by CBE of the arts indicates the degree of impact of the changes of the 1960s and early 1970s.

AESTHETIC EDUCATION

One of the most critical needs of the music education profession at midcentury was a central unifying philosophy to replace the philosophical support of progressive education. In 1954 the Music Educators National Conference organized the Commission on Basic Concepts. The work of the commission resulted in a decision by the National Society for the Study of Education to devote its 1958 yearbook to music education. Articles by distinguished authors in disciplines related to music education were published in 1958 under the title *Basic Concepts in Music Education*.[2] *Basic Concepts* was the first attempt to publish guidelines for the development of a philosophy of music education. It included articles on various philosophical systems upon which American education is based and papers on subjects that can help in the development of a philosophy of music education. Allen Britton cited historical justification for music education and supported the use of music in schools for its own sake:

> Music, as one of the seven liberal arts, has formed an integral art of the educational systems of Western civilization from Hellenic times to the present. Thus, the position of music in education historically speaking, is one of great strength. Unfortunately, this fact seems to be one of which most educators, including music educators, remain unaware. As a result, the defense of music in the curriculum is often approached as if something new were being dealt with. Lacking the assurance which a knowledge of history could provide, many who seek to justify the present place of music in American schools tend to place too heavy a reliance upon ancillary values which music may certainly serve but which cannot, in the end, constitute its justification. Plato, of course, is the original offender in this regard,

and his general view that the essential value of music lies in its social usefulness seems to be as alive today as ever.[3]

Another book that had significance for music education philosophy was published in 1959—*Foundations and Principles of Music Education* by Charles Leonhard and Robert House. Both books are significant because they expose the music educator to aesthetics, the philosophical field devoted to examining the value of the arts. Both books provide support in articulating the foundational values of music education.[4]

Charles Leonhard wrote:

When we speak of a philosophy of music education, we refer to a system of basic beliefs which underlies and provides a basis for the operation of the musical enterprise in an educational setting. . . . The business of the school is to help young people undergo meaningful experience and arrive at a system of values that will be beneficial to society. . . . While reliance on statements of the instrumental value of music may well have convinced some reluctant administrator more fully to support the music program, those values cannot stand close scrutiny, because they are not directly related to music and are not unique to music. In fact, many other areas of the curriculum are in a position to make a more powerful contribution to these values than is music.[5]

Another influential writer on music education philosophy was Abraham Schwadron, who stated:

The *real* problems in contemporary music education which are daily concerns are to a considerable extent value-centered. We are coming to realize that a new or alternate approach is needed for the construction of value-oriented curricular designs. The context of this emerging curriculum will focus on issues relevant to the nature of music and to the lives of the students. It will lead students to ask fundamental questions, to engage in intriguing musical activities, and to seek answers based on personal reflection, inquiry, discovery, and research; it will help them formulate their values of music on both logical and introspective levels. . . .

It seems very odd that the why of music has been investigated by those like Dewey, Mursell, Langer, and Meyer and yet categorically avoided by those directly responsible for daily musical instruction.[6]

Each of these writers encouraged music educators to teach music for its own value to enrich the lives of their students. The evolution toward aesthetic education was described by Bennett Reimer: "If music education in the present era could be characterized by a single, overriding purpose, one would have to say this field is trying to become 'aesthetic education.' What is needed in order to fulfill this purpose is a philosophy which shows how and why music education is aesthetic in its nature and its value."[7]

CONCEPTUAL LEARNING

At the same time that aesthetic education was beginning to influence music education philosophy, another viewpoint, conceptual learning, appeared. It had direct influence on the music curriculum. Before the 1960s the process of education used a variety of approaches to rote learning. Children were usually expected to memorize specific information from both the teacher and books. Educators thought that children developed understanding of a subject after learning its basic factual content. Jerome Bruner's book *The Process of Education*[8] was an important basis for curriculum development in all subject areas and influenced instructional practices in American schools. *The Process of Education* encompassed four themes related to teaching and learning: (1) the role of structure in learning and how it can be made central in teaching; (2) readiness for learning; (3) intuition; and (4) the desire to learn and how the desire can be stimulated.

The impact of Bruner's work, as well as that of other psychologists, on curriculum development was profound. Music educators studied the implications of conceptual learning, developed new ideas about teaching and learning music, and developed new practices and curricular materials. Getz described the influence of conceptual learning on music education:

> One of the greatest changes for better music teaching was the gradual acceptance by general music teachers of the concept approach, as compared to previous efforts, which were often more concerned with associative properties of music. Instead of emphasizing story-telling through program music and correlating music with geography, social studies, mathematics, and science, the heart of music education has become the study of music itself, the components of pitch, duration, dynamics, and timbre, and the resultant concomitants such as melody, harmony, rhythm, instrumentation, style, and form.[9]

One of the most important publications to relate conceptual learning practices to music education was *The Study of Music in the Elementary School—A Conceptual Approach*.[10] The book offered ideas to assist children in developing musical concepts that would permit them to discover the structure and meaning of musical works. An important contribution of the book was its discussion of concepts about rhythm, melody, harmony, form in music, forms of music, tempo, dynamics, and tone color. It also related conceptual learning of music to the general music and instrumental music programs, and is of special significance because it was developed by a group of practicing music educators (see Chapter 13).

NEW APPROACHES TO THE MUSIC CURRICULUM

During the 1960s, several new music curricula were introduced. Although they incorporated conceptual learning materials, techniques, and practices, they did not develop as a result of the new emphasis on conceptual education. Several were imported from other countries, where they had proved their success. Being compatible with the new conceptual learning movement, they fit well into American education.

Eurhythmics, or the Dalcroze Method, was based on the work of Emile Jaques-Dalcroze (1865–1950), a Swiss musician who stressed the importance of training what he called the musical faculties, as opposed to the common practice of his time of teaching technique but not emphasizing musicality. Eurhythmics came to the United States early in the twentieth century, and derivative ideas from it were incorporated in graded series such as Mabelle Glenn's *World of Music*.

Dalcroze studied at the Conservatoire of Music in Geneva, in Paris under Leo Delibes, and in Vienna under Bruckner and Fuchs. In 1892 he was appointed professor of harmony at the Geneva Conservatoire. To Dalcroze, the musicality of the individual was the basis for specialized musical study. His method emphasized tone and rhythm, using movement to express musical interpretation. Dalcroze was originally interested in training musicians, and was one of the first musicians to study the new science of psychology. He studied with his friend, the psychologist Edouard Claparede, who recognized the potential of the Dalcroze method in teaching children. Dalcroze wrote:

> It is true that I first devised my method as a musician for musicians. But the further I carried my experiments, the more I noticed that, while a method intended to develop the sense for rhythm, and indeed based on such development, is of great importance in the education of a musician, its chief value lies in the fact that it trains the powers of apperception and of expression in the individual and renders easier the externalization of natural emotions. Experience teaches me that a man is not ready for the specialized study of an art until his character is formed, and his powers of expression developed.[11]

In 1906 Dalcroze presented his first training course for teachers. It was repeated several times until 1909, when the first diploma was awarded. He considered it necessary to grant diplomas to his students because his method was used in other parts of the world by people whom he did not train and whose standards he felt were not equal to those of his own students.

Although the Dalcroze method has not become part of the American music curriculum, many American teachers have studied it, and some have earned diplomas. The philosophy of the method and many of its techniques have been incorporated into other methods and have contributed to American music education in that way. Hoffer wrote:

> The use of "walking" and "running" as designations for quarter and eighth notes is one common example in the elementary schools. By the 1930s a number of college music schools or physical education departments were requiring courses in *eurhythmics*, the term often used for Dalcroze-like instruction.[12]

Interest in the Dalcroze method leveled at that time, although there was a modest renewal of interest in the 1970s. Dalcroze instruction is now offered in about twenty colleges, four of which award Dalcroze certificates.

The Orff Approach of the composer Carl Orff (1895–1982) is based on his interest in folk song, nineteenth-century popular song, dance and theater music, and medieval, Baroque, and Renaissance music. In Munich, during the early days of his career, Orff was influenced by the dance-movement theories (eurhythmics) of Emile Jaques-Dalcroze. In 1924 Orff and the dancer Dorothea Gunther founded the Gunther Schule, an innovative ensemble of dancers and musicians that developed and trained teachers in new forms of movement and rhythm. Improvisation was a major part of the program of the Gunther Schule. Many of the students at the Gunther Schule were preparing to be physical education teachers. Orff's goal was to develop creativity in his students by means of Jaques-Dalcroze's principles.

Assisted by Curt Sachs and Karl Maendler, Orff developed an instrumental ensemble at the Gunther Schule, which he described as follows:

> In due course the Gunther school boasted an ensemble of dancers with an orchestra of their own. Music and choreography were supervised by Gunild Keetman and Maja Lex, respectively. Dancers and players were interchangeable. Suitable instruments (flutes, cymbals, drums, etc.) were integrated into the dance itself. The diverse and varied instruments employed included recorders, xylophones, and metallophones of all ranges, glockenspiels, kettledrums, small drums, tomtoms, gongs, various kinds of cymbols, triangles, tone bells; and sometimes also fiddles, gambas, spinettinos, and portatives.[13]

The ensemble traveled throughout Germany, playing for educational conferences and teachers' meetings and generating interest in the work of the Gunther Schule. World War II, however, interrupted plans to test the Orff-Gunther approach on a larger scale in German schools.

The Gunther Schule was destroyed during the war. After the war, a Bavarian radio official discovered an out-of-print recording from the Gunther Schule. His interest in the record led to the gradual rekindling of national interest in Orff's work. When Orff reflected on the method that he had developed before the war, he considered that rhythm education might be more effective with young children than with adults. Exploring the idea, he concluded that elemental (primeval or basic) music evolving from speech, movement, and dance could become the basis of early childhood music education. He and Gunild Keetman, his lifelong associate, began to test the idea in nursery schools and kindergartens.

A radio broadcast series in 1948, in which children performed elemental music on a small set of Orff instruments brought widespread interest in music that appealed to many children. Klaus Becker learned to reconstruct the Orff instruments and in 1949 opened a workshop, Studio 49, to build and improve them. Between 1950 and 1954, Orff published his five-volume *Music for Children*, a compilation and complete reworking of this prewar work. The method was called *Schulwerk*. It attracted international interest. The books were translated into eighteen languages, and the exercises were adapted to the native rhythms and music of the countries that imported Orff's techniques. The American (actually Canadian) adaptation by Doreen Hall and Arnold Walter consists of five volumes and a teacher's edition. It corresponds to the original Schulwerk in progression of subject matter, but the music was selected or written especially for English-speaking children.

The Orff approach was adopted in private and public schools throughout the United States. The American Orff-Schulwerk Association was founded in 1963 at Ball State University, Muncie, Indiana, to promote the dissemination of information about the Schulwerk and its uses in the United States through its publication, *Orff Echo*, and through workshops.

The Kodály Method of Hungarian composer Zoltán Kodály (1882–1967) reflects his belief that:

> Hungarian music education should be designed to teach the spirit of singing to everyone, to educate all to be musically literate, to bring music into every day use in homes and in leisure activities, and to educate concert audiences.

Kodály was concerned with the creative, humanizing enrichment of life through music and regarded the goal of music literacy for everyone as the first step toward his ideal.[14] He also desired to build a national music culture through his approach to teaching music in the schools, using nationalistic and folk songs. He was concerned that twentieth-century

Hungarian life was not as musical as that of the nineteenth century, when music was a part of everyday life. Society had lost its ability to stimulate musicality in individuals, and Kodály felt that the schools must remedy the situation. His pedagogical system was created to help the schools reawaken the musicality of the Hungarian people.

Kodály's method was adapted for use in the United States by several people, including Tibor Bachmann, Lois Choksy, Mary Helen Richards, and Denise Bacon. American music educators learned the method from numerous writings, workshops, and a variety of programs offered by colleges and specialized schools and from studying in Hungary. The Organization of American Kodály Educators (OAKE) was formed in 1974 to support Kodály education in the United States and to act as a catalyst for its growth and development. Its official journal is *The Kodály Envoy*. Ih 1984, OAKE became an associated organization of the Music Educators National Conference.

The three European methods found a place in American schools in the 1960 and 1970s through the process of adaption, rather than being adopted intact because the conditions of American education are different than those of the countries from which they came. Given the different conditions, such as having infrequent or irregular meetings of music classes or teachers being trained to offer a traditional curriculum, it was natural that music educators would seek the best parts of the methods and adapt them for use in their own curricula. The most attractive elements of Orff and Kodály, and to some extent Dalcroze, found their way into the eclectic American music curriculum and enriched it. Some American schools have also implemented the imported curricula in a relatively pure form.

The Suzuki Method was another imported curriculum that influenced American music education. Shinichi Suzuki was born Japan in 1898, the son of the owner of the first violin factory in that country. He learned about violin design and construction while working there. Suzuki's musical training began in Japan and later included eight years of study with Karl Klinger in Berlin. In Matsumoto, Suzuki had adopted a young orphan boy, to whom he taught the the violin. His success lead to the development of his method, called *talent education*. He called his method the "mother-tongue method." It is based on psycholinguistic development. Suzuki, aware that children learn their native language easily and naturally while adults do so only with great difficulty, realized the potential of young children to learn much more than they are normally taught. If children have the ability to master something as challenging as a language, the same ability must also allow them to master many other kinds of knowledge and skills if presented in the same manner as the mother-tongue—observation, imitation, repetition, and gradual development of intellectual awareness.

The American introduction to talent education occurred in 1958, when a film of 750 Japanese children playing the Bach *Concerto for Two Violins* was presented at a meeting of the American String Teachers Association at Oberlin College. Teachers at the meeting were so impressed that they sent a representative, John Kendall, to Japan to observe the method as practiced by Suzuki. Kendall went to Japan in 1959 and again in 1962 to continue his study of the method. In 1964 Suzuki and ten children traveled to the United States and performed at the Music Educators National Conference convention in Philadelphia and other places. The performances were a revelation to the American teachers, who did not know that young children had the potential to play so well. Four- and five-year-old Japanese children played music of professional caliber, while American children usually did not begin to study the violin until age nine or ten.

After the 1964 convention, talent education began to develop in the United States. Like the European methods, cultural differences prevented a wholesale adoption. Several American string educators, including John Kendall, Paul Rolland, and Tibor Zelig, developed solutions to problems that arose in adapting the method and developed their own successful Suzuki programs. Since then, Suzuki programs have found their way into some public schools and numerous private schools featuring Suzuki instruction have opened in all parts of the country.

Comprehensive Musicianship was an American development to improve the music curriculum by relating various aspects of music usually studied separately. Music history and theory, for example, are often taught as separate subjects, and some students have difficulty relating the two. A fragmented view of music often prevents students from developing insights necessary for true musical understanding. The integrated study of music was seen as the means to prevent fragmentation of musical knowledge and understanding.

The Contemporary Music Project was the catalyst for comprehensive musicianship. In 1965 CMP sponsored the four day "Seminar on Comprehensive Musicianship—the Foundation for College Education in Music" at Northwestern University. The participants, including scholars, educators, theorists, composers, historians, and performers, examined the content and orientation of basic college music courses in history and theory. The seminar resulted in six Institutes for Music in Contemporary Education (IMCE). Their purpose was to implement comprehensive musicianship as formulated at the Northwestern University seminar.

The realization of comprehensive musicianship in schools was slow and gradual. Relatively few colleges instituted comprehensive musicianship programs. More impact was felt in elementary and secondary schools, where performing ensembles were often exposed to comprehensive musicianship concepts and practices in an effort to counter the Yale Seminar criticism that performance-oriented music programs often did little to increase the musicality and musical appreciation of the individual musician. Traditionally. American school performance ensembles have had no formal curriculum. The music played by a group has usually served as the curriculum. The problem was described by R. Jack Mercer:

> There are few band curricula that take the student through the basics of music theory and history. Instead, scores are selected to meet the requirements of the next performance, and the curriculum is the score. Consequently, the content of the course of study is fortuitous, depending almost entirely upon whether it is football season or concert season. . . . The goal of musical training is to present a polished musical performance.[15]

The solution to the problem was in the music used by performing ensembles. It was the basis for broader musical learning, including analysis, theory, and historical information. This approach required much preparation by directors, and rehearsals became combinations of rehearsal, class, and laboratory.

Comprehensive musicianship was also applied to general music classes because the experiences children had in those classes were often too narrow to permit them to develop musical concepts and knowledge that could be transferred to various styles of music. General music students did not have in-depth performance experiences that validated the conceptual knowledge developed in class. Frequently, the curriculum was often based on the unit approach, which usually addressed such nonmusical topics as the lives of composers or plots of Broadway shows.

The Hawaii Music Curriculum Program, which began in 1968 under the sponsorship of the Hawaii Curriculum Center in Honolulu, was established "to create a logical, continuous educational program ensuring the competent guidance of the music education of all children in the state's public schools and to test and assemble the materials needed by schools to realize this program."[16] The program was designed to implement comprehensive musicianship concepts and practices in the public school music program. The term "comprehensive" in the context of this program meant that students were to be involved with music in school in the same ways that people are involved with it in the outside world because the school should be a microcosm of the outside world. The book *Comprehensive Musicianship Through Classroom Music*,[17] which resulted from the Hawaii Music Curriculum Program, was influential in imparting comprehensive musicianship concepts through the general music class.

The Manhattanville Music Curriculum Program (MMCP) was even more influential in developing comprehensive musicianship in school music programs. The premise of the Manhattanville curriculum is summarized in a statement by its creator, Ronald Thomas:

> If music is an expressive medium, learning involves expressing. If it is a creative art, learning means creating. If music has meaning, personal judgments are fundamental to the learning process. If music is a communicative art, the educational process must involve students in communication. Facts may be taught, but meaning is discovered. There is nothing antecedent to discovering meaning.[18]

The MMCP, funded by a grant from the U.S. Office of Education, was named for Manhattanville College, where it originated. Its objectives were to develop a music curriculum and related materials for a sequential music learning program for the primary grades through high school. MMCP was used in some schools, but the most common usage was the adaptation of its concepts and strategies for use in traditional music programs.

OTHER INFLUENCES IN MUSIC EDUCATION

Curricular influences were not the only catalysts for change in music education from the 1960s on. Others included new musical materials, the impact of technology, more realistic recognition of cultural differences between students, and students with special needs.

New Musical Materials began to influence music education as a result of the youth generation of the 1960s. Popular music and jazz had long been a peripheral part of the music program, but they had never found full acceptance among music educators because they were not considered respectable enough to be a regular part of the music program. While this was true in predominantly white schools, and in early integrated ones until after the Tanglewood Symposium, it was obviously not the case in predominantly black institutions. In 1928 James (better known as Jimmie) Lunceford was the music teacher and athletic director at Manassa High School in Memphis. That year he took ten of his students to play a summer job in Buffalo, which was the start of one of the great Big Bands.[19] Louis Armstrong's introduction to the trumpet in a New Orleans orphanage is well known. Other jazzmen had public school experience before joining professional bands. Milt Hinton (born 1910) learned the violin from his father but played bass, the instrument on which he earned his fame, in a Chicago high school. Charlie Parker (born 1920) played the saxophone in a Kansas City school.[20] James P. Johnson played ragtime piano with an amateur theatrical group in P.S. 69 in New York City.[21] By the 1950s, the dance band was a common extracurricular activity in many schools, and general music teachers often included units on jazz and Broadway music. No special importance was assigned to the music. It was a part of American life and was rarely examined in an academic setting.

Changes in American society in the 1960s persuaded many educators that the popular arts have a legitimate place in American education. The confrontational and sometimes violent protest tactics of the 1960s brought many changes to American culture, one of which was increased permissiveness toward the younger generation and acceptance of its taste in clothing, music, and other aspects of life-style. This affected the general academic atmosphere of music as well as other programs. For example, minicourses in many areas of interest were introduced. In general, Americans became increasingly aware of individual personal value in relation to school and society. Colleges that may or may not have recognized the popular arts earlier began to develop degree programs in jazz. Secondary schools that had previously offered elective courses only in music appreciation developed interest courses in jazz, rock, and other areas of music.

The Tanglewood Symposium supported the use of popular musics in the curriculum by recognizing the value of all kinds of music. The participants agreed that it is neither possible nor appropriate to recognize a hierarchy of kinds of music. The symposium stated, ''The music repertory should be expanded to involve music of our time in its rich variety, including currently popular teenage music.'' This opened the way for an infusion of popular musics in the curriculum, and many music educators began to adopt these musics.

The National Association of Jazz Educators (NAJE) was established in 1968 and accepted as an associated organization of MENC. Some of the founders were Stan Kenton, Louis Wersen, John Roberts, and Charles Gary. All had participated in the Tanglewood Symposium and saw NAJE as a means of implementing its recommendations. The affiliation was all but inevitable because the purpose of NAJE was ''to further the understanding and appreciation of jazz and popular music, and to promote its artistic performance.''[22]

Rock was also brought into the schools, but music teachers were less familiar with it than with jazz. The Youth Music Institute was held at the University of Wisconsin in summer 1969 to bring together rock-oriented young people and music teachers to communicate about rock music and music education. It was organized by Emmett Sarig, a participant in the Tanglewood Symposium, and sponsored by MENC, the U.S. Office of Education, and the Extension Music Department of the University of Wisconsin. The institute helped many music educators become more knowledgeable of the youth culture and of rock music.

The movement toward popular musics was summarized by David McAllester:

We affirm that it is our duty to seek true musical communication with the great masses of our population. While we continue to develop and make available, to all who are interested, the great musics of the middle class and aristocracy, we must also learn the language of the great musical arts which we have labeled "base" because they are popular. . . . When we have learned that any musical expression is "music," we hope to be able to reduce the class barriers in our schools and our concert halls. The resulting enrichment of our music will, we hope, give it a new vitality at all levels, and provide a united voice that can speak, without sham, of our democratic ideals.[23]

TECHNOLOGY AND MUSIC EDUCATION

By 1970 the United States had become a truly technological society, and the then-current generation of music students considered technology a normal part of the environment. The Tanglewood Symposium supported electronic music in the schools, as it did popular musics: "Music of all periods, styles, forms, and cultures belongs in the curriculum. The musical repertory should be expanded to involve music of our time in its rich variety, including . . . avant-garde music."[24]

Electronic Music had begun to find its way into school music education programs during the late 1960s. Only a few colleges offered courses in electronic music, and they dealt with composition, theory, and the techniques of musique concrete. The few music education courses in electronic music were usually limited to summer workshops. The cost of an electronic music studio was prohibitive for most educational institutions. Few music educators had the opportunity to learn much about the subject.

At first, electronic music was treated as music literature through the study of composed pieces. It had little relevance for the schools. A breakthrough came in 1967, when the Pilot Electronic Project (PEP) was established in eighteen schools in Connecticut by the state department of education. Funds were provided by Title III of the Elementary and Secondary Education Act. The project provided a medium of creativity for students. Curricula were established with the assistance of such consultants as Ussachevsky and Babbit. At the same time, synthesizers suitable for schools were being invented. The Electrocomp 200 was developed in response to the needs of the Connecticut schools. After that, as the prices of electronic equipment fell, schools in many parts of the country began to set up electronic music studios, some with complex collections of sophisticated equipment. Synthesizers became more readily available to the public, and at much lower prices. They were no longer considered exotic and lost some of their appeal in school programs. They continued to influence music education, though, as the

direction of electronic music programs shifted to become more functional in the curriculum. Some teachers used synthesizers to teach form
and analysis, theory, acoustics, and keyboard techniques without exploring the innovative electronic music aspect of the instrument. In
other cases, synthesizers were used for performance purposes with
stage bands, to accompany instrumentalists and singers, and in synthe-
sizer ensembles.

Computers also affected music education. One of the most common
usages was Computer Assisted Instruction (CAI). In music, as in other
areas of education, CAI was used to present material to students in a
manner that requires students to interact with the computer. A body of
material is presented, and the student selects the appropriate response
in order to progress to new material or to review material not yet
learned. CAI was used in elementary and secondary schools to assist
students in developing aural skills and to study musical form, theory,
and history.

The National Consortium for Computer-Based Music Instruction
(NCCBMI) was founded in 1973 to assist educators who use computers
in music instruction by providing materials, consultation, and a forum
for the exchange of ideas.

OTHER INFLUENCES ON MUSIC EDUCATION

Urban Schools had been examples of excellence in music education.
After midcentury, however, due to a variety of sociological factors, urban education suffered setbacks, and the quality of general education
and music education suffered. The problems of urban schools, especially those in the inner city, came to the attention of the federal government in the early 1960s, but the numerous attempts to improve them
met with little success. The quality of life in those parts of American
cities had deteriorated to the point where the schools could only reflect
those conditions. Such problems as drugs, teen pregnancy, and crime
were of such magnitude that the schools could do little to help improve
life in the inner cities. As late as the 1950s city schools were spending
about the same on a per-pupil basis as suburban schools. By 1962 cities
were spending an average of $145 less per pupil. This reflected the
growing disparity between the economic situation of the cities and the
suburbs. To make matters worse, the formulas by which state support
of education was determined favored the suburbs, which at that time
received an average of forty dollars more per pupil than the cities.[25]

Music in Inner-City Schools has been strong historically, although it
has suffered when budgets have been insufficient to maintain all school
programs. The Tanglewood Symposium Committee on Critical Issues

discussed the lack of relevant preparation of music teachers in inner-city areas. Recommendations were made for improvement of teacher education. One of the major problems is lack of appropriate education for students who plan to become inner-city music teachers. In many cases, colleges have prepared music educators to teach in all kinds of schools with little attention to the special problems of those in the city.

Before the social revolution of the 1960s, music in urban schools had not been appreciably different from that in other kinds of school systems. It consisted of the same performing and general music experiences that constituted most music programs and utilized the same materials. Although this was still the case in many places, in the late 1960s and early 1970s greater emphasis began to be placed on music that reflected minority cultures. In effect, music was taught for the attainment of a sociological goal—the awakening of self-awareness and development of self-pride through music. Wiley Housewright, president of the MENC, spoke of the use of a variety of musics:

> There is much to be gained from the study of any musical creation. Rock, soul, blues, folk, and jazz cannot be ignored. To delimit concert halls, schools, and colleges to a steady diet of the ''masters'' is as absurd as permitting only Euripides, Shakespeare, and Moliere to be performed in the theater. Music education must encompass all music. If student musical attitudes are to be affected by music education, the music teacher's openness to new music serves as a necessary model. The Music Educators National Conference through its Tanglewood Declaration not only accepts rock and other present-day music as legitimate, but sanctions its use in education.[26]

Housewright's statement reflected the changing attitude of music educators toward the uses of various kinds on music in school programs. The literature of many urban music programs changed in the late 1960s to ethnic, rock, pop, and jazz. The shift from Western art music was helpful to people who wished to learn more about themselves. These kinds of music are now commonly found in elementary basal series, general music texts, and in the music literature of school performance ensembles of all types. It is also not unusual to find in urban schools African, Hispanic, and other ethnic instrumental and vocal ensembles.

Music in Special Education has been of interest to music educators since Lowell Mason taught at the Perkins School for the Blind in Boston. The term ''special education'' refers to the process of educating exceptional children that is different from the process of educating normal children. Most well-developed programs of music education in larger school systems have provided music teachers for schools for handicapped children, as have state schools for the handicapped. Music in special education has developed significantly in American schools since midcentury and has been assisted greatly by the relatively new discipline of music therapy. Exceptional children include those whose abilities, because of physical, mental, or emotional abnormalities, deviate sufficiently from those of normal children to require special or modified educational experiences. They are intellectually gifted, emotionally disturbed, physically handicapped, and those who for unknown reasons achieve less than might reasonably be expected of normal children.

Various efforts in teaching music to handicapped students have been documented. Music for the deaf, both as a subject of study and as a diagnostic tool, is described by Solomon.[27] Heller and Darrow provide further documentation about historical music education programs for the deaf.[28] A performance by mentally retarded children under the direction of Richard Weber at the 1964 Philadelphia convention opened a new world for many music educators. Yet it was ten years before organized attention was paid to music instruction for retarded students on a widespread basis.

Public Law 94-142, passed in 1975, guarantees the rights of exceptional children. Since that time, those children have been legally entitled to a free public education with full educational opportunities. Music educators have devised numerous strategies to work with special students, and college music education programs usually include components on music in special education. Many states now require such courses for teacher certification.

SUMMARY

The recent past has seen the complexion of music education change in many ways. Attention to the teaching of music for aesthetic reasons has increased dramatically. New approaches to learning music, imported from other countries, have found devoted followers in the United States. A general loosening of the approach to music in the schools has characterized the period, but there has been no diminution in the quality of performance of the outstanding school ensembles. Music educators have become involved with utilizing the new equipment provided by electronic technology. The concern over the great body of secondary school students who are not affected by the music program continues.

NOTES

1. John I. Goodlad, *The Changing School Curriculum* (New York: Fund for the Advancement of Education, 1966), pp. 14–16.
2. Nelson B. Henry, ed., *Basic Concepts in Music Education*, Fifty-seventh Year-

book of the National Society for the Study of Education, pt. 1 (Chicago: University of Chicago Press, 1958).

3. Allen Britton, "Music in Early American Public Education: A Historical Critique," in *Basic Concepts in Music Education*, p. 195.

4. Bennett Reimer, "Music Education Aesthetic Education: Past and Present," *Music Educators Journal* 75 (February 1989): 22–24.

5. Charles Leonhard, "The Philosophy of Music Education—Present and Future," *Comprehensive Musicianship: The Foundation for College Education in Music* (Washington, DC: Music Educators National Conference, 1965), pp. 42–43, 45.

6. Abraham A. Schwadron, "Philosophy in Music Education: Pure or Applied Research?," *Bulletin of the Council for Research in Music Education* 19 (Winter 1970): 26.

7. Bennett Reimer, *A Philosophy of Music Education* (Englewood Cliffs, NJ: Prentice-Hall, 1970), p. 2.

8. Jerome S. Bruner, *The Process of Education* (Cambridge, MA: Harvard University Press, 1960), p. 3.

9. Russell P. Getz, "Music Education in Tomorrow's Schools: A Practical Approach," *The Future of Music Education in America* (Rochester, NY: Eastman School of Music Press, 1984), pp. 24, 25.

10. Charles L. Gary, ed., *The Study of Music in the Elementary School—A Conceptual Approach* (Washington, DC: Music Educators National Conference, 1967).

11. M. E. Sadler, in Émile Jaques-Dalcroze, *The Eurythmics* (Boston: Small Maynard, 1915), p. 32.

12. Charles R. Hoffer, *Introduction to Music Education* (Belmont, CA: Wadsworth, 1983), p. 123.

13. Beth Landis and Polly Carder, *The Eclectic Curriculum in American Music Education: Contributions of Dalcroze, Kodály, and Orff* (Washington, DC: Music Educators National Conference, 1972), p. 156.

14. Lorraine Edwards, "The Great Animating Stream of Music," *Music Educators Journal* 57 (February 1971): 38–39.

15. R. Jack Mercer, "Is the Curriculum the Score—or More?," *Music Educators Journal* 58 (February 1972): 51–53.

16. William Thomson, "Music Rides a Wave of Reform in Hawaii," *Music Educators Journal* 56 (May 1970): 73.

17. William Thomson, *Comprehensive Musicianship Through Classroom Music* (Belmont, CA: Addison-Wesley, 1974).

18. Ronald B. Thomas, "Rethinking the Curriculum," *Music Educators Journal* 56 (February 1970): 70.

19. Liner notes, "Jimmie Lunceford," *Big Band Series* (Chicago: Time-Life Music, 1986).

20. Carlo Bohländer and Karl Heinz Holler, *Reclam's Jazz Fuhrer* (Stuttgart: Reclam, 1970), pp. 314, 502.

21. M. E. Hall, "Jazz," *The Encyclopedia of Education* (New York: Macmillan, 1971), pp. 459–62.

22. John T. Roberts, "MENC's Associated Organizations: NAJE," *Music Educators Journal* 55 (March 1969): 44–46.

23. David McAllester, "Curriculum Must Assume a Place at the Center of Music," *Documentary Report of the Tanglewood Symposium*, (Washington, DC: Music Educators National Conference, 1968), p. 138.

24. The Tanglewood Declaration, article 2 (Washington, DC: Music Educators National Conference, 1968), p. 139.
25. "The Widening Gap in Quality," *Carnegie Quarterly* 14 (Fall 1966), quoted in *New Trends in the Schools*, ed. William P. Lineberry (New York: Wilson, 1967), p. 24.
26. Wiley L. Housewright, "Youth Music in Education," *Music Educators Journal* 56 (November 1969): 45.
27. Alan L. Solomon, "Music in Special Education Before 1930: Hearing and Speech Development," *Journal of Research in Music Education* 28 (Winter 1980): 236–49.
28. Alice-Ann Darrow and George N. Heller, "Early Advocates of Music Education for the Hearing Impaired: William Wolcott Turner and David Ely Bartlett," *Journal of Research in Music Education* 33 (Winter 1985): 269–79.

BIBLIOGRAPHY

Bruner, Jerome S. *The Process of Education*. Cambridge, MA: Harvard University Press, 1960.

"CMP in Perspective." *Music Educators Journal* 59 (May 1973).

Darrow, Alice-Ann, and Heller, George N., "Early Advocates of Music Education for the Hearing Impaired: William Wolcott Turner and David Ely Bartlett." *Journal of Research in Music Education* 33 (Winter 1985).

Edwards, Lorraine. "The Great Animating Stream of Music." *Music Educators Journal* 57 (February 1971).

Gary, Charles L., ed. *The Study of Music in the Elementary School—A Conceptual Approach*. Washington, DC: Music Educators National Conference, 1967.

———. "Why Music Education? NASSP *Bulletin*. Reston, VA: National Association of Secondary School Principals, 1975.

Getz, Russell P. "Music Education in Tomorrow's Schools: A Practical Approach." *The Future of Music Education in America*. Rochester, NY: Eastman School of Music Press, 1984.

Goodlad, John I. *The Changing School Curriculum*. New York: Fund for the Advancement of Education, 1966.

Henry, Nelson B., ed. *Basic Concepts in Music Education*, Fifty-seventh Yearbook of the National Society for the Study of Education, pt. 1. Chicago: University of Chicago Press, 1958.

Hodsell, Frank. *Toward Civilization*. Washington, DC: National Endowment for the Arts, 1988.

Housewright, Wiley L. "Youth Music in Education." *Music Educators Journal* 56 (November 1969).

Kirk, Andy. *Twenty Years on Wheels*. Ann Arbor: The University of Michigan Press, 1987.

Landis, Beth, and Carder, Polly. *The Eclectic Curriculum in American Music Education: Contributions of Dalcroze, Kodály, and Orff*. Washington, DC: Music Educators National Conference, 1972.

Leonhard, Charles. "The Philosophy of Music Education—Present and Future." *Comprehensive Musicianship: The Foundation for College Education in Music.* Washington, DC: Music Educators National Conference, 1965.

Liner notes, "Jimmie Lunceford," *Big Band Series.* Chicago: Time-Life Music, 1986.

Madeja, Stanley, ed. *Arts and Aesthetics: An Agenda for the Future.* Saint Louis: CEMREL, 1977.

Mercer, R. Jack. "Is the Curriculum the Score—or More?" *Music Educators Journal* 57 (February 1972).

Reimer, Bennett. "Music Education Aesthetic Education: Past and Present." *Music Educators Journal* 75 (February 1989).

Sadler, M.E., in Émile Jaques-Dalcroze, *The Eurythmics.* Boston: Small Maynard, 1915.

Solomon, Alan L. "Music in Special Education before 1930: Hearing and Speech Development." *Journal of Research in Music Education* 28 (Winter 1980).

Thomson, William. *Comprehensive Musicianship Through Classroom Music.* Belmont, CA: Addison-Wesley, 1974.

——. "Music Rides a Wave of Reform in Hawaii." *Music Educators Journal* 56 (May 1970).

17

REFLECTIONS

Teachers as Musicians. In tracing the long development of music education to the present, a few recurring themes can be observed. One of the more interesting has to do with the relationship of teachers, all teachers, to music. As graduates of medieval German universities, new teachers were expected to begin their teaching careers by lecturing on music. After doing that successfully, they were permitted to deal with the other liberal arts. Incompetence in treating music disqualified candidates for the teaching profession. It is hardly surprising that the German priest Martin Luther wanted all teachers to be musicians. Since music was the principal subject taught by the Spanish priests in the mission schools of the American West, it is likely that they were all musicians too.

Such ideas were not only found in the accounts of teaching in centuries long past. It occurred again as the United States prepared to build a system of common schools. One of the leaders of that movement was William Woodbridge of Connecticut. In his famous lecture of August 24, 1830, he said that we should "prepare every teacher to endeavor to introduce it [music] into his school and every parent to provide the necessary means of instruction for his children." Chauncey Holcomb of Pennsylvania was of like mind. When Timothy Mason and Charles Beecher reported on school music to the Western Literary Institute and College of Professional Teachers in 1837 they urged "that every teacher should be expected, as part of his profession, to teach vocal and instrumental music." While the college passed a resolution that strongly supported music as a part of daily instruction, it did not state specifically that musicianship should be required of all teachers in the common schools. What might have been the course of development of music education in the United States had the Ohio legislature, which listened with such interest to the report of Beecher's brother-in-law on the schools of Prussia and Wurtemburg, defined a professional teacher for the common schools as one who could teach reading, writing, 'rithmetic, and music?

There was such a requirement of lady teachers for a period in some school systems where music was not taught by experts until the fourth grade. Ability to play the piano and teach music in their classroom was a requirement of employment for teachers of kindergarten through the third grade. With the advent of programs of teacher education in normal schools, music courses were required of all elementary teachers. Some states continue this pattern. Unfortunately, earning six credits in music fundamentals and methods does not always make teachers into musicians. Beecher and Mason were suggesting competency, not credits.

The Purpose of Music Education. Many music educators are on record in regard to the purpose of school music instruction. A Moravian publication makes it clear that their very musical schools were not meant to make children into professional musicians. It would not even have been desirable to do so if possible. Rather, "music should be allowed to help form and refine the mind and the heart." Albert Mitchell, the leader of the class violin movement in America, defended his program by saying that he hoped simply to open the door to music and "to educate the sense of touch, sight and hearing. The school's job," echoed Earhart, "was not to fit the pupil into a musical life, but to fit music into the life of the pupil." There are many other similar expressions of this sentiment to be found in MENC yearbooks and in the pages of the *Music Educators Journal.*

The above themes relate to another that can be observed in this account of the development of music education—standards for admission to the profession of music educator. Singing masters sold their services on the open market. We only hear today of those who were good enough to attract paying customers and who persisted long enough to compile a book. The early school music teachers had to sell themselves to the school boards, but once hired they were frequently paid higher salaries than the classroom teachers—sometimes as much as the principal. Unless they were unfortunate enough to be caught up in a political situation, as was Lowell Mason, they were employed as long as they produced pupils who could sing at periodic concerts and demonstrate their music reading ability at the annual public examinations.

Within a generation, however, came a movement to raise standards of musicianship and educational practice among teachers. Summer schools of music and normal schools for music supervisors were followed by collegiate programs. In the second decade of the twentieth century Kansas began requiring two years of college for music teachers, and in a few years a four-year curriculum was in place. Almost simultaneously, the National Association of Schools of Music was created. One of its original purposes was to raise the standards of teacher education programs.

The MENC Council of Past Presidents, the official resolution-making body of the organization, called for higher standards of admission to the collegiate programs of teacher preparation in 1940. The MENC has continued to be active in this role, having issued several publications on teacher education and sponsored numerous sessions on the subject at meetings. It would be difficult to identify when during this continuum music education became a specialized profession, but like any true profession it persists in improving itself. In the process the profession is likely to serve more ably those committed amateurs it wishes to create.

Amateurism, in the original meaning of the word, is what Mitchell, Earhart, and many others hoped for from school music. Did they give America universal education in music? The truth is that we do not know how to measure the success of music education. Few music educators, however, would take exception to the position that their profession has been a positive force in American society, as it was in previous societies. There is little reason to think that will change in the future.

Index

Selected MENC Publications

National Standards for Arts Education: What Every Young American Should Know and Be Able to Do in the Arts. Content and achievement standards for music, dance, theatre, and visual arts for grades K–12. Developed by the National Arts Education Associations under the guidance of the National Committee for Standards in the Arts. 1994. 148 pages. ISBN 1-56545-036-1. Stock #1605.

Opportunity-to-Learn Standards for Music Instruction: Grades PreK–12. Recommends standards for the music teaching environment: curriculum and scheduling, staffing, materials and equipment, facilities. 1994. 32 pages. ISBN 1-56545-040-X. Stock #1619.

Performance Standards for Music: Strategies and Benchmarks for Assessing Progress Toward the National Standards, Grades PreK–12. Provides valid, reliable, and effective systems for assessing students' musical learning. MENC Committee on Performance Standards, chaired by Paul R. Lehman. 1996. 136 pages. ISBN 1-56545-099-X. Stock #1620.

Music Education Research: An Anthology from the Journal of Research in Music Education. A collection of 58 research articles selected for their impact on the field of music education. Designed for use in the classroom with graduate and upper-level undergraduate students. Edited by Harry E. Price. 1998. 840 pages. ISBN 1-56545-109-0. Stock #1680.

The Eclectic Curriculum in American Music Education. Analytical essays by noted music educators on Dalcroze, Kodály, and Orff and their contributions to music education, K–12. Edited by Polly Carder. 176 pages. ISBN 0-940796-77-5. Stock #1503.

Multicultural Perspectives in Music Education, 2nd edition. A pragmatic approach to teaching the music of other cultures. For upper elementary through high school classes. Adaptable for use in undergraduate college courses. Edited by William M. Anderson and Patricia Shehan Campbell. 1996. 436 pages. ISBN 1-56545-097-3. Stock #1509.

For further information on these and other MENC publications, write to:

MENC Publications Sales
1806 Robert Fulton Drive
Reston, VA 20191-4348
Credit card holders may call 1-800-828-0229.